Nine Nights of the Goddess

SUNY series in Hindu Studies

Wendy Doniger, editor

Nine Nights of the Goddess

The Navarātri Festival in South Asia

Edited by

Caleb Simmons, Moumita Sen,
and Hillary Rodrigues

SUNY
PRESS

Cover image: iStockphoto by Getty Images.

Published by State University of New York Press, Albany

Printed in the United States of America

For information, contact State University of New York Press, Albany, NY
www.sunypress.edu

Library of Congress Cataloging-in-Publication Data

Names: Simmons, Caleb, editor.
Title: Nine nights of the goddess : the Navaratri festival in South Asia / edited by Caleb Simmons, Moumita Sen, and Hillary Rodrigues.
Description: Albany, NY : State University of New York, 2018. | Series: SUNY series in Hindu studies | Includes bibliographical references and index.
Identifiers: LCCN 2017040335 | ISBN 9781438470696 (hardcover : alk. paper) | ISBN 9781438470702 (pbk. : alk. paper) | ISBN 9781438470719 (ebook)
Subjects: LCSH: Durgā-pūjā (Hindu festival)—South Asia. | Durgā (Hindu deity) | Fasts and feasts—Hinduism.
Classification: LCC BL1239.82.D87 N56 2018 | DDC 294.5/36—dc23
LC record available at https://lccn.loc.gov/2017040335

10 9 8 7 6 5 4 3 2 1

In memory of Kathleen M. Erndl, brilliant scholar,
gracious mentor, and loving friend

Contents

List of Figures and Tables xi

Acknowledgments xiii

Introduction: Movements of Navarātri 1
Caleb Simmons and Moumita Sen

Navarātri in the Court

1. The Splendor of the Sun: Brightening the Bridge between *Mārkaṇḍeya Purāṇa* and *Devī Māhātmya* in Light of Navarātri Ritual Timing 23
Raj Balkaran

2. Which Durgā? What Navarātra? Remarks on Reconfigurations of Royal Rituals in the Kathmandu Valley 39
Astrid Zotter

3. The King and the Yadu Line: Performing Lineage through Dasara in Nineteenth-Century Mysore 63
Caleb Simmons

4. Dasara and the Selective Decline of Sacrificial Polity in a Former Princely State of Odisha 83
Uwe Skoda

Navarātri on Display

5. Politics, Religion, and Art in the Durgā Pūjā of West Bengal 105
Moumita Sen

6. Durgā Pūjā Committees: Community Origin and Transformed Mediatized Practices Employing Social Media 121
Xenia Zeiler

7. Navarātri in Benares: Narrative Structures and Social Realities 139
Silje Lyngar Einarsen

8. Dolls and Demons: The Materiality of Navarātri 157
Ina Marie Lunde Ilkama

9. Ritual Complementarity and Difference: Navarātri and Vijayadaśamī in Kāñcipuram 179
Ute Hüsken

Navarātri Inside

10. Bengali Durgā Pūjā: Procedures and Symbolism 197
Hillary Rodrigues

11. The Internal Navarātri: Sarkar Baba of Benares and the Goddess Within 215
Jishnu Shankar

Navarātri at Home

12. *Kolus*, Caste, and Class: Navarātri as a Site for Ritual and Social Change in Urban South India 237
Nicole A. Wilson

13. Display Shows, Display Tells: The Aesthetics of Memory during Pommai Kolu 257
Deeksha Sivakumar

14. Royal *Darbār* and Domestic *Kolus*: Social Order, Creation, Procreation, and Re-Creation 275
Vasudha Narayanan

15. Navarātra and Kanyā Pūjā: The Worship of Girls as Representatives of the Goddess in Northwest India 299
Brigitte Luchesi

Conclusion 317
Hillary Rodrigues

Contributors 331

Index 335

Figures and Tables

Figures

Figure 2.1	Durgā as the eighteen-armed Ugracaṇḍā from the court of Bhaktapur (1707 CE).	51
Figure 3.1	"Everlasting Lotus" or "*Santanambuja*" from Raṅgamahal in the Jaganmōhan Palace.	73
Figure 3.2	"Family tree" or "*Vṛkṣa*" from Raṅgamahal in the Jaganmōhan Palace.	75
Figure 3.3	Untitled mural from Raṅgamahal in the Jaganmōhan Palace in which Kṛṣnarāja III sports with the women from his harem.	76
Figure 3.4	"Vijayadaśamiya Jambū Svāri" from Raṅgamahal in the Jaganmōhan Palace.	78
Figure 3.5	Procession on the eastern wall of Raṅgamahal in the Jaganmōhan Palace.	78
Figure 5.1	Mamata Banerjee's Durgā as public art in New Town, Kolkata, 2014.	111
Figure 5.2	A large signboard advertising the local club's Durgā Pūjā using the photograph of the minister consecrating the goddess image, E. M. Bypass, Kolkata, 2016.	114
Figure 8.1	Mrs. Padma worshipping an image of Kāmākṣī in front of her *kolu*. The pot in which the goddess is invoked is placed on the third step.	160
Figure 8.2	Paṭavēṭṭamman̲'s stone image decorated as an anthill (*pur̲r̲u Māriyamman̲ alaṅkāram*). As a form of Māriyamman̲, Paṭavēṭṭamman̲ is represented in her sanctum as a full statue with a head in front.	171

Figure 10.1 Devī embodied in a jar atop the Sarvatobhadra Maṇḍala. 201

Figure 10.2 The *purohita* prepares an *argha* offering to the Devī during the Durgā Pūjā. 205

Figure 10.3 The *kośa* and *kuśi* (*yoni*-shaped ritual implements) are visible as the *purohita* performs *mudrās* during the Durgā Pūjā. 209

Figure 11.1 The process of internalizing and releasing the Goddess during Navarātri. 230

Figure 12.1 An elaborate *kolu* constructed at the home of a middle-class Chettiyar family in Madurai, Tamil Nadu. 245

Figure 14.1 Singing and dancing before the *kolu* is a significant part of the *kolu* activities. 279

Figure 14.2 A *kolu* display with the deities—Viṣṇu with Lakṣmī and Bhū Devī (the Earth Goddess) on the top tier. 281

Figure 14.3 *Paṭṭada* (king and queen) dolls are set on the lowest tier of the *kolu.* 283

Figure 14.4 Women from Gujarat venerate the creative energies of the goddess. A clay jar (*garbo*) and freshly sprouted *jowar* plants are arranged at the altar. 290

Figure 14.5 Rice balls (*piṇḍa*) are kept in an outside area in Bangkok to venerate the ancestors in *pitṛ pakṣa,* the fortnight before Navarātri begins. 293

Figure 15.1 *Kanyās* being fed by a young man at the Cāmuṇḍā Temple in Kangra during the Navarātra 2017. 304

Tables

Table 1.1 Parallels between *Devī Māhātmya* and *Sūrya Māhātmya* 28

Table 2.1 Attributes held by Ugracaṇḍā in her eighteen hands 52

Table 2.2 Central configuration of deities worshipped in a mandala under the Malla dynasty on Navarātra according to handbooks 53

Table 4.1 Ritual changes to Dasara in Bonai 93

Acknowledgments

This book grew out of the Navarātri, Navarātra and Durgāpūjā in South Asia and Beyond research group, a joint venture between the University of Oslo and the University of Texas-Austin that was headed by Professor Ute Hüsken. This collaboration provided the foundation and funding for the formative workshop in Paris in August 2015, without which this volume would not have been possible. Several drafts and portions of the chapters included in this book were presented at the 2014 South Asia Conference (Madison, WI), the 2014 American Academy of Religion (AAR) Annual Meeting (San Diego, CA), and the 2015 International Association for the History of Religions Congress and Conference (Erfurt, Germany). Additionally, several of the chapters were presented in an exploratory session at the 2016 AAR Annual Meeting, which has since led to the establishment of a Navarātri Seminar which will convene at the AAR Annual Meeting between 2017 and 2021, supporting the continued study of Navarātri from 2017 through 2021. We extend our sincere thanks to the organizers of these conferences.

The Käte Hamburger Kolleg and the Centrum für Religionswissenschaftliche Studien at Ruhr Universität-Bochum are also owed a debt of gratitude for graciously providing Caleb Simmons support during the editorial process. Additionally, we are grateful for the support of the University of Lethbridge Strategic Opportunities Fund and the Department of Culture Studies and Oriental Languages, the South Asia Institute, University of Texas at Austin, the Norwegian Ministry of Education, and the Centre Universitaire de Norvège à Paris, all of which provided publication subvention for costs related to publication.

We are extremely grateful to Christopher Ahn, who recognized the importance and potential of this volume; Chelsea Miller, editorial assistant; and everyone at SUNY Press for guiding us through the publication process. We are also extremely thankful to the two anonymous reviewers for their close reading of our manuscript and their many helpful comments.

Last, we would like to thank all our families, friends, and colleagues, who have supported us throughout the process of putting this book together.

Introduction

Movements of Navarātri

CALEB SIMMONS AND MOUMITA SEN

The Navarātri festival, alternatively called Navarātra, Mahānavamī, Durgā Pūjā, Dasarā, and/or Dassain, is celebrated throughout South Asia, often with great fervor and massive public participation. The festival lasts for nine nights and ends with a celebration called Vijayadaśamī (tenth day of victory). Navarātri celebrations take place worldwide, wherever South Asians settle. While in some traditions several Navarātris are celebrated at different times of the year, the most widely known and publicly celebrated Navarātri festival takes place in the autumn month of Āśvina (September–October).

There exist many descriptions and historical accounts of different local celebrations of Navarātri, and there are also detailed analyses of individual texts or text groups pertaining to this festival. There is great diversity wherever one looks. Accordingly, the festival has been interpreted as a "counterpart of Holi," "autumnal equinox," "harvest festival," "prime festival of the kings, rulers, and warriors," "the celebration of the victory of good over evil," "the temporary return of the married daughter to her paternal home," "the start of the season for warfare," and/or "the celebration of the female divine power," depending on what aspect the investigator chose to look at (e.g., the classical Sanskrit sources, local enactments, historical accounts, or interpretations of the diverse celebrants).

While it seems that there are many recurring elements (goddess, royal power, weapons, the killing of demons, worship of young girls and married women, a *śamī* tree, communal dancing, etc.), the arrangement and performance and the interpretation of these elements and the festival as a whole varies greatly. Most likely this has always been the case with innumerable local, regional, and non-Brahminical versions of the festival and its narratives, although the Brahminical prescriptive texts suggest uniformity.[1]

This book brings together a variety of scholars who employ diverse methodologies to investigate Navarātri in its many manifestations throughout different historical periods. This book addresses the festival as a broader socioreligious phenomenon, which shares broad themes, without neglecting the particularities of each festival event or its representation in textual and literary accounts. The authors, who individually draw upon contextual and specific expertise, collectively demonstrate how Navarātri functions as a festival that negotiates different spaces linking the public (be it the palace, the temple, or contemporary public space) with the domestic by moving the context of the festival back and forth. Navarātri is then a "prime festival" for those interested in the categories of space as it demonstrates the movement between the internal and external worlds of festival and religious practice, a theme that runs throughout the book.

In this brief introduction to this volume, we set the stage for the individual chapters, beginning with a brief historical overview of the festival drawing upon the Sanskrit literary tradition. This is in no way meant to privilege the Sanskrit textual material as somehow more authentic or to suggest (implicitly or explicitly) that all celebrations of the festival are rooted in these texts. Certainly, there have always been manifold iterations of the festival throughout South (and Southeast) Asia with as much (if not more) diversity in practice and belief as exists today. Instead, we intend to demonstrate how some of the oldest extant sources about Navarātri and its attendant rituals and regulations viewed the festival, even if from a limited perspective. This introduction will conclude with a reflection on the contemporary debates that have arisen in the past decade concerning the practice of Navarātri as a form of cultural and caste hegemony over Dalit groups (including what the government of India defines as "Scheduled Castes, Scheduled Tribes, and Other Backward Classes") by "Brahminical society," especially regarding the observation of Mahiṣāsura Commemoration Day. Through this brief discussion, we hope to demonstrate the continued relevance of Navarātri within contemporary politics as veneration of the state is intertwined with veneration of Durgā. In the next section, we will discuss how the spaces of Navarātri are negotiated through the movement of people and deities to provide a broader theoretical lens through which the many different celebrations of Navarātri discussed within this volume can be understood. We are primarily concerned with problematizing the binary construction of space as "domestic" or "public" by demonstrating the ubiquity of Navarātri throughout South Asian life. We will conclude our introduction with a general overview of the book's sections and each of the chapters.

Navarātri, Its Textual History and Its Controversies

Since the chapters in this volume examine Navarātri from a wide variety of disciplinary perspectives and from a broad chronology, we have decided to provide this brief survey of the textual history of the festival to ground the individual chapters in a more "classical" study. This is in no way meant to be comprehensive; rather, it serves to provide a starting point for those interested in the festival's textual sources. While we believe that this textual background is important, it is only one part of the history of Navarātri. Indeed, many groups within South Asia and beyond have practiced and continue to practice the festival in ways that are not reflected in or even sometimes contradict the textual injunctions and/or descriptions. The following will briefly examine both the textual history of Navarātri and some of the claims against it.

The Early Sanskrit Textual History of Navarātri

The most accessible archive to trace the history of a popular festival like Navarātri is contained in references to the nine nights of the Goddess in the Sanskrit corpus. Indeed, it is within the *ślokas* (common Sanskrit verse) of many of these elite, priestly, and royal texts that we find the earliest references to the worship of the Goddess during the festival of the autumn equinox. Though this can at best give a vague and penumbral view of Navarātri's past, we think it will be of interest to many if we connect the chapters in this volume to a broad chronology of Navarātri as curated in Sanskrit texts.

Outside of the narratives that tell the deeds of the Goddess, Navarātri is perhaps most connected with the story of Rāma within the popular imagination of its celebrants. As the epic story goes, Rāma, the erstwhile prince of Ayodhyā, was engaged in a long and difficult battle with Rāvaṇa, the demon-king of Laṅkā who had abducted his wife, Sītā, and held her captive. Finding his adversary not easily vanquished, Rāma performed *pūjā* to the goddess Durgā. The Goddess, pleased with his worship since it was Navarātri, appeared and granted him victory over his foe. With the boon from the Goddess, Rāma was able to defeat Rāvaṇa on Vijayadaśamī. While many attribute this narrative to the Sanskrit *Rāmāyaṇa* of Vālmīki, it does not appear in that text. Instead in Vālmīki's *Rāmāyaṇa,* Rāma worshipped Sūrya, the Sun, at the behest of the sage Agastya. The praises used, however, are very similar to later Goddess-oriented (Śākta) narratives with the deity praised as the giver of victory (*namaḥ jayāya namaḥ jayabhadrāya*) (*Rāmāyaṇa* "Yuddha Kanda" 105.17). The narrative of Rāma's Durgā Pūjā, however, appears in later texts, including many from the vernacular traditions. For example, in the Bengali *Kṛttivāsa Rāmāyaṇa* (c. fifteenth century), Rāma conducts

Durgā Pūjā, offering the Goddess his eye to show the extent of his devotion.

In the Hindu ritual calendars, however, Navarātri and the Rāmāyaṇa narrative are intimately linked since the Vijayadaśamī (in some cases Navamī, the ninth day) is believed to be the day that Rāma killed Rāvaṇa *and* the Goddess killed Mahiṣāsura. In Benares, the first days of the bright fortnight of the Hindu month of Āśvin are full of pomp and pageantry as the famous performance of Tulsīdās's *Rāmcaritmanas,* the Rām Līlā, unfolds, along with the celebration of Navarātri (see Einarsen). This association has been in place for centuries and is rooted in the *Gautamacandrikā* (c. 1624), a biography of Tulsidās, by Kṛṣṇadatt Miśra, who writes that the first *Rām Līlā* performance was consecrated after the poet finished his Navarātri and Vijayadaśamī observations (Lutgendorf 1991, 255–56).

Many of the rituals associated with the royal celebration of Navarātri are also said to derive from the actions of the five Pāṇḍava brothers from the epic *Mahābhārata.* In the sixth book of the Virāṭa Parva, the brothers enter the thirteenth year of their exile, in which they must travel without being recognized lest they have to start another twelve-year cycle. To remain incognito, the Pāṇḍavas chose to take up residence in the court of king Virāṭa, each assuming a different guise. Before they could enter his kingdom, however, the brothers needed to hide their weapons. They found a *śamī* tree large enough to store their weapons and hung their battle accouterments and a corpse (so no one would bother the tree) among its limbs and branches. After this strange ritual at the *śamī* tree, Yudhiṣṭhira began praising the goddess Durgā, who appeared before him and offered him a boon of victory over his Kaurava cousins. While not exactly the same ritual of the *śamī* tree that is part of the royal celebration of the Navarātri and Vijaydaśamī festivals in medieval, modern, and contemporary India, there is clearly resonance between the Pāṇḍava story and the ritual of the Day of Victory.

Later (Bhīṣma Parva 23), we find another narrative that references Navarātri rituals and Durgā Pūjā. Just before the start of the great Kurukṣetra War, the text tells us that Arjuna praised Durgā as the giver of victory so she could likewise grant him the promise of victory. Like the narrative from the Virāṭa Parva and the narrative of Rāma in Laṅkā, the praise of Arjuna and his subsequent blessings are remarkably similar in style and tone to narratives from the later Goddess Purāṇas. Indeed, there is general scholarly consensus that both of these Goddess-oriented praise/boon narratives were redactions into the *Mahābhārata* that reflected later developments in Goddess devotion that included the increasing popularity of Navarātri in all levels of society (Mazumdar 1906, 356; Van Buitenen 1978, 5, 19–20).

Within the Purāṇic tradition, references to Navarātri and its attendant rituals steadily increase over time. One of the earliest discussions of the great autumn festival to the goddess comes from the *Mārkaṇḍeya Purāṇa* (discussed in much greater detail in Balkaran's chapter). Within the text is a smaller thirteen-chapter section commonly known as the *Devī Māhātmya* (also known as *Durgāsaptaśatī* and *Caṇḍīpāṭha,* c. sixth-century CE) that tells of the exploits of the Goddess as she embodies to fight demons for the sake of the gods and the maintenance of the cosmos. In the second of three episodes, the text relates the story of the manifestation of the Goddess from the brilliance of the gods and her subsequent defeat of the buffalo-demon Mahiṣa. It is, however, in the last episode that Navarātri is specifically mentioned. In this portion of the text the Goddess has just defeated the demons Śumbha and Niśumbha, which prompts praise and adulation from the rest of the pantheon, specifically exalting her role as the giver of boons. Beginning in chapter 11, the Goddess replies to their praise with a monologue in which she prescribes the most efficacious forms of worship for those seeking boons. In chapter 12, she transitions to a discussion of the *Devī Māhātmya* itself and proclaims that anyone who hears it recited during the great *pūjā* of autumn (*śaratkāle mahāpūjā*) will be healthy and wealthy with grain and with children (*Devī Māhātmya* 12.12). The text continues to be important for Navarātri not only for its narration of the deeds of the Goddess, but just as the text prescribes it continues to be chanted throughout the nine nights of the Goddess.

The *Devī Purāṇa* is perhaps the earliest of the Śākta (Goddess-oriented) Purāṇas, dating between the sixth and ninth centuries (Hazra 1963, 71–77). This text, unlike the *Devī Māhātmya,* explicitly connects the slaying of Mahiṣāsura and Navarātri and describes the proper celebration of the festival. The story of Mahiṣāsura, however, diverges from the story with which most are familiar. In the text's second *pada,* it narrates the rise of the demon named Ghora. After Ghora is deluded by his wife because of her conversion to a Digambara sect of Jainism, the demon devolves into sinful acts and in the twentieth chapter assumes the form of a buffalo (Mahiṣa). In the subsequent chapter, Ghora-as-Mahiṣa is slain by the Goddess, after which Navarātri is established. The following chapters (chapters 22–23) discuss the proper timing and performance of the rituals during the nine nights of Mahānavamī. Later in chapter 28, the text returns to the Navarātri rites and enumerates their benefits to the practitioner.

The *Kālikā Purāṇa* (c. tenth to twelfth centuries) reserves an entire chapter (chapter 60) to the proper celebration of the autumnal festival of Navarātri. In addition to describing the proper *mantra* and Tantras, the text also explicitly connects the *Rāmāyaṇa* narrative and the story of Mahiṣa with Navarātri. According to the text, the Goddess watched the first seven days of the battle between the armies of Rāma and Rāvaṇa, eating the flesh of the fallen at night. On the ninth day of the battle, Rāma conducted a special *pūjā* to Durgā after which she caused Rāvaṇa to be slain.[2] The text uses this narration to solicit kings to conduct the same *pūjā* to strengthen their armies (*Kālikā Purāṇa* 60.43). Later in the same chapter, the *Kālikā Purāṇa* narrates the Mahiṣa story but adds another portion in which Mahiṣāsura converts and takes refuge in the Goddess before she kills him (*Kālikā Purāṇa* 60.101–02). Going even further, the text equates Mahiṣa to an incarnation of the deity Śiva due to a curse from the sage Kātyāyana (*Kālikā Purāṇa* 60.151–53). Despite or perhaps due to its strong Śākta message, the *Kālikā Purāṇa* has remained an influential ritual text and is even the ritual *śāstra* used to determine issues of practice for pandits of the Mysore court (see Simmons).

The *Devī Bhāgavata Purāṇa* (c. eleventh to twelfth centuries) is roughly contemporaneous with the *Kālikā Purāṇa* and likewise places the celebration of Navarātri within both ritual and narrative contexts throughout the twenty-sixth to thirtieth chapters of its third book. In the narrative descriptions, however, the *Devī Bhāgavata Purāṇa* places Navarātri in a broader mythic context in which the *pūjā* to the Goddess not only gave Rāma his victory over Rāvaṇa but was also enacted by other deities ensuring victories for Indra over the demon Vṛtra, Śiva over Tripura, and Viṣṇu over Madhu, truly expanding the cosmic scope and efficacy of the festival (*Devī Bhāgavata Purāṇa* 3.30.25–26). Further, in the seventh book (chapters 31–40) of the *Devī Bhāgavata Purāṇa,* a philosophical treatise called the *Devī Gītā* expounds upon Śākta thought in a style that mimics the famous *Bhagavad Gītā.* In the *Devī Gītā,* the Goddess tells the mountain Himālāya the secrets of her worship, among which she lists both the spring and autumn Navarātris among the most effective celebrations of her power (*Devī Gītā* 8.42; Brown 1998, 251). In addition to the narrative and philosophical developments, *Devī Bhāgavata Purāṇa* expands the ritual prescriptions for Navarātri, especially in regard to the austerities of the festival's *vrata* (fast), which has become a major element of many celebrations of the festival (Hazra 1987, 242; see Shankar).[3]

Just as the Purāṇic tradition has maintained portions of the Navarātri tradition, the Navarātri tradition has preserved otherwise lost Purāṇic knowledge. The only remaining portions of the lost Śākta Purāṇa *Bṛhannandikeśvara Purāṇa* is known to us through twenty-five lines that were quoted in Raghunandana's text on the practice of Durgā Pūja, the *Durgāpūjātattva* (also known as *Durgotsavatattva,* c. sixteenth century) (Hazra 1963, 466–69). In the passage quoted by Raghunandana, it is said that the Goddess should be worshipped in earthen images and in the form of nine plants (*nava patrikā*) and should be bathed (*mahāsnāna*) with various ritual elements. He also describes ritual sacrifice of he-goats and buffaloes and the performance of fire rituals (*homa*). He concludes that the ninth day is to be celebrated with sacrifices, music, and general merry-making.

Beyond these texts, there are many more Sanskrit narrative texts that reference Navarātri and ritual treatises that discuss the proper celebration of the festival (e.g., *Durgotsavaviveka* of Śūlapāṇi, *Durgāpūjāprayogatattva* of Raghunandana, *Durgābhaktitaraṅgiṇī* of Vidyāpati, *Navarātrapradīpa* of Vināyaka, and *Durgotsavapaddhati* of Udayasiṃha; see Hazra 1963, 155). In addition to these, there are innumerable traditional narratives, prescriptions, and ritual treatises in vernacular languages throughout South Asia, not to mention the emerging visual media (film and television) and social media that are constantly recording and recreating the tradition today.

Contemporary Debates about Navarātri and Hegemonic Culture

In India, a country with a large majority of Hindus (79 percent according to the 2011 census), the symbolic nature of the nationwide celebration of Navarātri is contentious from the perspective of minority religious groups—Dalits (lit. "suppressed," "Scheduled Castes" in the Indian Constitution) and Ādivāsis ("Scheduled Tribes" in the Indian Constitution). Contestations over Navarātri and the observation of Mahiṣāsura Commemoration Day became a matter of national interest at the time of editing this volume. Since at least 2010, the demon Mahiṣāsura has been worshipped and commemorated publicly in villages and cities in India (Roy 2015). This commemoration of the demon-king reflects a perspective that runs parallel and counter to the hegemonic celebration of the nine nights of the Goddess. While the term *asura* means "demon" in most Indian vernacular languages, and Mahiṣāsura is the villain of the narrative for most Indians, Asuras are also members of an indigenous community (Scheduled Tribe) in different districts of eastern India. The members of this community believe that Mahiṣāsura, their hero, king, and venerable ancestor, was tricked and murdered by the fair-skinned, bejewelled goddess of the Aryan Brahmins. Mahiṣāsura Pūjā or Mahiṣāsura Smaraṇ Divas (Commemoration Day) is a provocative and proliferating religiopolitical festival where minority groups in metropolitan universities and villages (in Eastern and Central India) publicly worship Mahiṣāsura instead of the goddess Durgā. Under the current political regime led by the right-wing Bharatiya Janata Party (BJP), Mahiṣāsura Pūjā has been labelled "blasphemy" in the public sphere and in the Indian parliament because it contrasts the desired metanarrative of a homogenous Hindu tradition central to their political agenda (DNA 2016).[4]

One particular observation of Mahiṣāsura Commemoration Day on the campus of Jawaharlal Nehru University (JNU) in 2016 became the center of legal actions, political controversy, and multiple blasphemy accusations in the Indian parliament. The controversy was ignited when three students were arrested from the JNU campus on charges of sedition, beef-eating, and Mahiṣāsura worship.[5] Following their arrest and the ensuing debates, the Minister of Human Resources Development (de facto education minister) of India and member of the BJP, Smriti Irani, made an impassioned speech in the Indian parliament on February 24,

2016, denouncing the observance of Mahiṣāsura Commemoration Day. For the Hindu nationalist ideologues, the political contestation over the narrative of Durgā and Mahiṣa (and thereby Navarātri) is amplified by the equation of the goddess Durgā and the religiopolitical embodiment of the nation as Bhārat Mātā (Mother India) (Kovacs 2004, Guha-Thakurta 2006). In her speech, there was a clear line drawn that connects the violated honor of the vulnerable female deity and the security of the nation-state. Therefore, in a broad rhetorical sweep, she connected "blasphemy" against the goddess to treason against the nation.[6] At one point in her speech, she read aloud excerpts from a pamphlet circulated on campus by Dalit activists (DNA 2016):

> Durga Puja is the most controversial racial festival, where a fair-skinned beautiful goddess Durga is depicted brutally killing a dark-skinned native called Mahishasur. Mahishasur, a brave self-respecting leader, [was] tricked into marriage by Aryans. They hired a sex worker called Durga, who enticed Mahishasur into marriage and killed him after nine nights of honeymooning during sleep.

From exclamations of "shame . . . shame . . . shame" that were heard in Parliament as Irani read, it was evident that the comparison between the goddess and a prostitute garnered the strongest protest (Ranjan 2016).[7] Given the relationship between Durgā and the nation-goddess, the sexualisation of Durgā is a particularly contentious topic.[8] From the perspective of Irani and her political allies, Durgā's honor must be protected because it reflects the honor that is afforded to the sovereign state of India. The honor politics that are often applied to women's bodies are extended to that of the goddess's and the nation's as vulnerable, coveted entities to be protected militantly by her men. Therefore, creating a homogenous single narrative of Durgā and Mahiṣāsura and the enactment of Navarātri are deeply entrenched in discourses around Hindu nationalism and nation building.

Against the rise of such attempts to homogenize the tradition, the chapters in this book seek to display the multiplicities and dynamism within the Navarātri tradition. Indeed, it is through the divergent ways of enacting the festival that it finds ubiquity in the subcontinent and gives meaning for the variety of peoples who observe the nine nights of Navarātri.

Movements of Navarātri, Public and Domestic

Perhaps one reason for the ubiquity of the Navarātri festival within Indian and Hindu life is its presence in both the public and domestic spheres. As will be evidenced in this book, Navarātri exists in a variety of forms that manifest in both public and domestic ritual spaces, producing a myriad of overlapping and complementary, yet disparate performances and celebrations. Therefore, it is necessary to place the varieties of Navarātris and Navarātri spaces within a broader theoretical context regarding ritual practice in the domestic and public spheres.

Indeed, much has been written about religion and religious practice/performance within these two spheres of life in South Asia and elsewhere. One such writing that can be a helpful starting point is the essay "Here, There, and Anywhere" by Jonathan Z. Smith (2004, 323–39). In this essay, Smith contrasts the domestic/household or "here" religion with the religion of "there," which is public or civic religion. He is primarily concerned with location and argues that domestic religion is local. For Smith, domestic religion attempts to ground the family/household (including ancestors) in a network of relations within its community but remains primarily attached to one's domicile. He suggests that the central component of domestic religions is immediate and symmetrical relations between the ancestors, the living, and the fecundity of nature, often focusing on agricultural and ancestor rituals. He continues by describing public religions as those of which "most of us think first when we imagine ancient religion: the dominant deities and their attendant mythologies and liturgies, the impressive constructions associated with temple, court, and public square. Wherever one's domicile, these latter locales are someplace else, are 'over there' in relation to one's homeplace" (Smith 2004, 328). In public religion, he continues, relations are based in hierarchies of nested power and specialized knowledge, with kings and priests at their head. Public religion is a religion of unequals. Both domestic and public religions, however, are religions of place. Where "here" religions are interested in situating the family within a locale, "there" religion is about broadening the cosmos to include the earthly powers-that-be "over there" as well as celestial and nether-terrestrial powers that, like earthly overlords, are also not readily present but whose beneficent and maleficent effects can be felt. Last, he observes a third type of religion, religion of "anywhere." This type is particularly present in diaspora traditions and melds elements of the previous two. In "anywhere" religion, there is a dislocation that creates the need for new ideas of locale and a new and "true" home (often only seen after death), a new cosmology that aims to transcend earthly realms, and a new polity that relies on the king of the gods above and beyond earthly rulers.

Many of Smith's observations are supported by the descriptions of Navarātri rituals found in this book. Indeed, Navarātri, when celebrated in the home, has elements that ground the practitioner to their locale through symmetrical relations between fertility/virility of the earth, the ancestors, and living—all key components of the "here" religion. Navarātri is often referred to as a harvest festival, and it is celebrated immediately following the festival of the ancestors. Further, there is an emphasis on ritual use of grains and gifting of foodstuffs in many of the chapters that discuss home rituals (see Rodrigues, Luchesi, Sivakumar, Narayanan). Additionally, we see that part of the function of Navarātri in the home involves the relationship between the members of the family and their community, as they invite their neighbors into their home (see Wilson, Sivakumar, Narayanan), and their neighbors' daughters and sons become part of important domestic rituals (see Sivakumar, Luchesi).

Likewise, many of the chapters describe aspects of Navarātri that reflect the "over there"-ness of Smith's "there" religions, religions that serve to create and uphold the power of the king and priests. Navarātri is one of the central festivals for South Asia courtly life and served as the yearly affirmation of the king's power to rule, which was granted from the Goddess (see Balkaran, Zotter, Narayanan, Simmons). The festival is a highly visible performance of the hierarchic relations between various communities and political entities in which these asymmetrical affiliations are created, enacted, and reaffirmed (see Skoda, Einarsen, Sen). The public performance of stratified society is also on display, as ritual specialists from different groups negotiate their roles through their unique ritual apparatuses and their inclusion and exclusion from certain places and rituals (see Ilkama, Hüsken).

Last, Navarātri has many aspects of the "anywhere" religion. Navarātri is not only a religion of terrestrial power and locale, but for many practitioners the physical ritual complex is rooted in greater spiritual truths that transcend mere physicality (see Rodrigues, Shankar), what Smith highlights is "neither here nor there" (2004, 330). Navarātri is also often celebrated in the dislocation of diaspora contexts or even in virtual spaces (see Zeiler).

As we look more closely at Navarātri, however, the helpfulness of these categories begins to dissipate. In this work, we find that domestic rituals that are celebrated in the homes of the practitioners not only serve to ground the family within its locale, but they are also complex negotiations of power and prestige among neighbors, and entire cities are drawn to their very public *kolus* (doll displays) (see Wilson, Sivakumar). We also find that rituals to the young girls-as-goddesses are the same in the large temples and in the home, both containing public displays of means and generosity (see Luchesi). Additionally, even the connection to the fecundity of the earth is not without cosmological significance, creating both symmetrical relationships and a vertical hierarchical relationship between macro- and microcosms (see Balkaran and Rodrigues). In Navarātri, family and home life are often turned inside-out, and domesticity is inverted, becoming public.

The public performances of Navarātri also transgress the domestic/public binary as they intertwine royal and priestly rituals with domestic concerns. The imperial enactments of the festival are inherently tied to the king's family and ancestors as they display their lineage to the public (see Simmons). Furthermore, throughout India, palaces are seats of public religion, but they are also the domicile of the king, wherein domestic rituals are enacted in the living quarters to ensure the virility of the royal line. Further, not only is the temple a site of public worship, but it is transformed into the home of the deities, who themselves partake in rituals during which the space is closed from the public eye (see Hüsken). Thus, many of the spaces of public ritual are simultaneously sites of domesticity.

Navarātri, therefore, is a site through which the gendered boundaries of space can also be contested. Traditionally, domestic spaces were associated with women, and the public sphere, with men, with women being the harbingers of household religious practices and men controlling and performing goddess rituals in temples, courts, and public venues. Within the chapters of this book, there are many examples that uphold or implicitly comply with this gendered ordering of space; however, we invite our readers to pay close attention to the ways that gender dynamics change in the many examples of Navarātri in which spatial binaries are upended or reversed. Thus, as Navarātri blurs the boundaries of religious space, it simultaneously can be and has been a force of social critique and reform.

Moreover, the dislocation of the "anywhere" religions described by Smith is lost on Navarātri. In the Goddess-oriented traditions, locality is central. While Navarātri has cosmological significance, it remains rooted in specific sites and materiality. As many of the chapters in this volume demonstrate, though she may be connected with a greater pan-Indian tradition and goddess, many that celebrate Navarātri worship a local goddess, who is simultaneously regal, fierce, and loving. This goddess is the goddess of the locale, but she is also the Goddess. For the practitioner, then, the Goddess is not "over there" somewhere, she is always "here" and "there," simultaneously immanent and transcendent. As Ákos Östör has argued, "specific pūjās celebrate the timeless, limitless dimensions of the goddess . . . In all cases, however, the pūjās relate land, locality, and people to each other in a direct and particular way" (1980, 88). We, therefore, consider a fourth category—"everywhere"—that might help us to better understand the movement, multiplicity, and ubiquity of Navarātri. Instead of "anywhere," which is tied to no particular place, by "everywhere" we are suggesting that Navarātri is *both* domestic *and* public at once. It is firmly grounded in the family, home, ancestors, and earthly fecundity *and* publicly displays hierarchies (both terrestrial and cosmological). The relationships that the performance of Navarātri creates, confirms, and reaffirms are both symmetrical—in that they focus on the reciprocal shifting of power amongst related entities—*and* hierarchic—

in that they produce clear asymmetries within homes, neighborhoods, temples, and palaces and amongst spiritual entities (deities, gurus, etc).

Furthermore, the Goddess to whom the festival and its attendant rites are performed is not simply confined in one form. The same Goddess, who is worshipped in the image of Durgā slaying the demon Mahiṣa, is venerated in the form of prepubescent girls, resides in the clay vessel, and is cultivated within by the practitioners. These different forms are not even relegated to different ritual moments. As Hillary Rodrigues has shown,

> The casual observer might be inclined to think that the clay effigy (*mūrti*) is the only image of the Goddess worshipped during the Durgā Pūjā, when in fact, in the very same ritual, the Devī is actually worshipped under a plethora of other forms and names. Although closer observation of the ritual reveals several explicit images of the Goddess, such as an earthen jar and a cluster of plants, there are numerous other names and forms of the Devī not perceived by most votaries. (Rodrigues 2003, 11)

This unity yet variegation of the Goddess perfectly encapsulates the "everywhere"-ness of Navarātri. The festival is uniquely grounded within each city and town through its local goddesses and to individual homes through the power (*śakti*) that is embodied in its women and girls. Yet, it transcends space for those who are away from home connecting them to a broader tradition and with a new community of celebrants wherever they may be. Simultaneously, celebrations construct political and religious ideologies, empowering and disempowering people and communities; yet for many the Goddess and her festival transcend these mundane concerns.

In this way, our theory of Navarātri as an "everywhere" tradition resonates with the theory of space articulated by Kim Knott. Likewise, Knott diverges from Smith by conceptualizing space not as separate spheres but as unbounded and interconnected (2009, 156). Working with theories from postmodern geographers such as Doreen Massey (1992), she argues that space exists relative to many scales–such as the body, objects, locality, community, and global networks–through which the place of religion can be better understood (2015). For Knott, it is within the intersections of these scaled sites that "social relations occur, which may be material or metaphorical and which is necessarily interconnected (with places) and full of power" (2015, 134). Preferring "space" to "place" because of its connotation of openness, Knott's theory emphasizes the interconnectedness and fluidity of spatial categories such as public/private, local/global, and so on. Indeed, any clear demarcation of spaces into a binary of public and private is problematic for understanding Navarātri and South Asia more generally (Kaviraj, 1997). As will be seen in this book, within the frame of Navarātri, space is transformed, but its transformation is not from one type of space to another but as multilayered and co-existing spaces imbued with power and embroiled in issues of status.[9]

Therefore, when we consider the multiplicity of Navarātri and the ways that it is enacted and performed in its various contexts, we see a tradition that permeates various levels and scales of South Asian life, simultaneously. It is "everywhere" at once. It is within the simultaneity of the tradition—its "everywhere"-ness—that negotiations of status and power are displayed and worked out.

Form and Layout of the Book

This work is made up of contributions from a range of scholars from various disciplines who lend numerous perspectives to the celebration of Navarātri. The chapters are arranged thematically relative to the spaces in which the Navarātri practices discussed are performed. Through these different iterations of the festival, the similarity, diversity, and difference within each spatial theme will hopefully become evident.

The first section, "Navarātri in the Court," focuses on the performance of the festival within the context of the royal celebrations. This section begins with an essay by Raj Balkaran. Balkaran discusses Navarātri from a textual perspective by reading the *Devī Māhātmya,* arguably the most influential goddess-centered scripture, as a Navarātri ritual text. He argues that the text's interpolation into the *Mārkaṇḍeya Purāṇa* between narratives of the Sun situates the text as an account of the vernal and autumnal equinoxes that was purposefully intended for recitation. The next chapter, by Astrid Zotter, examines the textual sources for the Malla (1200–1768) and Shah (1768–2008) dynasties of Kathmandu through ethnohistorical method. In this chapter, Zotter compares the ritual procedures of both courts to reconsider the relationship between the two dynasties. She complicates the received history of Nepal's royal rituals by showing how the Shahs adopted rites, deities, and specialists of the previous dynasty while advancing their own ritual culture. In the next chapter, Caleb Simmons looks at the representation of Mysore's Dasara procession in courtly literature and mural paintings from the reign of Kṛṣṇarāja Woḍeyar III (1799–1868). He argues that Dasara was the public display of a larger project of king-fashioning in Mysore that sought to (re)establish the newly reinstalled Woḍeyar dynasty through genealogical accounts. Simmons suggests that Navarātri and Dasara became the Mysore festival *par excellence* because they enabled the display of a newly formed vision of divine kingship in light of colonial oppression. Uwe Skoda's chapter focuses on the royal fort-centered rituals of Dasara in the Bonaigarh region of Odisha. He demonstrates how the economic conditions after Indian national integration shape the religious landscape of the former princely states and the ritual life of its tribal inhabitants for whom the performance of the festival procession has been a site of identity formation. He then compares the decline of the rituals of fort-centered Dasara to the rise of market-centered Durgā Pūjā to show how post-liberalizaton economics has shifted ritual emphasis from the fort to the market.

The subsequent section, "Navarātri on Display," examines iterations of Navarātri that take place in the "public" displays of Navarātri and Durgā Pūjā in public exhibitions, performances, and temples. This section begins with two chapters that focus on clubs and committees involved in the planning and preparation of Durgā Pūjā displays. In her chapter, Moumita Sen looks at the organizers of Durgā Pūjā in Calcutta, specifically the patronage of local youth clubs. She examines the increasing political patronage of the festival since the dramatic victory of the Trinamool Congress in 2011. Sen argues that this political upheaval of the secularist position vis-à-vis religious festivals of the erstwhile communist government has been drastically revised. She shows how new alliances between the Goddess and the government in popular politics and popular religiosity have significantly impacted the practice of secularism in West Bengal. Conversely, Xenia Zeiler examines Durgā Pūjā committees through the emerging processes of mediatization. Her chapter analyzes the mediatized activities of the Durgāpūjā committee Mulund in Mumbai as it communicates, organizes, and negotiates the community's Durgā Pūjā via various forms of social media. She demonstrates Mulund's and other committees' ability to adapt to emerging media environments and how their mediatized activities serve as markers for identity as they negotiate community status, prestige, and authority.

In the next chapter, Silje Einarsen uses ethnographic research to illustrate recent changes in Navarātri celebrations in Benares, focusing on two types of cultural performance: the royally-patronized *Rām Līlā* play based on poet Tulsidas's Hindi rendering of the epic *Rāmāyaṇa* and the Durgā Pūjā installations creatively arranged by neighborhood youth clubs. Whereas the former represents tradition and Banarasi identity, the latter is perceived of as new and innovative, which manifests as skepticism and breeds some resistance to the celebrations. Like Skoda's findings, Einarsen shows us that the popularity of the traditional *Rām Līlā* is decreasing, whereas the Durgā Pūjā is increasing rapidly in both scope and public esteem, highlighting the dynamics of change, creativity, tradition, and innovation in the festival culture of Benares.

The final two chapters of this section examine the celebration of the autumnal festival within the context of the temple. Ina Marie Ilkama examines the ritual enactment of the Goddess's fight with the demon in the Brahmin Kāmākṣī Ammaṉ temple in Kāñchipuram, Tamil Nadu, and in the popular local non-Brahmin temple of Paṭavēṭṭammaṉ. Ilkama traces both performances to different local mythologies that inform the reenactments and practices of the festival. Particularly interested in the materiality of the festival, she argues that through their presence, material representations are imbued with agency within the context of Navarātri rituals. In the next chapter, Ute Hüsken also investigates the celebration of Navarātri in Kañcipuram, focusing on the Vaiṣṇava Varadarāja temple and comparing its ritual apparatus with that of the Kāmākṣī goddess temple. Hüsken demonstrates that the Varadarāja temple's enactment of Navarātri is rooted in the Sanskrit ritual texts the Pāñcarātra *saṃhitās*, in which the importance of this festival and the role of the goddess are downplayed. Yet in many oral (re)interpretations and in some of the temple's nontextual rituals, Varadarāja's Navarātri festival resembles the celebrations at the Kāmākṣī goddess temple much more closely. She argues that ultimately the rituals and festival performances of both temples are derived as much from shared local cultural values as they are from normative textual traditions.

The following section, "Navarātri Inside," examines Navarātri as an internal tradition that is embedded with symbolic meanings for the practitioner. In chapter 10, Hillary Rodrigues presents a summary of the main ritual actions of the Bengali Durgā Pūjā and offers interpretations of some of its symbolic features. He illustrates that the primary function of the Durgā Pūjā rituals is to establish the presence of the Goddess by installing her in a wide variety of forms, such as a jar, a cluster of nine plants, a clay image, a cosmograph, and a virgin girl. He argues that Durgā Pūjā in effect enlivens devotees and cleanses their faculties so that the Goddess may be perceived as ubiquitous in creation, thereby revitalizing themselves, their families and communities, and the cosmos itself. Similarly, Jishnu Shankar provides a closer look at the expressions of the spiritual element inherent in the celebration of the Navarātri festival. Shankar examines the teachings delivered by Aghoreshwar Mahaprabhu Baba Bhagwan Ram ji (a.k.a. Sarkar Baba) of Benares to individual practitioners over the course of the nine-day festival. He demonstrates that within these teachings, Sarkar Baba presented the body as the ultimate vessel of the Goddess and that through the processes of asceticism the practitioner seeks to become one with her. In both chapters in this section, the space of Navarātri is an internal space conceived within the ritualist.

The final section, "Navarātri at Home," moves the reader into the "domestic" spaces of the festival and into the private world of Navarātri performances. Nicole A. Wilson examines Navarātri as a device of identity construction and communication within a small suburban, middle-class temple and the homes of its middle-class devotees in Madurai, Tamil Nadu. She illustrates how performances of Navarātri rituals are being refashioned according to the changes in local social structure, particularly those relating to social mobility and socioeconomic status in an urban living environment. She argues that Navarātri ritual performances are moments during which caste-based customs, identities, and practices can be challenged, *class* stereotypes can be reaffirmed, and *class* identities can be constructed. In chapter 13, Deeksha Sivakumar explores the female-centered Brahmin ritual of Pommai Kolu during Navarātri. She shows how homes and possessions function like museums during Pommai Kolu, preserving personal and religious memories through aesthetic arrangement. Sivakumar demonstrates that the entire visual space of the display, the unique objects and dolls housed within it, the participants' organization around that display space, and the reflexivity evoked from their responses to the display all function together to enhance the performance of this festival. The final chapters, by Narayanan and Luchesi, show the overlap between domestic and public Navarātri performance. Narayanan's chapter demonstrates the overlapping aesthetics and concerns of the royal display of the king at the Dasara *darbār* and the arrangement of dolls in the domestic *kolu* by connecting many of the overlapping themes of the affirmation of life and conquest of death. The final chapter, by Bridgett Luchesi, demonstrates how Navarātri transcends the distinctions of public/domestic through a detailed ethnography and analysis of the ritual worship of girls and women both in the homes of practitioners and in the local goddess temples. She keenly demonstrates the ways in which the festival changes given the relationship of the participants, especially regarding the behavior and demeanor of those who are being worshipped.

The collection will then finish with concluding remarks by Hillary Rodrigues in which he brings together the themes of the chapters more closely and looks toward the future of Navarātri studies.

The chapters in this book demonstrate the wide range of practices and performances through which Navarātri is celebrated. They display the dynamic nature of the festival specifically and religious traditions more broadly. They lead the reader through the pomp of the court, public display and performance, and temple rituals, to the domestic and private space of the home, and back again, all the while destroying any such distinctions. Together, they provide a fuller picture of the complex ways that Navarātri is practiced, enacted, and understood by devotees in a variety of places and spaces.

Notes

1. These efforts to harness the heterogeneity of religious practices have important consequences in contemporary politics in India as well. See the discussion of Mahiṣāsura below.

2. This narrative and its connection to Navarātri and Durgā Pūjā are expanded in the Śākta *Mahābhāgavata Purāṇa*, a later Purāṇa that was influential for eastern India, especially Bengal (Hazra 1963, 270–72, 278).

3. Hazra suggests that the *vrata* portion of the celebration is a blend of Vedic and Tantric rites and that it most likely reflects the traditions of western and southern India (1987, 242; 1963, 357–58). This suggests that the popularity of Navarātri in Brahminical circles had expanded considerably.

4. Other parties have stood up in defense of the observation of Mahiṣāsura Commemoration Day. Sitaram Yechuri, a Communist Party of India (Marxist) leader, defended Mahiṣāsura worship in the lower house of the Indian parliament with two main points. First, Hinduism is marked by a practice of pluralistic traditions; he cites the example of Onam, in which the return of Mahābali, an *asura* who was tricked and killed by Viṣṇu in the form of Vāmana, is celebrated. Second, when BJP leader Atal Behari Vajpayee compared the erstwhile prime minister, Indira Gandhi, to Abhinav Caṇḍī Durgā, she rejected the comparison on the grounds that Bahujans, Dalits, and Ādivāsis worship Mahiṣāsura (Vincent 2016).

5. The first information report (FIR) lodged with the Delhi police by a BJP minister listed eating beef and the worship of the demon Mahiṣāsura upon university premises as legally punishable offences (Indian Express 2016). Cow slaughter is prohibited legally in most states in India. This makes the practice of Muslims and Dalits of consuming beef contentious (Chigateri 2011).

6. Within the political ideology of the ruling BJP-led National Democratic Alliance, ideas, personalities, symbols, sites, and geopolitical bodies are often sacralized for political mobilization (Freitag 1980; Ramaswamy 2009; Van Der Veer 1992). In this sense, ideas of the sacred, distinct from yet filtered through religion (Lynch 2014), tinge all the following legal charges of offense: sedition, prevention of insults to national honor, defamation of historically important personality, and hate speech.

7. This was not the first time such depictions had raised controversy at JNU. A similar debate over memorializing Mahiṣāsura had arisen over images published in a campus magazine that depicted Durgā having sex with Mahiṣāsura, which several right-wing student bodies deemed blasphemous (Lal 2014).

8. Muslim artist M. F. Hussain was charged under the Insult to National Honour Act for images that were said to depict Durgā having sex with Mahiṣāsura (Simmons 2011; Guha-Thakurta 2010; Chattopadhyay 2008).

9. Yet another way to view the space of Navarātri with its multitude of milling bodies, commerce, and ludic festivities and rituals would be Michel Foucault's theory of "heterotopia" (Foucault and Miskowiec 1986). Tapati Guha-Thakurta has used this Foucauldian concept to show how the everyday neighborhoods of Kolkata are transformed into multilayered and multifunctional spaces during the Durgā Pūjā (Guha-Thakurta 2004).

References

Brown, C. Mackenzie. 1990. *The Triumph of the Goddess: The Canonical Models and Theological Visions of the Devī-Bhāgavata Purāṇa*. Albany: State University of New York Press.

Chattopadhyay, Swati. 2008. "Contours of the Obscene, Architectures of the Visible." *Third Text* 22 (6): 769–85.

Chigateri, Shraddha. 2011. "Negotiating the 'Sacred' Cow: Cow Slaughter and the Regulation of Difference in India." In *Democracy, Religious Pluralism and the*

Liberal Dilemma of Accommodation, edited by Monica Mookherjee, 137–59. Dordrecht: Springer Netherlands.Coburn, Thomas B. *Encountering the Goddess: A Translation of the Devī-Māhātmya and a Study of Its Interpretation*. Albany: State University of New York Press.

DNA India. 2016. "Opposition Reacts Sharply to Smriti Irani Linking 'Mahishasur Martyrdom Day' to JNU Row," Diligent Media Corporation, February 25. URL: http://www.dnaindia.com/india/report-oppositionreacts-sharply-to-smriti-irani-linking-mahishasur-martyrdom-day-to-jnu-row-2182436.

Doniger, Wendy. 2009. *The Hindus: An Alternative History*. New York: Penguin.

Foucault, M., and J. Miskowiec. 1986. "Of Other Spaces." *Diacritics* 16 (1): 22–27.

Freitag, Sandria B. 1980. "Sacred Symbol as Mobilizing Ideology: The North Indian search for a "Hindu" Community." *Comparative Studies in Society and History* 22 (04): 597–625.

Guha-Thakurta, Tapati 2015. *In the Name of the Goddess: The Durga Pujas of Contemporary Kolkata*. Kolkata: Primus Books.

———. 2006. *Iconography Now*. New Delhi: SAMHAT.

———. 2004. "From Spectacle to 'Art': The Changing Aesthetics of Durga Puja in Contemporary Calcutta." *Art India* 9 (3).

Hazra, R. C. 1987. *Studies in the Purāṇic Records on Hindu Rites and Customs*. New Delhi: Motilal Banarsidass.

———. 1963. *Studies in the Upapurāṇas Volume 2*. Calcutta: Sanskrit College Press.

Indian Express. 2016. "Kanhaiya Kumar Arrest: The FIR filed by Delhi Police in Sedition Case." *Indian Express*, February 17, 2016.

Knott, Kim. 2015. *The Location of Religion: A Spatial Analysis*. London: Routledge.

———. 2009. "From Locality to Location and Back Again: A Spatial Journey in the Study of Religion." *Religion* 39 (2): 154–60.

Kovacs, Anja. 2004. "You Don't Understand, We Are at War! Refashioning Durga in the Service of Hindu Nationalism." *Contemporary South Asia* 13 (4): 373–88.

Lal, Ratnakar. 2014. "King Mahishasur's Martyrdom." *Forward Press* 4: 6–8.

Lutgendorf, Philip. 1991. *The Life of a Text*. Berkeley: University of California Press.

Lynch, Gordon. 2014. *On the Sacred*. London: Routledge.

"The *Mahābhārata*." *Bhandarkar Oriental Research Institute*. Accessed September 30, 2015. http://bombay.indology.info/mahabharata/statement.html.

Massey, Doreen. 1992. "Politics and Space/Time." *New Left Review* 196:65.

Mazumdar, B. C. 1906. "Durgā: Her Origin and History." *The Journal of the Royal Asiatic Society of Great Britian and Ireland* (April): 355–62.

Östör, Ákos. 1980. *Play of the Gods: Locality, Ideology, Structure, and Time in the Festivals of a Bengali Town*. Chicago: University of Chicago Press.

Rajagopal, Arvind. 2001. *Politics after Television: Hindu Nationalism and the Reshaping of the Public in India*. Cambridge: Cambridge University Press.

Ramanujan, A. K. 1991. "Three Hundred Ramayanas: Five Examples and Three Thoughts on Translation." In *Many Ramayanas: The Diversity of a Narrative Tradition in South Asia*. edited by Paula Richman. Berkeley: University of California Press.

Ramaswamy, Sumathi. 2009. *The Goddess and the Nation: Mapping Mother India*. Durham, NC: Duke University Press.

"The *Rāmāyaṇa*." *Bhandarkar Oriental Research Institute*. Accessed September 30, 2015. http://bombay.indology.info/ramayana/statement.html.

Ranjan, Pramod. 2016. Smriti Irani's Speech in Lok Sabha on JNU and Mahishasur and Durga [video]. https://youtu.be/_VGmzuwo_Ag.
Rodrigues, Hillary Peter. 2003. *Ritual Worship of the Great Goddess: The Litugy of the Durgā Pūjā with Interpretations.* Albany: State University of New York Press.
Roy, Indrajit. 2015. "The Imaginary of the Mulnibasi in West Bengal." In *The Politics of Caste in West Bengal,* edited by Kenneth Bo Nielsen, Geir Heierstad, and Uday Chandra. New Delhi: Routledge.
Sarkar, Bihani. 2017. *Heroic Shāktism. The Cult of Durgā in Ancient Indian Kingship.* Oxford: Oxford University Press.
Simmons, Caleb. 2011. "The Graphic Goddess: Mahiṣāsuramardinī in the Modern Art World." *Modern Art Asia* 8 (November 2011). http://www.modernartasia.com/issue8.html.
Sharma, Hari Krishna. 1984. *Durgāsaptaśati with Seven Sanskrit Commentaries.* Delhi: Chaukhamba Sanskrit Prathishthan.
Shasti, B. N. 2008. *The Kālikāpurāṇa.* Delhi: Nag.
Smith, J. Z. 2004. *Relating Religion.* Chicago: University of Chicago Press.Van Buintenen, J. A. B. 1978. *The Mahābhārata, Volume 3 Book 4: The Books of Virāṭa; Book 5: The Book of the Effort.* Chicago: University of Chicago Press.
Van Der Veer, Peter. 1992. "Ayodhya and Somnath: Eternal Shrines, Contested Histories." *Social Research* 5 (1): 85–109.
Vincent, Pheroze L. 2016. "Footnote to Fabled Story on Indira." *The Telegraph.* February 27, 2016.

NAVARĀTRI IN THE COURT

1

The Splendor of the Sun

Brightening the Bridge between *Mārkaṇḍeya Purāṇa* and *Devī Māhātmya* in Light of *Navarātri* Ritual Timing

RAJ BALKARAN

The *Devī Māhātmya* (*Glorification of the Goddess, DM*) is the first detailed Sanskritic account of the Hindu Great Goddess, extolling the magnanimous cosmic feats she enacts, in protection of the gods. It enjoys a robust independent life, particularly as prime liturgy during the "nine nights" autumnal festival of Navarātri. The festival pays homage to the cycles of dark and light upon which the cosmos is founded, cycles expressed through the rhythms of nature, oscillating between night and day, summer and winter, full and new moon. It occurs when light and darkness are equal on the earth. But, unlike its vernal counterpart (in March, on the first day of spring), the autumnal equinox occurs when darkness overtakes light, when the days grow darker and colder. This is the most inauspicious annual juncture, the midnight of the gods, when Viṣṇu, the protector of the world, slumbers, fast asleep since the onset of the monsoon season. It is a time when even the gods are vulnerable, when the forces of darkness are at the height of their power. Protection is crucial when the sun's light starts to wane; hence the festival marks the consecration of kings—sworn to protect—and the invocation of the Great Goddess, protectress bar none. Unsurprisingly, she plays a crucial role in rituals of royal consecration, one indispensable to an appreciation of the *DM*. Hence, as C. J. Fuller notes, the nine nights festival is *the* royal festival, reenergizing the earthly office of protection at an annual juncture so dark (both literally and figuratively), that the gods themselves are left vulnerable to the forces of darkness (Fuller 2004, 108–11).

The *DM* takes up residence within the larger *Mārkaṇḍeya Purāṇa* (*MkP*). In this broader text, Sage Mārkaṇḍeya tells of the previous six *manvantaras* (cosmic intervals), which are ruled by various mythical progenitors called manus. He then relates the details of our present cosmic interval, as the text transitions into the *DM*. The *DM* serves to elucidate the ascension of the next manu, who shall attain his reign at the end of this age and the commencement of the next. Thus, the *DM* proper begins, "Sāvarṇi, who is Sūrya's son, is said to be the eighth Manu. Hear about his birth from me" (*DM* 1.2; Coburn 1991, 32).[1] In like fashion, Mārkaṇḍeya concludes the *DM* by declaring, "[T]hus having received a boon from the Goddess, Suratha, the best of rulers, upon receiving another birth from Sūrya, will become the Manu known as Sāvarṇi" (*DM* 13.17; Coburn 1991, 84). Here within a text that is so central to the goddess tradition in India, the Goddess herself seems to be only an afterthought. In light of this frame narrative, the exploits of the Goddess in the *DM* are mere means for King Suratha to regain his earthly regime and to secure sovereignty over an entire age as the future Manu Sāvarṇi, son of the Sun. But what is the significance of conflating the glories of the Goddess with the story of solar succession? This chapter undertakes a synchronic analysis of the solar myths of the *MkP* to demonstrate their profound interplay with the *Devī Māhātmya*, encoding the astronomical configuration during which the Great Goddess festival occurs.

The bridge between the *DM* and *MkP* has been dimly lit throughout the history of Purāṇic study, and understandably so. Pargiter notes in the introduction of his 1904 translation of the *MkP* that "if the Devī-māhātmya is put aside, the Sun is the deity that receives the most special adoration, and his story is related twice, first, briefly in cantos 77 and 78, and afterwards with fullness in cantos 102–110" (Pargiter 1904, xv). He fails, however, to register the glaring similarities between the modes through which these two deities are glorified and the ways in which they explicitly harken to one another. His understanding of the relationship between the *MkP* and *DM* accounts for his inability to register the parallels between the larger text and its constituent parts:

> The Devī Māhātmya stands entirely by itself as a later interpolation. It is a poem complete in itself. Its subject and the character attributed to the goddess shew that it is the product of a later age which developed and took pleasure in the sanguinary features of popular religion. The praise of the goddess Mahā-māyā in canto 81 is in the ordinary style. Her special

> glorification begins in canto 82, and is elaborated with the most extravagant laudation and the most miraculous imagination. (Pargiter 1904, vi–vii)

For Pargiter, the *DM* was an incommensurate interpolation affronting the fabric of the oldest, most authentic, nonsectarian strata of the work. By deeming the *DM* as an inauthentic presence in the *MkP*, he compromises his ability to perceive the obvious interplay at work between the *DM* and its Purāṇic context. Furthermore, he dismisses the narrative frames within the *DM* itself, which serves to orient the exploits of the Goddess and to orient the *DM* within the *MkP* more broadly.

Pargiter's biased view of the *DM* as a later interpolation occluded his ability to register the parallels between solar and *śākta* (goddess) mythologies, even though the *DM* emphatically declares at its very outset and again at its conclusion that it shall elucidate the rise of the son of the Sun as the next manu. Pargiter's bias has remained entrenched thoughout the generations of his scholarly heirs (see Winternitz 1972, 560; Agrawala 1963, 832; Rocher and Gonda 1986, 195; Desai 1968, 109; Doniger 2014). This legacy must be thoroughly acknowledged to gain a fuller understanding of the relationship between the *DM* and the *MkP* and between the Goddess and the Sun in the Purāṇic tradition (cf. the rich discussion in Ramanujan 1989). Amid the dizzying frame narratives and seemingly intrusive interpolations lie thematic continuities that account for the content and composition of these narratives and their frames.

The Splendor of the Sun

The mythology of the Sun and his son, the manu Sāvarṇi, occurs at two junctures within the *MkP*. The first telling of the birth of the Sun's son Sāvarṇi (along with his several other children) commences the manu-interval discourse on the seventh manu, Sāvarṇi (*MkP* 78–79), and the second telling follows shortly thereafter (*MkP* 106–8) and contributes to a larger trilogy of episodes lauding the glories of the Sun (*MkP* 101–10). Interestingly, the second narrative acknowledges that the Purāṇa has already relayed the tale, saying "Manu Vaivasvata was begotten by Vivasvat of her then, and his nature has been already indeed declared particularly" (Pargiter 1904, 566). Yet the text does not eliminate the redundancy; instead, the second telling is much more elaborate than the first. It is perhaps not by chance that the first telling relays a condensed version of the Sun's exploits implicated in the birth of the manus Vaivasvata and Sāvarṇi. This tale is located directly prior to the *DM*, serving to introduce the *DM* and to nestle the myths of the Goddess betwixt the myths of the Sun. The first telling provides the necessary anteceding frame—a foreshadowing—so that the hearer is already aware of the solar circumstance under which Sāvarṇi is born. This allows for further elaboration of how he earns that prestigious birth through the worship of the Goddess in the longer retelling. Through an examination of the mythology of the Sun, we shall illuminate the relationship between the Sun and the Goddess and her role in solar succession.

Let us now examine the pertinent portions of the first telling. The Sun and his wife Saṃjñā beget a famous and learned manu, Vaivasvata, along with the deities Yama and Yamunā (*MkP* 77.1–7). Saṃjñā endures the sharpness (*tejas*) of the Sun for some time, and unable to bear it further, she decides to take refuge with her father, Viśvakarman. To do so, she fashions Chāyā, a double of herself (*chāyā* means shadow or reflection), who agrees to take her place with the Sun. Saṃjñā then goes to her father's abode where she is respectfully received. Having remained there for some time, Viśvakarman advises her to return to her husband (*MkP* 77.15–21). Agreeing to his counsel, she salutes her father and secretly departs for the northern Kurus unbeknownst to him, still fearing the sharp splendor of the Sun. She practices austerities there in the form of a mare (*MkP* 77.22–23).[2]

Meanwhile, the unsuspecting Sun starts a second (mirror) family with Chāyā, one reflecting the first family, consisting of two sons and a daughter: Manu Sāvarṇi, Śanaiścara, and Tapatī. Due to an altercation between Yama and Chāyā, the Sun sees through the ruse and pays a visit to Viśvakarman to reclaim his wife (*MkP* 77.36). Once there, he asks in vain about Saṃjñā's whereabouts. Viśvakarman was, after all, under the impression she had returned to the Sun. Upon hearing that her father thought she had returned home, the Sun concentrates his mind in yogic meditation and inwardly sees his wife in the form of a mare practicing austerities in the northern Kurus. He is furthermore able to perceive the purpose of her penance, namely, that her husband should acquire a beautiful, gentle form. The Sun subsequently asks of his father-in-law that his sharp splendor be pared down, and Viśvakarman complies.

Gods and divine seers assemble and offer praise at the monumental event: the paring down of the *tejas* of the Sun. Having successfully shed himself of his extraneous sharpness, the Sun assumes the form of a stallion and journeys to the northern Kurus, where he encounters Saṃjñā in her equine guise. Upon seeing the stallion approach, Saṃjñā, fearful of an encounter with a strange male, engages him face-to-face to guard her hindquarters. As their noses meet, two sons Nāsatya and Dasra, better known as the Aśvin twins, are born in Saṃjñā's mouth. At the end of the Sun's emission, Revanta is born. The Sun then reveals his benign form, to Saṃjñā's delight, whereupon she resumes her own form and accompanies him home.

While the first telling (*MkP* 77–78), occurs as a stand-alone segment, the second telling of the sequence of events between the Sun and Saṃjñā (*MkP* 106–8) occurs as part of a conglomeration of tales embellishing the virtues of the Sun, casting him as a supreme primordial power even above the gods themselves. Remarkably, the *MkP* dedicates a nine-chapter episodic trilogy to lauding the majesty of the Sun (Pargiter 1904, 553–87), which I shall refer to here as the *Sūrya (Sun) Mahātmyā* (*SM*).[3] For the purposes of the discussion at hand, I shall loosely plot the overarching parallels in formal and thematic features between the two *māhātmyas* (table 1.1 on pages 28–29).

Through a comparison of the overall structure and arrangement of the two *māhātmyas*, one can readily ascertain the similitude between the two glorifications that demonstrates a conscious compositional cross-pollination at play between the compilers/editors of each one. The content of these *māhātmyas* bespeaks a pronounced parity between the Goddess and the Sun. First, each *māhātmya* exhibits movement from the cosmic sphere at the time of creation, to the heavenly sphere, to the terrestrial sphere. The first portion of each *māhātmya* establishes the cosmic supremacy of its respective deity insofar as Brahmā, the creator deity, praises the Sun and the Goddess as a self-existent supreme cosmic principle, invoking them for the sake of preserving the universe within their respective *māhātmyas*. This is followed in each text by the gods of heaven calling upon the deity, who is being praised. Both texts also reestablish the reign of an earthly king at their conclusion—Rājyavardhana in the *SM* and Suratha in the *DM*. The association between these two *māhātmyas* of the *MkP* is undeniable, and the interplay between these two literary entities is central in the composition of the *MkP*. Of particular importance for our understanding of the relationship between the Sun and the Goddess and the two *māhātmyas* is the equine adventure between the Sun and Saṃjña to which we will now turn.

Equine Exegesis

Why does Saṃjñā not merely gallop away from the strange male if she was so intent upon guarding her rear? This face-to-face equine encounter is central to the overall composition, and the movement within the myth is crucial, not the narrative that surrounds it. This is what Doniger refers to as a "gloss" (Doniger 1980, 185). Though "untrue to the original spirit of the myth," Saṃjñā's fear serves as an impetus for a seminal plot development and is a clever narrative trope deployed for the sake of occasioning a crucial and lasting element of this myth cycle (Doniger 1980, 185). By protecting her rear, she spins around to enable intimate nose-to-nose engagement, which allows for the birth of equine twins through the nos-

Table 1.1. Parallels between *Devī Māhātmya* and *Sūrya Māhātmya*

Sūrya Māhātmya, MkP 101–10 [occurring within succession of kings discourse, MkP 101–136]		Devī Māhātmya, MkP 81–93 [occurring within succession of Manus discourse, MkP 53–100]	
Canto	Content	Canto	Content
SM Introduction 101	Sage Markaṇḍeya introduces the Sun; Krauṣṭuki asks to hear about his greatness in full (101.15–17).	**Introduction 81**	Sage Medhas introduces the Devī; Suratha asks to hear about her greatness in full (81.45–81.46).
SM Episode I 102–103	Describes the Sun's cosmic role at the dawn of creation: Brahmā hymns the Sun to save the universe from his overpowering luster. Hymn 1 by Brahmā (103.5–12)	**DM Episode I 81**	Describes the Devī's cosmic role at the dawn of creation: Brahmā hymns the Devī to save the universe from her overpowering darkness. Hymn 1 by Brahmā (1.54–87)
SM Episode II 104–105	The gods are overtaken by the demons and Aditi hymns the Sun so that he is born to her and combats the them and restores sovereignty to the gods. Hymn 2 by Aditi (104.18–29)	**DM Episode II 82–84**	The gods are overtaken by Mahīṣa and his demon forces and their collective wrath manifest the Devī who combats the demons and restores sovereignty to the gods. Weapons forged by Tejas (82.19.82.28) Hymn 2 by Indra and the devas (4.1–4.42)
SM Episode III 106–108	Srūrya-Saṃjñā-Chāyā story [recapitulation of Cantos 77–78]. Hymn 3 by Viśvakarman (107.2–10) Weapons forged by Tejas (108.3–5)		

SM Epilogue **109–110**	Krauṣṭuki interjects to ask for more details (109.1–2) Hymn 4 by the *brāhmaṇas* (110.62–74) Phalaśruti 110.37–43. The Sun reinstates King Rājyavardhana's earthy reign.	**DM Episode III** **DM Epilogue** **85–92; 93**	The gods are again overtaken, this time by Śumbha-Niśumbha and they invoke the Goddess again restores their sovereignty. Hymn 3 by the devas (5.7–5.36) Suratha Interjects to ask for more details (89.1–2) Hymn 4 by Agni and the devas (11.1–34) Phalaśruti (12.1–12.29) The Devī reinstates King Suratha's earthy reign.

trils of the equine Sun. The narrative of this birth is equally crucial as it bridges the *DM* and its solar framework. To understand the significance of this trope, we must turn to perhaps the most ancient avenue of mythic narrative: astrological mythology.

The Purāṇic form is generally attributed to the flourishing of the Gupta Empire (Doniger 2009, 370), as is classical Indian astrology Jyotiṣa (Pingree 1977 vol. 6, 11). At several junctures, the *MkP* demonstrates knowledge of and reliance upon the principles of Jyotiṣa in (1) ascribing categorical astrological signifiers for people and geographical locations (e.g., *MkP* 58; Pargiter 1904, 348–87); (2) ritual timing (e.g., *MkP* 33; Pargiter 1904, 168–170); (3) conjunction with life decisions (e.g., *MkP* 109.38; Pargiter 1904, 580); and (4) casting of horoscope at the time of birth (*MkP* 122.4; Pargiter 1904, 626). With respect to the fourth of the astrological applications to be found in the *MkP* (i.e., casting a horoscope at the time of birth), we find in the text a remarkable example that demonstrates the centrality of Jyotiṣa in the text. At the time of his son's birth, King Karandhama "asked the astrologers—who could read fate—'I trust my son is born under an excellent constellation, at an excellent conjuncture?' " (*MkP* 122.4; see Pargiter 1904, 626). The astrologers reported,

> When the moment, the constellation and the conjuncture have been excellent, thy son has been born to be great in valour, great in his parts, great in strength. O great king, thy son shall be a great king. The planet Jupiter, preceptor of the gods, has looked on him, and Venus which is the seventh and the Moon the fourth planet has looked upon this thy son and Soma's son Mercury also, which is stationed at the edge has guarded him. The Sun has not looked on him; nor has Mars or Saturn looked on thy son, O great king. Happy is this thy son! he will be endowed with all good fortune and prosperity. (*MkP* 122.4; Pargiter 1904, 626)

The king, of course, was gladdened by his astrologers' forecast. He appears to trust both the skill of his court astrologers and the principles of Jyotiṣa themselves to render accurate information about the nature and destiny of an individual. He makes a most remarkable reply to his astrologers at this point: "The preceptor of the gods has looked on him, and so has Soma's son Mercury. The Sun has not looked on him, nor has the Sun's son nor Mars. This word 'Has looked upon' of that ye, sirs, have uttered often,—celebrated by reason of it his name shall be Avīkshita" (*MkP* 122.4; see Pargiter 1904, 626). The faith that King Karandhama puts in his court astrologers is so central to this episode, that he ends up naming his son Avīkṣita, based on the astrological terminology. Given the usages of Jyotiṣa and the specific references to its mechanisms throughout the *MkP*,

I now turn to two standard Sanskrit treatises outlining the mechanics of classical Jyotiṣa—the *Bṛhat Parāśara Hora* (*BPH*; c. 600–750 CE) ascribed to sage Parāśara, and the *Bṛhat Jātaka* (*BJ*; c. sixth century CE), ascribed to Varāhamahira (Pingree 1977 vol. 6, 84–86)—to elucidate our understanding of the placement of the *DM* within the *MkP*.

According to these Jyotiṣa texts, the movements of the heavenly bodies are accompanied not only by techniques of interpretation and prediction but by rich and ancient narratives—narratives, which, as shall be made clear, find themselves at home in Purāṇic literature. An explicit example of this is to be found in Canto 75 of the *MkP*, which tells of the exploits of the constellation Revatī (technically, one of the lunar asterisms, or *nakṣatras*, discussed below), which fell to earth due to Sage Ṛta-vāc's curse (Pargiter 1904, 443–49).[4] Similarly, the symbolism of horses is not only thematically apropos to the mythology of the Sun insofar as "seven equally swift horses" draw the chariot of the sun across the sky (*MkP* 107.8; Pargiter 1904, 572–73) but particularly because horses symbolize the half-equine Aśvin twins whose genesis the myth relays and after which the lunar asterism (*nakṣatra*) Aśvini is named.

The use of lunar *nakṣatras* for ritual and predictive purposes has persisted since Vedic times. These lunar asterisms or mansions represent the oldest strata of Indian astrology and, quite possibly, encapsulate some of the most ancient extant South Asian narrative motifs in their mythologies. There are twenty-seven lunar asterisms, whose zodiacal arcs necessarily occupy 1/27 of the 360-degree orb of the sky. We must note further that of the twenty-seven lunar asterisms, Aśvini, astronomically known as the stars β and γ Arietis, is the first and commences the Zodiac, occupying the beginning of Aries, the first zodiacal sign (*BJ* 1.4; Varāhamihira 1995, 10–11). Unsurprisingly, within Jyotiṣa this asterism governs all things equine in the world. This can be seen within the *MkP* when the queen Madālasā informs her son Alarka that "one attains horses when performing the śrāddha [ancestor rites] while the moon is conjoined Aśvini nakṣatra" (Pargiter 1904, 170). The association between the lunar asterism Aśvini and all things equine is ubiquitous in Indian thought and myth and can be corroborated within all accounts of the birth of the Aśvins (the half-equine deities that preside over the Aśvini *nakṣatra*) where the Sun and his wife take on equine form to give birth to them and through the etymology of the term of the *nakṣatra*.

The *BPH* introduces the nine planets as "the Sun, the Moon, Mars, Mercury, Jupiter, Venus, Saturn, Rahu, and Ketu" (*BPH* 3.10; Parāśara and Sharma 1994, 16). Each planet serves as signifier for a multitude of aspects of the phenomenal universe. To put it differently, each aspect of the known universe is ascribed to the sway of one of the nine planets. The *BPH* specifies what is foremost represented by each planet with respect to human beings, stating that "the Sun is the soul of all. The moon is the mind. Mars is one's strength. Mercury is the speech giver while Jupiter confers knowledge and happiness. Venus governs semen (potency) while Saturn indicates grief" (*BPH* 3.12–13; Parāśara and Sharma 1994, 17; *BJ* 2.1; Varāhamihira 1995, 27).[5] Within this text and Jyotiṣa more generally, the Sun as the soul of all is afforded supremacy amongst the nine planets. Since the *MkP* at large seems concerned with the rules and mechanisms of Jyotiṣa, it is fitting that the Sun would be the father of the Aśvins, the foremost of these lunar mansions, especially in the *SM* in which he is lauded as the primal universal principle. Like the astrological myth found in Jyotiṣa texts in which he seeds the beginnings of the zodiac, in the myths of the *SM* the Sun seeds creation itself (the phenomenal universe).

However, his association with the Aśvins long predates the grandeur he is accorded in the Purāṇas and was present even when he was a mere mortal in Vedic times. Jyotiṣa informs us that all the planets acquire different degrees of strength in different signs. For example, Jupiter, being a watery planet, attains its peak performance in Cancer, the most watery of zodiacal signs. Whether or not these ascriptions were ever based on experience of the natural planets, there can be little doubt that the states accorded to the Sun as it passed through the zodiac were based on its palpable effect on the planet, particularly in an equatorial climate. The Sun, being fire itself, therefore acquires its state of peak performance or exaltation (*ucca*) in the fiery sign of Aries. The strength it acquires as it passes through Aries is expressed on earth as the coming of Spring. The *BPH* therefore states that "Aries, Taurus, Capricorn, Virgo, Cancer, Pisces, and Libra have been spoken of respectively from the Sun on, as the signs of exaltation of the seven planets" (*BPH* 2.49; Parāśara and Sharma 1994, 36). But given that there are twelve zodiacal signs and twenty-seven lunar asterisms, each sign will typically contain within it two and a fraction asterisms. For example, the sign of Aries is home to three lunar asterisms: *aśvinī, bharaṇī,* and the first bit of *kṛtikkā*. The question then arises, within its mythology why is the Sun tied to only the first of these asterisms? The answer again lies in Indian astrological understandings. There is a point within the entire sign, which is considered the chief star (*yoga tārā*) for exaltation. For example, if one were to visualize an astrological sign as warm room, the point of greatest heat would be the fireplace. The fireplace would be the *yoga tāra* of that room. This primary point of exaltation occurs at ten degrees of Aries, which falls within the arc of *aśvinī nakṣatra* (*BPH* 2.50; Parāśara and Sharma 1994, 36). Through a consideration of ancient Indian astrological mythology, the mythologist is, perhaps at long last, equipped to understand why the Sun and Saṃjñā take equine form and encounter each other in the Northern Kurus to birth the Aśvins. This narrative is a mythic representation of the annual exaltation of the Sun as it approaches ten degrees of Aries and conjoins in the asterism of Aśvini.

Corroborating the extent to which the myth of the Sun and Saṃjñā is inextricable to astrological understandings of the Sun's journey through the zodiac, we can again take direction from Jyotiṣa with respect to why the Sun and Saṃjñā encounter each other face-to-face. Each zodiacal sign is represented by a region of the body. The *BJ* specifies that on the scale of the full body Aries represents the head itself (*BJ* 1.4; Varāhamihira 1995, 10–11). Furthermore, each of the twelve zodiacal signs is symbolized by a part of the face.[6] The nose symbolizes the sign of Aries, in which sits the lunar asterism Aśvini. By having the equine Saṃjñā turn about, under the pretense of guarding her rear, the poet embellishes the nasal association wherein the Aśvins are conceived by sniffing the *tejas* of the Sun.[7] The myth subtly encodes that the Sun acquires its state of exaltation (*ucca*) when it sits in Aries (since this coincides with the coming of spring, around the time of the vernal equinox), conjoined the asterism of Aśvini, and likewise that the Aśvin twins originate in Aries (represented by the nose), powered by the sun's exaltation therein (represented by their spawning by the Sun's stallion form).

Another dimension of the astrological associations within this myth is Revanta, about which we know nothing more of than what we hear in the myth of the Aśvins' birth. This suggests to me he is merely a supporting actor in the story of the Sun and the Aśvins. The name Revanta might very well be read as a pun in the form of a contraction of "Revatī," the final asterism ending the constellation Pisces, immediately before the start of Aries, and "anta" or "the end" emphasizing the termination thereof. Therefore, the Aśvins are born (where Aśvini commences) in conjunction with Revanta, at the end of Revatī.

The myths of the Sun not only serve the *DM* thematically but also with respect to the ritual timing of its annual recitation at the Navarātri (nine nights) festivities dedicated to the Great Goddess. The Goddess festival takes place at two annual junctures, the first nine nights of Āśvina, when the full moon is in Aśvini (and the Sun is in Citrā), and in Caitra, when the full moon is in Citra (and the Sun is in Aśvini). To demonstrate this linkage, we again draw from texts on Jyotiṣa. As discussed above, the Sun attains its greatest power in Aries, conjoined Aśvini *nakṣatra*, in the springtime during its equine equinox.[8] This time of year brings with it the lunar month Āśvina, marked by the full moon in the constellation Aries (conjoined Aśvini *nakṣatra*) 180 degrees away from the "fallen" Sun, stationed in the constellation Libra.[9] It is this time of year when, due to the fallen state of solar energy in the cosmos, that the grand Goddess festival takes place. It occurs on the first nine nights of the waxing moon headed toward its fullness in the asterism Aśvinī and is a time when the *DM*, detailing the acts of Durgā, her reinstatement of the fallen kingship of Suratha, and her deliverance of the promise of a future manu, is ritually chanted throughout the Hindu world. The *DM*, as noted, commences and concludes with invoking the Sun. Therefore, the mythologies of the Sun offer more than a narrative corollary; they serve to contextualize its ritual life, affording direction and justification for the annual juncture that is most auspicious for the chanting of the text.

Hillary Rodrigues traces the Sanskrit liturgy of the pan-Indic autumnal festival in honor of the Hindu Great Goddess (primarily in the form of Durgā), which occurs during the first nine nights of the waxing moon commencing on the Indian (lunar) month of Āśvina (Rodrigues 2003 and this volume). In many homes, the *DM* (also referred to as the *Durgā Saptaśatī* in ritual context) is chanted daily during the festival (Rodrigues 2003, 10). This study constitutes an exhaustive description of a Bengali-style of ritual worship of Durgā Pūjā, as it is enacted in the sacred city of Benares. Rodrigues expounds the overt connection between the grand ritual and its mythic heritage in his discussion on the extent to which the clay image that is housed in temporary complexes (*pandals*) erected for the festival "clearly forges a relationship between Purāṇic myth and the ritual" (Rodrigues 2003, 50). These images and attendant motifs enact the demon-slaying exploits of the *DM*, particularly in its second episode, where Durgā slays Mahīṣāsura, an episode that also, as Rodrigues notes, echoes elsewhere in the Purāṇic corpus. In the context of the gathered masses at the Goddess festival, Rodrigues designates Durgā as

> the monarch for whom the people have gathered in a display of service, loyalty and devotion. In their numbers, and in their visible and verbalized sentiments of revelry and unity, they have a vision (*darśana*) of their own power, and with it, the certitude of being victorious in any undertaking. This vision of the victorious power (*vijayā śakti*) that permeates the community of worshippers, binding them in a union characterized by joy and fearlessness, is implicitly a view of the manifest form of the Goddess. (Rodrigues 2003, 296)

It is this spirit of motherly protection of sovereign empowerment that characterizes the Goddess of our text, the same characterization that, as Rodrigues notes, pervades her festival as well. It is quite intriguing that he elects the word "monarch" to describe the Goddess in this context. Through the ritual chanting of the *DM* at this annual juncture, the waning Sun is ameliorated by the grace of the Goddess, whose role it is to keep darkness (which, paradoxically, she also represents) at bay, and so too is the waning energy of sovereignty and of righteous regulation throughout the universe kept away. Therefore, in invoking the Goddess, one also invokes the very root of majesty and sovereignty.

Within Jyotiṣa texts, this royal majesty is specifically equated with the solar. For example, according the *BPH* "the Sun and the Moon are of royal status,"[10] a notion that is echoed verbatim in Varāhamahira's *BJ* (*BJ* 2.1; Varāhamihira 1995, 27). Royal figures in the Indian context not only carry associations of regality and magnanimity but equally carry sanguinary associations: to be a king in ancient India (and in the Indian literary imagination) is to necessarily be a warrior, bar none. Jyotiṣa texts are also happy to point this out. The *BPH,* while assigning castes to all the planets, unsurprisingly assign the Sun the warrior and royal caste of *kṣatriya,* a trope that is echoed in the *BJ* (*BJ* 2.6. see Varāhamihira 1995, 32).[11] It is perhaps for this very reason that both the Sun and Mars are described as "dark red" (*rakta śyāmaḥ*) in both the *BJ* (*BJ* 2.4; Varāhamihira 1995, 30) and the *BPH* (*BPH* 3.16–17; Parāśara and Sharma 1994, 20), despite only Mars appearing dark red to the naked eye. Thus, the majestic and sanguinary aspects of the Goddess are appropriately framed in the *MkP* by those of the Sun, since both Goddess and Sun are emblematic of the archetypal Indian sovereign.

The work of Goddess, Sun, manu, and king have in common a theme central to Indian religious thought: preservation. Unsurprisingly, the work of preservation is squarely shouldered by the Goddess throughout her exploits in the *DM,* and utterly underscored by the cosmic impetus behind the relaying of these episodes, for Suratha to secure a subsequent birth as the next manu, who will be the son of the Sun. Therefore, this outer intrinsic frame that grants the earthly king Suratha cosmic kingship formally clasps the *DM* to the body of the *MkP* and is commensurate with the primary frame of the exploits of the Goddess: the restoration of Suratha's earthly kingdom by means of his encounter with Sage Medhas. Within the *DM,* the frame narrative is not a haphazard entity. It necessarily imports significance to the tale it attempts to didactically contextualize. The *DM*'s making of a manu is therefore also the tale of solar succession, which may be understood as the lineage whose primary function is preservation within this realm. The invocation of the Sun therefore constitutes fitting symbolism for a narrative preoccupied by themes of preservation. Like the Goddess, both sovereign and Sun are charged with supporting this realm. Hence, the commencement of the glories of the Goddess invoke the glories of the Sun, where from we may receive both thematic direction in how to understand the glories of the Goddess and ritual direction about when to incant these glories. The bridge between *DM* and *MkP* is at long last brightened within the trajectory of Indological scholarship, owing to the splendor of the Sun.

Notes

1. All translations of the *DM* herein are Thomas Coburn's unless otherwise specified.

2. ityuktā sā tadā pitrā tathetyuktvā ca sā mune / saṃpūjayitvā pitaraṃ jagāmāthottarān kurūn // 77.22 //

sūryatāpamanicchantī tejasastasya bibhyatī / tapaścacāra tatrāpi vaḍa-vārūpadhāriṇī // 77.23 //.

3. Gonda notes that while *māhātmya* literature often centers around places of pilgrimage (i.e., *tīrtha*), it can, of course, center around "the figure of a god and the spread of his cult rather than the sanctity of a particular temple city or place of pilgrimage. A well-known instance is the Devī-Māhātmya" (Gonda 1977, 281). Therefore, since this conglomeration of myths details various exploits of the Sun, it is too elaborate to be called a *stotra* or *stava* (and indeed includes four such *stotras*) and lacks the requisite structure to be termed a *gītā* (indeed, there is an existing *Sūrya Gītā*), I deem *māhātmya* as the most apt appellation for the scope of these acts glorifying the Sun. To my knowledge, nothing has been written on this compilation of solar myths in the *MkP*, save for passing, general remarks that refer to sectarian materials lauding about the Sun in the *MkP*. For example, there is no mention of a *Sūrya Māhātmya* in Jan Gonda's discourse on *māhāmtyas* in the "Sanskrit Medieval Literature" section of his edited series *A History of Indian Literature*. With respect to works that praise the Sun, Gonda makes mention only of Mayūra's early seventh-century *Sūrya-Śataka* (see Gonda 1977, 251), which was contemporary with Bāṇa's *Caṇḍī-Śataka*, (see Gonda 1977, 250), along with praise of the Sun "attributed to a certain Sāmba" beginning in the middle of the eighth century (Gonda 1977, 252). He refers to a *Sūrya Gītā* in one lone sentence as follows: "The Surya-Gita must belong to the comparatively late works of this genre because it has undergone the influence of Rāmānuja's Viśiṣṭādvaita philosophy" (Gonda 1977, 276).

4. Given the explicit association of the manu Raivata and the asterism Revatī, along with the (less explicit, but still distinct, which this discussion shall elucidate) association between Vaivasvata and Aśvini, one wonders if the mythologies of the asterism and of the manus aren't intertwined in general. If so, this might account for the fact that there are fourteen manus (a highly obscure number) and twenty-eight Nakṣatras—perhaps they thematically associate in a 2:1 ratio.

5. Note that while the Sun is accorded primacy, as the soul of all, Venus represents sexuality and procreation. Venus is often personified as a goddess of fertility throughout the Indian (Lakṣmī) and Near Eastern world (e.g., Ishtar to the Babylonians; Isis to the Egyptians; Aphrodite to the Greeks; and Venus to the Romans, from whence the name comes down to us). It represents not only sexual reproduction, but also sensual and aesthetic experience at large. It is telling that the most common name for this planet in Sanskrit and its derivatives is śukra, the word for semen itself. It is understood as a moist planet since moisture is, of course, necessary for life. The Sun, on the other hand, represents heat and dryness, both of which threaten seminal health.

6. Aries is symbolized by the nose, Leo and Cancer by the right and left eye respectively, Libra and Taurus by the right and left cheek respectively, Scorpio by the mouth, Sagittarius and Pisces by the right and left ear respectively, Gemini and Virgo by the right and left forehead respectively, and Aquarius and Capricorn by the right and left chin respectively.

7. One wonders if this myth also symbolizes the Āyurvedic herb, *aśvagandha*, particularly given the association of *aśvini nakṣatra* and medicinal herbs.

8. Conversely, it is at its weakest (described in a fallen state or *nicca*) six months later at the time of the autumnal equinox, when the sun sits 180 degrees away, in the constellation of Libra. As stated in the *BJ*, the sun "is most exalted in the 10th degree of Aries" (*BJ* 1.13; Varāhamihira 1995, 17), and it is "considered as the most debilitated 180 degrees away from the degree of exaltation," that is, at the tenth degree of Libra (*BJ* 1.13; Varāhamihira 1995, 17).

9. The myth of Sūrya's hammering down is the myth of his movement from the constellation Citrā (which is owned by Aryamān, his father-in-law), to that of Aśvini, which is owned by the Aśvins.

10. The verse continues, "and Mars is the army chief; Mercury is the prince apparent and Jupiter and Venus are ministerial planets. Saturn is servant and Rahu and Ketu form the planetary army." See *BPH* 3.14–15 and Parāśara and Sharma 1994, 19.

11. The caste allotments for all the planets are as follows: Jupiter and Venus as the royal counselors (the former sacred, the later secular) are Brahmins, the Sun and Mars are Kṣatriyas, the Moon and Mercury are Vaiśyas, and Saturn is the *śūdra* (servant). See *BPH* 3.21; Parāśara and Sharma 1994, 24–25.

Bibliography

Agrawala, Vasudeva Sharana. 1963. *Devī-Māhātmyam: The Glorification of the Great Goddess*. Varanasi: All-India Kashiraj Trust.

Coburn, Thomas B. 1991. *Encountering the Goddess: A Translation of the Devī-Māhātmya and a Study of Its Interpretation*. Albany: State University of New York Press.

Desai, Nileshvari Y. 1968. *Ancient Indian Society, Religion, and Mythology as Depicted in the Mārkaṇḍeya-Purāna: A Critical Study*. Baroda: Faculty of Arts, M.S. University of Baroda.

Doniger, Wendy. 2014. "Saranyu/Samjna: The Sun and the Shadow." In *On Hinduism*, 269–87.

———. 2009. *The Hindus: An Alternative History*. New York: Penguin.

———. 1980. *Women, Androgynes, and Other Mythical Beasts*. Chicago: University of Chicago Press.

Fuller, C. J. 2004. *Camphor Flame: Popular Hinduism and Society in India*. Princeton, NJ: Princeton University Press.

Goldman, Robert P. 1969. "Mortal Man and Immortal Woman: An Interpretation of Three Akhyana Hymns of the Rgveda." *Journal of the Oriental Institute of Baroda* 18 (4): 274–303.

Gonda, Jan. 1977. *Medieval Religious Literature in Sanskrit*. A History of Indian Literature Series Volume II, Fasc. 1. Wiesbaden: Harrassowitz.

Lannoy, Richard. 1971. *The Speaking Tree: A Study of Indian Culture and Society*. London; New York: Oxford University Press.

Parāśara, and Girish Chand Sharma. 1994. *Maharishi Parasara's Brihat Parasara Hora Sastra*. New Delhi, India: Sagar.

Pargiter, F. Eden. 1904. *Mārkaṇḍeya Purāṇa*. Calcutta: Asiatic Society of Bengal.

Pingree, David. 1977. *Jyotiḥśāstra*. A History of Indian Literature Series Volume VI, Fasc. 4. Wiesbaden: Harrassowitz.

Ramanujan, A. K. 1989. "Is There an Indian Way of Thinking?" *Contributions to Indian Sociology* 23 (1): 41–58.
Rocher, Ludo. 1986. *The Purāṇas*. A History of Indian Literature Series Volume II, Fasc. 3. Wiesbaden: Harrassowitz.
Rodrigues, Hillary. 2003. *Ritual Worship of the Great Goddess: The Liturgy of the Durgā Pūjā with Interpretations*. Albany: State University of New York Press.
Varāhamihira, Sastri Pothukuchi Subrahmanya. 1995. *Brihat Jataka*. New Delhi: Ranjan.
Winternitz, Moritz. 1972. *A History of Indian Literature. 1*. New Delhi: Oriental Books Repr.

2

Which Durgā? What Navarātra?

Remarks on Reconfigurations of Royal Rituals in the Kathmandu Valley

ASTRID ZOTTER

After introducing the significance of Navarātra[1] and its relevance for the perpetuation of sovereignty in Nepal in general, in this chapter I will specifically look at what happened to the royal Navarātra rituals at the palace of Kathmandu after the shift of power from the Malla kings, reigning over the Kathmandu Valley in the medieval period, to the Shah dynasty, under whom Nepal developed into a territorial state. The fabric of royal rituals performed at this central seat of power had to be reworked considerably to cope with the changed political realities, as the two dynasties' ritual practices differed. Comparing the procedures followed under the two royal houses and the forms of Durgā worshipped by drawing on ritual specialists' texts, it is argued that in these reconfigurations, two opposing tendencies become visible. On the one hand, the Shahs adopted and included previous kings' rites, deities, and specialists, and on the other hand, they advanced their own ritual culture. From this process emerged a festival complex, which became paradigmatic for Nepalese religion as officially promoted by the national state.

Navarātra in Royal Nepal

The Nepalese autumnal Navarātra can, with all justification, be called the most important festival of the annual cycle. It has been compared to the Western Christmas season (Anderson 1971, 142), and, indeed, employees receive an additional month's salary, all government offices close for the holidays, and it is the major occasion for family visits. Unlike Indian territories, Nepal has never been colonized by European forces. By contrast, one may say that it has been colonized from within (cf. Holmberg 2000) or, as official diction has it, "unified" starting in the eighteenth century when the Shah dynasty, the royal house of the petty state of Gorkha, extended overlordship to its surrounding territories. This process led to a territorial state unprecedented in the region. The phase of expansion ended when Nepal's southern borders were fixed in the Treaty of Sagauli (1816) after the Anglo-Gurkha War. Under the Gorkhalis, an explicit Hindu agenda was one of the backbones of the Nepalese project of nation building, and one of the means to Hinduize the population living in the conquered territories was to make them celebrate Hindu festivals, above all the ("Great") Dasaĩ, as the autumnal Navarātra has usually been called.

Thus, preexisting religious practices among the diverse ethnic and social groups were, over time and to different degrees, dominated or encompassed by the ritual culture promoted by the Shahs. The latter styled themselves as Kṣatriyas, tracing their ancestry back to the Rājput House of Mewar (cf. Whelpton 1991, 14). They employed Nepalese-speaking Brahmins, who were raised to the top of the official caste hierarchy and were accorded the status of Upādhyāya Brahmins, pushing Brahmins and priests of other groups below. The ritual practice of these Parbatiyas (mountain people), as this dominant group in society is commonly called, was advanced from above and enforced on many levels. In the case of Navarātra and other festivals, even adherence to the state religion seems to have been monitored. As Hangen (2005, 120) reports, older people still remember that in the Rana period (1846–1951) officers were sent throughout the country to check whether the necessary rites had been performed. Emblematic for such "forced performances" are arguments raised in the anti-Dasaĩ movements, nowadays prevalent among the Tamang and other ethnic groups (Pfaff-Czarnecka 1996; Hangen 2005; Holmberg 2016):

> Tamang leaders, as those of many . . . groups, will often recount in their speeches and conversations that Hindu overlords forced their Buddhist elders to celebrate Dasain and to press imprints of their bloodstained hands onto the walls of their houses to prove that they had indeed participated in the required sacrificial rituals that enacted and instantiated the hierarchies of the Hindu state of Nepal from the royal centre, through district administrative offices, to villages where headman and local polities took form. (Holmberg 2016, 308)

Apart from being enforced from above, assimilation to the state religion also became a means for upward social mobility utilized from below (e.g. N. J. Allen 1997). Formal compliance with the demanded ritual practice and its reinterpretation has been used to stress specific ethnic identities and to reinforce local power structures (e.g., Holmberg 2006). As an outcome of this official policy and of its arbitrations in different settings, by the end of the twentieth century, Dasaĩ had been "celebrated country-wide by all castes and creeds" (Anderson 1971, 142). Accordingly, reference to the festival is a standard mention in ethnography on Nepal (Krauskopff and Lecomte-Tilouine 1996, 9 n. 1).

Apart from those who were newly "Hinduized" by the Gorkhalis, there were groups and local rulers who had already followed Hindu practices prior to conquest. Once conquered and without a king, such royal festivals, notably the Navarātra celebrations (see cases in Krauskopff and Lecomte-Tilouine 1996), turned into local memorial practices:

> All history, which the community gives itself is condensed in the ritual space directed to Dasaĩ, in a "cosmodrame" where it is the gods who tell the history of humans. Despite the disappearance of their king since two centuries, all communities maintain the tradition of a royal Dasaĩ also seeing in it a glorification of the locality's past. (Krauskopff and Lecomte-Tilouine 1996, 30–31, translation mine)

Former royals' Navarātras did not, however, just go on as before. They were, to some extent, reworked and made to conform to the new rulers' celebrations. Fitting into the royal "body politic" and quasi identity of king and country, Navarātra as central state ritual was performed at temples throughout the realm and linked back to the center by strategies assuring that the ruling king acted as the ritual patron (Zotter, 2018: 506–509). The most obvious (and probably most complex) case in point, which is also discussed in this chapter, is the Kathmandu Valley or the area known as "Nepal" before this latter designation was used to denote the whole territorial state. There, prior to the advent of Shah rule in 1768/69, kings of the Malla dynasty had been ruling from around 1200 over a predominantly Newari-speaking population. The Mallas' first palace was located at the city of Bhaktapur. From the late fifteenth century onward this royal seat was rivaled by the two newly independent city kingdoms of Kathmandu and Patan. The Malla family—the three kings being close relatives—followed Shaivite Tantric traditions with strong emphasis on Goddess worship.[2] Their rituals featured a combination of exoteric and esoteric practices, and in both forms of rituals the king held key roles, that of premier ritual patron (*yajamāna*) and that of foremost Tantric practitioner (*sādhaka*). These traditions were regularly "updated" by specialists and texts that either arrived from the south or were produced in Nepal itself.

The Malla palaces housed many temples of royal and lineage deities, particularly of goddesses, from whom the rulers drew their power, exemplifying a Tantric concept of rule as aptly described by Gupta and Gombrich (1986). Looking at these "seats of power" diachronically, they attest to the presence of deities and cults of still earlier dynasties (Sanderson 2003, 366–72; Toffin 1996). So, rather than superseding deities of preceding rulers, newly arriving kings seem to have left these powerful entities in place and adopted them, at least to some extent. To these traditions, they then added their own cherished deities, putting them at the center of worship. The main royal goddess whose introduction is associated with the Mallas is known as Taleju.[3]

In effect, the palaces of the Kathmandu Valley present veritable mazes of deities and places of worship that have been piled up over centuries. These labyrinths are confusing and impenetrable to any outsider, and quite intentionally so. The closer to the central power, the more restrictive Nepalese religion becomes. This "advertised secret" of Tantric practice is part of the game and a condition of its function (Levy 1990, 335–38). For the rulers of Nepal, at least from the Malla period onward, the autumnal Navarātra had been the prime occasion during which the different royal goddesses were worshipped, identified with each other, and made to disseminate their power to king and realm.[4]

The process of adding new worship practices to existing traditions continued when the Shahs entered Kathmandu in 1768. There they adopted the old Malla palace, called Hanuman Dhoka, as their own. The Shah kings brought new specialists and an alternate religious practice, as will be exemplified in this chapter with the ritual complex of Navarātra. For the kings of Gorkha too, the autumnal Navarātra was the climax of the annual ritual obligations and a prime occasion to celebrate the conjunction of divine and human power. The installation of their royal goddess Kālikā at their old palace at Gorkha is ascribed to Dravya Shah, their ancestor king who conquered Gorkha in the middle of the sixteenth century (Unbescheid 1996, 130). Interestingly, the shift of the capital to Kathmandu did not entail the relocation of this goddess. On Navarātra, the connection between the old and new palaces and the royal goddesses residing there was celebrated and ritually reaffirmed. So, when looking at the Navarātra at Kathmandu palace as it has been performed from the late eighteenth century onward, one faces elements of different origin. Although this is taken for granted in previous studies of the rituals, apart from some obvious examples (e.g., the Shahs' introduction of the Phūlpātī procession on the seventh day or their incorporation of the Mallas' sword exchange on the tenth day), the different layers of the rituals have not yet been fully examined.

Many parts of the rituals are private; however, there is an extensive textual tradition on royal Navarātra produced by and for the actors involved. This tradition is extraordinarily well documented,[5] even if so far understudied. It may be comparatively easy to access these materials physically, but the character of the texts themselves obstructs straightforward comprehension. The texts are written in different mixtures of Sanskrit with vernaculars and in different levels of rule-conformity. They are oriented toward their pragmatic ends and address specific circles of users, but certainly not the Western researcher. As the texts are deeply embedded in religious practice, they presuppose contextual knowledge. From my presently thus limited understanding of the texts and their contexts, I here still arrogate to present preliminary insights into the ritual complex of Navarātra, focussing on a comparison between the ritual procedures advanced under the Mallas and the Shahs and between their conceptions of Durgā Mahiṣāsuramardinī.

The Ritual Procedures

From an outward expectation, the two royal Navarātras under discussion should be very similar. Under both dynasties, the same Vedic school, the Mādhyandina branch of the White Yajurveda, has been dominant (Witzel 1976a). Furthermore, both royal houses worshipped a goddess as their lineage deity, and both ritual cultures refer to (often the same) Vedic, Purāṇic, and Tāntric texts as their authorities. Still, the practiced religion is strikingly distinct. These two Hindu ritual cultures continue to co-exist to the present and have served as identity markers that distinguish the Newari-speaking Newars from the Nepalese-speaking Parbatiyas, that is, the groups who provided the social and religious elites under the Malla and the Shah dynasties, respectively. The distinctiveness in terms of practiced religion also pertains to the ways of performing the Navarātra, as the following provisional comparison of the main ritual events demonstrates.

Although the Malla dynasty was defeated in the eighteenth century, the legacy of its Navarātra rituals can still be observed in the ritual performances of the Newar specialists in the old palaces (for Bhaktapur, see Levy 1990, 523–76; Śreṣṭha 2003; for Patan, see Toffin 1996; for Kathmandu, see Hoek 2004, 61–122; Pradhan 1986, 268–315; G. Vajrācārya 1976, 185–88). Moreover, texts from the Malla period are extant. Those that probably stand closest to the historical ritual practice are journals or diaries (called Newari *thyāsaphū* or *chāta*, or Sanskrit *ghaṭanāvalī*), which record dates and proceedings of major events, and ritual handbooks (called *paddhati*, *vidhi*, etc.) used by the priests. These two types of texts are closely interrelated. Sometimes handbooks contain dated diary entries, and sometimes diaries record ritual procedures to the extent that they resemble ritual handbooks. With the great deal of overlap, the boundary between these (and other) genres is often quite blurred. Together, however, the diaries and handbooks shed light on royal Navarātra performances in the late Malla period, roughly from the late sixteenth to the middle of the eighteenth centuries.[6]

Regarding the courts' Navarātra celebrations, typically the diaries only detail the auspicious moments (Sanskrit: *muhūrta*), which have been calculated for certain critical ritual elements (see list 1). Thus, they tell us about how the rituals have been anchored in time. At the same time, they give us chronological blocks around which the priestly ritual was structured. They also illuminate what were considered the main points of the overall ritual scheme, since only the key elements of a given ritual must be performed at particular auspicious moments.

List 1:

Āśvina, first *tithi* of the waxing moon (also if falling on the same solar day as the preceding new moon day)

"establishing the Navarātra (worship)" (Newari: *navarātra svaṃṅe*);

Āśvina, eighth *tithi* of the waxing moon (also if falling on the same solar day as the seventh)

"taking the deity down" (Newari: *devatā kvāhā bijyātake*);

"establishing the sword" (Newari: *khaṇḍa svaṃṅe*; Sanskrit: *khaḍgasthāpanā*);

Āśvina, ninth day of the waxing moon (also if falling on the same solar day as the eighth)

"the great ninth" (Sanskrit: *mahānavamī*);

"making sacrifices" (Newari: *bhoga biye*) of goats and buffalos;

Āśvina, tenth day of the waxing moon (also if falling on the same solar day as the ninth)

Sword Procession (Newari: *pāyāta*; Sanskrit: *cālana*) with noting the direction.

List 1: Key moments of the Navarātra celebrations at the Malla courts for the different lunar days (*tithi*), abstracted from the diaries published by Regmi (1966) and G. Vajrācārya (1966 and 1968).

Entries covering these details are found for all three major Malla cities of the Kathmandu Valley. Along with demonstrating the centrality of

Navarātra for Malla court religion, the diaries attest to the close interdependency of the three kingdoms in terms of ritual, despite their political rivalries and intrigues notoriously highlighted in history writing on the late Malla period. These ties manifest in different ways. First, the royal adherence to impurity regulations regarding death bears testimony to the rulers' familial connection. Mourning periods following a death in one of the courts were observed at the other two palaces, too. When this period of impurity interfered with the Navarātra celebrations, the ritual program was reduced considerably.[7] Second, a greater ritual network in which Bhaktapur was the center is displayed by a transfer of offerings. As shown in a text edited by D. Vajrācārya (1986) that records the annual festival schedule for the court of Kathmandu, the Navarātra performances there (as probably at Patan too) were bound to the ones at Bhaktapur court. The former court was required to send offerings daily to the deities at the latter over the course of Navarātra.[8] In this way the Kathmandu palace appeared as a kind of "branch office" of the royal and Navarātra deities, which was to be linked back to the "headquarters" at Bhaktapur. Thus, the primordial seat of Malla power, Bhaktapur, still formed the center of the ritual mesocosm.

Among the many Navarātra handbooks microfilmed in the NGMPP collection, there is a set of interrelated ones that appears to have been used for the performance of the royal Navarātra at the Bhaktapur palace (see appendix). So, the scaffold of the ritual construction inferred from the diaries (see List 1) can be fleshed out when read in conjunction with these Navarātra handbooks from Bhaktapur, at least regarding priestly action. They elaborately prescribe and delineate the rituals that are to be completed on the different days of the festival by different priests. Roughly speaking, on the first day, called "Navarātra day" (Newari: *navarātrakonhu*) or "first day of the lunar fortnight" (Newari: *paḍukonhu*), the Navarātra goddess, together with her retinue deities, is invoked and worshipped in a mandala and in other representations, notably a sword (Newari: *khaṇḍa*; Sanskrit: *khaḍga*). Furthermore, barley is sown (Nw. *tyaṃcho hole*).[9] After repeating the initial day's worship over the following days, on the eighth day, the main royal deity, whose name is not given in the handbooks and only called by generic titles such as Bhagavatī (Glorious One), probably to conceal her identity from the uninitiated, and the sword are taken down from the temple (located on the top floor of the palace) in a procession. The deity is bathed and installed on the ground floor, where the sword is also set up for worship (*khaḍgasthāpanā*). For the ninth day, the handbooks again detail an extensive worship program that includes sacrifices and an elaborate "worship of girls" (*kumārīpūjā*). The tenth day is called the "procession day" (Newari: *cālanakonhu*) and includes the dismissal of the deities, the procession of the royal goddess back to her temple, and a Sword Procession (Newari: *pāyāta*) from the palace. Moreover, the handbooks mention specific recitations of the *Devīmāhātmya* from the first to the tenth days and the worship of one of nine Durgās together with Bhairavas (fierce forms of Śiva) on each of the first nine days (see below).

Currently, textual equivalents of these Malla-period handbooks and diaries are still missing from the Shah period. To date, I have not found ritual texts from preconquest era Gorkha or the actual handbooks used in the Shah period at Gorkha or Kathmandu. Although Unbescheid (1996, 111) has noted that the priests at Gorkha use printed handbooks, he does not give details. The material used here, therefore, consists primarily of observational data on the performance at Gorkha (Unbescheid 1996) and at Kathmandu (Hoek 2004, 107–22; Lecomte-Tilouine and Shrestha 1996). These materials are complemented by texts foundational for ritual practice in the Shah period, especially two treatments of Navarātra in digests written by early Shah kings of Kathmandu. An extensive *Durgotsavavidhi* (*Instruction for the Durgā Festival*) is found in the *Puraścaryārṇava* (II.959–1129) that was written by King Pratapsimha (1751–77, r. 1775–77), the second in line of succession and son of the conquering Prithvinarayan. The *Satkarmaratnāvalī* (II.201–44) by Pratapsimha's grandson Girvanayuddha (1797–1816, r. 1799–1816) covers the treatment of Navarātra during the annual cycle.[10] Additionally, I refer to a handbook from the late Shah period, written as teaching material for courses in ritual practice (*karmakaṇḍa*) at the campuses of the Māhendra Sanskrit University (Upādhyāya Gautama and Dāhāla 2006, 133–68). These sources consistently prescribe a procedure that differs from the Malla ritual sequence and has many practices in common with what is known from texts and performances of northeast Indian origin (see list 2; cp. Rodrigues 2003; Sarkar 2012):

List 2:

Āśvina, first day of the waxing moon
"establishing the jar" (Sanskrit: *ghaṭasthāpana*);
"sowing barley" (Sanskrit: *yavanaropaṇa*);
at Gorkha: royal goddess taken down;

Āśvina, sixth day of the waxing moon
"invoking (the goddess in) the *bilva* tree" (Sanskrit: *bilvanimantraṇa*);

Āśvina, seventh day of the waxing moon
"introducing the nine plants" (Sanskrit: *navapatrikāpraveśa*; Nepali: *phūlpātī*);

Āśvina, eighth day of the waxing moon
"great eighth" (Sanskrit: *mahāṣṭamī*);
at night: Kālarātri worship;

Āśvina, ninth day of the waxing moon

"great ninth" (Sanskrit: *mahānavamī*) with sacrifices;

"worship of (a stallion as) Revanta" (*revantapūjā*);[11]

Āśvina, tenth day of the waxing moon

dismissal of the deities with a procession to discard the *phūlpātī*.

List 2: Main elements of the royal Navarātra celebration as performed for the Shah dynasty.

Further elements common to these prescriptions include the reading of the *Devīmāhātmya* and the worship of girls from the first to the ninth days.

The rituals the two dynasties performed are very similar and can be (and actually are) recognized as "the same thing." The core performances extend from the first to the tenth lunar days of Āśvina: the main implements are established on the first day, the main sacrifices take place on the eighth and ninth days, and the deities are dismissed on the tenth day. Furthermore, the royal goddess is "brought down" to the place of worship, either from her temple on high in case of the Mallas' Taleju or from the Kailāsakoṭhā, a room on the top floor of the palace in case of the Shahs' Kālikā. The performances also share two other well-established Navarātra elements, the recitation of the *Devīmāhātmya* (cp. Balkaran, this volume) and the "worship of girls" (*kumārīpūjā*) (cp. Luchesi, this volume).

The *kumārīpūjā* may be taken as a case study to illustrate the fact that, despite an outward conformity of elements, the differences in ritual practice are striking. For the Mallas, Kumārī is worshipped as a premenstrual girl, who is considered the embodiment of the goddess and initiated into this post for a longer period. In all three cities of the Kathmandu Valley, she was and still is selected from certain families of the two highest Buddhist castes (for more on caste dynamics in this process, see Levy 1990, 542–44). Her initiation takes place during the autumnal Navarātra, and on each following "Great Ninth," she is worshipped in a special room just above the Navarātra room where the royal goddess is installed (M. Allen 1975, 10–21). Her worship as "lone Kumārī" (Ekāntakumārī) is preceded by the *gaṇakumārīpūjana*, the worship of nine other Kumārīs representing the nine maṇḍalic goddesses (see below) along with two boys representing Gaṇeśa and Bhairava. All children involved are chosen for the occasion from the same Buddhist families entitled to provide the Ekāntakumārī. It seems that in Malla times the children were personally fetched by the king from their Buddhist monastery, and the ruler personally carried the Ekāntakumārī on his back to the palace (for more details, see Levy 1990, 539–46; D. Vajrācārya 1986, 82–83). The behavior of the girl-goddesses on these occasions was taken as an omen for the future faith of king and country (Levy 1990, 542–46). This is illustrated in following story:

> On Thursday, the eighth day of the dark moon of Bhādra of the year 768, one of the queens of Pratāpa Malla of Kāntipura [i.e. Kathmandu, A.Z.] passed away. The death ritual was . . . performed. . . . King Siddhinarasiṃha [of Patan, A.Z.], ignoring the death impurity, let the people celebrate Dasaĩ in the usual manner . . . On the day of Navamī-pūjā, he went to Hatako Bāhāla to take the Kaumārīs (to the palace), but he could not do so, since Maheśvarī of the Kumārīs was crying. After eight days . . . glorious Bhānumatī, the queen of double-glorious Siddhinarasiṃha Malladeva, passed away at midnight. (Bajracharya and Michaels 2016, 122)

Though the text does not feature any markers that establish causality between the events, any reader acquainted with the local traditions would probably understand that the king's neglect of the proper observance of the ritual mourning period leads to the death of his wife. Moreover, her untimely death appears to have been foreshadowed by the behavior of one of the Kumārīs.

At the Shahs' palace, too, the "worship of girls" has been integral to Navarātra. In contrast to the Mallas' worship of Buddhist girls, however, in the Shah ritual, girls are selected from Brahmin families. At the royal court of Gorkha, the worship of these Kumārīs is conducted at Kanyākoṭhā, a special worship arena.[12] As in the Malla palaces, the ritual takes place on the first floor of the palace. The worship starts on the first day and continues throughout Navarātra with an especially elaborate *pūjā* of the girls as a set of twenty-seven (three by nine) Kumārīs, which includes washing their feet and feeding them on the "Great Ninth." This is in accordance with textual evidence, which states that on each of the Navarātra days a girl of a different age should be worshipped under a different name.[13]

These examples should suffice to show that the two dynasties followed distinct ritual procedures. So, after the conquest of Kathmandu, when the Shahs left their deity and her rituals at Gorkha behind and established themselves at Hanuman Dhoka palace, how was their royal Navarātra celebrated and relocated? What happened to the preexisting Malla practices? Were two rituals performed side-by-side or were they fused? Although the present state of research does not allow for comprehensive and detailed answers, I venture some suggestions about where future analysis might lead. The available materials suggest that since the Shahs' take-over, at Hanuman Dhoka, two teams of priests have worked through the ritual procedures. There seems to be only a slight overlap in procedure between the Newar specialists attending to the Mallas' royal goddess and the Parbatiya priests handling Shah practice. This is reflected in a separation of worship spaces, though this separation is not always clear-cut. The Newar specialists officiate at the Taleju temple that is called the big temple (Tavadevala) and at the Mūlcok (main courtyard) in the inner palace, where the deity is brought during Navarātra. The Parbatiya priests use the royal Dasaĩghar, which was more recently constructed in the garden on the eastern side of the Mūlcok and where the jar is established and the barley is sown.[14] As one of the highlights, the Parbatiya priests and the king welcome the procession of the Phūlpātī ([a bundle of] flowers and leaves) at the outer Nasalcok (courtyard [with a temple] of Nāsaḥdyaḥ) on the seventh day. In this elaborate Phūlpātī ritual, one may see the repetition and reaffirmation of victory over the Kathmandu Valley, as the bundle is carried from Gorkha to Kathmandu retracing the "road of conquest" (Krauskopff and Lecomte-Tilouine 1996, 29). As I have pointed out elsewhere (Zotter 2016a, 274–76; 2016b, 236), it may also be interpreted as an attempt to shift the accents of the ritual and distract attention from Taleju, who is carried in procession on the same day to Mūlcok, the courtyard behind the Nasalcok.

The spatial divide between worship practices also pertains to the blood sacrifices. Again, the Mūlcok serves as sacrificial ground for the Newar specialists, whereas the Koṭ, the military headquarters just opposite the royal palace, is the focal point for the Parbatiya army sacrifices, which were again blessed by the attendance of the king (Hoek 2004, 108–09, 120–21). There is, however, also some interweaving in terms of ritual space and function, as the army decapitates goats and buffalos for Taleju at Mūlcok under the guidance of Parbatiya Brahmins. This is done on the morning of the ninth day, but, as Hoek (2004, 109) has pointed out, the doors of the shrine of the Mallas' goddess remain closed on this occasion.

All this points to the fact that the practices of the previous dynasty were, by and large, left in place, while the Shahs added their practices, their own specialists, and ritual spaces. While the divide of worship space and the attendance of the king at Parbatiya rituals might convey a message that denies centrality to the former practice and specialists associated with the previous dynasty, to outsiders unfamiliar to the nuances in the ritual performance, the festival is successfully presented as one united ritual. It seems that this image of unity was achieved by minute but effective reworking of the predecessors' rituals to blend into the frame set by the newly arriving elites.

A close reading of the texts produced in the early Shah period indicates one such change, pertaining to timing. It is well known that calculating the proper timings for rituals is a science in its own right, and learned opinions may differ vastly. Festival days are typically fixed to particular lunar days (*tithi*). The length of these *tithis* varies between nineteen and twenty-six hours, but in most cases, they are shorter than solar days (*vāras*). Accordingly, possible recalibrations for every festival exist in case the real lunar day is omitted in the calendar because it covers only the latter part of one solar day and stops before or does not sufficiently extend into the next one (*kṣayatithi*). Problems and possible solutions to this and other astrological problems multiply for a festival extending over ten lunar days. This also finds expression in the Shah Nibandhas's treatment of Navarātra, where long discussions of determining the proper moments (*nirṇaya*) are found. In these passages, strikingly much ink is spilled to stress certain points, at least two of which are pertinent to the present discussion. It is argued that the "establishing of the jar" (*ghaṭasthāpana*) is not to be performed when the first lunar day (*pratipad*) falls on the same solar day as the preceding new moon day (*amāvasyā*). In this case, the solar day on which the second lunar day of the month falls is preferred.[15] Likewise the rites of the eighth day should only be performed on the solar day during which no parts of the seventh lunar day fall (*Puraścaryārṇava* II, 981–86; *Satkarmaratnāvalī* II, 218–19).

What, at first sight, appears to be a specialists' discussion of astrological details assumes new meanings in the local context. The two options explicitly condemned are exactly those that were the standard practice in Malla time, that is, in case of a *kṣayatithi* performing the rites of the first day on the solar day, on which *amāvasyā* and *pratipad* are connected, and the rites of the eighth day on the day when *saptamī* and *aṣṭamī* occur together (see List 1 above). The early Shah texts here reveal an attempt to "rectify" the existing ritual practice and to establish ritual superiority and final authority through "proper" performance. The official reworking of ritual timings seems to be part of a larger strategy, by which preexisting Navarātra practices throughout the country were synchronized and made to conform to a central model (Zotter forthcoming). The timings (Nepali *sāit*) for Navarātra and other rituals were fixed by the king's astrologers, and as historical documents show these centrally calculated timings guided all rituals performed on behalf of the royal state. Even today, these *sāits* are announced in newspapers. Levy (1990, 527, 531, 533, 550) reports that in Bhaktapur, three *sāits* were centrally fixed: the sowing of barley, taking the deity down, and putting the deity up again. The Newar specialists, however, were free to fix other timings as needed. This may also explain why the Malla handbooks prescribe the taking down of the deity for the eighth day, while it is reported that throughout the Shah period the deity was taken down on the seventh day. Was the ritual procession of the former royals' primary deity switched to the previous day to coincide with (or rather happen in the shadow of) the elaborately staged procession of the Phūlpātī? The question remains, but similar adaptations are also present when considering the deity worshipped.

The Goddesses Worshipped

Under both royal dynasties Durgā has been honoured as the "killer of the buffalo demon" (Mahiṣāsuramārdinī). After all, Navarātra is the festival celebrating the warrior goddess's victory over her demon enemy. When looking at the concrete forms of Mahiṣāsuramārdinī, however, the two festival traditions again differ.

For the Mallas, Durgā was the eighteen-armed Ugracaṇḍā, as the famous image of her, established at the court of Bhaktapur by Bhūpatīndra Malla in 1707, eye-catchingly displays (figure 2.1).[16] The royal Navarātra handbooks describe the worship of Ugracaṇḍā at great length. She is the main deity invoked. She is described with her hands holding different

Figure 2.1. Durgā as the eighteen-armed Ugracaṇḍā from the court of Bhaktapur (1707 CE).

Table 2.1. Attributes held by Ugracaṇḍā in her 18 hands (cp. plate 1). The hand pair no. 7 (*ḍamaru* and *khatvaṅga*) is depicted raised upwards and is the one which distinguishes Ugracaṇḍā from the eight surrounding Caṇḍās.

Hand (top to bottom)	Right	Left
1	sword (*khaḍga*)	shield (*spheṭaka*)
2	arrow (*śara*)	bow (*dhanu*)
3	disc (*cakra*)	mace (*gadā*)
4	thunderbolt (*vajra*)	bell (*ghaṇṭā*)
5	goad (*aṅkuśa*)	noose (*pāśa*)
6	boon-conveying gesture (*varadamudrā*)	*tarjanīmudrā*
7	two-headed drum (*ḍamaru*)	skull-topped staff (*khatvaṅga*)
8	spear (*śūla*)	bundle of hair (*keśapāśa*) (of Mahiṣāsura)
9	vessel (*pātra*)	*bindumudrā*

weapons with each pair of arms featuring two interrelated items, such as sword and shield and bow and arrow (see table 2.1). Though Ugracaṇḍā as eighteen-armed form of Mahiṣāsuramardinī is known from many local sources, both in texts and in performative arts, I have found no parallel for this particular iconography in any Sanskrit texts from outside the Kathmandu Valley.[17]

As the palace handbooks say, during the Navarātra, Ugracaṇḍā is to be worshipped in different representations, including on an earthen mound (*sthaṇḍila*), in a sword (*khaḍga*), a book (*puthi*), a statue (*pratimā*), and a jar (*kumbha*). On the first day, a mandala is drawn on the *sthaṇḍila*. There Ugracaṇḍā occupies the center of an eight-petal lotus and is surrounded by eight sixteen-armed Caṇḍās starting with Rudracaṇḍā on the eastern petal. These Caṇḍās are identified with the Aṣṭamātṛkās, the Eight Mother Goddesses, and are grouped with eight Bhairavas (see table 2.2). Along with their worship as part of the Navarātra *maṇḍala*, the retinue deities surrounding the central Ugracaṇḍā are to be worshipped throughout the eight days from the first to the eighth, each with specific offerings. On Mahānavamī, this worship of the individual Caṇḍās culminates in worshipping Ugracaṇḍā at their center. Interestingly, she is worshipped as an independent goddess with no attending Bhairava or Mātṛkā.

Not only are the deities of the mandala worshipped in seclusion inside the palace, but they are also integral to the valley's iconographic traditions and to the ritual construction of urban space. Moreover, this mandala literarily comes to life during the Navarātra festival. Over the nine days, the aniconic seats (*pīṭhas*) of the Eight Mother Goddesses that surround the settlement continue to be worshipped today by the inhab-

Table 2.2. Central configuration of deities worshipped in a mandala under the Malla dynasty on Navarātra according to handbooks. The pairings of Mātṛkās and Bhairavas are standards in the Newars' iconographic tradition (see Blom 1989, 22–29).

tithi	Direction	Caṇḍā	Mātṛkā	Bhairava
1	E	Rudracaṇḍā	Brahmāṇī	Asitāṅgabhairava
2	SE	Pracaṇḍā	Māheśvarī	Rurubhairava
3	S	Caṇḍogrā	Kaumārī	Caṇḍabhairava
4	SW	Caṇḍanāyikā	Vaiṣṇavī (Bhadrakālī)	Krodhabhairava
5	W	Caṇḍā	Vārāhī (Vajravarāhī)	Unmattabhairava
6	NW	Caṇḍavatī	Indrānī	Kapālīśabhairava
7	N	Caṇḍarūpā	Cāmuṇḍā (Mahākālī)	Bhīṣaṇabhairava
8	NE	Aticaṇḍikā	Mahālakṣmī	Saṃhārabhairava
9	center	Ugracaṇḍā	—	—

itants of Bhaktapur, who visit one of the goddesses on each of the days of the festival. This sequence of worship starts with Brahmāṇī in the east on the first day and continues through a full circumambulation of the city until the eighth day, during which Mahālakṣmī is worshipped in the northeast. Opinions differ regarding the identity of the goddess who is worshipped on the ninth day in the middle of the city. For the visitors of the Mother Goddesses, this day's worship destination is often the centrally located *pīṭha* that is dedicated to Tripurasundarī (Levy 1990, 538; cf. Kölver 1976, 69). From the perspective of the handbooks, the deity worshipped on the ninth day is Ugracaṇḍā, who is identified with a goddess called in Newari *śrīpañcabhaḍiju* (probably linked to Sanskrit: *śrīpañcabhaṭṭārikā*; "five times venerable goddess"). Thus, the secret and elusive nature of the goddess at the center, the "real" *śakti* of the realm, is stressed here again while underlining her power and pervasiveness.

The goddesses are also worshipped as they awake in the form of the troupe of nine Durgās (*navadurgāgaṇa*) in the night from the ninth to the tenth days.[18] During the strictly secret nocturnal ritual, they are transferred from their aniconic seats (*pīṭhas*) into human dancers from the gardener subcaste. The nine Durgās, then, come to the palace gate during the Sword Procession on Daśamī and receive empowerment from the central goddess (Levy 1990, 525). Over the following months, they perform their dances in and around the city. Thus, the whole city becomes a living mandala that replicates the one worshipped throughout the Navarātra in the palace sanctums.

All divine configurations worshipped during Navarātra under the Mallas of which I am aware align within this ritual construction. According to the handbooks, Ugracaṇḍā is not only central to the rites at the

Navarātra room of the palace, but she is also identified with other royal goddesses residing there. Moreover, all groups of goddesses—the Mother Goddesses at their *pīṭhas*, the dancers who are transformed into the Durgās, the troupe of Kumārīs who are worshipped on the ninth day—are conceived as the same set of nine Caṇḍās. Thus, at least for Bhaktapur, it seems as if the rituals and city were constructed for one another. At Kathmandu, this situation may vary, as for example the lists of Mother Goddesses surrounding the territory differ (see Gutschow and Bajracharya 1977), but more research is needed to elucidate this case, which probably constitutes an "exportation" of Malla ritual to a new urban surrounding and into a preexisting sacred infrastructure at the end of the fifteenth century. Still, as shown above, the court ritual of Malla-ruled Kathmandu maintained ties to the ancestral seat of power at Bhaktapur.

The Shahs' primary royal deity, Kālikā of Gorkha palace, is part of another network of deities. She is conceived as the oldest of seven sisters, whose shrines mark the core territory of the petty state of Gorkha (Unbescheid 1996, 104–5). This territorial structure was also actualized on Navarātra through the exchange of offerings that were being sent back and forth. As Unbescheid (1996) has shown, on the occasion of Navarātra the palace of Gorkha was marked as the sacred and political center when material and personal tributes were delivered to the goddess. Additionally, the Shahs' Durgā is conceived remarkably differently from the Mallas' Ugracaṇḍā. Although there is no observation data to confirm the goddess's iconography, texts from the Shah period describe the Navarātra worship of Durgā in her ten-armed form called Kātyāyanī. The *Puraścaryārṇava*, though it also treats her sixteen- and eighteen-armed forms, foregrounds her worship in this form. As we saw with other parts of the Shah-period Navarātra rituals, the visualization of this goddess concurs with what is known from northeast India.

Apart from this central goddess, the texts of the Shah period also include groups of nine Durgās that are to be worshipped. While under the Mallas the strategy seemed to have been to activate and celebrate one configuration of goddesses into which all concrete forms merge as instantiations, under the Shahs the wealth of forms of Durgās was stressed. Thus, not only are the nine young girls worshipped as a set of nine goddesses, but nine other goddesses are invoked in the Phūlpātī, the bundle of nine leaves worshipped on the seventh: Brāhmī, Raktadantikā, Lakṣmī, Durgā, Cāmuṇḍā, Kālikā, Śivā, Śokahāriṇī, Kārttikī (Upādhyāya Gautama and Dāhāla 2006, 155; cf. Rodrigues 2003 and Sarkar 2012, 353).

Interestingly, when looking at the meditation verses (*dhyānaślokas*) of the central Durgā, a group of eight Caṇḍās is mentioned as her divine retinue, but their names differ from those found in the Malla handbooks: the first goddess (Rudracaṇḍā) is replaced with Ugracaṇḍā and the last goddess (Aticaṇḍikā) is replaced with Caṇḍikā. The *Puraścaryārṇava* (II.1022–23) reads:

> *ugracaṇḍā pracaṇḍā ca caṇḍogrā caṇḍanāyikā* |
> *caṇḍā caṇḍavatī caiva caṇḍarūpā ca caṇḍikā* ||[19]

while the Malla handbooks have:

> *rudracaṇḍā pracaṇḍā ca caṇḍogrā caṇḍanāyikā* |
> *caṇḍā caṇḍavatī caiva caṇḍarūpāticaṇḍikā* ||[20]

These two versions of the verse are also attested in other sources (cp. Sarkar 2012, 379–80). In the local context of the Kathmandu Valley, this variance may carry important implications. By citing the verse in the first version, Ugracaṇḍā, the central goddess of the Mallas, is reduced to a retinue deity subordinated to the form of Durgā favored by the Shahs. In other respects too, the texts of the Shah period, at least implicitly, challenge their predecessors' celebration of Navarātra. The worship of Ugracaṇḍā is mentioned in the *Puraścaryārṇava,* but the text prescribes a different time frame of worship, quoting other authorities which say that Mahiṣāsuramārdinī when worshipped as Ugracaṇḍā is to be invoked on the ninth day of the dark fortnight preceding the Navarātra. Together the reconfiguration of the ritual practice and timing can be read as an attempt to challenge the rule-conformity of the Malla celebration of Navarātra.

Conclusion

The Malla and Shah dynasties, who successively ruled over the Kathmandu Valley, adhered to very similar religious traditions. The focus on a particular royal goddess is common to both dynasties. Likewise, in both cases the palace was the central seat of power (of king and goddess) and was ritually linked with other important worship places, thus stressing the sacred topography of the realm. Ritual practice, as performed by their elites, however, was also strikingly different. This divide is mirrored up to the present day in the two ritual cultures of the Newars and Parbatiyas and pertains to the ways royal Navarātra has been celebrated. While the Mallas' festival practices focused on the worship of a sword and a mandala, centering on the Navadurgā with eight sixteen-armed Caṇḍās surrounding the eighteen-armed Ugracaṇḍā, the Shahs' rituals largely followed the more common procedure of invoking Durgā in a jar on the first, in the *bilva* tree on the sixth, nine plants on the seventh, and featuring the worship of ten-armed Durgā as Kātyāyanī.

Under these conditions, the dynastic break of the eighteenth century, which involved the shift of the Shah seat of power from Gorkha to Kathmandu, necessitated a thorough reconfiguring of royal Navarātra practices. In effect, the Navarātra rites, not only at Gorkha, but at Kathmandu too, appeared as parts of one ritual complex which formed one of the main "reinforcement rituals" (Mocko 2016, ch. 6) for the Shah kings of Nepal.

Two different strategies seem to have been at work in bringing about this unification of practices. On the one hand, the Mallas' rituals were largely left intact, not only in the other two palaces of the valley, but also in Kathmandu. With the Mallas' ritual specialists being financed by the state, the rituals that focused on Ugracaṇḍā and Taleju continued to be staged. On the other hand, new elements, specialists, and worship arenas were added. Rather than dropping older practices or letting the deities involved be worshipped by new specialists or new procedures, the previous dynasty's performances were "tuned in." The minor recalibrations with which this was achieved, however, were probably hardly noticed by common people and observers. They were made visible in the present contribution by putting the specialists' texts into dialogue. A comparison of the ritual timings recorded in Malla period diaries with the schedule advanced in the Shah period reveals a reworking, which was advanced as a rectification in accordance with what the authoritative textual tradition mandates. Thus, supremacy and authority were established through the means of ritual itself.

Such integration of previous rulers' rituals could, depending on standpoint, be reinterpreted as an honoring of local traditions or as acknowledging the preeminent claims of the territorial deities. Or one could argue that the new rulers sought to legitimize themselves in the local context with the local elites, while at the same time making a statement about absorbing the earlier kings' practices and submitting them under their own model. The reconfiguration thus carried the potential for different attitudes of rulers, specialists, and audiences toward different parts of the royal Navarātra rituals and toward each other, which—depending on the mind-sets of the actual persons involved and on historical circumstances—could be and were at times activated to different degrees. To study these and further points of conflict, conflation, or harmony in the royal Nepalese Navarātra rituals promises to be a fruitful field of study.

Appendix: Consulted Handbooks on Royal Navarātra of the Malla Period

I consulted the following handbooks to reconstruct the Navarātra practice under the Malla dynasty. All of them were microfilmed under in the

Nepal-German Manuscript Preservation Project (NGMPP). The originals are kept at the Nepalese National Archives, Kathmandu (NAK).

Navarātrapūjāvidhi (NGMPP B 532/21; NAK 8/868): dated 1570 (NS 690), 33 fols., written under the joint rule of Gaṅgādevī, Trailokya, and Tribhuvana Malla by the *vidyāpīṭhakarmācārya* (of Bhaktapur) Govindasiṃha for the royal priest Harṣadeva, disciple of Ulhāsarāja.[21]

Navarātrapūjāvidhi (NGMPP B 532/23; NAK 8/2267): dated 1639 (NS 759), 25 fols., written by the royal priest Mahādeva Rāja.

Navarātracāranavidhi (NGMPP A 1234/26; NAK 8/2196): dated 1694 (NS 814), 15 fols., written under King Jitāmitra Malla: only contains prescriptions for the tenth day (end: *iti śrīśrīrājakula-bhaṭṭārakasya pāraṃparyyakramena navarātradaśamīcālanavidhiḥ samāptaḥ*) and is possibly part of a set of handbooks composed for different parts of the ritual.[22]

Mahāṣṭamīnavamīdaśamīvidhāna (NGMPP B 195/2; NAK 3/56): undated, 166 fols., starts: *śrīśrīrājakulayā mahanīyā paripāti vidhāna lhāye* ("the instructions for the method of the *mahanī* (rituals) of the twice venerable royal palace are told"). The handbook contains historical notes.

Notes

Research for this chapter was carried out as part of my employment in the research unit Documents on the History of Religion and Law of Premodern Nepal of the Heidelberg Academy of Sciences and Humanities. I wish to thank Niels Gutschow, Hillary Rodrigues, Alexis Sanderson, Moumita Sen, Caleb Simmons, Christof Zotter, and the anonymous reviewers of SUNY for their comments on and revisions of this chapter. All mistakes are mine.

1. I mostly refer to the festival as Navarātra. This designation is neutral to the two different ritual cultures treated. Although in the modern context, the Nepali term "Dasaĩ" (or, if to be distinguished from Caitedasaĩ, the spring Navarātra, "Baḍādasaĩ/Mahādasaĩ"), related to Sanskrit *daśāhan*, is usually used, in medieval Nepal, the Newari designation "Mahanī/Mohanī/Mvaḥni" (related to Sanskrit *mahānavamī*) was much more prevalent. My use of "Navarātra" rather than "Navarātrī" follows the texts studied.

2. The place of Buddhism in state religion should not be underestimated. Although the Malla kings had been Shaivite Hindus, Buddhist religious institutions have played a vital role, especially in the Buddhist stronghold of Patan.

3. Her name, the "Venerable (*ju*) on High (*tale*)," is more apt to veil than to disclose her identity, which is a well-protected secret and has invited many speculations. However, this issue is too involved to be addressed here.

4. The earliest safe reference I am aware of stems from the late fourteenth-century chronicle *Gopālarājavaṃśāvalī*, where reference to the Navarātra celebration of 1375 (NS 495) is made (Vajrācārya and Malla 1985, fol. 55). Moreover, there is a Paddhati for a Buddhist *khaḍgapūjā*, featuring the worship of Trailokyavijaya in the bright half of Āśvina, dated 1271 (NS 391) (Zotter 2016b, 239 n. 38).

5. This situation owes a great deal to the efforts of scholars, archives, and, not least, the Nepal-German Manuscript Preservation Project (NGMPP), under which Nepalese manuscripts were microfilmed from 1970–2002 (https://www.aai.uni-hamburg.de/en/forschung/ngmcp/history/about-ngmpp.html).

6. The earliest handbook is dated 1570 (NS 690) and the most recent entry in the diaries consulted is from 1743 (NS 863).

7. An example is the case in 1674 (NS 794), when on the sixth day after initiating the Navarātra worship, a grandchild of the king of Patan (Yala) died. The royal deity Taleju was not taken down at Kathmandu. Sacrifices were made to her at her temple, and only the sword was established as usual (G. Vajrācārya 1966, 23). For a case when the mourning period was not kept across the courts, see below.

8. Offerings are to be sent to Dumāju, Vaṃkuli, Māneśvarī, "the Navarātra goddess" (Navarātrabhagavatī), Taleju, and the different rooms, in which Navarātra worship takes place at Bhaktapur palace, such as Yethakhaṇḍakuthi (D. Vajrācārya 1986, 82–87). This link-up to the old Malla palace is specified for other festivals as well.

9. This element is covered by the *Navarātrapūjāvidhi* from 1639, but not in the earlier one from 1570 (see appendix). Either in the latter it had been taken for granted, or the sowing of barley was added later.

10. It is hard to imagine how kings who died at the age of twenty-six or nineteen, respectively, could have compiled the two voluminous digests they are ascribed by themselves. The ascription of authorship is more likely to be due to the royal body politic, in which achievements of others merge into the figure of the king. The texts are possibly better understood as being part of a process of newly arriving court pandits (or of resident pandits now employed by new rulers) working through the extensive libraries of the Malla dynasty and tailoring the textual authorities to the requirements of the new ritual practice. The takeover of these mines of knowledge under the Shahs deserves a study of its own.

11. From the textual side, this element is only covered by the *Puraścaryārṇava* (II.1108–14). Still, it is quoted here, as it forms part of the rituals at Gorkha palace (Unbescheid 1996).

12. The description of the worship at Gorkha follows Unbescheid (1996: 123–24).

13. From the first to the ninth, girls shall be worshipped as Kumārikā, Trimūrti, Kalyāṇī, Rohiṇī, Kālī, Caṇḍikā, Śāmbhavī, Durgā, and Subhadrā, respectively, with the girls' age increasing by one year every day, beginning when they are two (one-year-old girls are not considered fit for worship) on the first (*Satkarmaratnāvalī* II: 207). This prescription tallies with the one quoted by Kane (1958, 5.1:170) from the *Skandapurāṇa*. Upādhyāya Gautama and Dāhāla (2006, 150–63) have Kāmākṣī for Rohiṇī and Samudrā for Subhadrā.

14. Judging from the architecture, Gutschow (2011, 344–45 no. 29), gives the twentieth century as the beginning of this building. If this is the case, there

must have been a predecessor to the building, as *in situ* an inscription of 1802 (VS 1859) records a queen's donation of a bell to please the deity of the Dasaĩghar (G. Vajrācārya 1976, 267).

15. *Puraścaryārṇava* II, 961–75, *Satkarmaratnāvali* II, 201–2; for pro and counter arguments see Kane (1958, 5.1: 182–83).

16. The inscription quoted by Pauḍela (1966, 29) gives the date as NS 827 Vaiśākha, the third of the bright half (i.e., Akṣayatṛtīya).

17. The same iconography is found in painters' model books from Nepal (Blom 1989, 41 pl. 49, 51–52). The *Agnipurāṇa* (50.6c–13b) has the same names and arrangement of Caṇḍās, but Ugracaṇḍā's attributes differ. In the *Kālīkāpurāṇa* both attributes and set of Caṇḍās are different (cp. n. 19).

18. For more on the Navadurgāgaṇa, see, for example, Gutschow and Basukala 1987; Śreṣṭha 2003.

19. Compare *Kālīkāpurāṇa* 59.22 (with the last quarter reading instead *cāmuṇḍā caṇḍikā tathā*), 65.42 (same verse as in *Puraścaryārṇava* in the accusative case).

20. The same verse is found in *Agnipurāṇa* 50.10c–11b.

21. This is probably the same Ulhāsarāja/Ullāsarāja to whom Bhaktapur Rājopādhyāyas, the Mallas' former royal priests, trace their ancestry in family trees (see Witzel 1976b). Witzel (1976b 162) quotes a note on the date of death as 1576 but raises some doubts, which in light of the present manuscript can be erased.

22. Other manuscripts of the set, all written in NS 814, seem to include the following: handbook for the sword room (A 1234/23 *khandakhutiyā vidhi*); handbook for the Mahāṣṭamī (B 199/8, ends: *iti śrīśrīrājakulabhaṭṭārakasya pāraṃparyakramena mahāṣṭamī antalavāṅa arccanapūjāvidhiḥ samāptaḥ*); handbook for the worship of the Gaṇakaumārīs on Mahānavamī in the north-eastern room (A 233/18, ends: *iti śrīśrīrājakulabhaṭṭārakasya pāraṃparyakramena gaṇakaumārārccanamahānavamīvidhiḥ samāptaḥ* || *īśānakothāyā*); handbook for the worship and praise of the lone Kaumārī on Mahānavamī (A 989/7 *mahanavamiyakatakaumārārcanastuti*); handbook for the sacrifice to the sword on Mahānavamī (D 1/16 (*Mahānavamīpārvaṇa)Khaḍgabhogārcanapūjāvidhi*) handbook for Mahādaśamī rites (E 814/30(1) *Mahādaśamīpārvaṇya(b)alivisar(j)anavidhi*, E 814/30(2) *Mahādaśamīkhaḍga(y)ātrāvidhi*). All information, including spellings, is cited according to the online catalogue of the NGMCP (http://catalogue.ngmcp.uni-hamburg.de/wiki/).

References

Agnipurāṇa. 1873–1879. *Agni Purána: A Collection of Hindu Mythology and Traditions*, edited by Rájendralála Mitra. 3 vols. Calcutta: Bibliotheca Indica (e-text: http://gretil.sub.uni-goettingen.de/gretil/1_sanskr/3_purana/agp_bi_u.htm).

Allen, Michael. 1975. *The Cult of Kumari: Virgin Worship in Nepal*. Kathmandu: INAS.

Allen, N. J. 1997. "Hinduization: The Experience of the Thulung Rai." In *Nationalism and Ethnicity in a Hindu Kingdom: The Politics of Culture in Contemporary Nepal*, edited by David N. Gellner, Joanna Pfaff-Czarnecka, and John Whelpton, 303–24. Amsterdam: Harwood.

Anderson, Mary M. 1971. *The Festivals of Nepal*. London: Allen & Unwin.

Bajracharya, Manik Lal, and Axel Michaels, trans. 2016. *Nepālikabhūpavaṃśāvalī: History of the Kings of Nepal: A Buddhist Chronicle: Introduction and Translation.* Kathmandu, Nepal: Himal Books for Social Science Baha.

Blom, M. L. B. 1989. *Depicted Deities: Painters' Model Books in Nepal.* Groningen: E. Forsten.

Gupta, Sanjukta, and Richard Gombrich. 1986. "Kings, Power and the Goddess." *South Asia Research* 6: 123–38.

Gutschow, Niels. 2011. *Architecture of the Newars: A History of Building Typologies and Details in Nepal.* Chicago: Serindia.

Gutschow, Niels, and Ganesh Man Basukala. 1987. "The Navadurgā of Bhaktapur: Spatial Implications of an Urban Ritual." In *Heritage of the Kathmandu Valley: Proceedings of an International Conference in Lübeck, June 1985*, edited by Niels Gutschow and Axel Michaels. Sankt Augustin: VGH Wissenschaftsverlag.

Gutschow, Niels, and Manabajra Bajracharya. 1977. "Ritual as Mediator of Space in Kathmandu." *Journal of the Nepal Research Centre* 1: 1–10.

Hangen, Susan. 2005. "Boycotting Dasain: History, Memory, and Ethnic Politics in Nepal." *Studies in Nepali History and Society* 10 (1): 105–33.

Hoek, A. W. van den. 2004. *Caturmāsa: Celebrations of Death in Kathmandu, Nepal.* Edited by J. C Heesterman, Bal Gopal Shrestha, Han F. Vermeulen, and Sjoerd M. Zanen. Leiden: CNWS Publications.

Holmberg, David. 2016. "Tamang Lhochar and the New Nepal." In *Religion, Secularism, and Ethnicity in Contemporary Nepal*, edited by David N. Gellner, Sondra L. Hausner, and Chiara Letizia, 302–25. Delhi: Oxford University Press.

———. 2006. "Violence, Non-Violence, Sacrifice, Rebellion, and the State." *Studies in Nepali History and Society* 11 (1): 31–64.

———. 2000. "Derision, Exorcism, and the Ritual Production of Power." *American Ethnologist* 27 (4): 927–49.

Kālikāpurāṇa. 1972. *Kālikāpurāṇam*, edited by Biśwanārāyan Śāstrī. Varanasi: Chokhambha Sanskrit Series Office.

Kane, Pandurang Vaman. 1958. *History of Dharmaśāstra: Ancient and Mediaeval, Religious and Civil Law in India: Vratas, Utsavas and Kāla Etc.* Vol. 5.1. Poona: Bhandarkar Oriental Research Institute.

Kölver, Bernhard. 1976. "A Ritual Map from Nepal." In *Folia Rara: Wolfgang Voigt LXV. Diem Natalem Celebranti Ab Amicis et Catalogorum Codicum Orientalium Conscribendorum Collegis Dedicata*, edited by Herbert Franke, 68–80. Wiesbaden: Steiner.

Krauskopff, Gisèle, and Marie Lecomte-Tilouine, eds. 1996. *Célébrer le pouvoir: Dasaĩ, une fête royale au Népal.* Paris: CNRS.

Lecomte-Tilouine, Marie, and B. K. Shrestha. 1996. "Les rituels royaux de Dasaĩ à Kathmandu: Notes préliminaires." In Krauskopff and Lecomte-Tilouine, *Célébrer le pouvoir: Dasaĩ, une fête royale au Népal*, 152–65Paris: CNRS, 1996.

Levy, Robert I. 1990. *Mesocosm. Hinduism and the Organization of a Traditional Newar City in Nepal.* Berkeley: University of California Press.

Mocko, Anne Taylor. 2016. *Demoting Vishnu: Ritual, Politics, and the Unraveling of Nepal's Hindu Monarchy.* New York: Oxford University Press.

Pauḍela, Bholānātha. 1966. "Bhūpatīndra Mallakā kṛtiharu." *Pūrṇimā* 10: 22–30.

Pfaff-Czarnecka, Joanna. 1996. "A Battle of Meanings: Commemorating the Goddess Durgā's Victory over the Demon Mahiṣā as a Political Act." *Kailash* 18 (3–4): 57–92.

Pradhan, Rajendra P. 1986. "Domestic and Cosmic Rituals among the Hindu Newars of Kathmandu, Nepal." Delhi: School of Economics.

Puraścaryārṇava. Pratāpasiṃhasāhadeva. 1985. *Puraścaryārṇava: Tantraśāstrānusārividhāna-paddhati-nirūpaṇātmakaḥ*, edited by Muralīdhara Jhā. 2 vols. Delhi: Caukhambā Saṃskṛta Pratiṣṭhāna.

Regmi, Dilli Raman. 1966. *Medieval Nepal. Part III. Source Materials for the History and Culture of Nepal*. Calcutta: Mukhopadhyay.

Rodrigues, Hillary. 2003. *Ritual Worship of the Great Goddess: The Liturgy of the Durgā Pūjā with Interpretations*. Albany: State University of New York Press.

Sanderson, Alexis. 2003. "The Śaiva Religion among the Khmers (Part I)." *Bulletin de l'École Francaise d'Extrême-Orient* 90 (1): 349–462.

Sarkar, Bihani. 2012. "The Rite of Durgā in Medieval Bengal: An Introductory Study of Raghunandana's Durgāpūjātattva with Text and Translation of the Principal Rites." *Journal of the Royal Asiatic Society (Third Series)* 22 (2): 325–90. Doi:10.1017/S1356186312000181.

Satkarmaratnāvalī. Gīrvāṇayuddhavīravikramaśāhadeva. 1969. *Satkarmaratnāvalī*, edited by Rāmanātha Ācārya and Dāmodara Koirālā. 2 vols. Kathmandu: Vālmīkī Saṃskṛta Mahāvidyālaya.

Śreṣṭha, Puruṣottamalocana. 2003. *Bhaktapurako Navadurgā Gaṇa*. Bhaktapur: B. Śreṣṭha.

Toffin, Gérard. 1996. "Histoire et anthropologie d'un culte royal népalais: Le Mvaḥni (Durgā Pūjā) dans l'ancien palais royal de Patan." In *Célébrer le pouvoir: Dasaĩ, une fête royale au Népal*, edited by Gisèle Krauskopff and Marie Lecomte-Tilouine, 49–102. Paris: CNRS.

Unbescheid, Günter. 1996. "Dépendance mythologique et liberté rituelle: La celebration de Dasaĩ au temple de Kālikā à Gorkha." In *Célébrer le pouvoir: Dasaĩ, une fête royale au Népal*, edited by Gisèle Krauskopff and Marie Lecomte-Tilouine, 103–51. Paris: CNRS.

Upādhyāya Gautama, Gopikṛṣṇa, and Śambhuprasāda Dāhāla, eds. 2006. *Karmakāṇḍa: Vyāvasāyika: Kakṣā 9: Saṃskṛtavidyālayanāṃ kṛte*. 2. reprint, first pbl. 2004. Sano Thimi: Pāṭhyakramavikāsakendra.

Vajrācārya, Dhanavajra. 1986. "Varṣakṛtti: Eka aprakāśita ṭhyāsaphū." *Contributions to Nepalese Studies* 14 (1): 65–90.

Vajrācārya, Dhanavajra, and Kamal Prakash Malla, eds. 1985. *The Gopālarājavaṃśāvalī: A Facsimile Edition Prepared by the Nepal Research Centre in Collaboration with the National Archives, Kathmandu: With an Introduction, a Transcription, Nepali and English Translations, a Glossary and Indices*. Wiesbaden: Franz Steiner Verlag.

Vajrācārya, Gautamavajra. 1976. *Hanūmānḍhokā rājadarabāra*. Kathmandu: CNAS.

———. 1968. "Aitihāsika ghaṭanāvali." *Pūrṇimā* 19: 189–96.

———. 1966. "Aprakāśita Ṭhyāsaphu: Aitihāsika Ghaṭanāvali." *Pūrṇimā* 12: 22–39.

Whelpton, John. 1991. *Kings, Soldiers, and Priests: Nepalese Politics and the Rise of Jang Bahadur Rana, 1830–1857*. New Delhi: Manohar.

Witzel, Michael. 1976a. "On the History and the Present State of Vedic Tradition in Nepal." *Vasudha* 12: 17–24, 35–39.

———. 1976b. "Zur Geschichte der Rajopadhyayas von Bhaktapur." In *Folia Rara: Wolfgang Voigt LXV. diem natalem celebranti ab amicis et catalogorum codicum orientalium conscribendorum collegis dedicata*, edited by Herbert Franke, 155–75. Wiesbaden: Steiner Verlag.

Zotter, Astrid. 2018. "Conquering Navarātra: Documents on the Reorganisation of a State Festival." In *Studies in Historical Documents from Nepal and India*, edited by Simon Cubelic, Axel Michaels, and Astrid Zotter, 493–531. Heidelberg: Heidelberg University Publishing.

———. 2016a. "State Rituals in a Secular State? Replacing the Nepalese King in the Pacali Bhairava Sword Procession and Other Rituals." In *Religion, Secularism, and Ethnicity in Contemporary Nepal*, edited by David N. Gellner, Sondra L. Hausner, and Chiara Letizia, 265–301. Delhi: Oxford University Press.

———. 2016b. "The Making and Unmaking of Rulers: On Denial of Ritual in Nepal." In *The Ambivalence of Denial: Danger and Appeal of Rituals*, edited by Ute Hüsken and Udo Simon, 221–55. Wiesbaden: Harrassowitz.

3

The King and the Yadu Line

Performing Lineage through Dasara in Nineteenth-Century Mysore

CALEB SIMMONS

Dasara in Mysore is a ten-day festival full of pomp and pageantry. The celebration is the official "state festival" of Karnataka, a state mostly situated on the Deccan plateau of South India in which Kannada is the spoken language.[1] Dasara has become a public celebration of the arts and culture of the city, the state, and all of India, featuring concerts, dance recitals, and exhibitions for all ages and backgrounds. The festival draws an increasing number of tourists, both Indian and international. Because it is such a highly visible celebration, this festival is also an important platform for politicians from the region to be seen by their constituents as they inaugurate various functions throughout the festivities. Dasara, therefore, has become a festival of modern democratic Indian politics of national and regional import. This public celebration of "culture," however, co-opts traditional practices of the Mysore kings and their courts, connecting the modern state and its politicians to erstwhile royal sovereignty, by maintaining the medieval and early modern roots of the festival, which focused on king, goddess, and conquest.

In 2012 and 2013 I attended Dasara in Mysore while conducting archival research on the Woḍeyar dynasty and its relationship to the goddess Cāmuṇḍēśvari. As I observed the *darbār*, the special *pūjā*s, and the Dasara procession, I realized Dasara is a dynamic period of the year in which the medieval modes of king-fashioning collide with and assimilate into the contemporary politics of the region and its culture. This produces an awkward dynamic within the hierarchy of the city in which power oscillates between the king and the democratic state.[2] The festival begins with a symbolic breaking of the normative political order when the Mahārāja is anointed with oil, performs *pūjā* (Kannada: *pūje*) to his throne, takes on the ornate royal investiture including the symbolic wristlet (*kaṅkaṇa*), and ascends the throne. Throughout Dasara in the twice daily *darbār* the Mahārāja again ascends the throne and is introduced with his traditional *biridus* (Sanskrit: *biruḍa*s; "honorific titles"), including "the conqueror of Coorg" (*kuḍuga jayantrī*), "the protector of the realm" (*dēśa pālankārī*), and "lord of the earth" (*bhūpati*). On Dasara, literally, the tenth day (i.e., Vijayadaśami/Sanskrit: Vijayadaśamī) itself, the king marches to the *śamī* (Kannada: *banni*) tree in the palace's Bhūbanēśvari temple and performs the same *pūjā* that had inaugurated the medieval military season by reenacting the Mahābhārata Pāṇḍava ritual after their period of exile had concluded.[3] The climactic Dasara procession on the tenth day, which once featured a convoy highlighted by *darśana* of the Mahārāja seated in a golden covered palanquin (*hoda*) carried by an elephant, is now a moment for the chief minister of the state to open the parade and perform *pūjā* to the goddess Cāmuṇḍēśvari, who is now atop the golden palanquin and the focal point of the procession. Thus, Dasara serves as a site of contestation through which hierarchies of political power and sovereignty can be constituted, articulated, and performed by the politicians, royal family, and people of Karnataka.

At each phase of the celebration, what I observed seemed vaguely familiar from my research on medieval and early modern Woḍeyar *vaṃśāvaḷi* literature and paintings, especially those from the period of Kṛṣṇarāja Woḍeyar III. Kṛṣṇarāja Woḍeyar III had been the Mahārāja of Mysore during the colonial period when the British governor devested the king's power and installed a British Resident in the palace to govern the affairs of the state. This period is central for the emergence of Mysore as an important princely state and the British political solidification of the region after the defeat of Ṭippu Sultān in 1799 and the subsequent "reinstallation" of the Woḍeyar line—a line that was being challenged by various factions throughout the kingdom. In this chapter, I will argue that the celebration of Dasara during the reign of Kṛṣṇarāja III was part of a larger project of performing the continuity of his lineage—a lineage that was constructed and traced back to the beginning of cosmological time. Through this construction of lineage, the king and his court justified their rule through divine sanction and simultaneously protected themselves against the rising trend of British laws of dynastic succession in the South Asian subcontinent.[4] Dasara was a principal component of this courtly project, as it allowed the Woḍeyar kings to perform power and lineage before their subjects and overlords. To display the performance of Dasara as part of the larger project of lineage construction, I will examine passages pertaining to the establishment of Dasara as a Woḍeyar festival *par excellence* in the *Maisūru Samsthānada Prabhugaḷu Śrīman Mahārājavara Vaṃśāvaḷi* or *The Annals [Genealogy] of the Royal Family of Mysore* (ca. 1850s) and the mural paintings in the Raṅgamahal (Hall of Color) in the Jaganmōhan Palace. Both the *Śrīman Mahārājavara Vaṃśāvaḷi* and the Raṅgamahal murals are courtly productions in which the genealogy of the Woḍeyar line is the central theme. In each of these courtly productions, lineage and the celebration and procession of Dasara are represented together as constant and continual reaffirmations of the Woḍeyar royal family as divinely sanctioned and perpetual rulers in the region. Using Kantorowicz's theory of the visible and invisible bodies of the king, I will argue that Kṛṣṇarāja III's Dasara procession was a performance of divine and perpetual lineage through which the invisible and abstract notion of kingly immortality was made visible.

Historical Context

The Woḍeyars had risen to power in the wake of the Vijayanagara Empire's demise. This rise to regional power started when the ruler Rāja Woḍeyar usurped power from the Vijayanagara viceroy at Śrīraṅgapaṭṭana in 1610 CE. Thereafter, the Woḍeyar kingdom slowly gained power and territory in the region, reaching its height under Cikkadēvarāya Woḍeyar in the last quarter of the seventeenth century. Throughout their ascent, the poets and artists of the Woḍeyar court were careful to fashion their kings and their kings' legacies through traditional dynastic motifs, often mimicking the modalities of their Vijayanagara predecessors very closely.

The period I discuss in this chapter was a tumultuous time in Mysore. The medieval rulers of the city/state had lost control of their realm in 1734 to their Kaḷale *daḷavāyi*s (prime ministers of war). Woḍeyar rule was briefly restored under the new *daḷavāyi,* Haidar Ali, although he too took control of most of the political and administrative power from the Woḍeyar rulers. The kingdom was again lost by the Woḍeyars to Haidar Ali's son Ṭippu Sultān, who famously led a Mysore-French coalition against the British in the last two of four consecutive wars, collectively referred to as the Anglo-Mysore Wars. After the defeat of Ṭippu Sultān in 1799, the victorious British "restored" the Woḍeyar line on the throne of Mysore, crowning four-year-old Kṛṣṇarāja Woḍeyar III king under a makeshift pavilion (*maṇṭapa*) on June 30, 1799.

Kṛṣṇarāja Woḍeyar III's reign was of varied success. It is widely regarded as a period in Mysore of unmatched promotion of arts and letters (Nair 2010, 62). Indeed, during this period, as will be discussed in more detail below, the Mysore court was rife with scholars of Sanskrit and Kannada literature and visual and performing artists. This has led scholars of the period to focus on Kṛṣṇarāja Woḍeyar III's rule as a "regime of visibility" during which the locus of power was shifted to the symbolic (Nair 2010, 62). The shift toward the symbolic was necessitated by the political structures and strictures under which the king operated after a series of poor administrative decisions, which led the British to seize most of his power. His demotion was a result of his donative patterns, which were prone to excessive charity to temples and his relatives. This culminated in the "peasant rebellion" in the Śimōga district of the kingdom. The British, who had already been closely monitoring the kingdom, took advantage of this opportunity to declare the king incompetent to administrate the kingdom and to place full administrative power in the hands of an appointed British Resident. Thereafter, the king mostly remained secluded, enjoying the luxuries afforded him by his royal stipend. The king continued to patronize temples and artists; however, the nature of his patronage changed as he began bestowing gifts of jewels and money on his beneficiaries instead of large tracts of revenue-supplying land over which he no longer wielded power.

He also continued to fight to have his political/administrative power restored through a series of legal and rhetorical strategies, including his campaign to be allowed to adopt an heir. While adoption of royal heirs was a common practice in India prior to British rule, the British East India Company had taken to seizing kingdoms with which it had standing contracts if the kingdom was deemed so unstable as to threaten British stockholders' stake. The most common causes for the seizure of kingdoms were contested claims to the throne because of the lack of direct heirs. This practice was quite common during the first half of the nineteenth century but did not become official company policy until the institution of the Dalhousie's Doctrine of Lapse in 1848.

Corona visibilis et invisibilis

In his foundational work on medieval European political theology, *The King's Two Bodies*, Ernst Kantorowicz explored the relationship between the mortality of the king and the immortality of kingship (Kantorowicz 1997). In this work, Kantorowicz traces the notion of the king, his role, and his very nature (physical and metaphysical) as perceived by jurists and theologians through late medieval and into early modern Europe. He suggests that over time the king was viewed to have two bodies, "not a Body natural alone, Body politic alone, but a body natural and politic together" (Kantorowicz 1997, 438). While Kantorowicz has painstakingly shown how this developed through a particular European context of Christian theology and jurisprudence, including the expansion of legal theories about public corporation, some of his insights can help us to more fully understand the performance of Dasara in colonial Mysore. Without a doubt, there existed an independent indigenous trajectory of political theology in India in which kings and their lines were associated with divine power directly and indirectly. It is not my goal to neglect this deep and rich history of Indian political theory relating to kingship in favor of a theory from an external source. However, Kṛṣṇarāja Woḍeyar III ruled in a context that was heavily informed by European (primarily British) political theory. The rhetorical (both literary and visual) products of his court reflect an extremely sophisticated blend of existing Indian modalities of king-fashioning and those imported by his British suzerain. Therefore, I will now turn to Kantorowicz's discussion of royal continuity as it will help us to understand the processes through which kingly power resides and from which the construction of a continuous line of power is derived.

In the seventh chapter of *The King's Two Bodies*, "The King Never Dies," Kantorowicz demonstrates how the natural mortal body of the king and the mystical metaphysical immortal body of the King were unified as the "the dynastic continuity of the natural body [was amalgamated] with the perpetuality of the Crown as a political body in the person of the ruling king" (Kantorowicz 1997, 381). He explains how these two bodies can be reconciled in the minds of the people and in political theories through a process in which the natural body of the king was seen as part of a continual dynastic lineage in which the biological matter of the king continued through succession. Kantorowicz argues that this biological succession was bolstered and given power by an abstracted notion of the king as father of his citizens and a microcosm of the realm and its subjects. Collectively, he refers to this abstract power of the king as the "Crown." It is in this nonbiological form that the king was associated with the divine with all the "attributes of an 'angel' or other supernatural being" and obtained the semblance of immortality, his immortal body (Kantorowicz 1997, 382). Therefore, for Kantorowicz there exist two "crowns," the visible ornament of mortal kingship and the "invisible Crown" (*corona invisiblis*) of the divine immortal King. These two crowns are intertwined in the popular imagination of kingship and embody the way sovereigns and rulers were viewed within the European context, especially in English jurisprudence.

Kantorowicz's theory of the two bodies of the king, the visible and the invisible crown, is also crucial for understanding the development of kingship in India under British rule, especially in the case of Kṛṣṇarāja Woḍeyar III, who was educated by English teachers alongside his traditional Indian gurus. Particularly, I am interested in the processes whereby the physical realm of politics and power and the metaphysical realm of territory, power, and kingship could be reconfigured and reassembled considering Kṛṣṇarāja Woḍeyar's lack of administrative and military power. In order to understand these processes, it is necessary to examine how notions of kingship, power, and divinity are represented and performed in texts, images, and rituals during the reign of Kṛṣṇarāja Woḍeyar III. Indeed, I believe that part of the overall project of Kṛṣṇarāja Woḍeyar

III and his court was to establish a new program of performance and visuality in which the *corona invisiblis* and the king's physical body were rearticulated as simultaneous and metaphysical as ruler of a divine territory that transcended the physical plane. In this context, the dynastic continuation *and* the divinity of the Woḍeyar kings are collapsed into the metaphysical realm that surpasses the physical, which for all intents and purposes belonged to the British. Dasara was the moment where this invisible world of the king was on full display. At this point, however, I do want to be clear. I do not believe this to be an empty performance of a "theatre state" or simply an "illusion of permanence in a period of political uncertainty" (Dirks 1987, 384; Nair 2010, 61). Instead, the Woḍeyar court was developing a new way of conceiving Indian kingship and royal politics in which Kṛṣṇarāja III's territory and power were reconfigured to ultimately transcend the physical and administrative political authority of his colonial overlords. The celebration of Dasara through its kingly rituals and public procession was the site through which this vision of kingship could be articulated.

Performing Yadu Vaṃṣa and the Reign of Kṛṣṇarāja Woḍeyar III

With a reestablished ruler and an indirect ancestry resulting from various royal adoptions, the court of Kṛṣṇarāja III was engaged in the project of constructing dynastic continuity by emphasizing the connection of the Woḍeyar line with the Lunar dynasty of the Yadu Vamṣa (the lineage of Yadu), particularly the association between the deity Kṛṣṇa and the king Kṛṣṇarāja III. Additionally, the divinity and authority of their common ancestry were reaffirmed in public performance of Dasara and its representation in text and mural painting. In this section, I examine the representation of Dasara in two royal genealogies, a genre known as *vaṃśāvaḷi* (lit. the family-line), that were created in the middle of the nineteenth century: the *Śrīman Mahārājavara Vaṃśāvaḷi*, a Kannada lineage text, and the mural paintings of the Jaganmōhan Palace's Raṅgamahal, which is now part of the Jayachamarajendra Art Gallery in Mysore. I demonstrate that the rhetorical program of displaying dynastic continuity was twofold. First, the products of the court constructed an unbroken biological and divine lineage of Woḍeyar kingship by framing the family's ancestry starting with the moment of creation by cosmic deity Viṣṇu and tracing their kings through Viṣṇu's *avatāra*, the deity Kṛṣṇa down to the historical Woḍeyar rulers culminating in Kṛṣṇarāja III. By doing so, they display Kṛṣṇarāja III as a ruler who is simultaneously the physical and visible king and the embodiment of the divine, immortal, and invisible, what Kantorowicz would call the invisible crown (*corona invisiblis*). Second, the dynasty's foundation in the divine and its inherent perpetuity—the simultaneous embodiment of the physical and divine-immortal bodies of the king—were displayed during his indirect rule through the increasing pomp and pageantry during the performance of the kingly rites during Dasara. Dasara was the moment when the invisible crown became visible as the outward celebration of the king and the perpetual rule of his lineage.

Śrīman Mahārājavara Vaṃśāvaḷi

The *Śrīman Mahārājavara Vaṃśāvaḷi* (*SMV*), a Kannada prose text from Kṛṣṇarāja III's reign, is the most detailed account of the Woḍeyar line of kings and their deeds and accomplishments extant. The text is attributed to Kṛṣṇarāja III himself. It was composed during the middle of the nineteenth century, but it was first published for public consumption in the Kannada periodical *Hithibodhini* in 1881. The text was subsequently compiled into a single edition in 1916 (a second volume detailing the rule of Kṛṣṇarāja III would be added in 1922) that bore the English title *The Annals of the Mysore Royal Family*, although the entire contents of the books, except a two-page preface, remained in Kannada. The text is an elaborate and long recounting of the lives and deeds of the entire Woḍeyar line and is the most detailed example of the genealogical (*vaṃśāvaḷi*) literature from Mysore. The *SMV* painstakingly describes in great detail many of the rituals of the court and various military feats of Kṛṣṇarāja III's predecessors. The account of the Woḍeyar history in the *SMV* begins by grounding the lineage in its divine context, opening with a scene of the creation of this cosmic age with the birth of the deity Brahmā from the navel of Viṣṇu, who reclines on Śeṣa, the cosmic serpent, on the primordial ocean. The entire first chapter is devoted to enumerating their mythic ancestors, including the *ṛṣi* Atrimunīśvara, King Daśaratha, and, of course, Kṛṣṇa and his son Pradyumna, all the way down to the legendary progenitor of the Woḍeyar clan, Yadurāya and his brother Kṛṣṇarāya, who, according to the text, have migrated from northwestern India, Dvārakā—Kṛṣṇa's kingdom in the Mahābhārata narrative—to find a new kingdom in the south (*SMV* 1916, 1–12). From this first chapter, we can see that the author of the text was interested in grounding the lineage in the mythic by incorporating the genealogical strategy found in the vast corpus of South Asian narratives of deities collectively known as the Purāṇas. By relating the creation of the cosmos, the genealogy of the gods, and a history of solar and lunar lineages, the *SMV* fulfills several of the criteria (*pañcalakṣaṇa*) to be considered a "Great Purāṇa" (*mahāpurāṇa*). The text, therefore, is explicitly and implicitly placing itself and its subjects, the Woḍeyar kings, into the realm of the divine. From the beginning, we see that the history of the Woḍeyars is inseparable from the history of the gods.

The text continues with relatively short chapters describing the reigns of the first kings, but slows considerably in the fourth chapter and gives a detailed account of Rāja Woḍeyar, the king who established the Woḍeyars by defeating the Vijayanagara viceroy (*mahāmaṇḍalēśvara*) of Śrīraṅgapaṭṭaṇa in 1610 CE. In previous accounts of Mysorean history found in literary texts and *praśāsti*s (panegyric introduction to inscriptions), Rāja Woḍeyar had been heralded as the "conqueror of Śrīraṅgapaṭṭaṇa"; the *SMV* reframes him as the chosen successor of the Vijayanagara crown, who had been hand selected by its viceroy in the region to take control of Śrīraṅgapaṭṭaṇa and his position in the imperium. The *SMV* explains that this selection was due to the viceroy's fading health and his lack of an heir. The narrative of the viceroy and Rāja Woḍeyar establishes both a justification of Woḍeyar rule in the region and a pattern of heirless rulers, whom custom allows to choose a successor and heir, the latter of which is one of the most important themes throughout the text.

It is also in this context that the text introduces the narrative of the "Curse of Taḷakāḍu" into the official Woḍeyar literary records.[5] In this narrative, Alelamma, the wife of the deposed Vijayanagara viceroy, "accidentally" left the capital with her husband for retirement wearing the royal jewels. Rāja Woḍeyar, the new king, however, required the jewels because they were used to ornament the goddess of Śrīraṅgapaṭṭaṇa's Raṅganāṭhasvāmi temple every Tuesday and Friday and requested that Alelamma return them. The queen took affront to his request because she thought Rāja Woḍeyar was questioning her honor and refused to return the jewels. In response, the king sent his ministers, accompanied by soldiers, to collect the missing ornaments, but seeing the oncoming men, the queen feared for her modesty and went to the edge of a river to commit suicide. Before she jumped in, she cursed the Woḍeyar kings so that their line could never have direct male heirs. According to the *SMV*, after the fateful events in Taḷakāḍu, Rāja Woḍeyar had an image of Alelamma installed in the palace to ward off the evil effects of her death. He also decreed that she ought to be worshipped by his family every year during the celebration of Mahānavami (*SMV* 1916, 31–32). His attempt to placate the curse of the deceased queen failed, however, and his eldest son died shortly thereafter on the final day of the month of Bhādrapada, before the commencement of the first Woḍeyar Śrīraṅgapaṭṭaṇa Dasara in 1610 CE. This new narrative, like the genealogy of the gods and kings, provides an intensely specialized commentary on Woḍeyar lineage and dynastic continuity. The "Curse of Taḷakāḍu" narrative provides a religiomythic explanation for seeming dynastic discontinuity by proclaiming that even when one of its rulers was heirless, it was the result of divine intervention. Thus, the story of Alelamma's curse was entirely focused on preservation of lineage and served to reinforce the perpetuity and divinity of the Woḍeyars' dynasty.

Interestingly, the narrative of the curse also serves as the prelude and segue to the long description of the first Woḍeyar celebration of Dasara/Navarātri/Mahānavami and reflects the reality of Dasara during the time of Kṛṣṇarāja III's reign. The *SMV* details at length the proper ritual celebration of the Dasara festival, earmarking it as the central ritual of the newly established regional royal power. The *SMV*, however, does not focus on the Dasara procession as we will see in the Raṅgamahal of the Jaganmōhan Palace. Instead, the focus is on ritual purity, the worship of weapons, and the charity performed by the king through his gifts to his ministers and priests throughout the first nine days (*SMV* 1916, 32–40).

According to the text, the king was distraught over the death of his son but was also faced with a ritual dilemma concerning this festival that is the *sine qua non* of kingship. Due to the death of his son, the newly crowned king had become ritually impure for fourteen days. Therefore, he called a pluralistic council of Hindu scholars from the Vedāntic philosophical tradition, including representatives from the Mādhva, Śrī Vaiṣṇava, and Smārta/Iyyer communities (*saṃpradāya*) to figure out how the court should go about conducting the rituals of the festival during this unclean and inauspicious period for the king. The court scholars searched through the *Vijñānēśvarīya, Manusmṛti,* and other *dharmaśāstra*s (treatises on *dharma* or law) and finally delivered their unanimous verdict:

> In all the *dharmaśāstras*, including the *Vijñānēśvari,* it is said that if the uncleanliness of birth or death befalls one, who has been crowned prior to Navarātri, then on the first day of Navarātri he should take a bath, put on the holy thread, perform the holy rituals which are part of the ascension of the throne, like the holy bath, etc. He should put on the bangle [i.e., take the vow], do the *pūjā* described in the *Kāḷikā Purāṇa,* and ascend the throne. Then he should perform the *pūjās* including the elephant, horse, weapon (*āyudha*), and *śamī pūjās*. After [the festival comes to an end and] the bangle is removed the uncleanliness will return as in the days prior [to Navarātri]. If the uncleanliness befalls you in the middle of Navarātri, then you ought to complete the rituals according to typical *dharma*. Then after removing the bangle, which is part of the *śamī pūjā* part of the festival, you should start your period of uncleanliness. (*SMV* 1916, 32–33)

Rāja Woḍeyar, then, questioned the scholars concerning the performance of parental rituals for a king whose parents had previously died. They answered that the role of the parent should be performed by the king's paternal uncle. Satisfied with the legal decision of his court advisors, Rāja Woḍeyar declared that Navarātri would commence and that in the future, the rituals should be conducted by all kings of Mysore in the same manner.

The text then transitions to a detailed description of the celebration of Mahānavami in the Mysore/Śrīraṅgapaṭṭaṇa court that reflects the "orders" of Rāja Woḍeyar. The text describes and prescribes the initial eight days of the festival in great detail, beginning with the daily baths of the king, his ascension upon the lion throne, special *pūjās*, gifts given to him, the procession of ministers and courtiers in the *darbār*, fights between pairs of male goats and buffaloes, gymnasts, wrestlers, and a firework display, culminating in the nightly donative rituals of the king, with little variation from the previous day. Then the text continues by describing the ninth day, which is dedicated to the veneration of weaponry (*āyudha pūjā*). This day begins very similarly to the rest but includes a special decree that the hundred names of Caṇḍi (*śatacaṇḍi japa*) are to be recited in Cāmuṇḍēśvari's hill temple during the second watch of the day. The text then transitions to Dasara, the tenth day of the festival. The day begins with the royal investiture like the other days but quickly changes as the ensuing *pūjās* are described as the "final" *pūjā*s and the wrestlers' fight shifts from the third to second watch.

The major change in the sequence of ritual events is the preparation for the procession that begins with the collection of accouterments for the *śamī pūjā* (veneration of the *śamī* tree) that is followed by sending food to the goddess Amaladēvate's *pūjāri*'s house. At the beginning of the third watch, the king and his army set out toward the *śamī* tree, where the king performs recreational hunting of various animals displaying his prowess before worshipping the tree. Fascinatingly, here the text points out that when the *pūjā* was completed, "he [Rāja Woḍeyar] performed victory (*bijaya māḍisi*) according to the Hindu style (*hindugaḍe*) through a procession (*savāri*)" (*SMV* 1916, 39). Then, after returning to the palace, the king gives gifts to the family historian (*vaṃśāvaḷi karaṇikanu* [sic]), the wrestlers, and others. He also receives men and women from many other countries and gives them offerings of clothes (*vastrā*) according to their rank. The description closes when Rāja Woḍeyar reiterates that the festival of Mahānavami ought to always be practiced by his family (*vaṃśa*) in this manner. Finally, the description is completed with a poetic simile stating that after his first Dasara, Rāja Woḍeyar built a palace in front of the Raṅgasvāmi temple in Śrīraṅgapaṭṭaṇa in what was formerly a field of millet, and from that time onward the Woḍeyar *darbār* continued to grow as had the millet.

In the Rāja Woḍeyar chapter of the *SMV*, the primary emphases are clearly focused on lineage, which is perpetual and divine in origin, and the performance of kingship through the rituals of Dasara. By casting the lineage within the cosmic scheme of existence as part of a divine line of god-kings and buttressing that claim with a discussion of their adherence to proper "Hindu-style" ritual found in the various *dharmaśastra*s and the *Kālikā Purāṇa*, the *SMV* has effectively placed the Woḍeyar line within the realm of the gods constructing the lineage as part of a continual and perennial line of proper Hindu kings who perform proper Hindu rituals. Of course, like the *SMV*, this line of illustrious kings culminates with king Kṛṣṇarāja III. But to see the how the program explicitly highlighted the association between Kṛṣṇarāja III and the divine, we must indeed look further into the productions of his court.

Raṅgamahal Murals

The Raṅgamahal mural paintings are located on the top floor of the Jaganmōhan Palace in Mysore's Kṛṣṇavilāsa neighborhood. This palace was constructed in 1861 and served as the primary royal palace during the construction of the Mysore Palace after the previous wooden structure was burned due to a kitchen fire. The entire mural project is a montage of various smaller murals, the largest of which are massive lineage paintings and a long, detailed representation of Kṛṣṇarāja III in his Dasara procession. The hall is comprised of three rooms, the largest (and the one through which one enters the hall) of which is in the center. As one enters the room, an enormous pictorial representation of the Woḍeyar lineage is depicted on the northern wall as a large "everlasting lotus" (*santanambuja*/read: *sanātanambuja*) that grows out of a small blue-green vase through a stylized image of the crescent moon, probably a reference to the Lunar origins of the lineage (figure 3.1). Within the leaves of this lotus, the kings of the Woḍeyar family (*vaṃśa*) are depicted with small

Figure 3.1. "Everlasting Lotus" or "*Santanambuja*" from Raṅgamahal in the Jaganmōhan Palace.

captions detailing their names and their place in the genealogy. Red tendrils connect the leaves and lead the viewer's eye from leaf to leaf and from one king to the next.

The visual depiction begins in mythological time, tracing the Yaduvaṃśa (mythic genealogy of the Lunar dynasty) from Vasudeva, who is depicted in the first leaf in the upper right-hand corner and begins the enumeration of the line as the fifty-fifth member of the lineage. The second Woḍeyar ancestor is Vasudeva's son, the deity Kṛṣṇa, who is labeled the fifty-sixth member of the family. The lineage continues following the same genealogy and chronology found in the *SMV* through many other legendary kings from the Indian epics eventually to the seventy-fifth person from the Yadu lineage "Ādi" (first) Yadurāya Woḍeyar, who is subsequently labeled the "first king" (*ondunē paṭṭi*). The painting then continues the record of Woḍeyar kings through the remaining historical rulers, ultimately culminating at the center of the composition with the ninety-sixth king, Kṛṣṇarāja III, whose image is twice the size of the portraits of the other kings. He is shown seated on his golden throne wearing clothes and a heavily bejeweled turban made of golden cloth. He looks directly at the viewer with one hand holding a handkerchief and the other one draped languidly on his lap. He is attended by two whisk-bearers and two ministers, one of whom clasps his hands in subservience to his ruler, while the other raises his sheathed sword in salute.

Above the lotus, all the Woḍeyar kings are showered with flower petals by two *apsarases* (celestial nymphs), as two *gandharvas* (celestial musicians) play on their *vīnas* (lutes). The deities Sūrya (Sun) and Candra (Moon) rest in each of the upper corners of the mural, a common visual motif in medieval genealogical epigraphy. At the very top of the composition, the Woḍeyar devotional deities Śiva and Viṣṇu, as Bāla (baby) Kṛṣṇa, flank their tutelary deity Cāmuṇḍēśvari, as Mahiṣāsuramardinī (slayer of the buffalo-demon). Below the Woḍeyar kings, men dressed in Mysore attire contemporaneous with the rule of Kṛṣṇarāja III and holding the various royal insignia of the court salute their king(s) at the beginning and end of their Dasara procession.

The genealogical theme is continued in the two small rooms that flank the central hall. In the small room to the east of the large room is another genealogical mural painting that depicts Kṛṣṇarāja III with twenty of his legitimate wives as a "family tree" (*vṛkṣa*) (figure 3.2). Like the "everlasting lotus," the "family tree" grows from a small vase through a stylized image of the moon. At the center of the composition, Kṛṣṇarāja III sits upon his golden throne but does not engage the viewer as directly. His right hand comfortably rests on the arm cushion of the throne, and his left gently grasps the hilt of his golden sword. Absent are his male attendants and ministers, who are replaced by two female

Figure 3.2. "Family tree" or "*Vṛkṣa*" from Raṅgamahal in the Jaganmōhan Palace.

whisk-bearers, a woman with a fan, one with a goblet, another offering the king betel nut, and yet one more who appears to be reaching for the king's resting right hand—all of whom must be depictions of his wives. On the largest leaves of this "family tree," the names and rank of his legitimate wives are inscribed. The smaller leaves bear the names of his fourteen children from these wives. Finally, the small pinkish buds relate the details of Kṛṣṇarāja III's grandchildren. This mural is an important addition to the overall project of displaying the continuity of the line. As the "everlasting lotus" image had shown the king's ancestry, this mural displays his virility and his role in the continuation of the line. It stands as a reminder for all that could view it that Kṛṣṇarāja III was indeed not sterile or impotent, but, due to Alelamma's curse, he was supernaturally powerless to produce a male heir.

In the opposite small room to the west of the large hall, a large mural painting further demonstrates the king's sexuality and virility (figure 3.3). In this image, Kṛṣṇarāja III is inside his palace, sporting and playing "color" with the many women of his harem (*antaḥpura*). The viewer gazes into the interior of the palace in which Kṛṣṇarāja III stands at the middle of the composition almost twice the size of the many women in the scene. He is dressed in all white except for his red shawl and red and gold Mysore turban (*pēṭa*). He holds a large gold squirt gun with which he sprays red-colored water into the air, drenching members of his harem. He is surrounded by women, who are dancing and spraying red water at each other and at the king. More women stand on the ground level of the palace hall with small squirt guns spraying toward Kṛṣṇarāja III, and even more women watch the activities from the second floor and balcony. Simultaneously, another Kṛṣṇarāja III serenely watches the scene unfold from the second floor, invoking the concept of multiple manifestations and *avatāras* in the mind of any knowledgeable viewer. While this painting does not have a title written on the image, I have heard it called the *Rās Līlā* mural. Indeed, the composition of the painting with Kṛṣṇarāja

Figure 3.3. Untitled mural from Raṅgamahal in the Jaganmōhan Palace in which Kṛṣṇarāja III sports with the women from his harem.

III at the center of three rows of dancing, playful consorts immediately conjures images of Kṛṣṇa and his *gōpī* lovers, a theme present in many mural paintings from his reign. The association with the love games of the deity and Woḍeyar ancestor Kṛṣṇa is fitting because it serves to bring the entire three-room composition full circle as the lineage begins with and continues through references to Kṛṣṇa(-rāja). Together these three large murals work together to ground the Woḍeyar lineage in the divine and to demonstrate the king's ability to perpetuate the line (except for the curse/supernatural intervention of a righteous woman).

There is considerable overlap between the genealogy found in the first chapter of the *SMV* and the Raṅgamahal's genealogical paintings, including the same chronology and enumeration of Kṛṣṇarāja III's ancestry and the incorporation of divine beings in the story of the kings. Given the similarities between both products of the nineteenth-century Mysore court, both the *SMV* and the mural of the Raṅgamahal must be viewed as parts of a larger project in which Kṛṣṇarāja III and his line were placed within the context of the divine and which could offer an explanation of their indirect dynastic continuity. However, as different styles within the same genre, we can see different emphases within both, particularly how they situate Dasara as a key component of their royal identity through ritual propriety (*SMV*) and pageantry (Raṅgamahal).

In the Dasara mural of the Raṅgamahal, we see that the artist was focused on the pomp and pageantry of Dasara as a display of royal power and prestige. The Dasara painting extends along the upper half of the remaining three walls of the hall's large middle room. The image shows the Dasara procession, which has been labeled by the artist as the "Vijayadaśami elephant procession" (*vijayadaśamiya jumbū svāri* [sic]). In the central position of the southern wall directly opposite the "everlasting lotus" is an image of Kṛṣṇarāja III along with a young man who is presumed by many to be his soon-to-be-adopted son Cāmarāja Woḍeyar X in their golden chariot pulled in procession by his royal elephants (figure 3.4 on page 78).[6] Within the large representation of the Dasara procession, the central image of the chariot is the largest and most captivating and holds the viewer's attention. As with the "family tree" in the eastern room, the inclusion of the young prince immediately opposite the "everlasting lotus" signals to the viewer that the lineage continues.

The Dasara procession is pictured in all its grandeur with the king's retinue of ministers, attendants, warriors, and royals marching before and behind his chariot, flaunting the wealth of the royal family for all to see. In the long mural, the procession begins below the base of the "everlasting lotus," with members of the court saluting the lineage and continues on the eastern wall. On the east wall, the procession is led by two royal elephants, upon which fly the royal banners of the Mysore kings (figure 3.5 on page 78). They are followed by four men mounted on camels and three rows of musicians and cavalrymen. The first and last

Figure 3.4. "Vijayadaśamiya Jambū Svāri" from Raṅgamahal in the Jaganmōhan Palace.

Figure 3.5. Procession on the eastern wall of Raṅgamahal in the Jaganmōhan Palace.

rows of mounted men are dressed in Indian attire and play traditional Indian instruments. The men in the middle row are dressed in British uniform and carry swords at attention. Flanking the horsemen are rows of infantrymen, some of which are dressed in British fatigues and carry single-shot rifles. Next is an empty golden palanquin carried by a lone elephant, who is followed by four drummers and several banner carriers. Behind them is a British military band led by a drum major, who rides a white stallion. The eastern wall concludes with several more squads of Mysorean soldiers, eight saddled white stallions, and an elephant carrying an empty golden sedan chair (*hōḍa*).

On the southern wall, the flow of the procession changes as those on the march turn their attention back toward the central chariot. In this section of the image, many musicians play flutes, trumpets, violins, and drums, as rows of dancing girls perform for their king. Many more banner bearers hold the insignia (*biruḍa*) of the Woḍeyar lineage: Hanuman, Garuda (Viṣṇu's eagle vehicle), a lion, a boar, a double-headed eagle (*gaṇḍabhēruṇḍa*), a peacock, a fish, a *makara* (seamonster), an ax, and a conch and discus (Vaiṣṇava symbols). Some in the procession offer food, some twirl fine cloth before the king, and some salute the king's large wooden chariot, pulled by six royal elephants. Directly behind the chariot are more banner bearers followed by twenty foot soldiers with spears. After the spearmen, a cavalry company marches after the king and wraps around the western wall. Toward the end of the cavalry is another large, and presumably empty, wooden chariot pulled by eight horses, three palanquins carried by men, two carts pulled by bullocks, and two more royal elephants.

The procession culminates at the bottom of the "everlasting lotus" mural on the center of the northern wall with yet more members of the retinue saluting the depiction of the Woḍeyar dynasty. In this way, the beginning and the end of the Dasara procession are performed as a salute to the Woḍeyar lineage *in toto*. The march of the Dasara procession is the quintessential ritual for exalting the perpetuity of the line.

In addition to the images that overtly depict the Dasara procession, another mural provides more scenes from the celebration of Vijayadaśami, "the tenth-day of victory" (Dasara), during the reign of Kṛṣṇarāja III. In an image directly below the painting of the chariot, Kṛṣṇarāja III and his ministers are shown engaged in a variety of hunts, including multiple scenes of tiger and elephant hunts, but also one that includes, a tiger, a boar, and a bear—all animals that were part of the Dasara day hunt described in the *SMV*. While these hunts are taking place in a variety of landscapes in different regions of the Mysore territory, they have to be read within the same context. Any viewer from the period that was familiar with the details of the procession would see these images and the hunt as inherently connected to the ritual procession. Additionally, the images encourage viewers to look down and allow their eyes to work around the lower half of the large hall, which is filled with images of the king's leisure activities. Thus, the hunting scene serves as a transition from the public display of lineage and performance of kingship to the private life of the Mahārāja just as the various rituals throughout the day take the king from inside to outside the palace. Additionally, as part of the project of performing dynastic continuity, the images in which he enacts the hunt demonstrate the obverse aspect of kingly virility, his martial prowess.

Together, the images of Raṅgamahal paint a portrait of dynastic continuity through the spectacle that is the wealth, power, and virility of the king Kṛṣṇarāja III. The lineage is shown to be rooted in the divine through the Lunar lineage and the deity Kṛṣṇa and culminating in and continuing through Kṛṣṇarāja III, who is shown to embody the kingly standard of sexual and martial virility. Furthermore, Dasara is represented in all its glory as a spectacle to behold. Here, it is not a ritual of purity and charity. Dasara is a performance of royal virility. In this way the Raṅgamahal, presents the strength, wealth, and sheer magnitude of the Woḍeyar lineage as proper and powerful.

Conclusion

Both the *SMV* and the mural paintings of the Raṅgamahal are designed to address the Woḍeyar claims to kingship during the British period of reign of Kṛṣṇarāja III. Building upon the indigenous and British-influenced notions of kingship, the court of Kṛṣṇarāja III produced its lineage (*vaṃśāvaḷi*) in text and image that not only reinforced the continuity of the Wodeyar lineage, but cast it in such a way that their dynastic continuity was "everlasting," rooted in the divine and continuing through Kṛṣṇarāja III and his progeny. They both connected their kings to the divine by tracing their ancestry through the Purāṇic Lunar dynasty through the deity Kṛṣṇa and by placing the divine into the lives of the Woḍeyar kings in their foundational myth, the "Curse of Taḷakāḍu," or allusions to Kṛṣṇarāja III as Kṛṣṇa in *Rās līlā*. Through these strategies, continuity of the mortal body of the Mahārāja fused with the divine immortal body of kingship as the biological physicality of the king was associated with the material of the divine. Furthermore, as the primary ritual performance of Woḍeyar kingship, Dasara became the ultimate visible presentation of that invisible crown.

The *SMV* demonstrates how Dasara connected Kṛṣarāja III with his Woḍeyar and Vijayanagara predecessors through the performance of the festival, but it also shows that their ritual was properly conducted according to the leaders of the Hindu communities and textual precedent. The depiction of Dasara in the Raṅgamahal murals is quite a contrast to the negligible attention that the *SMV* pays to the procession. The *SMV* focused on purity regulations, proper ritual timing, and donative practices of Dasara; it simply stated that the "elephant procession" was done in the "Hindu-style." The Ranġamahal murals, in contrast, depict Dasara only through the performance of the procession, focusing on the display of kingly virility through the pomp and pageantry of the festival parade. When read together as parts of the same holistic program of displaying dynastic continuity and performing lineage, the *SMV* and the Raṅgamahal murals present a complete picture of proper and powerful Indian kingship. In this picture of the king, all the subtle and explicit aspects of the king and his physical and abstract, divine and material, characteristics are on display. In each, however, that vision of kingship is performed through the paradigmatic ritual of the king, Dasara.

As Mysore's political festival *par excellence*, Dasara and its attendant rituals, processions, and displays actively create political structure. It serves as a ritual link to traditional forms of Indian sovereignty and as a public site for the performance of authority, through which hierarchies are worked out and displayed. As one of the central features of the festival in Mysore, Dasara is a site of political contestation wherein political power is constituted and articulated by placing the ritual actor within a genealogy of Indian sovereignty. Indeed, this function continues to be one of its defining features that is still harnessed even in contemporary democratic politics as the "state festival" of Karnataka.

Notes

1. Throughout this chapter, I use Kannada terms and transliteration unless otherwise specified. Therefore, certain familiar terms that appear with long vowel endings in Sanskrit are written with short vowel endings. For example, Sanskrit Dasarā is rendered Dasara; Cāmuṇḍeśvarī is Cāmuṇḍēśvari; and Vijayadaśamī is Vijayadaśami. However, I use Sanskrit for that are widely known in South Asian studies and that appear elsewhere in this volume. For example, I use the Sanskrit *pūjā* in place of the Kannada *pūje* and *śamī* instead of the Kannada *banni*.

2. This battle is both symbolic and very real, including many ongoing legal suits regarding land ownership surrounding Cāmuṇḍi Hills and other holdings that is rooted in the same debates of state versus royal property since Indian national integration. The tension between the two groups can be seen spatially within the palace grounds. The palace is operated by the Karnataka State Department of Archaeology and Museums; however, portions are maintained by the Woḍeyar family as the private residence of the royal family. There is a certain amount of animosity between the two sides over the ownership of the property of the erstwhile royal family and the state, which produces contestation that is equally symbolic and pragmatic. Both the state and the royal family have separate entrances (the Mahārāja's is on the north side of the palace, and the Palace Board maintains the south side) that allow for varying degrees of access to the royal functions. Therefore, as a researcher you must often chose which approach is necessary to attend certain functions either through the state or the Mahārāja's secretary. However, if one declined permission often the other would acquiesce.

3. In 2013, however, due to his poor health, the Mahārāja took his car from the palace to the temple.

4. Here I am referring to what is often called the "Doctrine of Lapse," which was first articulated as policy in 1834, though it would not officially be known by this name until 1848 when enacted by Lord Dalhousie. In a memo dated February 26, 1834, the EIC contended that it could intervene and depose a monarchy that had "lapsed" by either breaking dynastic succession or failure to uphold financial obligations.

5. The curse narrative is conspicuously absent from Wilks's account of Rāja Woḍeyar's acquisition of Śrīraṅgapaṭṭaṇa, even though he mentions the viceroy's retirement in Taḷakāḍu (Wilks 1930, 27).

6. While many have presumed that this image depicts Kṛṣṇarāja Woḍeyar III's heir Cāmarāja X, the painting was commissioned and completed prior to the adoption of Cāmarāja X. The prince shown in this painting is more than likely a prince by the name of Nañjarāja, the son of Kṛṣṇarāja Woḍeyar III's tenth wife and who is listed as the yuvarāja or "heir apparent" in the "Family Tree" or Vṛkṣa mural in the east room of the Raṅgamahal. As of the time of publication, I am unaware of the fate of Nañjarāja, but it is possible that he died, as had Rāja

Woḍeyar's son in the SMV, or that he was considered by the British to be an illegitimate because they only accepted the precedent of Hindu men only being allowed to have four wives as described in the *Baudhyāna Dharmasūtra* and the *Yājñavalkya Smṛti*.

References

Dirks, Nicholas. 1987. *The Hollow Crown: Ethnohistory of an Indian Kingdom*. Cambridge: Cambridge University Press.

Ikegame, Aya. 2013. *Princely India Re-imagined: A Historical Anthropology of Mysore from 1799 to the Present*. New York: Routledge.

Kantorowicz, Ernst H. 1997. *The King's Two Bodies: A Study in Mediaeval Political Theology*. Princeton, NJ: Princeton University Press.

Maisūru Saṃsthānada Prabhugaḷu Śrīmanmahārājaravara Vaṃśāvaḷi Volumes 1. 1916. Edited by B. Ramakrishna Row. Mysore: Government Branch.

Nair, Janaki. 2010. *Mysore Modern: Rethinking the Region under Princely Rule*. New Delhi: Orient Blackswan Private Limited.

Wilks, Mark. 1930. *Historical Sketches of the South of India in an Attempt to Trace the History of Mysoor from the Hindoo Government of that State to the Extinction of the Mohammedan Dynasty in 1799 Volumes 1 & 2*. Mysore: Government Branch.

4

Dasara and the Selective Decline of Sacrificial Polity in a Former Princely State of Odisha[1]

UWE SKODA

Whoever visits the former kingdom of Bonai and its capital, Bonaigarh, can hardly fail to notice roads and highways often jammed with trucks and dumpers (over-)loaded with ore, vehicles for which these roads were not originally constructed. Although it has been known for a long time that the area close to the borders of Jharkhand and Chhattisgarh is rich in minerals, with iron ore being supplied to the Rourkela Steel Plant for decades, only in the wake of the most recent industrialization has the valley been dotted with *sponge-iron* factories. Nowadays, Bonai is a rather far cry from the picture drawn in colonial accounts (e.g., Dalton 1865, 1–2) of an inaccessible and remote valley like other "jungle kingdoms" (Schnepel 2002) whose structural residues feature in the Dasara rituals, which one may easily overlook as they are performed in the former fort (*garh*) and palace located slightly away from the busy main road with court, high school, and bus stand.

Goddess Durgā, the presiding deity of the Dasara rituals, is one of the most well-known, most devoutly venerated, and arguably also one of the most multifaceted goddesses of India. Accordingly, she has received a good deal of scholarly attention devoted to her textual (e.g., Kinsley 1978), iconographic (e.g., Panda 2004), and, even more, ritual representation (e.g., Nicholas 2013; McDermott 2011; Östör 2004 [1980]; Pfaff-Czearnecka 1998;

Sontheimer 1981 et al.). In her manifold appearances, Durgā is believed to be a primary form of the "feminine sacred" and guardian of dharma (Tambs-Lyche 2004), the "feminine-cosmological energy" (Michaels 1998, 246), and the "power of the fecund earth" (Khanna 2000). Her warrior qualities are emphasized in relation to Dasara, one of her most central rituals, which is arguably "the most prominent ritual of kingship across India" (Fuller 1992, 108). Intimate relations between rulers and their tutelary deities, commonly associated with Durgā, have been documented especially in the Odishan context (Hardenberg 2000; Schnepel 2002). Often appearing as Bana Durgā (forest Durgā), she has also been linked to "tribal" deities through processes of "Hinduization" (Eschmann 1994 [1975]; Mallebrein 2004) that simultaneously "Kṣatriyaized" her royal patrons, elevating their status within the political landscape of Indian polities (Kulke 2001 [1984]).

In this chapter, I introduce the elaborate Dasara rituals in the capital of the former princely state of Bonai, which is now the headquarters of a subdistrict in northwestern Odisha.[2] Thus, I look at a crucial "state ritual" that continues to attract crowds decades after the abolition of the "princely state" (after the merger of the former kingdom with the Indian Union in 1948 and after revoking royal privileges—the so-called privy purses—in the early 1970s). In Bonai, Dasara, with its various rituals and sacrifices, revolves around Durgā, who is worshipped primarily in the form of iron swords. It has been a central performance for the Bonai raja to symbolically demonstrate his power and his claim to territory, to maintain and renew ties with communities through services and exchanges, and to construct what, following Nicholas (2013), I have called a "sacrificial polity."

As I will show, these ritual practices have never been static, but rather reflect shifting social and political realities in Bonai in which the political and cultural power of the raja is waning in recent decades. Though royal patronage is shrinking, and there are visible signs of a disintegration of the sacrificial polity, this decline is nonlinear and selective rather than absolute. Historically, the performance of Dasara has been characterized by various ups and downs. Currently, ritual elements involving Adivasis (indigenous or "tribal" peoples) and their goddess Kant Debī, who is also considered a manifestation of Goddess Durgā, are certainly very vibrant and appear to have become even more popular. At the same time, a new major challenge to royal rituals has emerged outside of the fort in the wake of the recent industrialization, namely, in the form of Durgā Pūjā. Celebrated simultaneously with Dasara but in the market area of Bonaigarh, it not only diversifies the worship of Goddess Durgā, but increasingly overshadows royal pomp. I discuss Durgā's older manifestations in and around the fort worshipped during Dasara and then I turn to her co-existent forms.

Dasara and Goddesses in Bonai

Goddesses in and around the Fort and the Raja's Swords

Various goddesses are present in and around the fort, and locals relate these goddesses to the opposition *śānti* and *caṇḍī*, that is, between relatively peaceful and benevolent goddesses like Lakṣmī on the one hand, and goddesses like Durgā on the other, who are rather ambivalent, motherly, but also fierce and potentially destructive or malevolent (see also Biardieu 1989 [1981], 140; Michaels 1998, 247). The goddesses guarding the fort and those worshipped by the raja and the Paudi Bhuiyan (Ādivāsī-*bhuiyan*, literally "earth people") during Dasara belong to this second category.

Mā Kumārī, as tutelary goddess (*iṣṭa debī*), plays the major role among them. She is described in the royal chronicles (*rājbaṃśāboli*) as the goddess of the fort (*garh debī*) and linked to the state's well-being (for example, worshipped during droughts). In her temple just outside the fort, she appears as a hardly recognizable stone idol, which, according to local beliefs, became disfigured after the goddess devoured a human being. Like other tutelary goddesses in eastern India, Mā Kumārī is associated with Goddess Durgā. This link is particularly stressed in a prayer in the royal chronicles that is dedicated to her in which she is addressed as "mother," "Mahiṣamardinī" (buffalo-slaying goddess), "caretaker of the whole world," and "caretaker of the fort" (a universal as well as a very specific context of protection) or as "tutelary deity of Bonai" and "Durgā of the forest" (Bana Durgā) (Pramanik and Skoda 2013, 38).

Inside the fort, not unlike other regions in Odisha, Durgā, is worshipped primarily in the form of swords, which signifies the sacrificial nature of the polity more broadly (Schnepel 2002; Mallebrein 2004). She also appears as a bracelet or bracelets, which represent the Nine Durgās (*naba durgā kaṅkaṇa*; see below), or in anthropomorphic form (for example, small metal figures that depict the goddess with eight arms), but these are of secondary importance compared to the swords.

Three swords (*khaṇḍa*) play crucial roles during Dasara: *kumārī prasād* (blessing of Kumārī); *patkhaṇḍa* the "main sword," and *mohana khaṇḍa*. While *kumārī prasād*, received from Mā Kumārī, was used by the raja for everyday representational needs, *patkhaṇḍa* figured more prominently during Dasara, being publicly displayed during the procession to the Dasara field. It is believed that *patkhaṇḍa* had been brought from Rajputana and had been an instrumental weapon in the establishment of the realm by killing autochthonous chiefs (except a Bhuiyan chief, who became an ally). This empowerment of the raja is also reenacted during the Dasara procession and rituals when he symbolically conquers his realm again.

Mohana khaṇḍa is kept inside the palace premises, while the other two swords were kept in the armory (nowadays in the Jagannāth temple). It is believed that *mohana khaṇḍa* had been taken from a tribal chief while the raja was conquering the realm (for similar myths in Odisha see Schnepel 2002, 259). *Mohana khaṇḍa* is considered a form of Durgā, but she is kept even more invisibly than the *patkhaṇḍa*. The public is only given *darśan* (sight) of her during the investiture of every new raja.

Especially with reference to the swords, the royal priest (*rājpurohit*) emphasized in conversations that the Goddess Durgā has a permanent seat inside the fort, something that distinguished the fort rituals from the temporary worship of Durgā in her Bengali form during Durgā Pūjā. Describing the continuous presence of Goddess Durgā inside the fort as *pīṭha*, he linked Bonaigarh to many other religious centers and a greater tradition, including the well-known mythological story of Satī, in which her body parts fell upon the earth, establishing her seats (*pīṭha*) across the India landscape (see Kinsley 1987, 186). This myth and the Bonai connection to it emphasize the localization of the goddess and her literal *grounding* within her territory (see Galey 1990).

Kant Debī (Kant Kumārī) as Allied/Visiting Goddess

The aspects of the earth and a claim to a territory are also stressed in relation to the goddess Kant Debī, who is also referred to as Kant Kumārī or Kant Mahāpṛ great protector) and considered by many to be a form of Durgā and a sister of Mā Kumārī. She stands out during the Dasara rituals, not only for attracting larger audiences, but as the only visiting goddess otherwise not firmly located in Bonaigarh (Bonai town), but instead being carried by Paudi Bhuiyans from the relatively peripheral hills surrounding the central valley of Bonai to the fort at the center.

The goddess's relationship with the court is explained in her legend in the royal chronicles (Pramanik and Skoda 2013, 39ff). Accordingly, she is believed to have come from the neighboring kingdom of Keonjhar. Like Goddess Durgā, in the form of a bracelet, she is linked to a holy man (*bābājī*) who was killed for not handing them over to the king voluntarily. She is connected to the Bhuiyans and to the Pano community (a large "Scheduled Caste" in the region), which plays a marginal role in her Dasara rituals. The chronicles state that a Pano discovered the goddess while ploughing who appeared in the form of the lower part (*sama*) of a husking pedal (*dhinki*) (Pramanik and Skoda 2013, 40)

This myth elaborates on how the presence of the goddess was revealed and on the peculiar "quaint shape" of the goddess, basically "a roundish fragment of some old metal object" (Roy 1935: 105), in which some see a snake with a cobralike hood. The story continues that a visiting money lender (*mahājan*) recognizes the value of the piece, but finally:

> The Pano . . . dreamed that he should give the sama to the King, otherwise his clan will be wiped out. That night the

> King also dreamed that whatever he sees in the morning, he should worship it. That night a Bhuiyan of Jala also dreamed that he should go to the King early in the morning and bring the sama from the Rajbati (palace). . . . The Bhuiyan kept it in Jala. After some days again the King dreamed that it . . . will be worshipped as Kant Debi. From that day onwards Kant Debi is visible on the day of pratipada (commencement of Dasara). (Pramanik and Skoda 2013, 40)

The whole narrative includes allusions to fertility with the reference to ploughing and the *dhinki* (husking pedal / grinder) and to wealth through the harvest and the expert moneylender. Perhaps the most important part is the divine intervention through dreams that resolves the various interests (moneylender, Pano, Bhuiyan, and raja). In this royal perspective, she is presented as an outsider goddess, who is first brought to the raja and afterwards to the Bhuiyan, contesting the Paudi Bhuiyan view that the goddess is their mother.

Kant Debī is also believed to be the sister of Mā Kumārī as the raja's "chief goddess," and the late Raja K. K. C. Deo referred to her as "personal deity" who preferred to stay in the hills on the fringes or borders of the kingdom with the Paudi Bhuiyan. This is indicative of the ambivalent tie created between raja and (Paudi) Bhuiyan through the goddess and the stated sisterhood may hint at an attempted, yet incomplete appropriation of the goddess. Unlike other tutelary deities elsewhere in Odisha, Kant Debī has never fully moved to the court (Kulke 2001 [1984])—possibly because of the power of the Bhuiyan community and chief, described in the chronicles as the supreme (*sreṣṭa*) group among the Adivasis and as "*matīśvar*" or "Lord of the Soil," respectively. In fact, according to the chronicles, it was the Bhuiyan chief who helped the first Raja establishing his realm and became his ally. He literally hands soil over to the raja during the latter's investiture, when the raja sits on the chief's lap. The discovery of Kant Debī seems to reiterate this crucial link between (Paudi) Bhuiyans as guardians of the goddess and raja without presenting Kant Debī as Bhuiyan goddess—an alliance apparently tinged with rivalry.

Dasara Ritual Complex in Bonaigarh

Dasara Rituals and Ritual Specialists in the Royal Chronicles and in Contemporary Bonaigarh

The contemporary Dasara in Bonaigarh starts on the sixth day, *Ṣaṣṭi,* and ends on the following Kumār Pūrṇimā (full moon) during the light fortnight of the month of Āśvina. The festival links the goddess, the former ruler, and his former subjects through offering their services creating a polity rooted in sacrifice. Thanks to the raja, who meticulously lists all expenditures, there is a clear budget and detailed information on how he engages in ritual exchanges and distributes money and sacrificial meat during this occasion. For example, he pays *dastūrī*, a customary payment or remuneration for a specific service rendered, especially to those central in the performance of Dasara, including (1) the *kant dehuri* (*dihuri*), that is the Paudi Bhuiyan ritual specialist in charge of Kant Debī, (2) the *amat* as non-Brahmin priest, and (3) the Brahmin *rājpurohit*.

From an Adivasi perspective, the most important part of Dasara is related to Kant Debī. Accordingly, the *kant dehuri* plays a major role in the rituals until the goddess is handed over to the raja (and later when she is returned to his charge). On Aṣṭamī, the eighth day, the raja (or his representative) and Paudi Bhuiyan meet in a village about two kilometers south of the fort to receive the goddess Kant Debī, a ritual known as *kant bhet* or "meeting the goddess Kant," expressing the close relation between *raja* and Bhuiyan. The second day of the fortnight, a group of Paudi Bhuiyan start a procession from her abode in the hills, moving clockwise from the hills to the plains and back again with overnight stays involving other Adibasi and non-Adibasi communities (see also Roy 1935, 107). The sequence largely corresponds to the royal chronicles outlining a royal perspective on the meeting:

> Before that the Bhuiyan comes and takes a handful of flowers . . . offered to the deity on the day of new moon. . . . Then the goddess comes along with her seat (*asan*) through [the prescribed villages to] . . . a place named Kantajodi [where] a ritual on a special platform . . . is performed for Kant Debi. Then the Raja Saheb goes with his watchmen . . . beating the *dhol* and playing the *muhuri* to her. The Bhuiyan leaves Kant Debi thinking that the king is coming to kill him. Then Raja asks his followers to search for the Bhuiyan to call him back, but he does not come. Then Raja does not wait for him, but takes Kumari Debi and hands her over to his priest named as Amat. This is called kant bhet. After finishing the Debi Puja at midnight she meets Kumari Debi and stays with her like a sister in the armoury in a bowl filled with blood (rakta handi). (Adapted from Pramanik and Skoda 2013, 41)

While the chronicles seem to assert the raja's power vis-à-vis the Bhuiyan and interestingly change the name of the goddess from Kant Debī to Kumārī Debī in the text after she has been handed over—similar to the name of the tutelary goddess—when I observed the ritual in 2007, the raja's grandson (deputed by the raja) had to wait quite some time for the Paudi Bhuiyan in order to receive the goddess. The raja became furious over the delay and later scolded them in my presence. Such things, according to general impressions, would not have happened earlier and may indicate the growing popularity of the goddess's procession and the changing power dynamics between the raja and Paudi Bhuiyan; that is, the latter seem to be increasingly aware of their bargaining power.

In contrast to the chronicles, while meeting the raja on the eighth day, the Paudi Bhuiyan, particularly the *kant dehuri,* inquire about the well-being of the raja, the *rāṇī* (queen), and his kingdom. The raja answers positively, and only afterward is the goddess handed over to him, who in turn offers a new silver umbrella that is attached to her image (*mūrti*). The dialogue between the young grandson and the equally young Paudi Dehuri seems to have been a shortened version of what Roy (1935) described for the premerger period:

> The Dihuri of Jolo comes up to the Raja with the image, salutes him, and enquires of him about the health and welfare, first of himself, then of his Rani, then of his children, then of his servants, then of his elephants, then of his horses, and last of all about the welfare of the land (Prithvi or Earth). The Raja answers "yes" to every question; and then in his turn, the Raja asks the Dihuri about the welfare of himself and his children and then of the Pauris generally; and to every question the Dihuri replies in the affirmative. (Roy 1935, 109–10)

In this form, the dialogue seems even more balanced and expressive of mutual care and alliance, although the raja took precedence, as underlined in Roy's account of the following sequence: "While the Dihuri hands over the image to the Raja, he addresses the Raja, saying, 'Here is your deity (Deota); we kept it in the hills. Examine and see if the image is broken or intact' " (Roy 1935, 110). The raja would then confirm the wholeness of the image. In any case, once the raja receives the goddess from the *bhuiyans,* he passes her on to the *amat* as non-Brahmin priest, who worships her on a specially erected platform and sacrifices two *bukas* (male goats) that are tied together. They are beheaded not by the *amat* or Paudi Bhuiyan, but by the *barik* ("sacrificer") in charge of the animal sacrifices. Belonging to the Keunt community as another community involved in the sacrificial polity in this way, he also receives *dastūrī* for this service.

Having handed the goddess over to the *amat,* the *kant dehuri* and his men stay in Bonaigarh but remain without ritual duties until Vijayadaśamī (the victorious tenth day), when the goddess is returned to their care after the *maṇḍal pūjā* (platform rituals) inside the fort, to which large audiences flock, are over. Afterward, Kant Debī bids farewell to Bonaigarh, leaving from the north side of the fort. Having arrived from the south, it is stressed that she should move only in one direction and should never return the same way, thereby implicitly involving more villages and people in the procession. She continues in this way and returns with the Paudi Bhuiyan to the hills, where she is supposed to reach her home on the following full moon. However, before leaving Bonaigarh, a special cake (*chakuli*) made of bitter neem leaves, should be offered by a person identified as "Patro," a title used by the Pano community, which had discovered the goddess according to the royal chronicles mentioned above. This expression of bitterness metonymic for the farewell was performed in 2016 by the Paudi Bhuiyan themselves, because the Pano community did not fulfil this customary duty.

The *amat*, belonging to the Sud community, oversees Kant Debī in Bonaigarh and Mā Kumārī and is involved in the Dasara rituals from the commencement of the rituals, that is, from the *Bel barni pūjā or "bel-*branch invitation," sometimes also referred to as *saṣṭi pūjā*. Moreover, it is him who worships the swords—*patkhaṇḍa* and *kumārī prasād*—together on the seventh day, when seats (*asan*) are established for them, and on the eighth day, when the *khaṇḍa pūjā* (sword ritual) is performed, while the Rājpurohit worships the Naba Durgā. After sunset on both days, the *amat* worships both swords along with other local deities. At the end of the rituals on the seventh day, the first male goat is sacrificed for *patkhaṇḍa,* while one is sacrificed for Naba Durgā on the eighth. The *amat* and others are convinced that buffaloes or even humans used to be sacrificed earlier on these occasions, although none of them has performed such a ritual.

On the ninth day, the procession of Kant Debī through Bonaigarh, which begins with the *kant bhet*, continues under the guidance of the *amat* along the fixed route passing the older market area (*patna*) and the outer part of the fort (*bāharī garh*), where she meets her sister, Mā Kumārī. The *amat* arranges this meeting, which remains invisible to the public. Even the *amat* leaves the temple for a while to let the sisters talk as he explained, without any disturbance. Here the practice in 2007 and 2016 differed from the chronicles, which state, "After finishing the Debi Puja at midnight she meets Kumari Debi and stays with her like a sister in the armoury (*khanda ghar*) in a bowl filled with blood (*rakta handi*)" (Pramanik and Skoda 2013, 41). Thus, in the chronicles, Kant Debī and Mā Kumārī appear even closer, but the closeness might be linked to the raja's strategic interest in appropriating the goddess.

However, in contemporary Bonaigarh, this *rakta hāṇḍī* is utilized in the rituals on the ninth day, when the Goddess proceeds toward the palace or *darbār* hall (now functioning as an armory), where she was placed in a pot (*hāṇḍī*) filled with rice (*chāvul*) between the two swords already installed there. It is widely believed that this pot was filled with blood (*rakta*) in former times and hence its name. Once the goddess has arrived, the raja takes *darśan* first of Kant Debī and *patkhaṇḍa*/*kumārī prasād* and then of Durgā/Naba Durgā, all while the public is excluded. In another small procession, the raja himself (or his son) carries the goddess Kant Debī publicly into the inner part of the palace, where she is worshipped at an altar (*bedi*) by the *amat*. He places the goddess in a pot filled with wine, which is distributed as a *bad bhog* (grand offering) among the audience that has gathered around the *bedi,* while another male goat is sacrificed for Kant Debī.

The third major role is played by the Brahmin *rājpurohit,* who receives the largest *dastūrī* payment (Rs. 150 in 2007) for his service.[3] He is solely in charge not only of the anthropomorphic forms of Durgā and the worship of her mythical *kaṅkaṇa* (bracelet), but also of the *mohana khaṇḍa* sword kept inside the palace. His ritual services are required particularly from the seventh day to the tenth, when he takes care of various rituals such as *sandhi pūjā* (a ritual that links one lunar day to the next) performed between Aṣṭami and Nabami, the eighth and ninth days. Like the *mohana khaṇḍa pūjā, the sandhi pūjā,* performed for the Nine Durgās (*nabadurgā*), should be performed without the general public being present and without other gods and goddesses. It is also the Rājpurohit, who, together with the raja, performs the *dasara pūjā* celebrated on the veranda of the former Rājmahal around sunset on Vijayadaśami (after Kant Debī has left). The raja (or his deputy), who is usually alone with the Purohit, is asked to hold the sword to perform *buliba,* that is moving it in all directions—symbolically showing the empowerment of the raja to wield this sword.

As mentioned, prior to it and simultaneously with the *kant beth,* the *rājpurohit* should perform the *mohana khaṇḍa pūjā,* which includes another sacrifice of a male goat. It is later cooked inside the palace premises and consumed exclusively by the male relatives of the raja (*birādrī*), indicating not only the involvement of various communities in the sacrificial polity but also of the royal clan. It is important to note that the largest part of the raja's expenses is for sacrificial goats, which accounts for almost half of his budget and is a crucial part of the royal exchanges. Compared to the rather nominal amounts spent on *dastūrī* and on *dārśani* (money, the raja offered through the ritual specialists during *darśan* in various rituals including *kant bhet*) the sacrificial meat is more valued and costly, and ritual specialists emphasize that they are entitled to it. Thus, out of the seven male goats offered to the goddess(es), for example, two goats sacrificed during the *kant beth* rituals customarily go to *amat* and *kant dehuri,* while the *rājpurohit* receives the goat sacrificed during the *maṇḍal pūjā* inside the palace premises. The last goat sacrificed at the very end of the Dasara cycle, on the day of Kumārī Pūjā, is kept by the raja.

In addition to the *kant dehuri, amat* and *rājpurohit,* other specialists perform duties and receive *dastūrī* in exchange for their services. For example, on the seventh and eighth days, the royal swords are washed, sharpened, and wrapped in a new white cloth by the Kathi, who comes from the Maharona community—*khaṇḍa dhua* (sword washing). The Behera, who belongs to the Hansi (weaver) community, prepares an umbrella that is presented to Mā Kumārī on Kumār Pūrṇimā, at the end of the Dasara cycle.[4] The *kumbar* (potters) receive a relatively high amount in return for providing all the pots required for the festival's rituals, but as the raja explained, the family who received land in order to provide pots for the rituals no longer did so, and all the pots are actually purchased in the market. Similarly, other communities, such as Parida, who were previously in charge of producing alcohol (*bad bhog*) for Kant Debī, no longer perform that duty, because it is regarded as degrading, which also shows an on-going disintegration of the sacrificial polity.

Changing Fort Rituals, Decline and an Increasingly Popular Goddess, Kant Debī

The royal chronicles written before the merger of the princely state with the Indian Union describe many other elements not performed nowadays:

> [A]rms and ammunitions are worshipped at the khanda ghar and Brahmins are fed (bhojana). When Kant Debi is taken to the opposite side of the river, Dasara festival is observed. Now the groups of Saanta, Dandapata and Mohapatra [Zamindar and Jagirdars] come to the Rajbati. . . . The Raja goes to the Dasara festival sitting on a silver sedan with a sword. Besides the Raja, Tikayat (eldest son), Patayat (second son), etc. also go, sitting atop an elephant on a silver palanquin. The British police escort them in front and behind the Raja's group. All of them head for dasara festival. At the Dasara field wrestling, exercises and archery contests are held among the different groups of soldiers. And at the end, the Raja distributes prizes. On his return from the Dasara field the Raja is welcomed back with dance and song and is worshipped with incense at every square. Returning to the Rajbati all the soldiers from different places are given a big feast (bhoji). (Adapted from Pramanik and Skoda 2013, 42)

This brief overview indicates a range of elements, such as the procession to the Dasara field, that are no longer performed. According to most people, this procession came to an end in the 1960s, presumably prior to the abolition of the privy purses under Indira Gandhi. In fact, by 2016, the Dasara field itself had largely disappeared after additional court buildings had been constructed on the grounds. However, these parts are vividly remembered by older locals and were photographed around 1935 and 1936. Showing the king *in state*, such photos allow a diachronic comparison. Several photos show the raja with his *divān* (prime minister) and many other important state officials, while some photos show the raja with Adivasis. For example, one photograph shows the raja receiving and holding Kant Debī, surrounded by *rājpurohit, amat,* his relatives, the Paudi Bhuiyan, and others—a scene not very different from the situation during my fieldwork.

Observing fort rituals from 2003 onwards, and keeping the splendor of the 1930s photographs in mind, one cannot fail to notice a certain decline in the enchanting display (see table 4.1). Not surprisingly, there is a widespread feeling of a general retrogression and that norms are no longer being maintained. A case in point was the final day of the Dasara celebrations in Bonai. The crowd gathered at the Mā Kumārī temple, the site of the final rituals, but many participants remarked that in earlier days many more devotees and spectators had come to partake in the event. As an advisor to the raja told me, in the old days, people feared the goddess and therefore would not commit any crimes. Lamenting a bygone era fits well with ideas of an age of strife (*kali yug*), which is sometimes even mentioned directly.

And indeed, in many cases expenditure on rituals has been cut to a bare minimum. For example, the *khaṇḍa ghar*, the armory, collapsed a few years ago, so the rituals had to be shifted to the former *darbār* hall. Even there the roof is damaged, and the walls of the room used for the rituals are completely black because of a fire lit by burglars. The wooden platform used for the Naba Durgā worship is broken. Arguably

Table 4.1. Ritual changes to Dasara in Bonai

Ritual element Dasara in 1930s	Present situation
Worship of Kant Kumari/Paudi Bhuiyans coming to the *garh*	Vibrant, perhaps even more popular nowadays, but royal gifts reduced
Nabadurgā Pūjā/Sandhi Pūjā	Performed with reductions
Tradition of Ankulia + Baktria/ symbolic human sacrifices	Completely abolished
Procession to the Dasara field/ public competitions at the field	Completely abolished
Bhuiyan darbār*	Completely abolished
Kant Pūrṇimā Pūjā—rituals for the tutelary deity after Dasara	Performed—gifts reduced

*The Raja remembers that initially during his "rule" six to seven Sardars (headmen) still attended the celebrations, offering gifts and receiving turbans.

even more importantly, the *mohana khaṇḍa pūjā,* the ritual for the most powerful and secret sword, was not performed as scheduled by custom due to the absence of the *rājpurohit,* who was in charge. In earlier times, the raja would engage two *rājpurohits* to avoid any disruption because of such unforeseen events in any one family. Nowadays there is only one priest responsible for the performance. Given the current state of affairs, in which rituals have been reduced or abolished, observers and actors sometimes refer to arrangements simply as "short-cut *pūjās.*" While this might imply that this is only related to a weakened financial standing, the postponement, shrinking audiences, and almost private nature of today's sword worship are indicative of the changing social and political realities and a disintegration of Bonai as a sacrificial polity.

Another clear indicator of the steady reduction of ritual splendor and royal largesse in more recent times is the number of sacrificial animals offered during Dasara. As the late raja recollected, during the princely state period, his father gave sixty-six male goats, as well as buffalos and rams; he "cut it all down" to eight in 2006 and further down to seven in 2007. Similarly, the musical performances, including the playing of drums for the first eight days of the half of the month and the playing of other instruments for another eight days, have all been discontinued.

However, the deviations or reductions from 2007 through 2016 should not lead one to the conclusion that there is a linear decline, that premerger rituals were performed in a completely satisfactory manner, or that accelerated change is a postmerger phenomenon. In fact, one might rather expect certain shortcomings and fluctuations in terms of splendor depending on the financial situation, or perhaps the presence of a photographer as in the 1930s. There are, for example, hints in a report of 1948 mentioning considerable changes in the expenditure just around the merger of Bonai indicating several ups and downs in the Dasara performance. Thus, the administrator of Bonai wrote to the additional secretary to government, Cuttack, on September 20, 1948:

> Prior to the merger in the year 1947 the Ruler drew a sum of Rs. 3.000/—for all his religious ceremonies and festivals for that year. Before that the annual grant from the State for Dessehra [sic] was Rs. 26/—only as sanctioned by the Political Agent from year to year. This amount was being drawn by the Ruler. All the celebrations were done inside the Rajbati. It thus appears that the Dessehra was being celebrated by the Ruler in his private capacity. (Office of the Administrator of Bonai, Record No. 10226, 20th of Sept., 1948)

If the report is correct, the budget for ritual activities was considerably inflated from Rs. 26 to Rs. 3,000 in 1947, with the raja using his new but short-lived financial freedom immediately after independence. As the report also suggests, the amount was considerably reduced to Rs. 1,000 a year later. This amount, the newly appointed administrator argued, should be spent on the Bhuiyan *darbār* during Dasara but not on the ritual activities. Thus, he hints at another ritual element during Dasara, a ritual of loyalty involving the most important Adivasi group that was also valued by the postcolonial state, but was neither included in the photographs, nor does it exist today. However, comparing the budget of Rs. 3000 in 1947 or Rs. 1000 in 1948 with Rs. 6000 spent by the raja in 2007, one can easily see that the raja organized his own rituals on a shoestring budget, saving money by reducing the number of sacrificial animals, although campaigns against animal sacrifices may have also led to changes.

Yet, while several parts of the premerger Dasara celebration have been abolished or considerably reduced, at least one aspect of the Dasara has certainly lost nothing of its popularity. The visit of Kant Debī to Bonaigarh continues to be a vibrant element and appears to become increasingly popular. In fact, it was during the *maṇḍal pūjā* in and outside of the fort that eager crowds flocked to the altars erected, usually on crossroads. Here everybody seemed to be keen to hold the goddess, believing in her blessings and healing power. Many devotees also made individual offerings to her, including animal sacrifices—often fulfilling earlier vows. The previous system of inviting the goddess into the houses was abolished during the late raja K. K. C. Deo's "rule." He said that the delay in the *pūjā* and procession was due to an increase in the number of people who wanted to worship the goddess in their home, and a combined ritual for several families at one platform was needed to save time.[5] In fact, the vitality of the Kant Debī rituals is also clearly expressed by wishes of whole villages to be included into the official route of the goddess's procession, though the raja rejected a proposal I witnessed to expand the route—again arguing that time constraints do not allow the inclusion of all villages that want to be part of it.

Durgā Pūjā: A Challenge to Royal Rituals

While Dasara rituals have been declining, though selectively, the Durgā Pūjā ritual has risen. Beginning as a rather small affair, when Mangovind Mohanty, a businessman with interests in mining, migrated to the area and initiated the worship around 1948, Durgā Pūjā has grown and is predominantly supported by comparatively recent and well-off migrants or their descendants, who have never been well-integrated into royal hierarchies. Instead, these, usually middle-class, members of the organizing committee promote a tradition with which they are familiar because of their migration and have successfully garnered the financial support of new power holders with increasing clout in the local society because of their "spending power"—namely, industrialists, mine owners, officers, and occasionally politicians—all donating for a tradition of Durgā worship in which the goddess appears as a temporary idol rather than the royal sword.

The rise of Durgā Pūjā is clearly linked to the tremendous industrialization in the area from 2003 onward—especially a rapid growth of mining and sponge iron or integrated steel plants. This growth was fueled by an expanding demand for steel globally and by the concurrent rise of the price of steel and the relatively low capital investment required to set up a plant, the promise of short-term high profits—all of contributing to ruthless industrialization (CSE 2011: 7). While India emerged as the largest sponge-iron producer in the world, Odisha became a hotspot of this industry with a concentration of a third of all Indian plants—twelve or thirteen of them located in Bonai.[6] The boom of the sponge-iron industry was mirrored by a similar boom of the mining industry—including many cases of illegal mining. [7] And while the boom might have peeked around 2008 or 2009, the industry continues to stagnate on a high level.

Thus, the recent emergence of the sponge-iron industry and new wave in mining occurred parallel to the rise of Durgā Pūjā in Bonaigarh and offered a substantial boost to ritual activities aggrandizing the Durgā worship and confirming Nanda's (2011) dictum that globalization has been good for the gods or rather goddess. The Durgā Pūjā budget multiplied in the same period. According to the Bonai Durgā Pūjā Committee, before 2007 the budget for the ceremonies was around Rs 40,000 and rose to around Rs. 300,000 in 2008, while being around Rs. 5 lakhs in 2013. This was achieved not only by collecting substantial donations from mines and sponge-iron factories but also from local officers—at times also subtly hinting at possible resistance from the local population if donors were not generous in their support. When compared to the royal Dasara, its budget is substantially higher than the raja's, ensuring a grander celebration that increasingly overshadows the smaller rituals inside the fort and palace.

Thanks to the massively inflated budget, the organizing committee can offer relatively spectacular and embellished rituals. It does not rely only on local tent houses to build a temporary temple or *maṇḍap*—though local tent houses provide raw materials—but can bring in workers from West Bengal to erect it. The designs are often suggested by artisans from West Bengal and selected by the Pūjā Committee. In 2007 a replica of the famous Sun Temple in Konark and in 2013 a Buddhist stupa supposedly in Nepal were chosen—the *maṇḍap* altogether costing around 2,5 lakh in 2013. The committee can also procure a rather costly clay *mūrti* like that used in Durgā Pūjā celebrations in Bengal (for more on Bengali-style Durgā Pūjā, see Sen and Zeiler this volume)—showing the victorious ten-armed Durgā triumphing over the demon Mahiṣāsur whom she is visually slaying and thus protecting the world from evil. It was prepared in the steel town Rourkela around 50km away, because it is believed that local potters would not have been able to create such an idol. While the offerings remain strictly vegetarian, the visual and acoustic spectacle during Durgā Pūjā in the market area also include extensive illuminations around the *maṇḍap* and decorations like carpets as well as musical performances that attracted substantial crowds especially during the evening ritual or *ārati*. The importance of the worship was also indirectly stressed by the blocking of the main road for this purpose and diverting the traffic by the several policemen—also showing a tacit support by the state. Not only the final immersion of the unfired clay idol and its temporary character but also the arrangements around the *maṇḍap* stand in stark contrast to the relatively modest worship inside the fort.

Conclusion

Seventy years after the formal abolition of kingship, raja, Adivasis, and other communities in Bonai continue to share an extensive ritual framework, a sacrificial polity, with Dasara as its prime occasion. While crucial ties to ritual specialists such as *kant dehuri, amat,* and *rājpurohit,* and others are maintained, and sacrifices—including blood sacrifices—continue to be performed, Dasara rituals have clearly undergone considerable change, with royal pomp increasingly disappearing. Instead, the worship of the Paudi Bhuiyan goddess Kant Debī, visiting the palace annually, forms arguably the most popular part of contemporary celebrations in Bonaigarh. While there have been various ups and downs in Dasara rituals, for example, around 1948 when Bonai merged with the Indian Union, it seems that the raja and Adivasis are equally interested in maintaining their close and historical tie—particularly in the light of the on-going industrialization and mining boom that threatens the "habitat" of the Paudi Bhuiyan and potentially undermines the raja's position as exalted sacrifier. As a "power ritual" Dasara expresses his royal centrality, and, despite financial constraints, the raja actively seeks to maintain his role and engages in exchanges with various communities by providing at least nominal remunerations or sacrificial meat in lieu of ritual services.

As McDermott (2011, 141, see also Biardieu 1989 [1981]: 137) argued, "Bengali Goddess worship is inextricably bound up with competition, be it artistic, social, or political." Similarly, the multitude of Durgās, encountered in Bonai perhaps most prominently during Dasara rituals, seems to have been tied to rivalries in several ways. The sister relationship between the raja's *iṣṭa debī* Mā Kumārī and the Paudi Bhuiyan goddess Kant Debī may well be understood in this way as many rajas attempted to integrate powerful "tribal" deities as tutelary deities into court rituals (c.f. Kulke (2001 [1984] and Mallebrein 2004). However, the visiting goddess

Kant Debī has, at best, been imperfectly appropriated, though both are linked as sisters and forms of Durgā. While earlier the raja and the Paudi Bhuiyan may have competed in terms of their position vis-à-vis the goddess, under the current circumstances their alliance as a relation of mutual care is clearly foregrounded in the rituals.

Nowadays, the older fort-centered tradition coincides with a rather new market-based tradition, and both compete in terms of audiences, attractions, and ritual efficacy. Possibly resonating with older Vaiśya (merchant) versus Kṣatriya (royal) rivalries (see also Tambs-Lyche 1996), and overlapping with distinctions between strictly vegetarian (Durgā Pūjā) versus blood sacrifices (Dasara). Durgā Pūjā presents a ritual challenge to the raja's power by a rising middle or upper class with considerable resources, which are boosted by global economic processes. While expressing and mediating new aspirations and degrees of outsider- and insider-ness (Pfaff-Czarnecka 1998), this most recent schism in the Durgā worship in the context of Dasara and Durgā Pūjā, however, does not simply appear as a clear-cut break. Rather, one finds occasional nominal references to the raja from the side of the Durgā Pūjā Committee. Although the committee members see their more spectacular rituals as independent of the fort ceremonies, there are still vague hints at the raja's authority, however fading it might be. As the president of the committee explained to me in an interview:

> *US: Has the raja been invited to the Durgā maṇḍap [ritual pavilion]?*
>
> *Pres: No, there is no such tradition.*
>
> *US: Has the raja ever been a member of the committee?*
>
> *Pres: The raja does not give time. So we do not keep him in the committee, but everything is run with his co-operation.*

Similarly, the late raja argued that there is no need for him to get involved with the committee or to worship at the *maṇḍap*, because he worships Durgā in the palace. The worship of Kant Debī would be "sufficient" for him, thus making a clear reference to the most popular part of the older Dasara rituals, namely, the visit of Kant Debī traveling from the fringe of the kingdom to the palace. The raja also emphasized that the government (through its Debottar department) is involved in the management of the major local temples of Lord Baneśvar and Lord Jagannāṭh and may indirectly support Durgā Pūjā, but it has nothing to do with Kant Debī rituals: "This is only between the Bhuiyan and me." He very consciously guarded his role and power, visibly expressed in the worship of the goddesses in the form of iron swords, while trying to keep the Indian state and wealthy newcomers at bay.

Notes

1. This chapter is based on discontinuous field research in the former princely state since 2003, focusing on Dasara especially in 2003, 2007, and 2016.

2. Although some locals use the terms "Dasara" and "Durgā Pūjā" interchangeably, there is a clear tendency to use "Dasara" for the rituals in the fort and "Durgā Pūjā" for rituals in the market (*patna/bāzār*). The lexical differentiation, however, is not absolute. In an inclusive way, both names may be used to signify the whole "festive season." The usage may also depend on the background in the sense that migrants may tend to use "Durgā Pūjā" more frequently, while more established families may use "Dasara."

3. The Rajpurohit considers the payment as *dakhina* and not *dastūrī*, as in the raja's records.

4. Although his remuneration was not listed as *dastūrī* in the official ledger, the raja called it *dastūrī* during conversations and explained that it would be handed over prior to the full moon.

5. In 2007 there were rumors that during the procession of Kant Debi to Bonaigarh people from a village a few kilometers away from the route had actually taken the goddess illegally on a motorbike to their home—deviating from the prescribed route and further delaying the procession, which outraged people in Bonaigarh.

6. However, precise information is scarce—the last survey of the Joint Plant Committee (JPC) being conducted in 2005. For more recent information on sponge-iron plants, one must rely on data provided, for example, by the Sponge Iron Manufacturers Association (SIMA) or its regional associations.

7. "M B Shah Commission Report: Odisha's Mine of Scams Exposed," *Down to Earth*, January 28, 2014. http://www.downtoearth.org.in/content/m-b-shah-commission-report-odishas-mine-scams-exposed.

References

Biardieu, Madeleine. 1989 [1981]. *Hinduism. The Anthropology of a Civilization*. Delhi: Oxford University Press.

Bourdieu, Pierre, Luc Boltanski, et al. 1983 [1965]. *Eine illegitime Kunst. Die soziale Gebrauchsweise der Photographie*. Frankfurt/M.: Suhrkamp.

Chatterjee, Partha. 2008. "Critique of Popular Culture." *Public Culture* 20 (2): 321–44.

Eschmann, Anncharlott. 1994 [1975]. "Sign and Icon: Symbolism in the Indian Folk Religion." In *Religion and Society in Eastern India*, edited by G. C. Tripathi and Hermann Kulke. Delhi: Manohar.

Fuller, C. J. 1992. *The Camphor Flame: Popular Hinduism and Society in India*. Princeton: Princeton University Press.

Galey, J. C. 1990. "Reconsidering Kingship in India: An Ethnological Perspective." In *Kingship and the Kings*, edited by J.-C. Galey. Chur: Harwood.

Gell, Alfred. 1997. "Exalting the King and Obstructing the State: A Political Interpretation of Royal Ritual in Bastar District, Central India." *The Journal of the Royal Anthropological Institute* 3 (3): 433–50.

Ghosh, Anjan. 2006. "Durgā Pūjā: A Consuming Passion." *India Seminar* 559. http://www.india-seminar.com/2006/559/559%20anjan%20ghosh.htm.
Goffman, E. 1981. "Bilder-Rahmen." In *Bilder-Rahmen,* edited by E. Goffman, 45–103. Geschlecht und Werbung, Frankfurt: Suhrkamp.
Hardenberg, Roland. 2000. *Ideologie eines Hindu-Koenigtums. Struktur and Bedeutung der Rituale des: Koenigs von Puri (Orissa Indien).* Berlin: Das Arabische Buch.
Khanna, Madhu. 2000. "The Ritual Capsule of Durgā Pūjā: An Ecological Perspective." In *Hinduism and Ecology,* edited by Christopher K. Chapple and Mary Evelyn Tucker, 469–98. Cambridge: Harvard University.
Kinsley, David. 1987. *Hindu Goddesses: Vision of the Divine Feminine in the Hindu Religious Tradition.* New Delhi: Motilal Banarsidass.
———. 1978. "The Portrait of the Goddess in the Devī-māhātmya." *Journal of the American Academy of Religion* 46 (4): 489–506.
Kovacs, Anja. 2004. "You Don't Understand, We Are at War! Refashioning Durgā in the Service of Hindu Nationalism." *Contemporary South Asia* 13 (4): 373–88.
Kulke, Hermann. 2001 [1984]. "Tribal Deities at Princely Courts: The Feudatory Rājās of Central Orissa and Their Tutelary Deities (*istadevatās*)." In *Kings and Cults: State Formation and Legitimation in India and South East Asia,* edited by Hermann Kulke, 114–36. New Delhi: Manohar.
———. "Kshatriyaization and Social Change: A Study in the Orissan Setting." In *Kings and Cults: State Formation and Legitimation in India and South East Asia,* edited by Hermann Kulke, 82–89. Delhi: Manohar.
Mallebrein, Cornelia. 2004. "Entering the Realm of Durgā: Pātkhandā, a Hinduized Tribal Deity." In *Text and Context in the History, Literature and Religion of Orissa,* edited by Angelika Malinar, Johannes Belt, and Heiko Frese. New Delhi: Manohar.
McDermott, R. F. 2008. "The Pujas in Historical and Political Controversy: Colonial and Post-Colonial Goddesses." *Religions of South Asia* 2 (2): 135–59.
———. 2011. *Revelry, Rivalry, and Longing for the Goddesses of Bengal: The Fortunes of Hindu Festivals.* New York: Columbia University Press.
Michaels, A., ed. 2006. *Die neue Kraft der Rituale.* Heidelberg: Universitätsverlag Winter.
Michaels, Axel. 1998. *Der Hinduismus. Geschichte und Gegenwart.* Muenchen: Beck.
Nanda, Meera. 2011. *God Market: How Globalisation Is Making India More Hindu.* Delhi: Random House India.
Nicholas, R. W. 2013. *Night of the Gods: Durgā Pūjā and the Legitimation of Power in Rural Bengal.* Delhi: Orient BlackSwan.
Office of the Administrator of Bonai, Record No. 10226 from Administrator to Additional Secy to Govt, Home Department, States Section, Cuttack, September 20, 1948.
Östör, Ákos. 2004 [1980]. *The Play of Gods: Locality, Ideology, Structure, and Time in the Festivals of a Bengali Town.* New Delhi: Chronicle Books.
Panda, Sasanka S. 2004. "Durgā Worship in Upper Mahanadi Valley." *Orissa Review,* October 2004: http://orissagov.nic.in/e-magazine/Orissareview/oct2004/englishPdf/Durgāworshipinupper.pdf.
Pfaff-Czarnecka, Joanna. 1998. "A Battle of Meaning: Commemorating Goddess Durgā's Victory over Demon Mahisā as a Political Act." *Asiatische Studien: Zeitschrift der Schweizerischen Gesellschaft für Asienkunde* 52 (2): 575–610.

Pramanik, R., and Uwe Skoda. 2013. *Chronicles of the Royal Family of Bonai (Odisha).* Delhi: Manohar.

Schnepel, Burkhard. 2002. *The Jungle Kings: Ethnohistorical Aspects of Politics and Ritual in Orissa.* New Delhi: Manohar.

Shah, Alpa. 2008 [2007]. "Keeping the State Away." In *Power Plays: Politics, Rituals, Performances in South Asia,* edited by Lidia Guzy and Uwe Skoda. Berlin: Weissensee Verlag.

Singer, M. 1964. *When a Great Tradition Modernizes.* New York: Praeger.

Singh, Prabhas Kumar. 2006. "Sakta Pithas of Purusottama Kshetra." *Orissa Review* (June): 91–95.

Sontheimer, Guenther-Dietz. 1981. "Dasarā at Devaragudda: Ritual and Play in the Cult of Mailār / Khandobā." In *South Asian Digest of Regional Writing 10: Drama in Contemporary South Asia: Varieties and Settings,* edited by Lothar Lutze. Heidelberg: South Asia Institute.

Tambs-Lyche, Harald. 2004. *The Feminine Sacred in South Asia.* New Delhi: Manohar.

———. 1996. *Power, Profit and Poetry: Traditional Society in Kathiawar, Western India.* Delhi: Manohar.

Vasudevan, Sreelatha. 1990. "Deity as a Social Prism: A Study of Korravai (Durgā)." *Proceedings of the Indian History Congress* 51:122–26.

NAVARĀTRI ON DISPLAY

5

Politics, Religion, and Art in the Durgā Pūjā of West Bengal

MOUMITA SEN

During the Durgā Pūjā of 2014, the chief minister of West Bengal, Mamata Banerjee, was doing her usual rounds of inaugurations of the *pandals* (*paṇḍāl*), the temporary templelike marquees that house the goddess. At Hindustan Park, an elite neighborhood of south Kolkata (Calcutta), she appeared on stage accompanied by minister Sovandev Chatterjee, a monk from the Ramakrishna Mission, the CEO of a private real estate company, and a popular singer from Bengal. In her inaugural speech, she quoted lines from popular songs of Rabindranath Tagore[1] to address two major themes: the importance of festivals or *utsaba* in the life of the community and the greatness of Bengal. She defined "dharma" (loosely translated, in this context, as religion) as festivals, flows of creativity, and the coming together of a diverse community. Religion, in her speech, is something that brings to the street several self-contained, isolated individuals and groups. In other words, dharma became coterminous with the idea of *utsaba* in her speech. Significantly, she asked the enthusiastic audience not to let their spirits dampen when the goddess is immersed, the lights of the city have dimmed, and the music has stopped. She asked her audience to keep up their spirits for the other *utsabas* to follow: Lakṣmī Pūjā, Kālī Pūjā, Bakr-Īd, Jagatdhātri Pūjā, Chaṭ, and finally Christmas. She finished her speech by reciting a *stotra* dedicated to Caṇḍī in the *Devī Māhātmya* after apologizing to the monk for performing some of his tasks.

The adoration of gods and goddesses, including the temples built to them and the proliferation of devotional practices in South Asia, has been deeply rooted in the history of political regimes. The stories of the power and valor of gods and goddesses is never free from the story of their patrons, powerful men in possession of great wealth and status. The history of monumental temples built in medieval India shows us that monarchy and devotional practices are imbricated in each other (Appadurai 1977; Spencer 2008). In the history of Durgā Pūjā in Bengal, we see a similar operation of capital, power, and status-building. While the royal *pūjās* of the eighteenth century marked the power and sovereignty of kings, the aristocratic *pūjās* by the land-owning *zamīndārs* and other native elites of the nineteenth century were concerned with rivalry and prestige garnered by attracting British officers and people of wealth and significance to their festivities (McDermott 2011, 40–41; Guha-Thakurta 2015, 3). Several accounts written by the British at the time report the pomp and grandeur of the "Gentoo" (Gentleman Hindoo) *pūjā*s of Calcutta complete with *saṁ* (clown) performances, Hindustani classical music,[2] and the dance of "nautch" (Bengali: *nāca*) girls (McDermott 2011, 27). In fact, in the early nineteenth century, the aristocratic families advertised their yearly programs in British newspapers in hopes of attracting foreign guests (McDermott 2011, 41). Given this history, it is not surprising that when the goddess moves from the aristocratic courtyard to the streets, the politics of rivalry and grandeur remain the same.

The present organizers of the Durgā Pūjā are youth clubs located in the *pāṛās* (neighborhoods) of West Bengal, and the funds are raised by subscriptions collected from the residents of the *pāṛa* (Sen 2016). However, these local clubs now have implicit or explicit affiliations with the political parties that operate in the state of West Bengal. This is most obvious in the common practice of reserving the position of the president of the club for a minister, be it a local councilor, minister of parliament (or minister of the legislative assembly). The Durgā Pūjā of Kolkata, which the media has christened as the "megaevent" of the state, is clearly rooted in what the advertising agencies call the "intangibles" or "emotional quotient" of a community and the clubs call the "emotional core" of the city (interviews with Bates Advertising Agency 2012 and Forty One Pally Club 2015). But to stage this event, a well-known club typically spends from 10 to 20 million INR (US$1,542,458 to US$3,084,916). The production of the mega-event today is based on a network of funding from private sectors, political interest of the ruling party, the local clubs' bid for status, and a large group of professionals (artists, *pandal*-makers, flower-sellers, etc.), who find employment during the preparations for the spectacular festival city.

Over the last two decades, both popular and academic studies of the Durgā Pūjā have shown its "nonreligious" aspects (Guha-Thakurta

2015, 4)—from ethnographic accounts of the civic event, to art catalogs (Dasgupta, 2013). A new community of highly skilled art-school-trained visual artists—called "*pūjā* designers" began to use the *pūjā* as a platform for public art installations around the beginning of the 2000s. The Durgā Pūjā of Kolkata transforms the city into a museumlike space of artlike installations. I use "artlike" and "museumlike" because while the Durgā Pūjā clearly becomes deeply invested in the aesthetic discourse of art and design, its claim to the status of Art remains contentious. Following Homi Bhabha's understanding of the "mimic man" (1984), Guha-Thakurta shows how it becomes "Art, but not quite" (Guha-Thakurta 2015, 288). Nonetheless, the *pūjā* designers became the face of the Durgā Pūjā on promotional literature circulated by the clubs, and the people of the city—both elite and nonelite—follow their works in different parts of the city. The media and the private companies create panels of judges comprised of artists and important members of civil society, who grade their works and award them on the grounds of aesthetic merit and conceptual excellence. This aesthetic judgment is further propelled into popular public discourse through electronic and print media and a host of signage on the streets. It has been demonstrated that the Durgā Pūjā of Bengal has shifted from a ritual to a spectacle around the sixties and the seventies in Calcutta (Agnihotri 2001). Around the turn of the century, there was a further shift from the visual language of the spectacular to that of the artistic in the material production of the *pandal* and the Durgā *mūrti* (literally "image" or "figure") (Guha-Thakurta 2004).

Given the magnitude and ubiquity of the festival in West Bengal, in this chapter I discuss the ways through which Durgā Pūjā has become a vehicle of political parties to promote and promulgate their agenda and ideologies. I use three case studies through which this new form of politicization of Durgā Pūjā, in the electoral sense, clearly can be seen in *pandal*s set up by local clubs that enjoy the political patronage of the chief minister, Mamata Banerjee. I argue that since 2012, after the Trinamool Congress (TMC) came into power, the party has appropriated different aspects of the Durgā Pūjā to bolster its foothold in West Bengal.[3] I argue that the Durgā Pūjā of Kolkata is now experiencing another shift from the language of art to that of party politics. Not only is the political patronage of Durgā Pūjā in Kolkata a model for other festival cultures in the region under the TMC government, but it has paved the way to shaping of a modified practice of secularism in the state.

The Goddess and the Government: Three Case Studies

Since 2012, there has been a subtle yet obvious shift in the way clubs advertise for their Durgā Pūjās. On the promotional signs, we now see the names of ministers or local councilors of the TMC as the club president, vice president, or "chief patron" in bold letters, a phenomenon that was absent in earlier years. These promotional signs, slowly but surely over the last few years, replaced the name of the artist with the name of the minister, who was the president, chairman, or chief patron of the club. The minister's name is now featured in the foreground. In this section, I look at the relationship between the chief minister, Mamata Banerjee, and Durgā Pūjā with three examples. These examples, I argue, demonstrate the party politicization of Durgā Pūjā through the allegorical entanglement of the body of the female political leader with that of the goddess.

Political Power as Śakti: The Female Leader as Durgā

The new TMC government came into power supported by the ardent hope for *paribartana* (change) among the millions of voters in West Bengal after more than three decades under the same Communist Party of India, Marxist (CPIM) government. Since *paribartana* was a key idea in media and popular discourse, it was not surprising that it became the theme for Durgā Pūjās that year as well. The most striking case was that of the Mohammad Ali Park club in central Kolkata. As the media reported, the theme of the Durgā Pūjā was "Mamata Banerjee" herself. The club claimed that Mamata Banerjee stood for *śakti*, the embodiment of divine feminine energy. The LED tableaux laid out on the street leading up to the *pandal* showed portraits of Mamata Banerjee in a string of blinking lights, but the ultimate portrait of Banerjee was the goddess herself. The *mūrti* presented the goddess overpowering unique metaphorical demons: evil civil servants and other uniform-clad men, who certainly referred to the CPIM-orchestrated violence unleashed on the peasants and their families in Nandigarm and Singur (Ghatak et al. 2013). If the metaphorical demon is explicitly represented as the agents of the erstwhile CPIM government, it is implicit that the goddess herself is metaphorically represented as the woman who single-handedly caused the downfall of the leftist government in the popular imagination.

Political deification is common both in the history of the Indian independence movement and contemporary Indian politics (Amin 1984; Dickey 1993). Whether it is the deification of B. R. Ambedkar (Kirby 2008) or the temple built to Narendra Modi, the rhetoric of political obeisance often overlaps with ritual veneration. However, the images of goddesses, particularly Durgā slaying the buffalo-demon, have been employed regularly in political struggles. The Bhārat Mātā (Mother India) icon reverberates with similarities to the militant-goddess Durgā in its sentimental portrayals in a plethora of popular prints and bazaar art. Subhas Chandra Bose called for women to act as Durgā and come to the rescue of the nation from the demonlike colonizers (Bo Nielsen

2016, 98). The erstwhile prime minister Indira Gandhi refused the praise of BJP leader Atal Bihari Vajpayee, comparing her to "Abhinav Chandi Durga" after the Bangladesh war, saying that there are many Dalits and Bahujans who worship Mahiṣāsura (Vincent 2016). However, M. F. Husain, the controversial national modernist painter, portrayed her as Durgā on her lion mount in the act of slaying demons; however, he was eventually criticized for courting political patronage through his sycophantic portraits of Indira Gandhi (Guha-Thakurta 2011).

The icon of Durgā as inspiring *śakti* has been appropriated into singularly militant images among the women's organization affiliated with the Viswa Hindu Parishad called the "Durgā Vāhinī" (Vehicles of Durgā) (Kovacs 2004). In this organization, the ideal of Durgā's *śakti* is employed in terms of both moral and muscular power to hone the female members' bodies and minds so that they can defend the "Hindu Nation." The case of Jayalalitha is particularly interesting in the way popular notions of *śakti*, stardom, and role-playing as actress are used in the style of her political leadership.

Jayalalitha started representing herself as a goddess during an election campaign in 1991. Alleging that she had been assaulted by members of a rival party, when she referred to the incident, she presented herself as Draupadi, the heroine of the *Mahābhārata*. Years later, during Christmas, she appeared as the Virgin Mary on huge cut-outs all over Chennai, and in 1998 she was portrayed as Kali, wearing a garland of skulls depicting M. Karunanidhi, the leader of the rival party. In her home state of Tamil Nadu, there are temples where she appears as the central deity (Bo Nielsen 97–98).

When this chapter was written, Durgā and her relationship with female politicians were under discussion in Indian Parliament, with Human Resource Development minister Smriti Irani defending the goddess's honor as a "Durgā worshipper" against the caste rights activists, who claimed that the demon Mahiṣāsura is the real fallen hero of the Adivasis (tribal peoples) and Bahujans ("many people," India's "Scheduled Tribes," "Scheduled Castes," "Other Backward Classes," and other minority groups) (ANI 2016, Feb 25). In a speech at the Lok Sabha (Lower House of India's Parliament), opposing Irani's charge of blasphemy against the Dalit activists, CPIM minister Sitaram Yechuri recalled an incident in which Indira Gandhi was compared to Durgā by the media, and she had denounced the comparison (Shrivastava 2016). Goddess symbolism regarding female politicians is pervasive in the media and public opinion (Kishwar 1999), and women themselves can use or reject this comparison to their advantage in the Indian political arena. In the next case, I will look at the way in which Mamata Banerjee is not only compared to the goddess but she is also the artist who molds the so-called "*ārṭēra-mūrti*" (art-image) of Durgā herself.

Molding the Body of the Goddess: The Minister as Artist

In 2010, Mamata Banerjee, chief minister of West Bengal and former railway minister of India, was invited by the Bakul Bagan club to design the *pandal* and model the *mūrti* of Durgā. As the media reported later, this was not the first time she had been invited by the club, but this *was* the first time she accepted the invitation. The minister found time in her busy schedule to design the *pandal* and the *mūrti* along with Dhiren Ghosh, her assistant. It remains unclear in the media coverage and in my own interviews with the club whether the minister used her own hands to model the clay and paint it, or if she gave Ghosh a design on which he modeled the *pandal* and the *mūrti*. To the masses who came to this *pandal* to see the goddess made by the charismatic female leader of the TMC, she was the artist. On the sixth day of the Durgā Pūjā, the minister inaugurated the *pandal* with much fanfare. The urban crowd of Kolkata saw a painted panorama that showed a picturesque *grāma-bāṅgalā* (Village-Bengal) around the *pandal*. The ceiling was painted with white nimbus clouds, and the walls showed a landscape overflowing with *kāśa phūla* (*Saccharum spontaneum*), two signifiers that bring to most middle-class Bengali minds the autumn season. At the altar stood a *mūrti*, which the club called "modern art Durgā," an abstract, nonanthropomorphic representation of the goddess.

The idea of artistry is particularly important to the Bakul Bagan club in south Kolkata. This small club, on a tiny street in the old part of south Kolkata, became famous for the cultural capital it accrued almost a decade before the Durgā Pūjā of Bengal became a megaevent with many stars (politicians, actors, artists, etc.) under the media glare. For years, Bakul Bagan has invited renowned artists and sculptors from the world of high Art to make their *mūrti* of the goddess. Unlike the new crop of Durgā Pūjā "designers" whose status as "real artists" is questioned by the world of high art, the *mūrtis* made by the celebrity artists of the city were considered, in some sense, works of art. The term *ārṭēra ṭhākura* (artistic goddess) was coined first in the context of Bakul Bagan to find a suitable way of describing this new kind of goddess image, which functioned as both a work of art and a ritual object. In the years following the boom of "theme Pūjās" (c. 2002), Bakul Bagan has maintained its high cultural capital (or what Bourdieu would call "symbolic capital") through the list of names of the important artists who have designed and created *mūrtis* for the club, such as Shanu Lahiri and Paritosh Sen. While "theme" *pandals* created by other clubs—made of chilies, nails, and so on—were considered by the elites of the city to be gimmicky, spectacular, and without any real aesthetic value, the *pandals* of the Bakul Bagan club were distinctly "artistic," even high-brow because of their association with these artists. Therefore, the announcement of Mamata Banerjee as the *śilpī* (artist) of the year was somewhat distinct in the history of the Bakul Bagan club. What is crucial, however, is the location of the club in the constituency of south Kolkata where Banerjee has had many landslide victories in the elections, even during the CPIM regime.

The world of high art did not care much for Banerjee's "modern art" Durgā. The city did not even hear much about the *mūrti*. It was reported, however, that this Durgā was not ritually immersed. Instead, it spent three years in government storage. After the CPIM government was overthrown in the phenomenal election of 2011, and Mamata Banerjee came into power, several new projects related to the beautification of the city were initiated. At this point Banerjee's *mūrti* resurfaced as part of the beautification projects and found its pride of place as public art in an important crossroad at New Town, the emerging industrial wing of the growing city (figure 5.1).

The attempts to designate Mamata Banerjee as *śilpī* is part of her conscious self-(re)fashioning. Her predecessor, bitter rival, and current opposition party, the CPIM, is composed primarily of male, elite *bhadraloks* (aristocracy), who have over the years been associated with the "cultured" in West Bengal.

> A *bhadralok* is the embodiment of a particular combination of cultural capital, manners and dress code. A quintessential *bhadralok* is educated, refined, eloquent and with a good knowledge of English. He is a high caste Hindu, often a Brahmin, and has style, manners and dignity, although he will usually display a measure of modesty and moderation in public life.

Figure 5.1. Mamata Banerjee's Durgā as public art in New Town, Kolkata, 2014.

> His uniform is the crisp white *dhoti* and *kurta,* and a genuine *bhadralok* will be well versed in the world of arts, literature and poetry. Virtually all of West Bengal's chief ministers from B.C. Roy to Siddhartha Shankar Ray, Jyoti Basu and Buddhadeb Bhattacharya have conformed to this model of a *bhadralok* politician. (Bo Nielsen 2016, 91)

By contrast, Mamata Banerjee holds a "reputation as an unsophisticated and unpolished political maverick" (Bo Nielsen 2016, 83). Her lower-middle-class origin in an ordinary family as opposed to a political dynasty and her lack of facility with the English language make her particularly vulnerable to accusations of being "uncultured." She has tried to counter this accusation by cultivating an alternative image of a creative individual. She has molded the persona of an activist artist—a poet and a painter—living among the masses close to the grassroots and practicing general austerity in her lifestyle. A popular article portrays her in this manner:

> Ms. Banerjee is a street fighting, rabble rousing, plain living populist politician living in a slummy red-tiled one storey home on the banks of a stinking canal in a run-down Calcutta neighbourhood. She turns out in cheap, pale, sometimes-tattered saris. If there is one honest political leader in India who has lived like a common person and the Indian oligarchs could never bribe her with money and other things, she is Mamata Banerjee of West Bengal. (Chadda 2005, qtd by Bo Nielsen 2016, 90)

On the one hand, she is gentle, emotional, and caring, while on the other hand, she is rebellious, feisty, and confrontational (Bo Nielsen 2016, 89). Her public speeches and political rhetoric are typically a medley of quotations from well-known Bengali poems and songs. This rebel-poet persona has led to much popularity among the masses if not the elite of the city.

Banerjee has published seven books of Bengali poetry, thirty-three fictional and nonfictional books, and nine English poems and is the creator of several paintings which are easily accessible in an official internet archive run by the TMC (TMC 2015). Over the years, Mamata Banerjee's paintings have been auctioned for various charitable causes. After TMC came into power in 2011, the Durgā Pūjā map issued by the Kolkata Police, which shows all the club *pandals* in the municipality, began to feature a drawing made by the minister on its cover. The same image was printed on all large billboards and signboards issued by the Kolkata Police during the *pūjā*. While she ceaselessly writes and paints, the elites of the city continue to mock her attempts (Bo Nielsen 2016, 92).

What is of interest to me is the relationship between the aesthetic dimensions of Durgā Pūjā and the minister's individual style of political leadership. Confronted with the deeply gendered and elite opposition party, Mamata Banerjee uses her image as an artist and intellectual to compensate for her class and gender. While the other female political leaders of India find a way out of the patriarchal structure of Indian politics, either through their alliance to elaborate dynasties, political families, or cinema and television stardom, Mamata Banerjee's political career has been an exception. Bo Nielsen argues that in her grassroots activist persona, her "emotionality becomes as asset" (2016, 89). I add that her insistence on cultivating the artistic and intellectual dimensions of her public persona, despite the mockery of the elites, is a major aspect of her style of political leadership.

Bringing the Goddess to Life: Public Consecration Rituals by the Minister

In this final brief example, I want to point out the intersection of art, politics, and popular religiosity in contemporary West Bengal by citing an example from the Durgā Pūjā of 2014. The style of political speeches delivered by Mamata Banerjee is not traditional when compared to the comported style of the leftist leaders. In several of her inaugural speeches, she recited parts of popular *stotras* dedicated to goddesses, as I discussed at the beginning of this chapter, but in a particular incident from 2014, she performed the eye-painting ritual, which is popularly understood to consecrate and enliven the goddess.

For at least two decades, the front page of the popular newspapers has carried a picture of a traditional clay modeler performing *cakṣudāna* or the eye-painting ritual on the Durgā *mūrti*. In 2014, however, the front page of the newspaper the day after *mahālaẏā* showed the chief minister painting the third eye of the goddess. This was not just any *mūrti*; it was the *mūrti* made by the most important Durga Pūjā artist, Sanatan Dinda, in the Chetla Agrani Club, which is the neighborhood club of Bobby Hakim, the minister of Urban Development and Municipal Affairs.

Sanatan Dinda, the most famous Pūjā artist, stepped aside as Mamata Banerjee "finished" his *mūrti* by ritually opening its eyes under the watchful gaze of members of electronic and print media. The image of Mamata Banerjee performing *cakṣudāna* on Sanatan Dinda's *mūrti* appeared on the front page of the most popular newspapers, marking the beginning of *dēbī-parba* (fortnight of the goddess) in Bengal. When asked if he had any anxiety about the chief minister ruining his image, it is striking that the artist replied with a smile, ""Not at all! After all, Didi is also an artist herself" (Banerjie 2014). This photograph was later converted into an

Figure 5.2. A large signboard advertising the local club's Durgā Pūjā using the photograph of the minister consecrating the goddess image, E. M. Bypass, Kolkata, 2016.

advertisement for the club, which was reproduced in innumerable public places in Kolkata (figure 5.2).

Through these case studies, we can see how images of the goddess during Durgā Pūjā can be used in the context of electoral politics in West Bengal. In the first example, we see a metaphorical representation of the minister as a goddess demolishing figures that symbolize the CPIM. In the second, we see the self-fashioning of the minister as an artist. She created an abstract form to the body of the goddess in a club, which is historically known for annually inviting well-known sculptors and painters from the world of high art to create "*ārṭēra* Durgā" or "artistic Durgā." In the third example, we see the minister replacing the clay modeler as the one who conjures life into the clay body of the goddess. These examples coalesce the body politics of the female leader and the goddess, reverberating with metaphorical interpretations of the idea of *śakti*.

Between Money, Power, and the Community

In this section, I examine the vested interest that the political parties and the local clubs have in each other. Indeed, the relationship is so intertwined that Subrata Mukherjee, the former mayor of the city, once said that he does not organize the Durga Pūjā because he is a minister, but he is a politician because he learned how to organize a *pūjā* as a young member of the local club (conversation with a filmmaker, Kolkata, 2014).

Sociologically speaking, a neighborhood club is a voluntary civic organization built with a specific neighborhood in mind. Typically, a local club "takes care" of its neighborhood, looking out for lonely elderly people, sorting out disputes both within and among the families, and so on (interview with Ajeya Sanhati, 2014). Arguably the most visible if not the most important thing that the club does in contemporary Kolkata is organizing Durgā Pūjā.

A common theme that emerged in my interviews with some of the prominent clubs of Kolkata was that, in the context of the Durgā Pūjā, the clubs see themselves as mediators, who redistribute resources by generating funds from the private sector and creating employment opportunities for a series of creative professionals, artisans, laborers, and so on. This accumulation of funds is the primary reason that the local clubs affiliate with a political party by christening a minister of parliament or minister of the legislative assembly as their "chairman," "president," or "chief patron." This position is usually token or symbolic, but the club requires this symbolic position to buoy sponsorship negotiations with private companies. A private company is more likely to trust a club that is associated with a minister and might feel obliged to accept a proposal particularly because it has the minister's name on it. In other words, the sponsorship from the private sector is influenced by the political patronage of local clubs.

Along with the redistribution of resources, the primary interest of the club in staging a spectacular Durgā Pūjā seems to be two-fold. First, the Durgā Pūjā is one of the very few ways of heightening the status of a neighborhood irrespective of class by using cultural capital. In fact, some of the finest award-winning Durgā Pūjās of Kolkata are hosted by lower-middle- or middle-class neighborhoods. Second, even though the clubs claim that they do not accept any remuneration for their work, the people of the neighborhood complain about the mismanagement and unaccounted flow of funds.

While the clubs' interest in affiliating with the political party might be easily perceived, the interest of the political party in its involvement with the festival takes more careful consideration. Here we turn again to Mamata Banerjee to see how she has politicized the patronage of Durgā Pūjā in West Bengal. In 2013, the chief minister made it mandatory for different departments of the municipality to patronize at least ten *pūjās* in clubs in Kolkata and its suburbs. She requested that the prominent and wealthy clubs patronize at least five *pūjās* organized by smaller clubs. In 2014, she allocated state funds to supply free electricity to the city's Durgā Pūjā *pandals*. What is of interest to me is her mandate on further tax exemptions for *pandals* that use blue and white—the colors representing her TMC government. The TMC government has realized that the Durgā Pūjā is the emotional core of the Bengali middle-class community (Interview with Bates advertising agency, 2012). The appeal of the *pūjā* also spills over to other classes and religious groups and is used by the TMC government to secure political capital.

The Blue and White State of Relentless Festivity

This relationship of the government to the festival is not limited to the Durgā Pūjā. The TMC government patronizes other *pūjās* in smaller towns of West Bengal, such as the Kartik Pūjā in Bansberiya and the Saraswatī Pūjā in Magra Haat in the Hoogly district, using the template of Durgā Pūjā. It would, however, be a mistake to liken this relationship of the government with religious festivals to the forces of Hindu nationalist politics that are present in the nation today. The strategy of the TMC government, as is most obvious in Banerjee's inaugural speech quoted earlier, is to mobilize the religious festivals of all religious communities. Regarding the troublesome idea of governmental engagement in a religious festival that is frequently raised by communists, Banerjee's position is: "Durga *Pūjā* is not just about some religious rituals; the governing principle is a cultural connect between people of all religions and from all walks of life" (Basu 2011). The TMC government also extends its patronage to public celebrations beyond the religious festival, and in 2013 the government introduced sixty new nonreligious festivals in West Bengal that are centered on crafts, agriculture, cottage industries, education, and so on. Indeed, the idea of celebrating festivals is central to Banerjee's mission and political philosophy. In a conversation with a filmmaker, I was told that Mamata Banerjee, of all the leaders of Bengal, has understood best the power and the craft of advertising. In a consumerist neoliberal democracy, ideas of branding are used for efficacious mass communication; some have argued for the use of similar techniques of communicative efficacy even by Gandhi (Mazzarella 2010). By using the logic of branding, Banerjee has framed herself as an icon in association with a series of nationalist great men of Bengal: poets, thinkers, intellectuals, and martyrs. For instance, with every initiated or completed project, a new portrait of the chief minister is installed in the public space. To overwrite the city with the presence of the government, the municipal buildings, public walls, footpaths, and trunks of trees have been painted blue and white, constantly reinforcing the TMC brand within its city. The government announced in 2014 that every homeowner who paints his or her home blue and white will be privy to reduced property tax. Those who design their Durgā Pūjā *pandals* in these two colors are exempted from paying for electricity and the services of the police and fire brigade. Therefore, Durgā Pūjā falls into a larger branding strategy of the TMC in West Bengal.

No aspect of life in West Bengal is untouched by its political parties (Chatterjee 1997). Familial, social, and cultural life is permeated at every stage by the presence and influence of the reigning party. Durgā Pūjā of Bengal has in an obvious way emerged as a tool of mobilization of many publics. One of the conditions of the political society, according to

Chatterjee is "the widening of the arena of political mobilization . . . from formally organized structures such as political parties with well-ordered internal constitutions and coherent doctrines and programs to loose and often transient mobilizations, building on communication structures that would not be ordinarily recognized as political for instance, religious assemblies or cultural festivals" (Chatterjee 2004, 47). And these processes are prompted by electoral considerations and often only for electoral ends.

Conclusion

As I have shown above, the TMC government has adopted a larger strategy, like advertising techniques, where its potential voters see the portrait of the chief minister in her blue and white sari in every street corner in a city painted in blue and white. Her portrait stands next to the names of all the ministers in the posters issued by the government for local constituencies. Mamata Banerjee appears not only as a portrait but also as an infinitely repeated icon in the public spaces among her voters through the color-schemed cityscape. The photograph of her *body natural* in flex prints competes and forms alliances with the *body politic* of other nationalist icons in the city (Marin 1988). In this way, the ubiquitous presence of the image of Mamata Banerjee as the TMC brand captures the senses of the consumer citizen in the competitive democratic politics of West Bengal.

The Durgā Pūjā of West Bengal has a dynamic quality; it has been a ritual affair in domestic spaces, a courtly ritual, a spectacular public carnival, and a space for artistic creativity. In the hands of the TMC, the ritual significance of the Durgā Pūjā is undermined and translated into a mass festival—a spectacular event that thrives on the viewing of masses—that is then used as a tool of governmentality and mass mobilization. Like the festival, the Durgā *mūrti*, over the years, has also achieved a multidimensional polyvalence. She is at once the image of Śakti and Umā, the image of an everywoman who returns to her paternal home every autumn as is enacted during the celebration of Durgā Pūjā. She is a metaphor for social messages and political propaganda. She is a traditional icon and also an art object for museumization. It is this polyvalence that has led to the building of the large Durgā Pūjā industry throughout India. It is not surprising, then, that the artist community, which utilized the massive spectatorship of the Durga Pūjā to create artistic pavilions and *mūrtis*, is now receding to the background to make way for the political players who are mobilizing it for the same reasons: *janasaṃyog* or mass communication.

Notes

1. Popular songs composed by the national poet Rabindranath Tagore were played in public transport, traffic signals, and public parks.

2. Understood as a predominantly Muslim form with Muslim practitioners.

3. This appropriation applies to the larger domain of popular religiosity, which includes Muslims, Sikhs, Christians, and non-Bengali Hindus, all of whom the erstwhile Marxist party was ideologically opposed to engaging. In this sense, the TMC government also marked a new definition and practice of secularism in West Bengal.

References

Agnihotri, Anita. 2001. *Kolkatar Pratimashilpira*. Kolkata: Ananda.

Amin, Shahid. 1984. "Gandhi as Mahatma: Gorakhpur District, Eastern UP, 1921–2." *Subaltern Studies* 3:1–61.

ANI. 2016. "Opposition reacts sharply to Smriti Irani linking 'Mahishasur Martyrdom Day' to JNU row." Diligent Media Corporation. February 25. http://www.dnaindia.com/india/report-opposition-reacts-sharply-to-smriti-irani-linking-mahishasur-martyrdom-day-to-jnu-row-2182436.

Appadurai, Arjun. 1977. "Kings, Sects and Temples in South India." *Economic and Social History Review* 14 (1): 47–74.

Banerjie, Monideepa. 2014. "Mamata Banerjee Begins Durga Puja with a Brushstroke." NDTV. http://www.ndtv.com/india-news/mamata-banerjee-begins-durga-puja-with-a-brushstroke-669953.

Basu, Kinsuk. 2011. "Tussle for Didi in the Time of Devi—They've Got Mail, from Mamata!" *The Telegraph*, Friday, September 23, 2011.

Bhabha, Homi. 1984. "Of Mimicry and Man: The Ambivalence of Colonial Discourse." *October* 28: 125–33.

Bo Nielsen, Kenneth. 2016. "Mamata Banerjee: Redefining Female Leadership." In *India's Democracies: Diversity, Co-optation, Resistance*, ed. Arild Englesen Ruud and Geir Heierstad. Oslo: Universitetsforlaget.

Chadda, Sudhir. 2005. "Witch-hunt on Mamata Banerjee—Communists Blame Her for Instigating People against Sikhs in 1984 Riot—Shame on Communists." *India Dality*, August 19, 2005.

Chatterjee, Partha. 2004. *The Politics of the Governed: Reflections on Popular Politics in Most of the World*. New York: Columbia University Press.

———. 1997. *The Present History of West Bengal: Essays in Political Criticism*. Delhi: Oxford University Press.

Dickey, Sara. 1993. "The Politics of Adulation: Cinema and the Production of Politicians in South India." *The Journal of Asian Studies* 52 (2): 340–72.

Ghatak, Maitreesh, Sandip Mitra, Dilip Mookherjee, and Anusha Nath. 2013. "Land Acquisition and Compensation." *Economic & Political Weekly* 48 (21) (2013): 33.

Guha-Thakurta, Tapati. 2015. *In the Name of the Goddess: The Durga Pujas of Contemporary Kolkata*. Kolkata: Primus Books.

———. 2011. "Superstar of Indian Art Forced into Exile by the Controversy His Work Aroused." *The Guardian*, Wednesday, June 15, 2011.

———. 2004. "From Spectacle to 'Art': The Changing Aesthetics of Durga Puja in Contemporary Calcutta." *Art India* 9 (3.3): 34–56.

Kirby, Julian. 2008. "Ambedkar and the Indian Communists: The Absence of Conciliation." Winnipeg: University of Winnipeg.

Kishwar, Madhu. 1999. "Indian Politics Encourages Durgas, Snubs Women," *Manushi* 111.

Kovacs, Anja. 2004. "You Don't Understand, We Are at War! Refashioning Durga in the Service of Hindu Nationalism." *Contemporary South Asia* 13 (4): 373–88.

Mazzarella, William. 2010. "Branding the Mahatma: The Untimely Provocation of Gandhian Publicity." *Cultural Anthropology* 25 (1): 1–39.

McDermott, Rachel Fell. 2011. *Revelry, Rivalry, and Longing for the Goddesses of Bengal: The Fortunes of Hindu Festivals.* New York: Columbia University Press.

Sen, Moumita. 2016. "Clay-Modelling in West Bengal: Between Art, Religion and Politics." PhD Monograph, Department of Culture Studies and Oriental Languages, University of Oslo.

Shrivastava, Rahul. 2016. "Smriti Irani Row Leaves Rajya Sabha Truce over Bills in Tatters." NDTV.com. Hhttp://www.ndtv.com/india-news/fate-of-bills-uncertain-as-government-opposition-fight-over-smriti-irani-comment-1281450.

Spencer, George W. 2008. "Religious Networks and Royal Influence in Eleventh Century South India." In *Roots and Routes of Development in China and India,* 358–72. Leiden: Brill.

Trinamool Congress. 2015. http://aitcofficial.org/publications-by-didi/.

Vincent, Pheroze L. 2016. "Footnote to Fabled Story on Indira." *The Telegraph,* Saturday, February 27, 2016.

6

Durgā Pūjā Committees

Community Origin and Transformed Mediatized Practices Employing Social Media

XENIA ZEILER

Durgā Pūjā has not always been celebrated as a community or public event as it is today. Instead, it started as *pūjā* restricted to homes and temples (see Parpola 2015, 171, 214). All instructions for worship of Durgā during the Navarātri festival discussed in textual sources, such as the *Devī* (22.1–24), *Devī Bhagavata* (3.24.19–20; see McDermott 2011, 12), *Agni* (185.3–15), and *Skanda Purāṇas* (1.2.47.77–82, 5.1.14.4, 5.1.18.4, 7.1.83.39–60; see Einoo 1999, 34), highlight domestic practice and individual actor-centered ritual with no hints of community celebration. The festival, however, grew to become one of or maybe *the* most popular and widespread festivals in India. Partly, the rise in the popularity of Durgā Pūjā can and must be linked to the growth of community participation that began in the early seventeenth century.[1] Since then, Durgā Pūjā has developed into a celebration that spans the domestic, ritual, and public spheres. The festival has continued to (intensively) develop, especially since the second half of the twentieth century, as organizational and practical proceedings, including advertisement strategies, transformed, and as metaprocesses such as economization and globalization arose. This chapter acknowledges all influences that contribute to the current transformations, but it focuses on one particular process among these factors that continuously reshape the festival, namely, mediatization. Durgā Pūjā committees are frequently put in charge of the community-driven organization of the festival and as such are paradigmatic for the intended discussion. Therefore, this chapter discusses the mediatized activities of one exemplary group of actors, namely, a Durgā Pūjā committee group (rather than of individual actors), and focuses on the community aspects of the festival and how they have been mediatized. The Durgā Pūjā Committee Mulund, Mumbai, serves as the case study for this chapter.[2] Its mediatized activities are presented and discussed using media analytical and anthropological (i.e., participant observation and interview) methods. The case study is discussed applying Jäger's critical discourse analysis (Jäger 2004).

This chapter first gives a brief overview of the historical development of Durgā Pūjā as a community festival. It then proceeds to layout the theoretical concept of mediatization and mediatized religion, as understood and applied in the context of this study. After setting this theoretical frame, it turns to introduce and present the case study in which the Durgā Pūjā Committee Mulund, Mumbai, and its mediatized activities in the various levels of organization, hosting, and advertising the annual festival are discussed, using examples from both Internet sources and interviews. A conclusion recaptures the findings and summarizes the current transformation processes and their potential impact on the development of the festival as a practice, in general, and of status and authority negotiations via the festival, in particular.

Community Aspects in the History of Durgā Pūjā and the Origins of Durgā Pūjā Committees

Elaborate Durgā Pūjā celebrations involving complex organization have been part of the Hindu festival calendar since late medieval times. The festival spread to become one of the most popular pan-Hindu festivals and today is celebrated all over India and in many places around the globe that are homes to the Indian diaspora. Although it is not entirely clear, indicators point at the fact that the first elaborate public worship in the context of Durgā Pūjā may be traced back to the late sixteenth or early seventeenth century in Bengal in northeast India. Possibly the first public celebrations of the autumn Durgā Pūjā go back as far as 1583, when the Zamīndār of Tāhirpur in present Bangladesh sponsored a festivity (McDermott 2011, 14). Since the eighteenth century, the interest in Śākta (goddess-centered practice) deities increased in Bengal, and with this, festival celebrations took on a grander scale. Several historical sources report that *zamīndārs* began to host extensive festivities in their homes, in which their family and invited guests took part. Many grand and public Durgā Pūjā celebrations were inaugurated, including Gobindarām Mitra's grand festival, which began in his home in 1720; Rājā Nabakṛṣṇa Deb's large *pūjā* in 1757 to felicitate the British in their victory at Plassey; and

Rājā Kṛṣṇacandra Rāy's public worship of Durgā, which began in the 1730s (McDermott 2011, 14; Bhattacharyya 2007, 933–34).

Early public Durgā Pūjā celebrations were closely (and perhaps exclusively) linked to both *zamīndār* families of Bengal and issues of politics and status or authority. We also have to keep in mind that these early celebrations were only "public" to a limited extent, as only invited guests could take part, and these guests were invited to negotiate or secure the *zamīndārs'* authority, political or otherwise. The origin of Durgā Pūjā celebrations beyond the traditional domestic ritual context then lies in a form of agenda-motivated, semi-public display of devotion. Selected guests were invited, allowing the event to be a display of status and a field of negotiating that status and claims to authority, which continues into the contemporary period (e.g., Nicholas 2013). That Durgā Pūjā became an established festivity of status negotiation, concerning many more aspects than religion alone, is maybe best illustrated by the fact that it was one of the Hindu festivals hosted by non-Hindu patrons as well. Bhattacharyya argues:

> The sponsorship of elaborate Shakta rituals by the Hindu zamindar/raja in the Nawabi era may not have been the articulation of a solely *religious* identity as it is understood in the modern sense. It is more likely that these festivals were a display of several elements of regal authority: political, material, as well as religious. As late as the nineteenth century, there is evidence of Hindu festivals being patronized by Muslim zamindars and vice versa. (2007, 936)

Due to the status of Durgā Pūjā celebrations, the audience for the festival even began to expand beyond the wealthy elite. A major shift in the public or community involvement occurred as the patronage system shifted toward a community-centered celebration with the origination of Durgā Pūjā organizing groups in 1790. As McDermott writes it:

> It was in this context that the *bāroiyāri* Pūjā, or Pūjā sponsored by twelve (friends), was first introduced in 1790. Instead of the expenses of the festival being defrayed by one zamindar family alone, the Pūjā was democratized, its costs spread out and shared among people not necessarily of the hereditary aristocracy. The *sarbajanīn* (or public) Pūjā of Kolkata today is heir to this intermediate, *bāroiyāri,* type; now, instead of twelve or so friends, the Pūjās are sponsored by neighborhood groups and civic associations that vie with each other to produce the best, most opulent, and most beautiful displays. (2011, 19)

Thus, the festivities were "democratized" with new patrons and new practical administrative measurements to cope with financial shortages. Ultimately, this shift massively transformed Durgā Pūjā organizational patterns. Durgā Pūjā, though, remained a highly important field for negotiations of authority in which hosting a pompous festival became a status symbol. Clearly the late eighteenth century transformed the practice and celebration of Durgā Pūjā to a community-oriented festival. Consequently, the festival also became more popular and widespread, and many aspects of the festivities underwent enormous changes, including practical areas such as preparations and organization.

The joint effort and community celebration of Durgā Pūjā in the public sphere, however, did fully develop as part of a Durgā Pūjā revival that took place in the late nineteenth and early twentieth centuries (Bhaduri 2004). This revival developed in connection to both Hindu identity-finding and anticolonial nationalist developments in India at the time (see McDermott 2011, 51–64; Bhattacharyya 2007, 938–44; Banerjee 1989; Kopf 1969). It was during this period that Durgā Pūjā as a community institution was finalized. The first all-public, that is publically founded, organized, and funded Durgā Pūjā can be traced back to Kolkata (Calcutta) in 1910:

> The baro-yaari puja gave way to the sarbajanin or community puja in 1910, when the Sanatan Dharmotsahini Sabha organized the first truly community puja in Baghbazar in Kolkata with full public contribution, public control and public participation. Now the dominant mode of Bengali Durga Puja is the "public" version. (Bhaduri 2004, 83)

The *sarbajanīn* (public) *pūjās* are the predominant form of festival celebrations today, all over India and worldwide.

In this form of community-centered festivity, a committee consisting of volunteers is elected representing a locality, neighborhood, and increasingly other units such as corporations. Durgā Pūjā committees' work by nature mainly consists of organization, primarily the preparatory activities, including raising funds needed to host the festival. Traditionally, and in many parts of India still today, donations are collected by volunteers making rounds door-to-door and by including local temples or cultural institutions that may collect donations in the name of the respective committee or by hosting fundraising cultural events, for example concerts. Most funds raised go into the creation and hosting of the *paṇḍal* and in festive activities. These expenditures often include artistic construction and erection of the *paṇḍal*; rental of the location where the *paṇḍal* is established for the time of Durgā Pūjā (often rented halls); rental of technical and other equipment (e.g., music and light systems, musical instruments or bands, chairs and tables, and possibly trucks to transport the *paṇḍal* and buses to transport visitors accompanying the *mūrti* on its way to the immersion in water); and payment of celebratory and ritual activities, such as food for the visitors of the *paṇḍal* or payment for the ritual specialists. Since the 1990s, the collection of funds from individual or family donations has changed significantly, when larger economic units, especially local firms and corporations (e.g. banks, etc.) became increasingly involved in the sponsorship of *paṇḍals*. Though private funding from neighborhoods has not entirely vanished, the largest source of funding for urban *paṇḍals* in India by today is from corporate entities (see e.g., McDermott 2010, 153).

The geographical spread of the Bengal-originated community *sarbajanīn* (public) *pūjā* began as early as 1911 with the shift of the capital of British India from Calcutta to Delhi. Further migration of Bengalis contributed to a quick and successful spread of the Bengali-style community festival all over India. That spread continues even today in the Hindu diaspora, where public Durgā Pūjā celebrations make it one of the biggest festivals worldwide.

A massive increase of the public celebration of the festival continues. In Kolkata alone, the number of *sarbajanīn pūjās* raised from 300 in 1954 to 1,120 in 1995 (Ghosh 2000, 298), and 4,000 in 2010 (Guha-Thakurta 2015). This exponential growth also is a result of the rapidly increasing processes of mediatization. Today, all aspects of Durgā Pūjā are highly mediatized. Not only is Durgā Pūjā a common theme in modern mass media (e.g., Bollywood and films by regional film industries, journalistic media, popular music, Internet blogs and forums, etc.), but the festival is also increasingly organized, participated, and negotiated via and in a variety of media.

Mediatization and Mediatized Religion

But what exactly is mediatization? The term and concept of mediatization have been discussed in media and communication studies since the mid-2000s, from which two prominent traditions were shaped. The institutionalist tradition regards media as an independent social institution with its own set of rules (Hjarvard 2013) and assumes that various fields of culture and society, such as religion, are determined by an inherent "media logic" of separate media genres (Altheide and Snow 1979). In contrast to this, the social-constructivist tradition "highlights the role of various media as part of the process" and "refers to the process of a communicative construction of socio cultural reality and analyzes the status of various media within that process" (Couldry and Hepp 2013, 196). Mediatization as understood and applied in this chapter is interested in everyday communication practices—especially related to digital media and personal communication—and focuses on the changing communicative construction of culture and society. The mediatization approach that is the base for this chapter's case study aligns with the social-constructivist tradition using Couldry and Hepp's general definition:

> . . . the contours of a shared, basic understanding of the term have emerged. On that fundamental level the term "mediatization" does not refer to a single theory but to a more general approach within media and communications research. Generally speaking, *mediatization is a concept used to analyze critically the interrelation between changes in media and communications on the one hand, and changes in culture and society on the other.* At this general level, mediatization has quantitative as well as qualitative dimensions. With regard to quantitative aspects, mediatization refers to the increasing temporal, spatial and social spread of mediated communication. . . . With regard to qualitative aspects, mediatization refers to the specificity of certain media within sociocultural change: It matters what kind of media is used for what kind of communication. (2013, 197)

Furthermore, the definition of mediatization by the communications scholar Friedrich Krotz as a metaprocess, which shapes modern societies and publics, along with various sociocultural processes as globalization or individualization, also underlies the approach of this chapter. As a logical consequence, mediatization research as used here focuses on the actors, individuals or groups of individuals, in their mediatized worlds, rather than focusing on the influence or effect of one singular medium on people. In short, mediatization in the social-constructivist understanding means a shift from media-centered to actor-centered research. For the study presented here, this means, for example, that the starting point of investigation was not one media genre, such as Facebook, but a group of people, namely, the Durgā Pūjā Committee Mulund, Mumbai. Furthermore, media alone cannot be the only reason of transformation processes, but they exist in a combination of various sociocultural processes in which mediatization is one process among others. As Krotz has written:

> Today, we can say that mediatization means at the least the following:
>
> (a) changing media environments . . .
>
> (b) an increase of different media . . .
>
> (c) the changing functions of old media . . .

(d) new and increasing functions of digital media for the people and a growth of media in general

(e) changing communication forms and relations between the people on the micro level, a changing organization of social life and changing nets of sense and meaning making on the macro level. (2008, 24)

Naturally, mediatization is as relevant for religion and religious practice as it is for any other field of study. Religion today is rapidly transforming, in large part due to mediatization processes. Notably, debates and discussions regarding religion are no longer restricted to religious institutions, but religious actors actively contribute to shape religion and religious practice on manifold levels (e.g., religious groups and individual actors increasingly use media to discuss and negotiate religious authority and identity, dogmatic doctrine, and belief itself). Religion today is deeply mediatized, by various media genres, and thus research on mediatized religion needs to be no longer simply media-centered but expanded into actor-centered research. When it comes to religious festivals such as Durgā Pūjā, this is true not only for the study of religious practice in a narrow sense (e.g., for the study of the festival's rituals) but also for the study of social practice around religion (e.g., for the study of the festival's communication and organizing practices).

The theoretical and methodical approach of mediatization today is established in Europe and primarily has been used to conduct research in European and American contexts. But for geographical contexts beyond these, including Asia in general and India in particular, the concept of mediatization has yet to be applied on a broad scale. More studies that examine the actors, that is, individuals or groups of individuals, and their mediatized worlds from various parts of the globe are much needed. Mediatization may not have the same meaning or function in the same way everywhere in the world; it is to be expected that it is determined by regional or cultural specifics. For India, future research projects must take into account the intensified media production, use, and reception especially in the past ten to twenty years and how that has led to a rearrangement of the religious settings. Today in India, details of religious beliefs, symbols, practices, and so on are (re)interpreted and (re)constructed in new media just as much as in historical texts with new media serving as platforms for (re)negotiations of religious and cultural heritage. This intensified media use may have effects reaching from consolidations of existing structures, in some cases, to their restructuring, in other cases. However, it is important to note that for many religious actors in India today, the information given in popular new media genres, such as TV, films, or the Internet, is just as important and formative as information in classical established texts. Within this ongoing mediatization, along with its new scale, a new quality of (re)negotiations takes place. Recent Hinduism is thus actively reshaped by and in new media (see Scheifinger 2015; Zeiler 2014). As the following case study will demonstrate, individual actors, as well as groups of actors, actively embrace the possibilities offered by digital media, especially social media. As a result, new transformed (i.e., mediatized) practices emerge.

The Durgā Pūjā Committee Mulund, Mumbai, and Its Mediatized Practices

The Durgā Pūjā Committee Mulund organizes the annual festivities for the Bengali community in the Mumbai suburb of Mulund. It is associated with and functions under the umbrella of the local nonprofit and volunteer-run organization Bengal Institute of Art & Culture, which is part of the same community. "Established in 1982, the Bengal Institute of Art & Culture is a not-for-profit organization engaged in preserving and nurturing traditional arts. One of the important activities of the Institute is organizing the Sarbojanin Durga Puja at Mulund every year" (Mulund Blog, "About Me" section). The organization today has about six hundred members who regularly celebrate Bengali culture and lifestyle together, including religious festivals and events. For instance, they meet every second Sunday to worship together in the premises of the organization's office, which also offers space for ritual or festive get-togethers, including annual Kālī, Lakṣmī and Sarasvatī Pūjās.[3] But their most important activity is to organize the annual autumn Durgā Pūjā of the community: "Every autumn, the Sarbojanin Durga Puja at Mulund (Mumbai, India) is organized by the Bengal Institute of Art & Culture at Kalidas Natya Mandir Complex" (Mulund Facebook page info). The committee consists of volunteer and unpaid members who are officially elected and appointed. In 2015, eighty-two committee members were elected, eighteen of whom served in the capacity of president, vice president, general secretary, joint secretary, or treasurer. The remaining elected volunteers filled positions in nine subcommittees that ranged from two to twelve members respectively: souvenir subcommittee, entertainment subcommittee, collection subcommittee, decoration subcommittee, *pūjā* subcommittee, *prasād* (blessed offering) subcommittee, *Mā bhog* (Mother-food) subcommittee, *bhog* (food) subcommittee, and reception subcommittee. Their annual expenditure is approximately Rs. one million (approximately US$15,000), and theirs is among the most popular of Durgā Pūjās in Mumbai. In 2015 the treasurer of the committee stated: "It's a middle-class Pūjā by middle-class people." One of the joint secretaries responsible for social media added:

> In terms of the budget, we would figure maybe among the bottom 25 percent. . . . In popularity, because of online presence, it's pretty huge—whenever I meet friends or strangers even, Bengalis, and I tell them that I'm from Mulund, they say: oh, Mulund, Bengali Pūjā. That's very famous. . . . In terms of popularity, I'd place this Pūjā maybe at about 40 percent, I'd say. (2015)

The general work and objective of the Durgā Pūjā Committee Mulund, Mumbai, in many ways are paradigmatic for neighborhood festival organizing and hosting groups. Such committees that are appointed by a local community and consist of unpaid helpers differ from corporate organizing groups in many ways. They are usually smaller and often host more modest festivities, as their budget is mainly provided by donations from private persons and some small businesses of the respective community (although sponsorship by larger firms is increasingly popular; see McDermott 2010, 153). Historically, such committees have been organizing Durgā Pūjās for a certain locally- and community-defined space, such as a village, city quarter, and the like (Sarma 1969). Such neighborhood committees today exist all over India (Nakatani 2015).

So, while in its general objective and activities this committee is a typical example for Durgā Pūjā committees, what is not so typical for all or even most Indian neighborhood or *sarbajanīn* committees (though it points to an emerging trend) is this group's strong use of social media, such as Facebook. Also, the language chosen for all Internet representations by the committee is neither Bengali nor Hindi, but exclusively English. Certain media, such as mobile phones are, of course, very common and used in probably each and every Durgā Pūjā committee in the country for organizational purposes, especially for communication among committee members and with selected affiliated persons such as ritual specialists or artists. However, major parts of committees' practices, like reaching out for the fundraising and advertising, are often still not very mediatized. This is especially true for Durgā Pūjās in rural contexts. In contrast to this and not surprisingly, urban Durgā Pūjā committees especially in bigger cities with reliable Internet access, increasingly communicate, organize, negotiate, and advertise via digital media (smartphones, emails, Facebook, etc.). The joint secretary responsible for social media was very aware of the current trends in social media and tries to remain updated on new forms of media:

> The thing with social media is, it evolves very fast. Today, there is Facebook, tomorrow, we don't know. You have to be on your feet all the time, and use whatever media is popular.

> We have this internal group on WhatsApp now, to keep sharing. During Pūjā it's certainly very active, we keep sharing information. (2015)

The mediatization of Durgā Pūjās today also extends beyond the work of Durgā Pūjā committees and organizational contexts, in general. As a major cultural, religious, and social event Durgā Pūjā is heavily represented, discussed, advertised, displayed, and reported on in entertainment media (e.g., in print media such as comics or belletristic writings, and in filmic media such as TV serials, Bollywood, or regional film industries) and in all existing journalistic media, (i.e., in print media such as newspapers or magazines, in TV news reports and magazines, or in Internet journalistic formats such as online newspaper, blogs, etc.). Individual Durgā Pūjā committees are especially eager to advertise through journalistic media coverage. In today's highly competitive Durgā Pūjā scene, especially in urban centers, advertisement through various media is required to attract more visitors, which is the point of pride for most *pūjās*. Therefore, all possible media channels, social and journalistic media, are employed to accomplish this. The 2015 president of the Mulund Durgā Pūjā Committee believes that social media and local print media were both critical to the Pūjā's success:

> We use both. We have a WhatsApp group for this club as well as we have our small writer in a local newspaper, *Times of India*. . . . So that is also another way that we communicate that what we are doing, how we invite people, how we organize this three to four days program, so we use both the media. . . . If I'm not mistaken, it could have been for the last ten years. . . . There are also emails which connect the group members. (2015)

The Durgā Pūjā Committee Mulund thus is one group that intensively works with social media. Since August 2010, it has a well-designed and maintained Facebook page (Mulund Facebook), which is updated on a regular basis. Around the nine nights of Durgā Pūjā (i.e., some weeks before, during, and some weeks after the event) the page is updated frequently (up to several posts daily, including information posts on upcoming events and photos or videos of the past festivities). Certain posts, which might contain text and/or photos and videos, are selected and then uploaded on the committee's blog (Mulund Blog). Occasionally some of the videos will also be posted on YouTube (e.g., Mulund YouTube). The committee began utilizing social media for the Mulund Durgā Pūjā in 2010 as a result of careful reflections by the committee's members. According to the joint secretary responsible for social media, the committee's incorporation of new media has made the group more visible and has been an unmitigated success:

> . . . in the corporate world, it's different. I mean you have a very supportive ecosystem in place, which helps you do things, and you don't need to worry about a lot of things. Out here there is no such help, and there is no money. Of course, there is no budget, and we wouldn't like to spend on marketing ourselves. . . . So I thought of what is the best way of doing it. If you look at most Durgā Pūjā websites, even in Mumbai or anywhere else they are not updated, in the way they should be. You wouldn't find the latest information *et cetera*. And it's not really their fault, because it is difficult to maintain a website on your own, and especially for an occasion like Durgā Pūjā, where people come together for a few months and then they go back to their daily things. So I thought, better than a website because it is difficult to maintain, let us create a blog so that we keep posting stuff whenever you have something. I mean it doesn't look bad if you don't have anything, because it is a blog, right? So we put up this blog. . . . And this blog, because the content was fresh and it was authentic, it started doing very well on search engines. So while corporates spend a lot of money on search engine optimization *et cetera*, if the content is fresh and the content is relevant people are visiting your site and it does well on its own. So there was a time, a year ago, if you typed in Durgā Pūjā Mumbai, our site would come up Number One, on all the search engines. And it's not through some agency or something. (2015)

The group's representation on Facebook was given intensive thought. To most effectively advertise the Durgā Pūjā and to provide more information on all aspects of the festival (e.g., host community, committee's work, and details on times, places, etc.), the committee decided to create a Facebook page rather than a Facebook group. The page was created in August 2010 and since has been updated on a regular basis.[4] The committee's choice of a Facebook page, which allows for very limited participation by visitors (as compared to a Facebook group, which stresses the interactive element), clearly points to the intended function of the group's Facebook presence: it is about self-representation and advertisement; it is not seen as a tool for organization. The joint secretary responsible for social media explained their choice:

> Then of course a Facebook page was the way to go, because that's where most people were. . . . People tend to make groups,

> and to understand the difference between a Facebook page and a group, being a professional helped there. . . . Groups are more about interacting with each other. . . . Our whole idea was to reach out to more people which is why we created a page, not a group. And of course, initially you had to be careful about the content that you are posting. If you left everything for the public to post it could go havoc. . . . We now have been giving rights to people, to tag their pictures now; so once we get a feeling of comfort, that this page is doing well, it's not much disturbing activity going on. . . . Social media is kind of part of me, I'm on it all the time; so it happens sort of on its own. So that's the Facebook story, and the Facebook and the blog helped us a lot in getting recognition in terms of people knowing about us. (2015)

The possibility to reach out to members of the community (family and friends) no longer living in Mumbai or even India was one unanimous reason for why the committee chose to intensively employ social media and why it chose English as its primary language. Not surprisingly, since keeping a community's diaspora in the loop is one key advantage of social media, it is often why religious groups go online. The treasurer of the committee was explicit about the its desire to connect the Mulund Durgā Pūjā with its community worldwide:

> For four to five years now we do Internet advertisement. Not everybody is doing this. We have some NRI [nonresident Indian] members in UK, in USA, they made us aware of this. The Internet is mainly used for the purpose that we advertise, that the members away from us, that they are informed, that they are not deprived of what's happening. (2014)

The president of the committee confirmed:

> First of all, you know, we are basically all from West Bengal. This is the place where we are all connected, and many of our next generation senior people they are out of Mumbai. They may be within India. They may be outside of India. If there are media then everybody is well connected, easily connected. So that is one of the major reasons for us to decide to go for the media where people can see the photographs even if they are not physically present in Mumbai. (2015)

The desire to share with those outside of Mumbai was not the only cause for the committee's decision to go online; their ambition and desire to effectively advertise within the Mulund community and greater Mumbai area also played a major role. The committee deemed it unacceptable that people living in and near Mulund could be unaware of the local Durgā Pūjā celebration, especially if they belonged to the Bengali community and/or had recently moved to the neighborhood. The committee views itself as the local authority and its Durgā Pūja as the predominant or even the only Durgā Pūjā in terms of both its territory (Mulund and neighboring areas) and its community (especially Mulund's Bengali residents). The joint secretary responsible for social media suggests that their online presence helps make people aware of their own community celebration, lest they are enticed by some lesser Pūjā:

> Mulund Durgā Pūjā was, you could say, it was a well-kept secret. Bengalis especially would want to get involved in the Pūjā in their vicinity, and Mumbai being Mumbai sees a lot of floating population of new people coming, and they don't know, and they would want to be involved, and because this particular Pūjā takes place inside a complex and you don't see it while passing by, unlike most of the Pūjās which are held very close to highstreets, or outside parks *et cetera,* this is one Pūjā if you didn't have the information you couldn't find out. So we thought we must get online. . . . We have these meetings, and I put forth the idea and of course, everybody welcomed it. (2015)

Finally, the competition among Durgā Pūjās in Mumbai plays a visible role in committee members' comments about why the group went online. This is not only evident in Mumbai but is interwoven into the fabric of public Durgā Pūjās. As McDermott has noted in the Bengali context, "Sarbajanin Puja organizers freely admit that they want to clobber their competitors. . . . and during the celebrations they anxiously watch the papers" (2010, 153). The question of status and authority is prominent in the context of competition. While the Durgā Pūjā Mulund cannot keep up with the top prominent Mumbai Durgā Pūjās in terms of size or splendor, the committee makes claim to authority and prestige through direct competition with highly prominent *pūjās*. To do this, the committee stresses certain unique aspects that are absent in the larger festivals. The claim that their *pūjā* is special and a sense of pride that comes with being part of it resonates in statements made by the joint secretary responsible for social media:

> While this may not be a commercially big budget Pūjā, it got its own uniqueness. So we thought, yes, we should get online because at least people who are looking for Pūjās in

> their vicinity, they should be able to find us. Because we are a small scale Pūjā, while we do a lot of things differently, people didn't know about it. . . . For instance, this *bhog* lunch that we have. Making people sit, that's a tremendous task by itself, as you would have witnessed in the three days. And the bigger Pūjās, they are not able to execute that because there is a rush of crowd. . . . And then we try to maintain as far as possible to remain ecofriendly. For instance, we use leaf plates. (2015)

Given the feedback on their various social media accounts, the committee's decision to employ social media, such as Facebook and its blog, as means for advertising and disseminating information has proven valuable. Because the committee has never kept accurate statistics and its social media presence is still very recent, there are no statistics that verify an increased number of visitors so far, but it is clear by the personal communications on both Facebook and the blog that potential visitors are being reached. The joint secretary responsible for social media sees a direct correlation between the website activities inaugurated by the committee and people inquiring about the *pūjā*:

> We keep getting mails, and on the page you can see the statistics, likes and so on. Especially during Pūjā you get a lot of interested people, you know, wishing to do cultural programs. Some singer would want to come and sing. Generally people coming and saying "ok, it was great." And there are lot of people from different communities. . . . In fact the other day I got an email from a Tamil lady in Mulund, asking "have you drawn up a schedule, when is Aṣṭamī, can we come?" . . . It feels good that people are starting to recognize the Pūjā. Generally with social media, people spreading the word around, it's working well for us. (2015)

The Durgā Pūjā Committee Mulund with its extensive employment of social media foreshadows new trends in the development of urban Durgā Pūjā organization, advertising, and celebration practices. Although this development is just beginning and has by no means reached all Durgā Pūjā committees in India yet, it is certainly spreading. The use of social media will greatly contribute to further transformations and shape the face of Durgā Pūjās. The committee's treasurer comments on the benefits of employing social media:

> It's an intangible benefit. I cannot exactly quantify right now. . . . Right now the benefit may be like a child. When

> it grows up, it might become a mighty man. Right now it's a small newborn child. You cannot exactly quantify what is the benefit of a newborn child. Tomorrow, he may become Einstein, and he brings benefit to the entire mankind. (2014)

Conclusion

Looking at mediatized advertising, organizational, and celebratory practices of Durgā Pūjās in India, we can decipher two primary factors for why (so far especially urban) Durgā Pūjā committees have begun to turn to social media. First, social media is seen as an effective tool to reach out to people who are not present. This has special importance for the involvement of diaspora members of the community in the festivities. Second and more prominently, the advertising advantages of social media is identified as a major benefit. In an ever more mediatized world, all channels possible are employed to reach out to as many people as possible. This may increase the reputation and/or raise the position of the community. Mediatizing Durgā Pūjā in a mediatized world also means gaining religious, cultural, and social prestige. If a Pūjā is cleverly advertised in many media channels, its prominence may substantially go beyond the recognition it had before. In the case of the Durgā Pūjā Mulund, the blog created by the committee appeared as the top result when searching for "Durgapuja Mumbai" in search engines in 2014, thus increasing the *pūjā's* visibility and attracting the attention of potential visitors.

In general, a community's and committee's religious, cultural, and social identity and authority are renegotiated through the new mediatized channels. Creating a Facebook page and a blog dedicated to the committee's Durgā Pūjā involvements can, and in the case of the Durgā Pūjā Mulund did, contribute to its fame and attractiveness relative to the 140 highly competitive *paṇḍals* in Mumbai. Especially in megacities like Mumbai, a large number of middle- and upper-class residents frequently use the Internet and social media as tools for information about ongoing events including religious festivals, instead of more traditional channels like print newspaper, TV, or radio. A strategy of employing these emerging media can result in higher visibility and prestige for one's own *pūjā*. This may then even lead to chain reactions, as word spreads and more visitors and more news media are attracted. The result can be a shift in the community's hierarchical position. Via the mediatized Durgā Pūjā, the status of the whole community is enhanced.

In the case of the Durgā Pūjā Mulund, then, no more is authority negotiated via the traditional channels. Rather, the Durgā Pūjā Committee Mulund claims a position among the prominent Durgā Pūjās in Mumbai, and thus it stakes its claim to authority in specific ways. In the classical tripartite categorization of Max Weber (1958), religious authority may be legitimized in three major forms: tradition, rational dominance, and charisma. It must be gained through approval, and often authority is successfully claimed by persons or groups, which make use of outstanding means. Instead of competing with more prominent *pūjās* in scope, décor, or in general, the Durgā Pūjā Committee Mulund constructs its value through its unique "selling points," especially the traditional elaborate feeding (*bhog*) of the visitors. Today, this is complemented by another very effective means, the extensive employment of social media. So far, this strategy has proven very successful.

As mentioned before, the way and intensity in which Durgā Pūjā committees employ social media is an emerging phenomenon in India. While most Durgā Pūjā committees in the diaspora set up their own websites, blogs, or Facebook pages or groups (e.g. Berlin Durgā Pūjā or London Durgā Pūjā), so far mainly urban Indian committees tend to use social media intensively (e.g. New Delhi Facebook Group and North Bombay Facebook Group). Durgā Pūjā committees today are very competitive, and they increasingly communicate, organize, and negotiate via different media, including social media, to, at least partly, create and organize, but especially to advertise the festival activities. Self-representation in social media is an increasingly important factor for public outreach and to secure attention and prestige that support both the committees' and the community's status. Thus, social media will contribute to further transformations and will play an active role in shaping the face of Durgā Pūjās on many levels in the future.

Notes

I thank the Durgā Pūjā Committee Mulund for its welcome. Especially, I thank the members of the committee, as well as numerous visitors of the Durgā Pūjā Mulund celebrations 2015, who spent time and energy in answering my questions.

1. This is not to say that Durgā Pūjā celebrations do not include rituals. Rituals are part of every community *sarbajanīn* (public) *pūjā*. For a detailed account and discussion of the Durgā Pūjā ritual, see Rodrigues 2003.

2. I visited the committee premises in March 2014, following up on media research I had done before and on contacts via phone and email. After following the committee members' work via their media representations and email and phone conversations, I returned to take part in the Durgā Pūjā celebrations in 2015. Additional talks took place in January 2016.

3. See, for instance, http://mulunddurgapuja.blogspot.fi/2014/02/saraswati-puja-on-4-february-2014.html.

4. The page includes information and reports, mainly in the form of photos and videos, including activities other than Durgā Pūjā, in which the group is involved, for example on Kālī, Lakṣmī and Sarasvatī *pūjās*.

References

Altheide, David L., and Robert P. Snow. 1979. *Media Logic*. Beverly Hills: Sage.

Banerjee, Sumanta. 1989. *The Parlour and the Streets: Elite and Popular Culture in Nineteenth-Century Calcutta*. Calcutta: Seagull Books.

Bhaduri, Saugata. 2004. "Of Public Sphere and Sacred Space: Origins of Community Durga Puja in Bengal." In *Folklore, Public Sphere, and Civil Society*, edited by M. D. Muthukumaraswamy and Molly Kaushal, 79–91. New Delhi and Chennai: Indira Gandhi National Centre for the Arts and National Folklore Support Centre.

Bhattacharya, Tithi. 2007. "Tracking the Goddess: Religion, Community, and Identity in the Durga Puja Ceremonies of Nineteenth-century Calcutta." *The Journal of Asian Studies* 66 (4): 919–62. http://www.jstor.org/stable/20203237.

Chakrabarti, Indranil. 2007. "Local Governance: Politics and Neighbourhood Activism in Calcutta." In *The Meaning of the Local: Politics of Place in Urban India*, edited by Geert De Neve, and Henrike Donner, 68–89. London and New York: Routledge.

Couldry, Nick, and Andreas Hepp. 2013. "Conceptualizing Mediatization: Contexts, Traditions, Arguments." *Communication Theory* 23: 191–202.

Einoo, Shingo. 1999. "The Autumn Goddess Festival: Described in the Purāṇas." In *Living with Sakti: Gender, Sexuality and Religion in South Asia*, edited by Masakazu Tanaka, and Musashi Tachikawa, SENRI Ethnological Studies 50: 33–70.

Ghosh, Anjan. 2000. "Spaces of Recognition: Puja and Power in Contemporary Calcutta." *Journal of Southern African Studies* 26(2): 289–99. doi:10.1080/03057070050010129.

Guha-Thakurta, Tapati. 2015. *In the Name of the Goddess. The Durga Pujas of Contemporary Kolkata*. Delhi: Primus Books.

Hjarvard, Stig. 2013. *The Mediatization of Culture and Society*. London: Routledge.

Jäger, Sigfried. 2004. *Kritische Diskursanalyse. Eine Einführung*. Münster: Unrast Verlag.

Kopf, David. 1969. *British Orientalism and the Bengal Renaissance: The Dynamics of Indian Modernization*. Berkeley: University of California Press.

Krotz, Friedrich. 2008. "Media Connectivity: Concepts, Conditions, and Consequences." In *Network, Connectivity and Flow: Key Concepts for Media and Cultural Studies*, edited by Andreas Hepp, Friedrich Krotz, and S. Moores, 13–33. New York: Hampton Press.

McDermott, Rachel Fell. 2011. *Revelry, Rivalry, and Longing for the Goddesses of Bengal. The Fortunes of Hindu Festivals*. New York: Columbia University Press.

McDermott, Rachel Fell. 2010. "Playing with Durga in Bengal." In *Sacred Play: Ritual Levity and Humor in South Asian Religions*, edited by Selva G. Raj, and Corinne G. Dempsey143–59. Albany: State University of New York Press.

Nakatani, Tetsuya. 2015. "Durga Puja and Neighbourhood in a Displaced Persons' Colony in New Delhi." In *Cities in South Asia*, edited by Crispin Bates, and Minoru Mio, 159–79. New York: Routledge.

Nicholas, Ralph. 2013. *Night of the Gods: Durga Puja and the Legitimation of Power in Rural Bengal*. New Delhi: Orient Black Swan.

Parpola, Asko. 2015. *The Roots of Hinduism: The Early Aryans and the Indus Civilization*. New York: Oxford University Press.

Rodrigues, Hillary Peter. 2003. *Ritual Worship of the Great Goddess: The Liturgy of the Durgā Pūjā with Interpretations*. Albany: State University of New York Press.
Sarma, Jyotirmoyee. 1969. "Puja Associations in West Bengal." *The Journal of Asian Studies* 28 (3): 579–94. doi:10.2307/2943180.
Scheifinger, Heinz. 2015. "New Technology and Change in the Hindu Tradition: The Internet in Historical Perspective." In *Asian Religions, Technology and Science*, edited by István Keul, 153–68. New York: Routledge.
Weber, Max. 1958. "The Three Types of Legitimate Rule." *Berkeley Publications in Society and Institutions* 4 (1): 1–11. [Translated by Hans Gerth.]
Zeiler, Xenia. 2014. "Ethno-Indology Expanded: Researching Mediatized Religions in South Asia." In *Banāras Revisited: Scholarly Pilgrimages to the City of Light*, edited by István Keul, 173–90. Wiesbaden: Harrassowitz.

Digital Media Sources

Berlin Blog Durgā Pūjā, http://www.durgapujaberlin.de/.
London Durgā Pūjā, http://www.londonpuja.com/.
Mulund Blog, http://mulunddurgapuja.blogspot.in/.
Mulund Facebook, https://www.facebook.com/MulundDurgaPuja.
Mulund YouTube, https://www.youtube.com/watch?v=Qn2Pm5zPs4w.
New Delhi Facebook Group, https://www.facebook.com/pages/B-Block-Durga-Puja-CR-Park-New-Delhi/169498589790157.
North Bombay Facebook Group, https://www.facebook.com/NBDurgapuja/.

7

Navarātri in Benares

Narrative Structures and Social Realities

SILJE LYNGAR EINARSEN

In Benares (Vārāṇasī), as in many other places in India, the autumn Navarātri is particularly associated with "she who slew the demon Mahiṣa" (*Mahiṣāsuramardinī*), commonly known as Durgā.[1] Durgā visits the various neighborhoods (*muhallā*) of Benares at this time of the year. In the streets, she inhabits numerous large *mūrtis* (images) that the neighborhood *pūjā* committees have installed for the annual public (*sarvajanīnā*) celebration of Durgā Pūjā. The celebrations take place in *paṇḍāls* (marquees) that, for the duration of Navarātri, house installations depicting Durgā in the act of slaying Mahiṣa. However, the goddess is not the only one celebrated publicly during Navarātri; the earthly ruler and the divine king, the Mahārāja, accompany her. The glory and power of the Mahārāja is thematized in the annual *Rām Līlā* (play of Rāma) of Benares, which starts about two weeks prior to the Navarātri festival. This theatrical performance of Tulsīdās's *Rāmcaritmānas* is staged at various locations in Benares, each night presenting a new part of the narrative. The audience follows the movements of Rāma as he adventures through years in exile, the battle on Laṅkā, and finally, his defeat of Rāvaṇa, which restores social and cosmic balance. Both *Rām Līlā* and Durgā Pūjā culminate on *Vijayāsaśamī*, the tenth day of victory (also known as Dussehra or Dasara), which celebrates the victory of good over evil. *Vijayādaśamī* commemorates Durgā's triumph over Mahiṣa and Rāma's victory over Rāvaṇa, and is the climax of both public festivals. People crowd the streets, parading the images of Durgā from the *paṇḍāls* to the river Gaṅgā, and in the evening, they may rub shoulders while watching the annual burning of a giant Rāvaṇa effigy. These narratives, which present themes of power and victory, are at the core of Navarātri and are realized through the festival organization. Thus, not only are the victory and power of deities emphasized though Navarātri, but also the power of humans assuming various forms of patronage over the festivals.

This chapter analyzes the dynamics of tradition and change in the recent historical developments and the current expression of the public *Rām Līlā* and Durgā Pūjā festivals in Benares. I discuss the extent to which these festivals may be understood as competitive means of forging power relations and contesting social structures through the creative appropriation of their narratives and their forms of ritual and aesthetic presentations. Discussions of the connection between rituals and social power are recurrent topics in ritual and festival studies. Scholars have argued that public festivals and parades are thought to mirror and reinforce social order and organizations but that they are also occasions on which to rebel against hegemony and existing structures (e.g., Bell 1992; Durkheim 1915; Geertz 1980; Sax 2010; Tambiah 1979). The public nature of festivals makes them important arenas for the dominant parties. However, the Durkheimian view that festivals were solely conservative forces in the face of social change has been challenged, as now, emphasis is on the dynamic nature of festivals as arenas for innovatively creating culture and tradition and thereby forging new power structures. We will see in this chapter that festivals serve both ends. For instance, the *Rām Līlā* is imbued with notions of authenticity and *banārsipan* (Benares-ness), but was once a ritual invention created by political interest. The play enacts the Hindi vernacular *Rāmāyaṇa* composed by the famous poet-saint Tulsīdās (1532–1623). As Tulsīdās was himself a Banārasi, it is widely held that he was responsible for the very first *Rām Līlā* performance *in* Benares. Thus, *Rām Līlā* invokes a sense of authoritativeness and nostalgia central to the construction of tradition and communal identity (Bell 1992, 122). The important role of the *Rām Līlā* in the Banārasi collective memory of a shared past stands in stark contrast to the *paṇḍāl*-based Durgā Pūjā, which is considered modern, foreign (imported from Bengal), and provocative. Locals often characterize these *pūjās* as "commercial," "just an excuse to party," and "having nothing to do with religion" or "the true spirit" of Navarātri. The *paṇḍāls* are not only contrasted with the *Rām Līlās* in terms of their modernity, but there is also a subversive element to them, as will be described below. Yet, the *Rām Līlā* tradition in Benares seems to be undergoing a slow decline, whereas the Durgā Pūjā is growing rapidly in terms of costs, power, and prestige. The *paṇḍāl* celebration has exploded since the latter part of the twentieth century and is now an undisputed part of the Navarātri scene in Benares. Therefore, the annual Durgā Pūjā and its role in the festival culture of Benares calls for our attention.[2]

Royal and Military Background

The month Āśvina concludes the monsoon season of heavy rains and initiates a season of religious festivals in Benares. Temples and schools reopen, and everyday life is about to fall back into place. Now gods and ancestors are to be appeased, and order—cosmic, religious, political, royal—is to be marked out in public. Historically, it was the season for regal military campaigns, and Navarātri is deeply connected with concepts of royal power and warfare (Fuller and Logan 1985, 99). It is hardly a coincidence that the military season coincided with the festival of Durgā, who has been connected to success in warfare from early times (Yokochi 2004). Among the earliest references to Durgā, we find two hymns in the *Mahābhārata* (*Mbh* IV.6 and VI.23), both of which are inserted into the text preceding narratives of battle. In these hymns, Durgā is invoked by Yudhiṣṭhira and Arjuna to ensure victory for the Pāṇḍavas.[3] We thus see developed an idea of earthly power being dependent on the goddess, who is power personified and the source of all might—divine and earthly. The Sanskrit term for this primordial, universal, and all-pervading power is *śakti*. As the festival of the goddess, Navarātri is the most effective time to manipulate and access *śakti* through ritual. The relations between rulers and goddess extended to the sociocultural reality, and the worship of *śakti* manifested as the royal tutelary goddesses has been institutionalized at the royal courts from north to south India since the twelfth century, reaching its peak during the Vijayanagara empire (Gupta and Gombrich 1985; Stein 1983; also see Fuller and Logan 1985, and Simmons 2014). The sovereignty of the king was dependent on his relationship with the goddess, who represented power. This relationship was annually reinforced during Navarātri. In present-day Benares, Navarātri's legacy as a festival of power is evident both in the *Rām Līlā* and in the Durgā Pūjā. In both these public festival traditions, famous narratives of battle and victory are recreated and presented aesthetically. Let us now briefly consider these narratives.

Narratives of the Goddess and Rāma

In a distant, mythological past, the mighty buffalo-demon Mahiṣa drove the gods from their heavenly abodes and made himself ruler of the universe. He assumed the post of their king, Indra, and overtook the cosmic functions of the Sun, the Wind (*Vāyu*), Fire (*Agni*), and so on.

This implies that dharma (here: cosmic order) was gravely threatened. Unable to defeat Mahiṣa, the gods—Viṣṇu, Śiva, and the rest—gathered in frustration and despair, and the goddess Durgā suddenly manifested from their fierce energies (*tejas*). Equipped with all the weapons of the gods, Durgā rode her lion into battle against the army of demons. She managed to do what the gods could not: she slew Mahiṣa and restored dharmic balance to the universe.

In a less distant mythological past, the demon Rāvaṇa was born on earth and disrupted the performance of the fire sacrifice. Again, this implies that dharma was threatened. The gods pleaded with Viṣṇu to do something, and he descended (*avatāra*) to earth and was born as Rāma, prince and heir to the throne of the kingdom of Ayodhyā. According to the epic, Rāma's cunning stepmother, Kaikeyī, conspired to have the young crown prince exiled from Ayodhyā, knowing that this would make her own son, Bhārata, king. Therefore, Rāma spent fourteen years in exile with his wife, Sītā, and his brother, Lakṣmaṇa. They met ascetics, tribes, members of the high and lower castes; they fought demons and built alliances with animals. One day, Sītā was abducted by Rāvaṇa, king of the island of Laṅkā. Thus, war broke out between Rāma, allied with Hanuman and an army of monkeys, and Rāvaṇa with an army of demons. Rāvaṇa was ultimately defeated and the victorious Rāma returned to Ayodhyā at the end of his exile and assumed his title of king. Dharmic balance was restored to earth, and a period of *rāmrājya* (Rāma's righteous rule) began.

Despite their many differences, the two narratives presented above are structured around the same themes of cosmic crisis, victory over forces of chaos, and the resultant reestablishment of a structured world with healthy power relations. Concepts of such structures and power relations not only are part of mythological narratives and theological discourse, but they also extend to sociocultural realities through the performance of collective rituals and public festivals. Such festivals and parades are often specifically understood as arenas where existing power relations are reinforced and where communal values, customs, and social structures are reconfirmed and preserved by a culture over time. As others have demonstrated before me, the *Rām Līlā* clearly reinforces a Brahmanical hierarchy, underpinned by conservative notions of gender and caste in the *Rāmāyaṇa* narrative. For instance, Nita Kumar (1995) has convincingly argued in her analysis of the nose-cutting (*nākkaṭayyā*) episode in *Rām Līlā* that traditional gender roles are reinforced through the performance of this narrative. This story of the "nose-cutting," familiar to any Banārasi you might ask, recounts how the demon Śūrpanakhā—sister of the narrative's main villain, Rāvaṇa—attempted to seduce Lakṣmaṇa, who punished her by cutting off her nose. In response to the mutilation of his sister, Rāvaṇa went to the forest where Rāma, Sītā, and Lakṣmaṇa lived in exile, where Rāvaṇa managed to abduct Sītā because she disobeyed Lakṣmaṇa's request, and stepped over the magic line he had drawn to protect her.[4] The point Kumar makes, with which I agree, is that this famous and popular part of the *līlā* reinforces traditional gender roles by telling the "story of two women who transgress the bounds set on them by men . . . and how their trespassing leads them to fates worse than death, not to speak of overall warfare, wastage of resources, destruction of men, and turning upside down of society" (Kumar 1995, 164). Narratives are important sources of knowledge about culture, hierarchies, values, and structures, and performance practices are specific means by which this knowledge is transmitted to groups and internalized by individuals. A conscious appropriation of the narrative and symbolism of the great mythical Hindu king Rāma was, as we will see, the motivation for the inauguration of the royal *Rām Līlā* in the eighteenth century. The *Rām Līlā* ritually re-establishes the *rāmrājya*, the dharmic, righteous rule of the idealized king. Not only does the narrative exemplify the dharma of the king, but also of all his subjects: *brāhmaṇas*, *śūdras*, ascetics, women, indigenous people. They all have a role to play in the narrative in which their dharmas are exemplified and performed. Thus, *Rām Līlā* not only re-enacts the life and deeds of Rāma, but it models the ideal Hindu society.

Power and Performance in the *Rām Līlā*

Demonstrations of power structures are embedded in the organizations of festivals. For example, the fact that only *brāhmaṇas* are allowed to play the important roles such as Rāma, Lakṣmaṇa, and Hanuman indicates a pronounced awareness of caste. The boys who play these roles are regarded as becoming *svarūpa*s, god's "own form," and worthy of being worshipped throughout the festival. Schechner has furthermore argued that since the Mahārāja has no actual political power, just as the boys become gods for the duration of the play, likewise, the Mahārāja temporarily becomes an actual king. He thus writes of Vibhuti Narayan Singh, father of the present-day Mahārāja, "his existence as Maharaja is confirmed by his function as sponsor-producer of Ramlila. For the month of Ramraj [i.e. the *Rām Līlā*] is when the Maharaja of Benares is most visibly and demonstrably a king" (Schechner 1983, 242). Despite his lack of power, the Mahārāja still figures as an important symbol of Banārasi tradition and values. The Mahārāja's patronage of the *Rām Līlā* and his presence as center of attention in the Dussehra parade may be seen as important arenas where his power and relationship with the residents of Benares are negotiated.

When Mahārāja Udit Narayan Singh (1770–1835) began to host the *Rāmcaritmānas* performance at Rāmnagar fort facing Benares from the eastern banks of Gaṅgā, he forged new power relations with the rulers and citizens of Benares by inaugurating a new tradition. In the early nineteenth century—when the *Rām Līlā* in Benares developed into its present day form under royal patronage—Rāmnagar was a Muslim dominated area, a political situation that probably impelled the Mahārāja to "cultivate an explicitly Hindu symbol of royal legitimacy, and thus to achieve ideological as well as political independence from the Nawabs" (Lutgendorf 1995, 41; cf. Awasthi 1980).[5] This was a time when Hindu nationalism was on the rise, and the righteous dharma king Rāma was then, as now, a much-favored ideal.[6] The ritual timing connects the performance of *Rām Līlā* to military campaigning, which allows for the combining of military rituals with the narrative of the idealized king, Rāma. Thus, during the *līlā* on *Vijayādaśamī* we find the most important demonstration of royal power during the year: In previous years, the Mahārāja used to march with his military forces to the borders of neighboring Mirzapur, demonstrating the extent of his kingdom (Schechner 1998, 47). Today, the Mahārāja's procession on his elephant and the ritual display of *pūjā* to the king's weapons are the symbolic remnants of this lost demonstration of power.

In order for something to present itself as tradition, it must be imbued with authenticity, forging connections with the past (cf. Hobsbawm 1992). Udit Narayan Singh and his royal entourage managed to create the impression of a continuous tradition of the Rāmnagar *Rām Līlā* by suggesting that it directly continued the *līlā* tradition initiated by Tulsīdās himself.[7] Thus, the dynasty of Udit Narayan Singh invented a new tradition, a demonstration of royal power, but created it so it seemed as though it had always existed. The history of *Rām Līlā* that traces its origins to Tulsīdās is part of a Banārasi shared cultural identity, and is a tradition in which people seem to take great pride. Rāmnagar *Rām Līlā* is probably the best-known of all *Rām Līlās* of North India, and it is famous for preserving the authentic "mānas" tradition of Tulsīdās without intervention of modern-day technical equipment and effects. For decades it has attracted a large number of pilgrims, tourists, and devotees. However, several other *Rām Līlās* are staged in Benares, and most Banārasis have grown up attending a local *Rām Līlā* organized by elected committees in their neighborhoods (*muhallā),* including the Tulsī *ghāṭ līlā,* which is believed to be that very first *līlā* that Tulsīdās established. Thus, the Banārsis proudly claim the *Rām Līlā* tradition as their own. It is a vital part of their individual childhood memories, and it continues to form part of the Banārasi collective memory of tradition.

Emergence of Durgā Pūjā

Western observers have characterized *Rām Līlā* as the most spectacular and important festival in Benares. The Reverend M. A. Sherring, a missionary residing in the city in the nineteenth century, took little notice of the Durgā Pūjā, but described the *Rām Līlā* as the most popular and widely attended festival in Benares (Sherring 1868). Diana Eck described the *Bhārat Mīlāp* scene (reuniting with Bhārata) on the day after *Vijayadaśamī* as the most popular of all Benares fairs and festivals throughout the year, allegedly attracting crowds of tens of thousands (1983, 269). Schechner characterized the *Rām Līlā* at Rāmnagar as "one of Benares's greatest events . . . a display of the maharaja of Banaras's splendor" (1998, 19).

The past few decades have witnessed changes in the public Navarātri celebration in Benares, with a decline in the *Rām Līlā* and an increase in the popularity of the celebration of Durgā Pūjā. Schechner and Hess (1977) already noted a decline in the Rāmnagar *Rām Līlā* in the late 1970s, and my fieldwork confirms that this perception is present in contemporary discourse in the city. The perceived decline in *Rām Līlā* performance and attendance seems to be connected to the actual declining economy of the Mahārāja following Indian independence. Lutgendorf (1991) has challenged this conclusion, pointing out that valuing the past over the present is a common trope. Although I agree that we need to be cautious of confusing a "golden age" mentality with factual developments, the numbers presented by Schechner and Hess (1977, 73), and the visual of decay in Rāmnagar today supports the narratives of a royal *Rām Līlā* tradition in decline. In 2005 UNESCO labeled the Rāmnagar *Rām Līlā* a "Masterpiece of the Oral and Intangible Heritage of Humanity," recognizing both the uniqueness of the *līlā* and its vulnerability ("Ramlila" 2005). However, the focus on tradition and resistance to change may be precisely what make the Rāmnagar *Rām Līlā* vulnerable. With the rise of mass media and modern popular culture, and their roles in Durgā Pūjā, one might ask, can the *Rām Līlā* still compete?

My informants suggest that the rise of neighborhood Durgā Pūjās is supplanting the neighborhood *Rām Līlās* "everywhere," because the *pūjās* meet the expectations and demands of a globalized, modern audience. Although I am unaware of any statistical data that supports the claim that the Durgā Pūjās are in fact supplanting the *Rām Līlā*, it is beyond doubt that numerically, the annual *paṇḍāl* celebration of Durgā Pūjā is increasing rapidly, while also the amount of money spent on them and their creation is increasing. According to a police survey conducted in 2013, the number of *paṇḍāls* in the Benares district had reached 397, with 233 in the city alone.[8] If the numbers are correct, when compared to the estimated 70 to 80 community Durgā Pūjās in the late 1970s (Rodrigues 2003, 292), we could be talking about an increase of at least 250 percent over a period of forty years. Furthermore, it appears the number of *paṇḍāls* is still increasing, despite legislative efforts to control their growth (this is discussed in further detail below). The boom of the Durgā Pūjā and other similar annual *pūjās* (such as the *Gaṇeśa Caturthī* and *Viśvakarman*

Pūjā) may be intrinsically related to the rapid social changes in the postcolonial era of global modernity, which, according to Meera Nanda, is bringing about a new, market-based "rush hour of the gods" in India (2011, 61–107). It is worth noting that Nanda, too, sees this development in relation to the modern tendency to understand Hinduism as not only a majority religion, but as a "national ethos" that is politically favored in terms of economy and infrastructure (2011, 64). She argues that the neo-Vedantin "secular humanist version of Hinduism" of the educated middle and upper classes has lost its appeal:

> They are instead looking for jagrit (or awake) gods who respond to their prayers and who fulfill their wishes—the kind of gods who are personal, caring, and loving. (. . .) [W]hat is changing is simply that it is becoming fashionable to be religious in the theistic (saguna bhakti) tradition of popular Hinduism and to be seen as being religious in this manner. (Nanda 2011, 74)

Nanda' s analysis accounts for forces that may have contributed to the changes in Benares' festival culture. Durgā is awakened in a specifically theistic, *saguṇa* (embodied) form in the *paṇḍāls*. She is *śakti* personified, and is a goddess that "does the work," meaning she responds to prayers and fulfills wishes. This view was repeatedly confirmed in interviews: Durgā "does the work" of fulfilling wishes because she is *śakti*, and therefore is the most powerful one.

Discussions concerning the difference between the *Rām Līlā* and the Durgā Pūjā in Benares typically evolved around the latter being more "in style" and fashionable.[9] I was told, "In *Rām Līlā*, you only find old men in *dhoti* [traditional Indian clothing] and children, but in Durgā Pūjā people can show off their expensive clothes and their wealth."[10] The limited possibilities of alternative creative expression and artistic recognition in the *Rām Līlā* could also factor in, resonating UNESCO's 2005 act stating, "In families that have traditionally been engaged in these performances, the young members are no longer keen to take over because of the lack of artistic recognition and the limited remuneration." Displays of affluence and prestige may be key aspects that explain the popularity of the Durgā Pūjā. As the Banārasi *paṇḍāls* have grown in number, they have also grown in terms of expenses. For example, in October 2012 the *pūjā* committee of the Nati Imli area reported to the *Times of India* that it had raised its budget from INR 80,000 to more than INR 200,000 in just one year ("Grandiose Themes," 2012). Amid the joyful mood of the festival, informants also expressed a sense of unease related to these sudden shifts in neighborhood economics and the new power relations to which this testifies. The *pūjā* is funded by the committees that raise money by collecting funds from neighbors and by obtaining commercial sponsors, with increasing patronage from the city's wealthy and powerful men. A group of informants half-humorously and half-seriously called these *pūjās* "mafia *paṇḍāls*," indicating their speculation that the "dons" of the city influence neighborhood politics by patronizing the *pūjās*.[11]

Durgā Pūjā and Innovation

Just like the *Rām Līlā*, the festival of Durgā has deep roots in the festival culture of Benares. Whereas *Rām Līlā* was always a *public* performance, and was invested with notions of tradition and authenticity, the communal Durgā Pūjā is generally regarded as "new" and nontraditional. In Benares, the festival of the goddess is traditionally observed through personal austerity and as a domestic, family event. A traditional Banārasi way of observing Navarātri is to take vows (*vrata*), to fast and to embark on pilgrimages within the city limits (as prescribed in the Durgājaya chapter of Kāśikhaṇḍa, *Skandapurāṇa* IV.ii.72), *darśana* (viewing of a deity) at temples and/or *śakti pīṭhas* (seats of the goddess) dedicated to the goddess, particularly the Navādurgā pilgrimage (Wilke 2006 and Rodrigues 1993). However, the most important aspect is the performance of daily *pūjā* and *āratis* (ritual waving of lamps) before the home shrine. Here, the goddess is invoked in a pot (*kalaśa*) filled with mud and water from the Gaṅgā, which is then placed on the shrine and worshipped throughout the festival. The rituals are performed by a member of the family or, perhaps preferably, by the family *purohita* (professional ritualist), and involve the recitation of the *Durgāsaptaśatī* each day, the worship of prepubescent girls (*kumārīpūjā*), and a fire oblation (*havana*) on the ninth day.

Mirroring the developments in Bengal, the Durgā Pūjā in Benares has moved from the domestic to the public sphere (McDermott 2011). Although it is common to observe the traditional and domestic Navarātri *pūjā* in private, taking *darśana* of Mahiṣamardinī in the *paṇḍāls* has become an important part of the Banārasi's public Navarātri practices. The *paṇḍāls*, originally a Bengali tradition, traveled to Benares sometime during the first half of the twentieth century and was confined to the Bengali community (Rodrigues 2003, 24). In these *paṇḍāls*, the goddess worshipped was ritually awakened in a clay statue (*mūrti*), which was traditionally the center of attention in the *paṇḍāl*. However, focus has gradually shifted from the traditional *mūrti* to the aesthetic aspects of the *paṇḍāl* installations. These days, the actual *mūrti* that is worshipped is almost invisible, compared to the large "artlike" Durgā installations placed above it (see Sen in this volume). Even though this *pūjā* is modeled on the famous Bengali Kolkata (Calcutta) Durgā Pūjā, the *paṇḍāl pūjā* concept has been embraced by the general population and may no longer be seen as a strictly Bengali phenomenon in Benares.[12] The younger generations of

Banārasis have especially embraced the public *paṇḍāl pūjā* concept. Boys and young men from particular neighborhoods come together in so-called "sporting clubs" that collect funds and appoint the professionals involved in creating what is hoped will be the year's most impressive theme-based Durgā installation.

There seem to be almost no clearly-formulated limits to artistic creativity when designing and decorating the theme-based *paṇḍāl*s, and thus they serve as important platforms for conveying religious, social, and political messages. We now come to an important point that I wish to emphasize, concerning the difference between the *Rām Līlā* and the Durgā Pūjā today: whereas *Rām Līlā* has been "tamed," to use Nita Kumar's choice of words (see below), the Durgā Pūjā is an arena for the young men of the Benares neighborhoods to empower themselves and influence their environments. These celebrations are more open to innovation and creativity, and they can challenge social structures and the established voices of the public sphere, as the *Rām Līlā* cannot. I will now focus on two arenas in which the differences become clear. One is in the *paṇḍāl* itself, or rather, in the design of the Durgā tableau; the other is the communal aspect of the public immersion (*visarjana*) parade, and the government's attempts to control the festival.

The *paṇḍāl* tableau inevitably depicts Durgā as Mahiṣamardinī slaying the buffalo-demon, which is the very center of attention in the *paṇḍāls*; however, the *pūjā* committees consciously decorate them to communicate statements about social and political concerns through their chosen theme. Such theme-based *paṇḍāls*, charged with political statements, existed in Kolkata long before they appeared in Benares; a quite recent example is the 2011 *paṇḍāl* of the Mohammad Ali Park club in Kolkata, which portrayed "corrupt" politicians as the demons being slain by Durgā (see Sen in this volume). Themes are relatively new in the *paṇḍāls* of Benares, and are not as provocative—perhaps yet. However, examples of politically and socially conscious themes have clearly made an entrance on the Banārasi Durgā Pūjā scene. The 2012 *paṇḍāl* of the Machodari neighborhood *pūjā* committee, for example, was decorated with paintings allegedly depicting the rise of petrol prices and its effect on the common people. Other *paṇḍāl* themes relate to terrorism, environmental issues, and city planning. If the Banārasi *paṇḍāls* are to follow the developments of the festival culture of the rest of UP, there will certainly continue to be more of these *paṇḍāls* that reflect contemporary issues in the years to come. In 2014, for instance, the local media reported that several *paṇḍāls* in the state featured themes centering on women's issues, such as female feticide and acid-attack victims. It appears that the use of the aesthetics of the *paṇḍāls* as means of challenging the norms, values, and organization of the establishment is increasingly becoming part of the festival culture in Benares. At the same time, one might ask to what extent such social and political statements are reflected in the organization of the Durgā Pūjā. On the basis of a 2003 survey, Singh and Singh suggested that the Durgā Pūjā *paṇḍāl* celebration provides lower-caste youth with an opportunity for creating their own *pūjā* committees, thereby "using the traditions and symbols of higher castes as a means for upward mobility" (Singh and Singh 2006, 50). Likewise, Katz describes a "Harijan" committee consisting only of Dalit children (Katz 2007, 149). The very organization of these *pūjās*, whether to Durgā or the similarly structured *sarvajanīnā pūjā* to other deities (i.e. *Kālī Pūjā, Sarasvatī Pūjā* and *Gaṇeśa Caturthī*) is democratic in the sense that anyone, regardless of caste or status, can initiate and patronize a *pūjā*. Thus, there are Dalit *pūjā* committees, caste-heterogenous committees, and even *pūjās* organized by Hindus and Muslims alike. Katz (2007) has thus argued for an all-inclusiveness of these *pūjās* in Benares, understanding them as arenas where brotherhood is emphasized across the boundaries of caste and religion. Still, the most publicly dominating aspect of these *pūjās*, the *visarjana* parade, has a long history of hosting communal power demonstrations and breeding Hindu-Muslim riots in Benares. In fact, as Rodrigues has pointed out, the presence of Banārasi *paṇḍāl* Durgā Pūjās increased after violent clashes between Hindus and Muslims in 1978, as a *visarjana* parade through a Muslim-dominated *muhallā* sparked riots.[13] The growth of Durgā Pūjā *paṇḍāl* committees in the aftermath of these incidents therefore reflects, as in the case of the *Rām Līlā*, a need to cultivate a powerful Hindu symbol in the face of a perceived Muslim threat. The picture is therefore complex, which calls for a more thorough study of the inner dynamics and organization of these *pūjās*.

Attempts to Curb Durgā Pūjā

Whether the authorities feel challenged by the *paṇḍāl* themes, they are definitely concerned about the communal aspects of the festival, particularly those related to the immersion (*visarjana*) parade on *Vijayādaśamī*, the final day of the Durgā Pūjā. This is evident from the increased police presence during the important festival days, and the attempts to curb elements of the celebration through legal means. Communal religious identity is a strong aspect of the *pūjā* organizations, and governmental concerns over communal tensions arise each year. Ever since the installation of *paṇḍāls* boomed in the 1990s, the state and local government has tried to control the celebration through law enforcement. First, by requiring *pūjā* committees to annually register with local government in an attempt to curb the growth of the *paṇḍāl* scene, which, according to local media, has not succeeded. More successfully, the immersion parade has been regulated and expanded over several days following *Vijayādaśamī*. As a public performance, the immersion parades are highly charged power demonstrations and powerful public statements. Therefore, attempts to curb this part of the festival may be understood as an attempt to limit the impact of these statements. Part of this regulatory scheme has focused on the environmental impact of the festival on the Gaṅgā, the river in which the images of Durgā are immersed. A ban on the immersion of statues has been debated for years, but only after the present Indian prime minister, Narendra Modi—who campaigned on a "save the Gaṅgā" platform in Benares—came to power was a 2013 High Court decision to ban the immersion of *mūrtis* in the river officially enacted. This decision seemingly removed the central element of the *paṇḍāl*. One cannot awaken the goddess for a festival without having the opportunity to ritually dismiss her afterward. Even though in the huge *paṇḍāls* attention is focused on visual tableaus, the clay image of Durgā is considered the ritual *raison d'être,* as it receives the *pūjā*. Furthermore, without the Durgā *mūrti* to immerse, there is no need for an immersion parade to the Gaṅgā. The effects of the ban were evident and led to protests and violent clashes between Hindu organizations and the local law enforcement officers over the issue of the immersion of Gaṇeśa *mūrtis* a few weeks prior to the 2015 Navarātri. The conflict quickly escalated from a religious protest to a politically charged power struggle in the city, and members of *pūjā* committees were allegedly arrested. Among them was the patron of the Hathua Market Durgā Pūjā committee, the controversial member of the legislative assembly, and one of Modi's few rivals in Benares, Ajay Rai, who claims to have had no part in the riots and to have been the victim of a political conspiracy. In the aftermath of these events some Durgā Pūjā committees found ways around the ban by installing and immersing *kalaśas* (clay pots) instead of the large clay images, while other committees eventually accepted immersion of their *mūrtis* in substitute ponds.

At this point, it is appropriate to turn our attention back to the *Rām Līlā* and Nita Kumar's (1995) analysis of the nose-cutting episode. The highlight of the nose-cutting episode—or of the whole *Rām Līlā,* one could argue—is the procession of Rāvaṇa's forces in response to the cutting off of Śūrpanakhā's nose. The most famous of these takes place in the *Rām Līlā* of the neighborhood of Chaitganj. This processional performance has led a life of its own. Instead of showing the demon forces, the procession consists of an interesting mixture of performers: a *hijra* (a member of the third-sex, transgender community), musicians, Durgā dancers wielding fire and swords, elephants and camels, and—the highlight—many impressive floats (*vimāna*), with children dressed up as gods and other characters from history and myth, in acrobatic balancing acts (e.g., a child dressed as Śiva balances other children dressed as deities on the top of his *triśūla*). However, these floats have not always portrayed innocent images. According to Kumar, the history of the Chaitganj *nākkatayyā* shows that this demon parade was once appropriated to invert social structures, partly following the logic of a carnival, and that as such it challenged social norms and the hegemony in Benares. It portrayed for one night all the things that were prohibited the rest of the year, presenting a unique opportunity for social criticism. A description of the parade from the beginning of the twentieth century tells of floats portraying couples engaged in intimate acts and people dressed as though belonging to the lower castes, scenes of domestic violence, people acting as alcoholics, gamblers, and so on. Kumar also argues that the nose-cutting episode underwent a purification process at the hands of the nationalist government beginning in the 1920s. Gradually, the powerful nose-cutting procession came under government control, expressing only their consensus discourse: "It assumes Rightness, Naturalness, and Representativeness, and has no spaces where those who believe in bigamy, for example, or the naturalness of drink and drugs, may make their statements" (Kumar 1995, 54). It is tempting to draw a parallel with the social themes of the present-day Durgā *paṇḍāls*. If Kumar is correct, and the *Rām Līlā* has been rid of subversive and rebellious elements by the government, could we see the government's attempt to control the Durgā Pūjā as driven by similar interests? Whereas the *Rām Līlā* reinforces traditional and conservative structures, may the Durgā Pūjā be understood as rebelling against these same structures?

Final Thoughts

In Benares, Āśvina Navarātri provides an opportunity to observe the dynamics of tradition and innovation in the city's festival culture. Throughout this chapter, I have sketched the invention of traditions and the recent developments pertaining to the public aspects of the festival, exemplified by *Rām Līlā* and Durgā Pūjā. I have shown that the *Rām Līlā*, although deeply embedded in Banārasi collective identity, may be losing ground to the Durgā Pūjā. However, there are many reasons why a claim that the public Durgā Pūjās and the *Rām Līlās* are directly competing for attention is problematic. First, as both festivals are staged in public over several days, it is absolutely possible—and common—for people to attend both festivals. One could walk in the immersion parade, then proceed to Laṅkā to watch the burning of Rāvaṇa in the evening, and return to the *ghāṭs* to party with the sporting clubs throughout the night. Second, age and generation are issues. As one informant told me, "I was forced to go to our neighborhood *Rām Līlā* when I was a child, and I saw all the people there dressed up and looking ridiculous. I used to tell myself: When I grow up I will not bother with this anymore." However, the same informant admitted that his children took great joy in watching the local *Rām Līlā* of Assi, something he considered to be an essential part of their upbringing. Therefore, resistance to the traditionalism of certain narratives and practices does not necessarily imply that these traditions are not transmitted through generations.

Power negotiation, a central aspect of public festivals in general, is particularly at the forefront of Navarātri in Benares. Through the Navarātri festival, the power of the goddess and the divine king enters the physical world of groups and individuals. The history of the Rāmnagar *Rām Līlā* exemplifies the dynamic nature of festivals as occasions when traditions may be created or appropriated. But the *līlā* also shows how festivals may be controlled and "fixed," annually reinforcing the same structures. *Rām Līlā* presents a model of the traditional Banārasi society, where kings, *brāhmaṇas*, and Dalits are structured and united under the power of King Rāma. By contrast, Durgā Pūjā strikes one as presenting democratic organization, reflecting a free-market-based and modern society, where traditional social structures and ritualism are put in the background, and intercommunal brotherhood is foregrounded. But how far can we follow this reasoning?

Although it may be tempting to suggest that the popularity of the communal Durgā Pūjā testifies to a lower-class protest (cf. Singh and Singh 2006) against the Brahmanical hegemony of the *Rām Līlā* during Navarātri, there is no reason to assume that caste and gender bias are absent from the organization of the Durgā Pūjā, and the data presently available does not support such a claim. Benares is still a "*puruṣon ka sahar*" (city of men, cf. Kumar 1995), where girls largely are excluded from the communal parts of the Durgā Pūjā. This is reflected in the names of the *pūjā* committees, such as the Premier Boys' Club of the Hathua market area, and the Young Boys' club in Sonarpura. Furthermore, the role of communal identity and history of Hindu-Muslim tensions related to the public Durgā Pūjā in Benares suggests that these celebrations could best be seen as yet another platform of Hinduizing secular public spaces. Recalling Nanda's analysis (above) of the ritualistic, nationalistic, and publicly dominating Hinduism of the modern middle classes, it is hardly an insignificant fact that Durgā herself is a strong Hindu nationalist symbol. Apart from being a demon-slaying heroine, she also manifests as Mother India (Bhārat Mātā), the land of (Hindu) India in the form of a goddess. Nevertheless, there is a transgressive element to these *pūjās*. The civil structure of the *sarvajanīnā pūjā* youth organizations has potential for establishing inclusiveness across the boundaries of caste and religion. Furthermore, the aesthetic dimension of the *paṇḍāl pūjā* format creates an arena where progressive political or social statements may be made public in a popular ritual context. Durgā Pūjā in Benares creates new opportunities for expression—expression through which various social realities may be challenged and contested.[14]

Notes

1. There are four Navarātris during the year. Most people celebrate two: the Navarātri in Caitra in the spring, and the autumn Navarātri in Āśvina, which by far is the most popular. The two remaining Navarātris, in the winter and in the summer, are considered "gupta" (hidden) and, according to informants, are only celebrated by Tantric *sādakhas* and others devoted to fierce aspects of the goddess.

2. Furthermore, although there are substantial publications on the *Rām Līlā*, based on field research done in Benares in the late 1970s and 1980s (see Schechner 1983; Hess 1988; Lutgendorf 1991; Sax 2010; and Kumar 1995), and studies of the Bengali domestic Durgā Pūjā in Benares by Hillary Rodrigues (2003), to my knowledge no work has been done on the most recent developments in the public festival culture of Benares.

3. These Durgā hymns are regarded as late interpolations and are confined to the appendix of the critical edition. As Yudhiṣṭhira and Arjuna in the *Mahābhārata* praised Durgā before going to war, so does Rāma in the later *Rāmāyaṇa* traditions. Unable to defeat Rāvaṇa, Rāma seeks help from Durgā on *mahāṣṭamī*, the eighth day of Navarātri. After triumphing in battle, he performs a *śamī* tree *pūjā* on Dussehra (Biardeau 1984, 6). This *pūjā* is a royal ritual performed by the Mahārāja on Dussehra. The meaning of the tree is somewhat mysterious, but it seems to be associated with the goddess (particularly in the form of Aparājitā, "the invincible" warrior-goddess), victory, and "prosperity of the kingdom (jfr. Biardieu 1984). I found that it is generally believed to contain the *śakti* (energy) of the goddess. Thus, the relationship between the earthly god-ruler Rāma and the cosmic ruler Durgā exists both in narratives and in sociocultural performance spaces.

4. This version differs from other versions of the story where Ravaṇa's brother Khara leads the demon army against Rāma and Lakṣmaṇa.

5. Interestingly, there is a similar explanation for the rise of Durgā Pūjās among the zamindars in eighteenth-century Bengal: "Aparna Bhattacharya, a modern-day historian, writes that the worship of the powerful goddess Durgā attracted the Hindu *rājā*s as a means of overcoming their inferiority complex vis-à-vis the *nawābs*; further, they hoped to imbibe some of Durgā's strength, which could be used for political purposes" (McDermott 2011: 16).

6. For more on the role of Rāma and the Rāmāyaṇa narrative in modern Hindu nationalism, see Rajagopal 2001.

7. Hein (1958) concludes that the earliest *Rāmcaritmānas* performances may have occurred during or shortly after Tulsīdās's lifetime.

8. Numbers presented in the local news, see "Durga Puja: Counting of pandals" 2013. I have not had the chance to confirm these numbers with the Varanasi Police.

9. I conducted qualitative interviews during Navarātri in 2011, 2012, 2013, and 2014.

10. Interview with Vipin Singh during the *paṇḍāl* visits on Mahāṣṭamī, October 1, 2014, BHU area, Benares.

11. Group interview with revelers at the Hathua Market *paṇḍāl* on Mahāṣṭamī, October 1, 2014.

12. Bengalis themselves clearly distinguish their *paṇḍāl* from the Banārasi ones, claiming that their *mūrti* and their performances are more correct and authentic.

13. According to Rodrigues, this incident was related to the Durgotsava Sammilini community Durgā Pūjā of Pandey Haveli in 1978. The clash "resulted in city-wide rioting and deaths" (Rodrigues 2003, 292).

14. Although I am not aware of *paṇḍāls* in Benares being characterized as obscene in the same way as the *nākkatayyā* was, it could be worthwhile to look at the debate in the rest of the subcontinent. I am thinking of the debate going on as I write, involving Smriti Irani, JNU, and the so-called Mahiṣāsur Pūjā.

Bibliography

Awasthi, Induja. 1980. "Rāmcaritmānas and the Performing Tradition of Ramayana." In *The Ramayana Tradition in Asia*, edited by V. Raghavan, 505–16. New Delhi: Sahitya Akademi.

Bell, Catherine. 1992. *Ritual Theory, Ritual Practice.* New York: Oxford University Press.

Biardeau, Madeleine. 1984. "The Śamītree and the Sacrificial Buffalo." In *Contributions to Indian Sociology* 18: 1, 1–23.

Devi Mahatmyam (Glory of the Divine Mother). 700 Mantras on Sri Durga. 1953. With English translation by Swami Jagadiswarananda. Chennai: Sri Ramakrishna Math.

"Durga Puja: Counting of Pandals an Eyewash till 2012." 2013. *Times of India.* October 9. http://timesofindia.indiatimes.com/city/varanasi/Durga-Puja-Counting-of-pandals-an-eyewash-till-2012/articleshow/23783623.cms.

Eck, Diana.1983. *Banaras: City of Light.* New Delhi: Penguin Books.

Freitag, Sandria B. 1992. *Culture and Power in Banaras: Community, Performance, and Environment, 1800–1980.* Berkeley: University of California Press.

Fuller, C. J., and Penny Logan. 1985. "The Navarātri Festival in Madurai." In *Bulletin of the School of Oriental and African Studies* 48 (1): 79–105.

Geertz, Clifford. 1980. *Negara: The Theatre State of Ninteenth Century Bali.* Princeton: Princeton University Press.

"Grandiose Theme Makes Puja Pandal Budget Soar." 2012. *Times of India.* October 22. http://timesofindia.indiatimes.com/city/varanasi/Grandiose-themes-make-puja-pandal-budget-soar/articleshow/16914476.cms.

Gupta, Sanjukta, and Richard Gombrich. 1986. "Kings, Power and the Goddess." In *South Asia Research* 6 (2): 123–38.

Hein, Norvin. 1958. "The Rām Līlā." *The Journal of American Folklore* 71 (281), 279–304.

Hess, Linda. 1988. *The Rāmlīlā of Rāmnagar: An Introduction and Day-by-Day Description.* Berkeley: Published at the request of the Maharaja of Banaras.

Hobsbawm, Eric, and Terence O. Ranger. 1992. *The Invention of Tradition.* Cambridge: Cambridge University Press.

Kumar, Nita. 1995. "Class and Gender Politics in the *Rāmlīlā.*" In *The Gods at Play: Līlā in South Asia*, edited by William S. Sax, 156–76. New York: Oxford University Press.

Lutgendorf, Philip. 1991. *The Life of a Text: Performing the Rāmcaritmānas of Tulsīdās.* Berkeley: University of California Press.

Mahābhārata. With the commentary of Nīlakaṇṭha. 1929–1936. 10 vols. Poona: Chitrashala.

McDermott, Rachel Fell. 2011. *Revelry, Rivalry and Longing for the Goddess of Bengal: The Fortunes of Hindu Festivals*. New York: Columbia University Press.

Nanda, Meera. 2011. *The God Market: How Globalization Is Making India More Hindu*. New York: Monthly Review.

Piliavsky, Anastasia. 2014. *Patronage as Politics in South Asia*. New York: Cambridge University Press.

Rajagopal, Arvind. 2001. *Politics after Television. Hindu Nationalism and the Reshaping of the Public in India*. Cambridge: Cambridge University Press.

Ramlila: The Traditional Performance of the Ramayana. 2005. United Nations Educational Scientific and Cultural Organization (UNESCO), *Third Proclamation of Masterpieces of the Oral and Intangible Heritage of Humanity*. Retrieved from www.unesco.org/culture/intangible-heritage/16apa_uk.htm.

Rodrigues, Hillary Peter. 2003. *Ritual Worship of the Great Goddess: The Liturgy of the Durgā Pūjā with Interpretations*. Albany: State University of New York Press.

———. 1993. "The Image of the Goddess Durgā and Her Worship in Banāras." PhD thesis, McMaster University.

Sax, William S. 2010. "The Royal Pilgrimage of the Goddess Nanda." In *Pilgrimages Today*, edited by Tore Ahlbäck, 334–52. Abo, Finland: Donner Institute for Research in Religious and Cultural History.

Schechner, Richard. 1998. "Crossing the Water: Pilgrimage, Movement, and Environmental Scenography of the *Ramlila* of Ramnagar." In *Living Banaras: Hindu Religion in Cultural Context*, edited by Bradley R. Hertel and Cynthia Ann Humes, 19–72. New Delhi: Manohar.

———. 1983. *Performative Circumstances from the Avant Garde to Ramlila*. Calcutta: Seagull Books.

Schechner, Richard, and Linda Hess. 1977. "The Ramlila of Ramnagar." *The Drama Review* 21 (3): 51–82.

Sherring, Rev. M. A. 1868. *The Sacred City of the Hindus: An Account of Benares in Ancient and Modern Times*. London: Trübner.

Simmons, Caleb. 2014. "The Goddess and Vaiṣṇavism in Search for Regional Supremacy: Woḍeyar Devotional Traditions during the Reign of Rāja Woḍeyar (1578–1617 CE)." *Indian History* 1 (1): 27–46.

Singer, Milton B. 1972. *When a Great Tradition Modernizes: An Anthropological Approach to Civilization*. London: Pall Mall.

Singh, Ravi S., and Rana P. B. Singh. 2006. "Goddesses in Kāśī (Vārāṇasī): Spatial Patterns Symbolic Orders." In *Visualizing Space in Banaras: Images, Maps, and the Practice of Representation*, edited by Martin Gaenszle and Jörg Gengnagel, 41–68. Wiesbaden: Harrassowitz Verlag.

Skandapurāṇa (kāśīkhaṇḍa). Translated and Annotated by Dr. G. V. Tagare. 1996. *Ancient Indian Tradition and Mythology Series*. Delhi: Motilal Banarsidass.

Stein, Burton. 1983. "Manhānavamī: Medieval and Modern Kingly Ritual in South Asia." In *Essays on Gupta Culture*, edited by Bardwell L. Smith, 69–90. Delhi: Motilal Banarsidass.

Tambiah, Stanley J. 1979. "A Performative Approach to Ritual." *Proceedings of the British Academy* 65: 113–69.

Wilke, Annette. 2006. "The Banarsī Navadurgā Cycle and Its Spatial Orientation." In *Visualizing Space in Banaras: Images, Maps, and the Practice of Representation*,

edited by Martin Gaenszle and Jörg Gengnagel, 69–94. Wiesbaden: Harrassowitz Verlag.
Yokochi, Yuko. 2004. "The Rise of the Warrior Goddess in Ancient India: A Study of the Myth Cycle of Kauśikī-Vindhyavāsinī in the Skandapurāṇa." PhD thesis, University of Groningen.

8

Dolls and Demons

The Materiality of Navarātri

INA MARIE LUNDE ILKAMA

Navarātri, the nine-night festival of the goddess, is celebrated in many homes and temples throughout Tamil Nadu. Based on ethnographic fieldwork in Kāñchipuram, this chapter will investigate the contemporary festival as it is celebrated domestically and in goddess temples. This is done particularly by looking at materiality, by which I mean a broad array of actions and objects associated with the material world, or more specifically, the material representations of the goddess and the demon in the corporeal environs of the ritual space.

I will start by exploring the domestic festival and its characteristic display of dolls (*kolu*), before proceeding to selected rituals of two goddess temples, namely, the well-known Brahmanical Kāmākṣī Amman̲ temple and the small but popular temple of the village goddess Paṭavēṭṭamman̲. The temple rituals that are addressed are the enactment of the goddess' fight with the (buffalo) demon and subsequent cooling or atonement rituals. Along with the *alaṃkāras* (ornamentation) of the goddess, which are considered highlights of the festival, these rituals provide Navarātri with its special character in the temples in question, and the investigation of these rituals and their attendant practices illustrate the many ways Navarātri rituals are performed and the manifold interpretations that follow.

My aim in this chapter is to draw attention to the material aspects of the ethnography: how the Navarātri festival is manifested and played out in the world and, more specifically, how it affects and is affected by its surroundings. Materiality of religion consists of "the stuff through which 'the religious' is manifest . . . how God, or the gods, or the spirits, or one's ancestors can be recognized as being present and/or *represented*" (Engelke 2011, 213). Like Engelke, I see materiality as including not only physical *things*, but also actions, gestures, words, texts and everything else that can be taken as communicating a message, or is recognized as a semiotic form (Engelke 2011, 218). In this chapter, however, I will focus primarily on physical objects and the agency with which they are imbued within the Navarātri ritual context. Through exploring various Navarātri rituals, I will show that materiality frequently concerns presence rather than representation and that material representations in turn encompass agency, or the ability to foster consequences in interaction with the material world.

Background

Navarātri is centered upon the worship of the goddess in various forms and is known for commemorating Durgā's victory over the Buffalo Demon, as famously portrayed in the Sanskrit *Devī Māhātmya*. Despite the persistence of this overarching Pan-Indian "theme," we find that in the temples of local and regional goddesses, the celebrations are centered upon the local manifestations of the goddess and her mythology, as is the case with Kāmākṣi and Paṭavēṭṭamma<u>ṉ</u>. Thus, the celebrations of the goddess festival in Kāñchipuram continue to have strong local connotations in which devotees enact rituals of local significance.

Tamil celebrations of Navarātri take place both domestically and in temples. These celebrations, however, take quite different forms in the two spheres and might at first glimpse even seem to be two distinct festivals. In the homes, family, auspiciousness, and harmony are emphasized, and women perform most rituals and visit each other for nine days, admiring the *kolus* set up in each other's homes for the occasion. In addition to going "*kolu* hopping," it is common to visit one or several goddess temples for *darśana* (auspicious viewing of the deity) and worship of the goddess during the festival. Some temples enact the fight of the goddess and the demon and thus have a stronger emphasis on battle and the goddess's supremacy over the demonic forces; yet far from all temples do. The different ornamentations (*alaṃkāras*) of the goddess that are changed each night of the festival are, however, an integral and popular part of Navarātri in almost every temple.

An important aspect of materiality during the festival is the increased accessibility of the goddess through her diverse material presences, as she manifests in several forms. She is invited home abiding on the *kolu* in the form of a pot. She is worshipped in the form of visiting females. *And* she is worshipped in temples, where her ornamentations depict and transform her into various forms each day of the festival. Devotees are thus able to interact with her in a variety of ways through various forms of her materiality.

Domestic Navarātri

The day before the new moon in the Tamil month of Puraṭṭāci (September–October), Mrs. Padma's family assemble their dolls (*pommai*) from boxes that have been stored for the year.[1] These dolls will be carefully arranged and displayed on a structure of seven stepped levels (*kolu*, lit. royal presence, court) during Navarātri. Most of their dolls represent deities and figures from Hindu mythology, but their collection also includes saints, humans, animals, fruits, vegetables, and sets depicting various religious and cultural scenes, like weddings, temple festivals, rural scenes, and famous pilgrimage sites. Ranging from about a meter to the size of a finger, the dolls are placed hierarchically on the steps according to size and level of consciousness, with inanimate objects on the bottom and the gods on top. Some dolls date twenty-five years back, to the time of Mrs. Padma's marriage, and include the *marappācci* (prepared from wood) dolls, a man and a woman, which are traditionally received as wedding gifts. Other dolls are even older and inherited through the family, but a few are new, as there is an obligation to buy at least one new doll for each Navarātri. Thus, their collection has grown steadily since their marriage and takes up a huge part of their spacious living room.

At an auspicious time during the new moon day at the beginning of the festival, Mrs. Padma cleans the floor in front of the *kolu* steps, which are now replete with colorful dolls, and draws a *kōlam* (geometrical drawing of rice flour) in front of it. Then she invokes the goddess Kāmākṣī in a pot (*kalaśa*) the form through which she is worshipped for the duration of the festival.[2] Mrs. Padma puts water, rice, *tōr dal* (pigeon peas), five betel nuts, five turmeric pieces, betel leaves, silver and gold into the pot. Mango leaves and a coconut are placed on its mouth, and she drapes the pot with a blue cloth and decorates it with a jeweled necklace, a jeweled *bindi*, and garlands of fresh jasmine flowers.[3] Once the pot is ornamented, Mrs. Padma places it in the middle of the *kolu*, and neither it nor the dolls can be rearranged or moved until Vijayadaśamī (the tenth day of victory), when the *marappācci* dolls are laid flat and the pot moved to the north.

During each of the festival's nine mornings, Mrs. Padma worships the *kolu* with fresh flowers, specially prepared food, lights, and incense,

Figure 8.1. Mrs. Padma worshipping an image of Kāmākṣī in front of her *kolu*. The pot in which the goddess is invoked is placed on the third step.

and she recites various goddess *stotras* (hymns) (figure 8.1). Afterward, she eagerly awaits visits from auspicious married women (*sumaṅgalī, suvasinī*) and prepubescent girls (*kanyā, kaṉṉi*), whom she and her husband will worship as representatives of the goddess.[4] When the female visitors arrive, Mrs. Padma and her husband wash the females' feet and offer them turmeric, a dress or a sari blouse piece, food, betel nuts, betel leaves, and buttermilk. Finally, the couple waves the camphor flame in front of the females and prostrates before them. It is widely believed that the goddess will come to one's house in the form of a young girl during Navarātri, so these *pūjās* directly reach the goddess.

In the evenings, women bring their children to view Mrs. Padma's *kolu*, sing devotional songs, and exchange gossip and stories connected to the dolls' history and mythological background. They receive *prasāda*, the food prepared and first offered to the goddess, who is installed on the *kolu*. This *prasāda* commonly consists of nine types of pulses (*cuṇṭal*), one for each Navarātri evening. Within the Tamil typology of food, *cuṇṭal* is considered a "hot" dish, increasing the *śakti* (female power) of the consumers and further strengthening the connection between the devotee and the goddess (Fuller and Logan 1985; Tanaka 1999; cf. Beck 1969). As they leave, Mrs. Padma presents the women with gifts connected to feminine beauty, auspiciousness, and domesticity: a sari blouse piece, fresh jasmines, turmeric, *kuṅkuma*, betel nuts, a coconut, bangles, a comb, and a mirror (cf. Hancock 1999, 3). She explains, "It is like giving to the goddess herself."

When the festival is over, Mrs. Padma cooks the rice from the pot along with the coconut, makes coconut *pāyacam* (a sweet dessert), and offers it to Kāmākṣī. Finally, the food is consumed as *prasāda*. Thus, her family partakes in the powers of the goddess, as she is absorbed in them through the consumption of the rice in which she was temporarily installed.

Material Aspects of the *Kolu*

While talking to various women in Kāñchipuram, many different explanations came up in response to my question of *why* a *kolu* is erected during Navarātri. Many connected the *kolu* to the goddess's fight with the demon and regarded the dolls as the army of Durgā helping her in the cosmic battle or as sources of empowerment for her during the nine days of battle until Vijayadaśamī, drawing on the doll's powers. This empowerment of the goddess leading up to the cosmic fight is also reflected in the offerings of "hot" *cuṇṭal* to the goddess in the pot and thereupon to the visiting women. This food makes both the goddess and the women, among whom the goddess also will be manifest, "hot" for the duration of the festival day by day increasing their *śakti*, enhancing the fierceness of the goddess in her fight with the demon. In response to this increased energy level of the women, the ingredients in the pot are used for making "cool" *pāyacam* once the festival is over, not only conferring the goddess's powers to the family who consumes this dish as *prasāda* but also cooling the women after the battle is over.

Returning to the dolls, others explained how the world stood still as "mere dolls" as the goddess attacked the demon, while others again told me the dolls were alive throughout the Navarātri festival. In turn, they need to be put back to sleep after the festival (cf. laying the *marappācci* dolls flat before the others can be removed). The most frequent answer, however, to the question of why the *kolu* is erected, was that keeping a *kolu* is equal to inviting the goddess into the home, and you *do* so by invoking her presence within the pot and receiving guests among whom the goddess is manifest. This is considered an auspicious ritual that brings prosperity to the household and the family and ensures women long lives as auspicious married women. As long as the woman remains *sumaṅgalī*, her husband will be alive, so this end ensures the welfare of the entire family. In tune with this wholly auspicious nature of the *kolu*, the dolls that are on display should consist only of benevolent deities.

It became clear to me early on that the *kolu* dolls are considered *more* than just dolls and that many people share an intimate relationship with them. Many women told me how the dolls are imbued with powers and divinity or spoke of them in terms of gods or close family relations. According to these powers and the auspiciousness of the *kolu*, prayers directed to the dolls and the goddess are said to have the ability to fulfill certain wishes, in particular, the wish to get married or conceive children. To achieve this end, women need only buy certain sets of dolls: sets depicting marriage (*kalyāna*) and the prenatal rite of passage of parting the hair (*sīmanta*) or baby Kṛṣṇa dolls.[5] Other people explained that if an unmarried young girl did *pūjā* to a *kolu* and received *prasāda*, or if she merely *saw* a *kolu*, she would get married within the next year. These material representations of dolls and the presence of the goddess on the *kolu* are widely believed to cause auspicious results, one of the main reasons for performing this ritual. In other words, according to the women I interviewed, these dolls have agency and are imbued with magical powers (cf. Bado-Fralick and Norris, 2010, 31).

The types of dolls on the *kolu* (some dolls and sets are more popular than others, and some dolls are rarer than others), their quality (they should ideally be made out of terracotta,but papier-mâché and plastic dolls are also available), and their maintenance (many dolls are inherited through the family and commonly repainted as the years pass to look fresh) are important not only for the owners of the dolls but also the women who attend the *kolu* viewings in the evenings. In her essay in this volume, Nicole Wilson compares the *kolu* viewings she attended in Madurai to the conspicuous consumption of Hindu weddings, as they represent an opportunity for families to highlight their expendable wealth in front of neighbors and friends. This wealth is manifested in the dolls and the gifts presented to visitors. Wilson further describes how the gifts are taken home and shown to the other family members (especially males) who did not attend the *kolu* viewing, who draw conclusions about people's class status and socioeconomic standing. Through displaying these dolls, materiality is very much on display as homes are opened up for visitors for the limited period of the festival. Here, we see how materiality of religious ritual not only represents, but also contributes to establish or enhance social positions: you climb up the social ladder if you perform or exhibit, according to certain standards.

By investigating the ritual of *kolus*, we have seen how divinity is embodied in the materiality of Navarātri. But while the dolls merely represent divinities and other figures, the goddess is present among them in the form of a pot. She is invited into one's home during the festival through this temporary auspicious installation, as well as through the worshipped *kanyās* and *sumaṅgalīs*, or "regular" evening guests, as it is widely believed that one among them "will surely be the goddess herself."[6] According to the women who partake in the domestic Navarātri celebrations of Kāñchipuram, the dolls and the goddess on the *kolu* have agency. They empower the goddess for her fight with the demon, which is also reflected in the food offerings consumed by women. They confer auspiciousness to married women and prosperity to the households who keep *kolus*. They grant wishes to those who ask. In addition, their display contributes to people's and families' status in society and makes upward social mobility possible.

Navarātri in the Kāmākṣī Temple

Along with the Brahmotsava celebrated in the month of Māci (January–February), Navarātri is considered one of the two major festivals of the ritual year in the Brahmanical temple complex of Kāmākṣī Ammaṉ. The Kāmākṣī temple is dedicated to the principal goddess of Kāñchipuram and follows the *śrīvidyā* (School of "Auspicious Wisdom") mode of worship based on the ritual manual *Saubhāgya Cintāmaṇi*, ascribed to the sage Durvāsa. The text prescribes the installation of the goddess and her attendant deities in pots, *homas* (fire sacrifices), the festival's framing rituals, the worship of young girls and auspicious married women, and various processions. Two of the central rituals performed during Navarātri that will be discussed below—the fight between Kāmākṣī and the demon and the subsequent worship of the *vaṉṉi* tree—are not mentioned in this handbook.

Around noon each Navarātri day, after the priests have performed all morning rituals to the goddess in the sanctum as well as the pots in which Kāmākṣī and her attendant deities are invoked during the festival, they worship a prepubescent girl, along with an auspicious married woman, in a manner similar to the domestic *pūjā* described previously. These *pūjās* are performed behind closed doors in front of the goddess's sanctum, and the girl and the woman are worshipped *as* the goddess, who is invoked in them with a mantra. Although my impression is that it is not always the case, the girls should be between one and nine years old and are worshipped in increasing order. According to one of Kāmākṣī's priests, this rite of worshipping young girls is conceptually linked to Kāmākṣī's fight with the dreadful demon Bandhāsura, which is enacted for the festival's first eight evenings as a large public spectacle. According to local mythology (*Kāmākṣīvilāsa* 12.16–114), the demon was killed by Kāmākṣī, who had incarnated in the form of a young girl (Balā Kāmākṣī, who is five years old in the text and nine according to the priest).

The evening rituals during Navarātri are mainly staged in a special Navarātri pavilion (*maṇḍapa*) used only for the festival. When I attended, for several evenings, I stood amidst a crowd eagerly awaiting the festival image of Kāmākṣī to be brought to the pavilion. Each evening the festival image of Kāmākṣī wears a new *alaṃkāra*, an elaborate ornamentation of fresh flowers and garlands, new clothes, and shining jewelry, and for a few evenings she is seated on a stuffed lion or a tiger, resembling the warrior goddess Durgā. Such *alaṃkāras* are a major attraction for the devotees during Navarātri.

Reaching the pavilion, Kāmākṣī is placed on a dais, opposing a man-sized effigy of the demon erected at the other end. This effigy has three interchangeable heads (red, black, and a buffalo head) that are alternated each evening. After *pūjā* for the goddess, a wire is set up between them, and three firecrackers are sent back and forth along the wire to the enthusiastic cheering of the crowd. As the demon is "hit," he shakes his head, and when he is beheaded with the final firecracker, a group of boys who impersonate the demon run up to Kāmākṣī with his weapons and head. The priests smear the head with red *kuṅkuma* powder, garland it, and place it at Kāmākṣī's feet as a token of his surrender. Next, the entire group of devotees who have witnessed the fight pushes and rushes to be blessed with the *kuṅkuma* powder and the flame of the ritual lamp (*āratī*).

The eighth day of Navarātri is called Durgāṣṭamī (Durgā's eighth [day]) and is considered the day the demon *dies*. On this day, Durgā's festival image is carried out along with Kāmākṣī and placed beside her during the fight. This evening the procedure changes slightly as the battle intensifies. Altogether, seven firecrackers are sent along the wire between the goddesses and the demon, and the demon changes his head three times before he is beheaded, wearing the head of a buffalo, pointing to the myth of the Devī's destruction of the demon Mahiṣa recounted in the *Devī Māhātmya*.

On the evening of Vijayadaśamī, I joined devotees for the *vaṉṉimarapūja* (worship of the *vaṉṉi* tree), which is closely connected to Kāmākṣī's fight with the demon. Prior to the arrival of Kāmākṣī and her procession, a branch of a *vaṉṉi* tree is tied to a grate in the street in front of the main temple entrance. Kāmākṣī is placed about ten meters in front of the branch, and the main priest retrieves three flower arrows and a flower-clad bow from the goddess and shoots them at the *vaṉṉi* branch on her behalf. Very few devotees attended this ritual compared to the numbers that show up for the fight: although the temple courtyard is filled to the brim with people eager to watch the goddess's procession in her golden chariot immediately afterward, the worship of the *vaṉṉi* tree has a certain aura of solitude to it. This *pūjā*, which is performed at dusk outside of the temple premises, is not announced in the festival program and is attended mostly by priests and temple musicians. Clearly, the *vaṉṉi* tree *pūjā* is performed for the sake of Kāmākṣī with a sole focus on her, not contributing to public spectacle.

Interestingly, Kāmākṣī's priests offered me different explanations for *why* the *vaṉṉi* tree *pūjā* is performed. One priest holds that this is an atonement ritual that Kāmākṣī must perform after committing the sin of killing the demon. According to him, the *vaṉṉi* tree has the power to relieve her of this particular sin. Two other priests, however, did not mention any atonement, but told me that the demon did *not* die on the eighth day, but that he took the form of a *vaṉṉi* tree. Therefore, Kāmākṣī must kill the tree on Vijayadaśamī. Only the *vaṉṉi* tree *pūjā* accomplishes killing the demon Bandhāsura. In the interpretations of the priests, then, the *vaṉṉi* tree carries two roles: it is considered either an atonement "device" *or* the final form of the demon himself.

Navarātri in the Paṭavēṭṭammaṉ Temple

The small Paṭavēṭṭammaṉ temple is a non-Brahmin temple that houses Paṭavēṭṭammaṉ, a form of the better-known Māriyammaṉ. She is a so-called village goddess (*grāmadevatā*), known for curing pox diseases. This is a private temple, and her priest belongs to the *ceṅkuntar mutaliyār* community. Even though the Paṭavēṭṭammaṉ temple is rather modest and slightly outside of the city center, it is known in Kāñchipuram for its magnificent and elaborately themed *alaṃkāras* depicting the goddess in various forms each night of the festival. The crowd attending Navarātri celebrations here grows rapidly from year to year.[7]

While there exist no written texts pertaining to this Paṭavēṭṭammaṉ temple, a rich mythological tradition surrounds the goddess residing here. According to her priest, the reason for Paṭavēṭṭammaṉ's fight with the demon Makiṣāsuraṉ (Tamil for Mahiṣāsura) is that in one of her carnations, she was born as Kalkattā (Calcutta) Kāḻi. The fight is enacted only once in this temple, on the evening of Vijayadaśamī.

As is common in smaller temples of independent goddesses, the ritual is carried out by the ritualized slaying of a banana tree, which substitutes for the rarer *vaṉṉi* tree. First, the priest performs *pūjā* to the tree, which for the occasion is placed in line with the sanctum just outside the temple. He dresses it in a *dhoti* (traditional clothing for men) and offers it an oil lamp, incense, puffed rice, a cigar, a banana, and coconuts. Ablutions are performed to it, and the trunk is smeared with turmeric and dotted with *kuṅkuma* powder. Next, the priest installs Makiṣa in the tree by reciting a mantra while circumambulating the tree with the *āratī* chandelier and a bell. Then his feet are washed by his son and painted with turmeric and *kuṅkuma* dots, before he enters the sanctum. Inside, to a mounting crescendo of drums and the barely restrained anticipation of the crowd outside, he silently recites another mantra, which makes him fierce and possessed by the goddess. He then runs out of the sanctum wielding a sword and cuts the banana tree in two before he collapses and is quickly carried back into the sanctum. In this way, the goddess, in the form of the priest, kills the demon, in the form of the banana tree. Thereafter, as in the Kāmākṣī temple, *kuṅkuma* and the *āratī* flame are distributed to an eager audience.

While, at least according to one priest, Kāmākṣī must atone for the sin of killing the demon with the *vaṉṉi* tree *pūjā*, implying that she committed a transgression and has to appease other forces, the response to Paṭavēṭṭammaṉ's killing of the demon seems to go in the opposite direction: *she* has to be appeased and cooled down with several ablutions the following day. For this ritual, I joined a group of devotees for a milk pot procession (*pālkuṭam*) and a piercing ritual (*vēltarital*), which are performed simultaneously the morning after Paṭavēṭṭammaṉ's fight. The devotees partaking in these rituals have all tied a protective cord (Tamil: *kāppu*; Sanskrit: *rakṣabandha*) to their wrists, signifying that they are taking up a vow (*vrata*) during the festival to fulfill a prayer.

In an early-morning ritual reserved for women, a group of women start preparing their milk pots, which they will carry in procession and finally pour over the goddess's image. The pots are filled with milk and decorated with turmeric and vermillion, with *nīm* and mango leaves and a coconut on their mouths. The piercing ceremony follows, during which the main priest functions as the lead singer and piercer, accompanied by a group of musicians. Both genders can take part in the piercing ceremony. For hours in the midday heat, there is a palpable tension as some devotees are possessed by various deities while they are pierced. The most common piercing is a spear or a trident through the cheeks, but a few devotees have more elaborate piercings such limes sewn onto their bodies, hooks inserted into their backs to pull small carts housing images of the goddess, or a structure of 108 spears pierced into the stomach, chest, and back.

When the piercings are done, and the milk pots are ready, the procession starts, including the pierced devotees, the women carrying milk pots, and the musicians, some of whom dance as they move along. Among them is also a man who carries a bigger pot that is dressed with a full-sized sari and with a face attached to it in which the goddess Paṭavēṭṭammaṉ is installed through water from the Ganges River.

Reaching the temple, the atmosphere is still ecstatic with drumming and singing, and the women standing in line outside the temple waiting to pour their milk over Paṭavēṭṭammaṉ repeatedly shout, "om *śakti*, om *śakti*." Meanwhile, as the piercings are removed, devotees who were possessed collapse on the ground and are carried into the temple. Several ablutions of the goddess in the sanctum follow, including the milk from the pots, water from 108 conches, and finally the Ganges water from the pot housing Paṭavēṭṭammaṉ. At last, the devotees themselves are sprinkled with water from a specially prepared pot which has been kept in the temple during the festival.

These ablutions, I am told by the priest, cool down the goddess and make her peaceful again after she was ferocious during Navarātri due to her fight with the demon. As the milk pot procession and the piercing ritual also signify the individual vows of the participants who have tied the protective cord, we thus note a double meaning within these rituals: they are performed both for the goddess and for the devotees.

Materiality of the Goddess

Temple Images

In temples of a certain size, there will be at least two images of the main deity (and in some cases of other deities as well): the immovable stone image in the sanctum (*mūlamūrti*, literally "root image") and a portable procession image made of metal (*utsavamūrti*, literally "festival image"). Both are invested with the power of the deity, through elaborate consecration ceremonies bringing forth the divine presence (*pratiṣṭhā*). Both images continually receive worship, although the attention alternates between the two images in ordinary and festival times. Diana Eck has argued that "for most ordinary Hindus, the notion of the divine as 'invisible' would be foreign indeed" (1998, 10). The temple deities in Hinduism are considered forms of the divine brought about and manifested in the statues in their own temples. Accordingly, the temple deities need to act themselves and they need to be acted upon, such as waking them up in the morning and putting them to bed at night, bathing them, adorning them, feeding them, or fanning them and pushing them while seated on swings. The images are in turn treated as if they are affected by their actions and experiences in this world. Eck further suggests that these acts may be seen as constituting "a human grammar of devotion" and that ultimately, God does not *need* them (1998, 48–9).

We have seen how Kāmākṣī (according to one priest) is afflicted with sin from her actions of killing the demon and how she must atone for this on Vijayadaśamī by shooting arrows at the *vaṉṉi* tree, which can relieve such sins. While one could argue that the supreme divine *ultimately* cannot be tainted, the temple deities in rituals are indeed treated as if they could (and likewise, mythology is filled with countless examples of gods doing deeds that affect them).

Particularly during festivals, which usually include public processions, there is an enhanced possibility for both the deities and the priests to attract pollution and the evil eye. Many unforeseen events could happen that could disrupt a festival: the deities could, for example, encounter a funeral procession during their procession through the streets, or ritual pollution could go on unnoticed by the performers, such as menstruating women entering the temple. The purity of the temple, its priests, and deities is highly important, as it is a precondition for the effective performance of ritual within the South Indian Hindu temple (Hüsken 2006, 11). The ritual handbooks used in Brahmanical temples are therefore full of atonement rituals (*prayāścittas*) for "repair" in case something goes wrong in ritual.

In contrast to Kāmākṣī, who needs to atone for killing the demon, the non-Brahmin goddess Paṭavēṭṭammaṉ is not thought to have sinned by the ritual killing, but she must be cooled down from a ferocious "hot" state with ablutions of milk. I argue that the different treatment of the goddesses after the demon killing has to do with the different types of goddesses in question. First, it is important to note that deities are vulnerable to temperature changes and thus affected by hot and cool substances. Although the following is a simplification of a highly ambiguous picture, village goddesses are in general thought to be particularly hot, and the married consorts of the Sanskritic deities (e.g., Sarasvatī, Lakṣmī, Pārvatī) are particularly cool. This is reflected in the village goddesses' lust for nonvegetarian offerings, her heightened sexual energy and malevolent potential (e.g. to inflict diseases), while the cool deities are exclusively benevolent. While the Brahmin interpretation of the *vaṉṉi* tree *pūja* would be that Kāmākṣī as a woman (even more so, a Brahmin woman) is not supposed to kill and needs to atone for it, the interpretation prevalent in non-Brahmin temples is that the tree *is* the demon and needs to be killed. The ferociousness is invoked in the priest by chanting the *mantra* that brings about the possession and the decapitation of the demon (the tree trunk is still outside of the temple as a reminder).[8] The goddess, then, needs to be cooled down and appeased to her calm (*śānta*) year-round state, preventing the unpredictability of the hot and fierce (*ugrā*) village goddess, who was temporarily manifest during the festival.

Here we see how presence is linked to actions of the deities, or their agency, or in the words of Matthew Engelke, "presence is linked to materiality quite closely" (2011, 227). During Navarātri, the goddesses need either atonement or cooling because they have been affected by their fights with the demon. This needs repair through further ritual action in her material and embodied form. Whether affected by pollution, sin, or the need is to be cooled from a "hot" state, it requires further ritual to rectify. The need for atonement and its solution are directly related to the goddess's agency and her interaction with and through her materiality.

Temple Images' Decorations and Transformations through *Alaṃkāras*

One of the most important features of Navarātri is how the goddess is represented in different forms of the divine each day through her evening *alaṃkāras*. For instance, Kāmākṣi is in a Durgā *alaṃkāra* (seated on the lion) on Durgāṣṭamī, and Paṭavēṭṭamma<u>n</u> will be in a Kalkattā Kā<u>l</u>i *alaṃkāra* for Vijayadaśamī (these are the days the demon is considered to be killed in the respective temples). *Alaṃkāras* are part of *pūjā* in temples and not at all particular to Navarātri, but the more elaborate *alaṃkāras* during Navarātri, often depicting the goddess in various forms each day, are specially made for this occasion. Indeed, Navarātri is known for its excellent *alaṃkāras*. As Krishna master, the *alaṃkāra* maker of the Paṭavēṭṭamma<u>n</u> temple told me, one aspect of this practice is didactic: it educates the audience about the various forms of the divine.[9] Moreover, the goddess is considered to actually assume different forms each day of the festival, and the respective *alaṃkāras* leading up to her fight on Vijayadaśamī reflect her changes. Thus, divinity is *present* in the goddess's *mūrti* (image), but awareness of this presence is generated through her *alaṃkāra*.

My impression of the *alaṃkāras* in the Brahmin temples of Kāñchipuram during Navarātri is that they adorn the goddess rather than transform her through the process. Moreover, they are not planned beforehand, as the priests told me that the goddess decides what *alaṃkāra* she wants after her evening ablutions, and they make it accordingly with the flowers, clothes, and jewelry at hand. In the Kāmākṣī temple, the exceptions are the Durgā *alaṃkāra* on the eighth day and the Sarasvatī *alaṃkāra* on the ninth (Sarasvatīpūjā), which are standard every year. The independent goddesses, such as Paṭavēṭṭamma<u>n</u>, on the other hand, tend to have themed *alaṃkāras* that are announced beforehand in the temples' festival program. The *alaṃkāras* of the non-Brahmin goddesses are often very innovative and experimental compared to the more traditional, stereotypical *alaṃkāras* in Brahmin temples.[10] The *alaṃkāras* can take hours to finish, as they are elaborately made with a variety of ingredients. In the Paṭavēṭṭamma<u>n</u> temple they are the results of months of preparations and are among the highlights of the ritual year. Importantly, they also require money, and people sponsor them (according to the priest, the *alaṃkāras* of Navarātri in 2014 each cost up to Rs. 20,000 (approximately US$300; approximately an average monthly salary). While some donors are individuals, others are silk businesses in Kāñchipuram who in turn get their brands exposed in relation to the temple, on huge posters and in the festival program.

One priest connected the difference in *alaṃkāra* styles and practices to the fact that independent goddesses assume ferocious forms to slay the demon, while the Brahmin goddesses, who represented as consorts of male gods, do not (in other Brahmin temples in Tamil Nadu the ritual of conquering the demon may be enacted with either the husband or the son of the goddess shooting arrows at a *vaṉṉi* tree; see Hüsken in this volume and Hernault and Reinchie 1999). In other words, in contrast to the Brahmin goddesses, we find that the independent goddesses are *transformed* through the *alaṃkāras;* here they are not considered mere decorations. Accordingly, Paṭavēṭṭammaṉ, who has manifested in her temple as a peaceful goddess, is considered ferocious during the Navarātri period, until she has killed the demon. Day by day, says her priest, "one *śakti* after another is getting formed in her."

An independent goddess can be depicted as various distinct goddesses (such as Mīnākṣī, Kāmākṣī, Annapūrṉa, or the female saint Āṇṭāḷ), as different forms of herself (i.e., various Māriyammaṉs), or as attributes of the divine (such as the *paṉiliṅka mūrti,* where an ice phallus is constructed around the image, or the *tiriculanāyaki* (lady of the trident) *alaṃkāra,* where the image is depicting a trident, a main weapon of the goddess; rarely, she is also depicted as male gods). In Navarātri 2014, the *mūrti* of Paṭavēṭṭmmaṉ was dressed up in twelve different *alaṃkāras,* some of which transformed the entire sanctum or even the temple.[11] These included the *śrī puṟṟu* (anthill) *Māriyammaṉ alaṅkāram,* in which the goddess is clad into a huge *kuṅkuma* dotted termite hill (figure 8.2) and the *Maḻaimāri* (rain) *alaṅkāram,* in which the temple is turned into a rainstorm with sprinklers and thunder and lightning devices installed on the ceiling. Through her Navarātri *alaṃkāras,* then, Paṭavēṭṭammaṉ, along with her surroundings, is transformed into various manifestations of the divine.

The two final *alaṃkāras* during Navarātri neatly depict the goddess's transformation from ferocious to benevolent, and these two *alaṅkāras* are the only two that stay the same each year (the actual artistic expression, however, is subject to change). On Vijayadaśamī, she is the fierce Kalkattā Kāli, slayer of the Buffalo Demon, pointing her trident toward a figure of the demon (*viṣvarupa taricaṉam alaṅkāram,* "showing of all forms"), the following evening after her milk pot ablutions, she is again the peaceful Paṭavēṭṭammaṉ (*cānta corūpinī alaṅkāram*). In this form, she is adorned with flowers and placed on a swing inside the temple, which for the occasion is clad with leaves and fruits to resemble the peaceful atmosphere of a soothing forest.

Darśana (ritual viewing) of the goddess in her various *alaṃkāras* was emphasized by priests and laypeople alike as the primary reason for devotees come to the temple during the festival. Much like the face masks applied to pots, I argue that the *alaṃkāras* enhance the goddess' presence for the worshippers and make her more prominent in her various forms and appearances. Like an elderly woman said to me, "It is

Figure 8.2. Paṭavēṭṭammaṉ's stone image decorated as an anthill (*puṟṟu Māriyammaṉ alaṅkāram*). As a form of Māriyammaṉ, Paṭavēṭṭammaṉ is represented in her sanctum as a full statue with a head in front. Picture by V. Krishna.

like the goddess herself is walking in front of us." This enhancement of her presence holds true for the traditional *alaṃkāras* as well as the more innovative transformative *alaṃkāras*. These special decorations place form on top of form, and in the case of the non-Brahmin goddesses, presence upon presence (perhaps we could call this "layers of presence"), leading up to the Vijayadaśamī battle and the conquest of the demon.

Prepubescent Girls and Auspicious Married Women

Apart from temple images and pots, another form through which the goddess is worshipped during the festival in homes, *maṭhas* (monastic establishments), and temples is as prepubescent girls (*kanyā, kaṉṉi*) and auspicious married women (*sumaṅgalī*). The unmarried girl and the *sumaṅgalī* are the two most powerful female categories in Tamil Nadu, corresponding to the two types of goddesses mentioned earlier, the ambivalent village goddess and the wholly benevolent wifely goddess. These are the two auspicious and desirable states for females, the *kanyā* being a potential *sumaṅgalī*.[12]

As we saw when discussing the *kolu*, it is generally believed that *pūjās* to the prepubescent girls and the *sumaṅgalīs* reach the goddess through these human females during Navarātri, as temporary manifestations. Unlike in the homes where females are worshipped and honored as representatives of the goddess, however, the goddess is actually invoked and made present in the prepubescent girls and *sumaṅgalīs* who are worshipped in the Kāmākṣī temple. The presence of the goddess is brought about by the priests by means of *mantras* as Kāmākṣī's manifestation as a prepubescent girl, who killed the demon, is invoked in the young girls, and Kāmākṣī "herself" in the women. Then they are worshipped as the goddess. As explained earlier in this chapter, the age of the girls should ideally increase daily during the festival, in accordance of the myth of Bālā Kāmākṣī (Child Kāmākṣī) and the belief that the demon could not be killed by any other than a child younger than nine. The morning after the demon is considered dead, nine girls and nine women are worshipped (along with a young boy) as a tribute to the victorious goddess. One interpretation of this ritual is that along with the increase in age, these *pūjās* empower and mature the goddess for her fight with the demon that is enacted in the temple courtyard the first eight evenings of the festival. There is a direct link between these temporary forms of the goddess and her empowerment that is transferred and manifested through her festival image during Navarātri. Through the materiality of human embodiment, the goddess has agency and provides her own conduit through which she gains the power to kill the demon.

Materiality of the Demon

In the rituals described, the demon is represented as a tree and, in the Kāmākṣī temple, an effigy that needs to be killed to maintain the world order. The *vaṉṉi* tree used for this ritual is particularly interesting, as it carries several layers of interpretation (see Biardeu 1984). We have seen how one priest interprets the *vaṉṉi* tree *pūja* as an atonement "device" for Kāmākṣī, and how others, working alongside within the same temple complex, see it as a form of the demon. As the actual killing of the demon, the purpose of the *vaṉṉi* tree *pūjā* bears similar connotations as the cutting of the banana tree prevalent in non-Brahmin temples. In the Paṭavēṭṭammaṉ temple, the banana tree is, moreover, a stand-in for the rarer *vaṉṉi* tree. We here have an instance of a tree representing another tree representing a demon! Similar rituals, here represented by shooting arrows at or axing a (*vaṉṉi*) tree, can carry totally different interpretations or be considered varieties of the "same" ritual, depending on who is asked, even among ritual specialists. At this point, it becomes tempting to invoke the theories of Frits Staal (1979, 1996), who claims that ritual, because of the diverse meanings attached to one single ritual *has* no inherent meaning, symbolism, or purpose. For Staal, ritual is pure, rule-governed activity, without function, referring to nothing outside of itself, even though he admits that ritual has "useful side effects" such as the ability to create bonds between participants, boost morale, and constitute links with ancestors (Staal 1979, 11).

Whether any ritual *ultimately* carries any meaning I leave as an open question. Rituals may be performed because they have been performed in the same manner for generations, or modeling other rituals. But that does not mean that one cannot project meaning onto a ritual and the substances or material used in ritual action. Indeed, Turner (1967, 50) has written of the "polysemy or multi-vocality" of material symbols and suggests how this attribute explains their value for ritual communication. For the performers and participants of the festival, in homes as well as temples, it is evident that Navarātri consists of meaningful events, as many rituals are performed to cause direct results. As we have seen, the materiality of ritual can affect the participants and the material manifestations themselves. This holds true for the *kolu* dolls, widely believed to cause auspicious results such as marriage and childbirth and general prosperity of the household. It is also the case for the ablutions of Paṭavēṭṭammaṉ that cool down the goddess and finalize the individual vows of the participants. Rituals can also function on a symbolic level, as when a young woman in the Kāmākṣī temple told me, "I think [the fight between the goddess and the demon] is [about] getting rid of evil. Curaṉ (the demon) represents evil, and it is the destruction of that by the divine. So then we can understand that if there is any evil within us and we pray for these nine days, we can eradicate it." Although open to a multiplicity of meanings, then, when applying an emic perspective (which is ignored by Staal), I would therefore not characterize these rituals as meaning*less*, but they are replete with multiple and complimentary meanings for those who participate in them.

Final Remarks

This chapter has explored Navarātri in Kāñchipuram from the domestic auspicious *kolu* assembly of dolls to the fights of the goddess and the demon and its related rituals in temples, in the light of materiality and various manifestations of the divine. The goddess is available for her devotees in many forms during Navarātri and is installed in pots, invoked in females, inaugurated in images, and summoned through possession. Likewise, the demon is present in trees and effigies and is killed by the goddess. While some of the manifestations we have encountered are permanent, such as the deities' temple images, others are installed particularly for the festival, including the pots (both on *kolus* and in temples), the human representatives of the goddess, and the demonic trees. In the case of the *alaṃkāras*, we have seen how ritual ornamentations project layers of presence onto the image of the goddess, enhancing her presence in the devotees' experience of *darśana* (ritual viewing). Moreover, in the case of Paṭavēṭṭammaṉ, fierceness is temporarily projected onto the goddess as she assumes different forms each night, leading up to her battle with the demon on Vijayadaśamī. Finally, she is brought back to her calm year-round state through the final *alaṃkāra* and by means of ablutions.

Further, we have seen how there is a close connection between materiality and action. Materiality very often concerns more than *representing* something else; rather, it is about *becoming* something else (cf. Engelke 2011). Through the presence of the divine, various objects become subjects, possessing agency. That is, through material the goddess and the demon can cause effects and foster consequences, and in turn be affected, in that they become and not merely represent the goddess (or the demon). This agency occurs in interaction with the material world, as the divine both affects and is affected by its surroundings, be it by *mantras*, deeds (such as killing the demon), or in contact with substances like various foods or fluids. In connection with this, we have seen how the two goddesses are offered different ritual "treatments" for killing the demon: Kāmākṣī atoning by shooting arrows at a *vaṉṉi* tree, and Paṭavēṭṭammaṉ cooled down through ablutions. Finally, whether it is through the girls worshipped in the Kāmākṣī temple or by the dolls surrounding the pots on the *kolu*, material representations of the goddess empower her for her fight with the demon.

Notes

I would like to thank Matthew Engelke, Ute Hüsken, and Silje Einarsen for comments on earlier versions of this chapter.

1. Mrs. Padma and her family are Brahmins connected to the Kāmākṣī temple of Kāñchipuram. Most of the practices described here are applicable to many households throughout town, although not all *kolus* will contain the pot housing the goddess, and not all families perform the *pūjās* to girls and women. While keeping a *kolu* has mainly been a practice of Brahmins and other higher castes, the practice is currently being taken up by non-Brahmin communities and seems to rapidly increase in popularity. See Wilson (2015 and this volume) and Ilkama (forthcoming) for more.

2. While Mrs. Padma invokes Kāmākṣī in her pot, others told me that they invoke the three goddesses Durgā, Lakṣmī and Sarasvatī, corresponding to the general idea that the first three days of the festival are reserved for worshipping Durgā, slayer of the Buffalo Demon, the following three days for Lakṣmī, goddess of wealth and prosperity, and the final three for Sarasvatī, goddess of learning.

3. In some homes, these pots are transformed to resemble dolls themselves with spare limbs attached to their pot "body" and jewel-filled hair and faces attached to the coconut "face" that is placed on top of the pot because the goddess, being a fine woman, should be adorned beautifully. Haberman (2013, 149–52) has argued that applying faces on aniconic forms makes a more intimate connection between the divine and the worshipper, as *darśan* becomes easier within an anthropomorphic form.

4. Tamil women are regarded as specific kinds of powerful beings with specific ontological statuses, corresponding and ranging from benevolent goddess to malevolent demons or spirits, depending on their marital status and condition of fertility (Reynolds 1980, 36–37). Apart from the unmarried girl and the auspicious married woman, possibilities in this scheme include unmarried mothers, barren women, women who die during childbirth, and widows. The ideal female status is that of the *sumaṅgalī*, whose auspiciousness is dependent on her possession of a husband and of children.

5. Buying specific dolls for specific purposes is generally a practice found among non-Brahmin households. However, the *kolu* is generally connected to a wish for prosperity of the household and for women to remain *sumaṅgalīs*.

6. Some women even considered *me* (the ethnographer) a form of the goddess. During an interview, while speaking of how the festival is auspicious for married women, an elderly lady blurted out, "See now we have met you! We never thought we would meet you! It is like a *devathai* (divinity) has visited us from another country. So the goddess will come to the house in somebody's *rūpa* [form of a person] only."

7. I observed the festival in the Paṭavēṭṭammaṉ temple in 2009, 2011, 2014, and 2015.

8. Bloch compares words used in ritual settings with things and states, saying that "if words in ritual have little explanatory power but much socially useful ambiguity and are little separated from their context, they begin to perform less as parts of a language and more as *things*, in the same way as material symbols" (1974, 75). Thus, ritual words, including mantras, have a material dimension and function much like material substances used in ritual. For instance, it is *mantras* that bring forth the actual awakening of the goddess in the substances of the pots installed on the *kolu* and in temples, as well as in the body of the priest. For the possessed devotees, songs, and not *mantras*, bring forth the goddess in a similar manner.

9. Note that in the same manner, a *kolu* can be read as a didactic device. Many people told me how they used the set up of dolls for telling mythological stories to their children.

10. By "stereotypical," I mean that the *alaṃkāras* of Kāmākṣī look more like *alaṃkāras* you will find in several other temples and also for other occasions than Navarātri: they are not themed or planned in advance, and fewer ingredients are used (mainly flowers, spare limbs, clothes, and jewelry). The priests take great

pride in fashioning the *alaṃkāras* beautifully, and Kāmākṣī's *alaṃkāras* are equally appreciated by her devotees.

11. Although Navarātri "proper" lasts for nine days with Vijayadaśamī in addition, the festival in this temple is celebrated for twelve days altogether (including, e.g., the tying of the protective cords and the milk pot procession).

12. Rodrigues argues that the Durgā Pūjā elicits the maturation of the pre-pubescent girl into a fertile woman and impels the fertile woman toward marriage and motherhood (2003: 267; see also Rodrigues 2005 and 2009).

References

Primary Sources

Kāmākṣīvilāsa. 1968. Beṅgalūr: Bhāratalakṣmī Mudraṇālayam.

Śrīsaubhāgyacintāmaṇiḥ. Year unknown. Pudukkottai: Sarma's Sanatorium.

Secondary Sources

Bado-Fralick, Nikki, and Rebecca Sachs Norris. 2010. *Toying with God: The World of Religious Games and Dolls*. Waco, TX: Baylor University Press.

Beck, Brenda E. F. 1969. "Colour and Heat in South Indian Ritual." *Man* 4 (4): 553–72.

Biardeau, Madeleine. 1984. "The Samitree and the Sacrificial Buffalo." *Contributions to Indian Sociology*, 18:1.

Bloch, Maurice. 1974. "Symbols, Song, Dance, and Features of Articulation: Is Religion an Extreme Form of Traditional Authority?" *European Journal of Sociology* 15 (1): 54–81.

Eck, Diana L. 1998. *Darśan: Seeing the Divine Image in India*. New York: Columbia University Press.

Engelke, Matthew. 2011. "Material Religion." In *The Cambridge Companion to Religious Studies*, edited by Robert A. Orsi, 209–29. Cambridge: Cambridge University Press.

Fuller, C. J., and Penelope Logan. 1985. "The Navarātri Festival in Madurai." *Bulletin of the School of Oriental and African Studies*, University of London 48 (1): 79–105.

Haberman, David L. 2013. *People Trees: Worship of Trees in Northern India*. New York: Oxford University Press.

Hancock, Mary. 1999. *Womanhood in the Making: Domestic Ritual and Public Culture in Urban South India*. Boulder: Westview.

Hüsken, Ute. 2006. "Pavitrotsava: Rectifying Ritual Lapses." In *Jaina-Itihāsa-Ratha: Festschrift für Gustav Roth zum 90. Geburtstag*, edited by Ute Hüsken, Petra Kieffer-Pülz, and Anne Peters. Marburg: Indica et Tibetica Verlag.

Ilkama, Ina Marie Lunde. Forthcoming. "The Play of the Feminine. Navarātri in Contemporary Kāñchipuram." PhD thesis, University of Oslo.

L'Hernault, Françoise, and Reiniche, Marie-Louise. 1999. *Tiruvannamalai, un lieu saint çivaïte du Sud de l'Inde*, vol. 3: Rites et fêtes, Paris, EFEO.

Reynolds, Holly Baker. 1980. "The Auspicious Married Woman." In *The Powers of Tamil Women*, edited by Susan S. Wadley. Syracuse, NY: Maxwell School of Citizenship and Public Affairs, Syracuse University.

Rodrigues, Hillary. 2009. "Women in the Worship of the Great Goddess." In *Goddesses and Women in the Indic Religious Tradition*, edited by Arvind Sharma. Leiden: Brill.

Rodrigues, Hillary Peter. 2005. "Fluid Control. Orchestrating Blood Flow in the Durgā Pūjā." *Studies in Religion/Sciences Religieuses* 38 (2): 263–92.

Rodrigues, Hillary Peter. 2003. *Ritual Worship of the Great Goddess. The Liturgy of the Durgā Pūjā with Interpretations.* Albany: State University of New York Press.

Shulman, David. 1980. *Tamil Temple Myths: Sacrifice and Divine Marriage in the South Indian Saiva Tradition.* Princeton, NJ: Princeton University Press.

Staal, Frits. 1996. *Ritual and Mantras. Rules without Meaning*. Delhi: Motilal Banarsidass.

Staal, Frits. 1979. "The Meaninglessness of Ritual." *Numen* 26, fasc. 1, 2–22.

Tanaka, Masakazu. 1999. "The Navarātri Festival in Chidambaram, South India." In *Living with Śakti: Gender, Sexuality and Religion in South Asia*, edited by Masakazu Tanaka and Musashi Tachikawa. Osaka: Museum of Ethnology.

Turner, Victor. 1967. "Symbols in Ndembu Ritual." In *The Forest of Symbols: Aspects of Ndembu Ritual.* Ithaca: Cornell University Press.

Wilson, Nicole Alyse. 2015. "Middle-Class Identity and Hindu Women's Ritual Practice in South India." PhD thesis, Syracuse University.

9

Ritual Complementarity and Difference

Navarātri and Vijayadaśamī in Kāñcipuram

UTE HÜSKEN

Kāñcipuram is an old religious center of South India that is characterized by countless sacred buildings and spaces, from small roadside shrines to monumental temples, housing many gods, goddesses, and saints. Among the many different religious traditions present in Kāñcipuram today, Vaiṣṇavism, Śaivism and Śāktism stand out, as their main deities preside over the city from their monumental temples: Viṣṇu as Varadarāja in the Varadarāja Perumāḷ temple, the goddess as Kāmākṣī in the Kāmākṣī Ammaṉ temple, and Śiva as Ekāmbareśvara in the Ekāmranātha temple.

Paying special attention to the representation of the goddess vis-à-vis diverse feminine ideals and to the relationship of gender and power, this chapter first looks into the Navarātri (Tam. *navarāttiri*) celebrations at the Vaiṣṇava Varadarāja Perumāḷ temple, where the ritual prescriptions of the normative texts (Pāñcarātrasaṃhitās) are followed meticulously. As it turns out, the role of the main goddess of the temple, Peruntēvi Tāyār (Tam.; Skt. Lakṣmī), is prominent compared to other festivals of the same temple, yet rather passive when compared to the corresponding Navarātri celebrations in goddess Kāmākṣī's temple in Kāñcipuram.

However, when focusing on the actual performances of the Varadarāja temple—rather than starting from the textual norms—one detects many ritual similarities between the two traditions, accounting for shared cultural values informing the festival performances independent from sectarian affiliation. In addition, at the site of what was to become the model for the South Indian version of the festival (Vijayanagara, today's Hampi), the royal aspects of the festival are enacted by the male god Virūpākṣa, whereas the goddess Pampā assumes a role like that of Kāmākṣī in Kāñcipuram. Like Virūpākṣa's and Pampā's roles in Hampi, Varadarāja's and Kāmākṣī's roles within the festival in Kāñcipuram complement each other. Even though there is no direct interaction between the two deities during the annual ritual calendar, Navarātri defines the sacred space of Kāñcipuram as *one* ritual arena, in which only Kāmākṣī's and Varadarāja's performances together make the festival complete.

The Performative Realization of Normative Texts at the Varadarāja Temple

I shall here first give an outline of the contemporary festival practices at the Varadarāja temple and show how these practices are related to the prescriptions of normative ritual texts.

The rituals in the Vaiṣṇava Varadarāja temple in Kāñcipuram are performed according to the Pāñcarātra mode of worship (see Colas 2013; Rastelli 2013; and Hüsken forthcoming). Yet the two Pāñcarātra texts considered normative in the Varadarāja temple, *Jayākhyasaṃhitā* (ca. ninth century CE; see Sanderson 2009, 69) and *Pādmasaṃhitā* (ca. twelfth century CE; Schwarz Linder 2014, 31) do not mention the festival Navarātri. However, another Pāñcarātra text, *Īśvarasaṃhitā,* deals with this festival in some detail. This text is also well known to the priests at the Varadarāja temple, since many of them receive priestly education in Melkote in Karnataka, where the *Īśvarasaṃhitā* is followed.

According to *Īśvarasaṃhitā* (13.91–146) a festival dedicated to "Hero-Lakṣmī" (*vīralakṣmyutsava*) is to be celebrated in the month *āśvayuja* (September–October; Tam. *puraṭṭāci*). Vīralakṣmyutsava is preceded by a nine-day festival (*navāhotsava*),[1] which starts on the eighth or ninth day of the bright half of the month (*Īśvarasaṃhitā* 13.92.; cf. *Śrīpraśnasaṃhitā* 48.47b–65a; Kane 1958 [5.1], 154, fn. 393). The text prescribes elaborate inaugural rituals of *aṅkurārpaṇa* (planting of the seedlings) and *rakṣabandha* (tying of the protective thread [to the main priest]; *Īśvarasaṃhitā* 13.98–99) at the beginning of the festival, and very elaborate daily worship of the goddess (*Īśvarasaṃhitā* 13.101–11; cf. *Śrīpraśnasaṃhitā* 48.49–50).[2] Of these textually prescribed rituals, today only the daily ablution (*abhiṣeka; Īśvarasaṃhitā* 13.100) of Lakṣmī (Peruntēvi Tāyār; Varadarāja's main consort in the temple) is performed. The festival images of Lakṣmī and Varadarāja spend the nine nights of the festival not in their usual place for the night, their respective shrines' inner cellas, but together in the "mirror hall" close to the temple entrance. Each of the nine festival days, Lakṣmī receives public *abhiṣeka* (an elaborate ablution with water) in front of this mirror hall.

This public ablution of Lakṣmī is a specific element of Navarātri in the temple's annual ritual cycle: during all other festivals, Varadarāja takes center stage. Yet for Lakṣmī's ablutions during Navarātri, Varadarāja usually stays inside the mirror hall. Only on the day of his birth *nakṣatra* (lunar mansion) and on the festival's final day (see below) Lakṣmī shares the stage with him.

Viśvarūpadarśaṇa (literally "viewing of the universal form"), a ritual not specifically mentioned for Navāhotsava in the texts,[3] is an extremely popular feature of this festival at the Varadarāja temple. *Viśvarūpadarśaṇa* takes place before Lakṣmī's daily morning ablution. It is the first sighting of the two deities after they awake. At that time, the devotees can see the deities in their full form, since they are not yet covered with heavy flower decorations, jewelry, and clothes. For this ritual, every morning at six o'clock during Navāhotsava, a milk cow with her calf is brought to the mirror hall, where Varadarāja and Lakṣmī spend the festival nights. When water for the morning worship arrives and the god and goddess are ready, the door of the mirror hall is opened with great fanfare, and the priest performs *ārati* in front of the god and goddess, in sight of the back part of the cow. This ritual is very popular, especially with the Vaiṣṇava Brahmin women living close by. They bring small vessels of fresh cow milk and offer it to Varadarāja and Lakṣmī. After *viśvarūpadarśaṇa* the devotees can enter the mirror hall for individual worship. When the worshippers leave the mirror hall, they receive sips of the offered milk, which some have poured into a vessel to take home.

For the evenings, the text prescribes a procession of the goddess through the village, mounted on a golden palanquin or a portable pavilion decorated with flowers (*puṣpamaṇḍapa*; *Īśvarasaṃhitā* 13.112–13). In actual practice, *both* Lakṣmī and her husband, Varadarāja, are taken in procession out of the temple building, though not beyond the limits of the temple compound. The limitation of Lakṣmī's movements to the temple compound is closely connected to the goddess's status as exemplary chaste and subdued Brahmin wife, who never leaves the house (i.e., temple compound).[4] The text continues that after the procession, the goddess is to be placed on a golden seat in the *āsthānamaṇḍapa* (audience pavilion), where she receives elaborate decoration and is fed lavishly. One part of her food is given to the priest, and the remainder is distributed among the devotees, while verses in her praise are recited and songs are sung. Then Lakṣmī is to be taken back inside the temple (*Īśvarasaṃhitā* 13.113–20). These textual prescriptions are perfectly reproduced in present-day performances with the significant difference that Lakṣmī throughout the evening rituals is *together* with her divine husband. In the evening, both Varadarāja and Lakṣmī leave the mirror hall together and are slowly carried through the large temple courtyard to the hundred-pillar pavilion accompanied by *nātasvaram* music. When they arrive at the pavilion, they are taken up the steps, placed on two swings, and swung for some time to the sound of gentle music. Then they receive food (Tam. *naivetiya*) behind a closed curtain. Next, both are taken onto the platform in the center of the hundred-pillar pavilion. After elaborate ritual services, the water sanctified by the use of the deities (Tam. *tīrttam*) is distributed among the devotees, and the divine couple holds court, while the public is allowed to come near to admire and circumambulate the deities. At that time, women of Vaiṣṇava families, especially those living near the temple, gather in the courtyard, dressed in their best saris. They are often accompanied by their small children, who are dressed up as Vaiṣṇava saints or even as deities. Small boys are often dressed as girls and girls as boys, and young women close to marriageable age wear a sari for the first time. First steps toward marriage arrangements are often made.

At the end of the evening, the divine couple is carried down the stairs of the hundred-pillar pavilion. Then the so-called *pattiyeṟṟakattikkey* is performed. In this ritual, the deities are gently carried down the flight of steps as verses in Varadarāja's honor are recited. These *pattiyeṟṟam* verses praise the male deity and refer to his mythology. Then Varadarāja and Lakṣmī retire for the night into the mirror hall in the temple building. As required by the text, this procedure is followed every day.

The *Īśvarasaṃhitā* (13.121–24) ordains that at the end of the ninth day, a ritual sequence called *mahotsava* is performed: At night, the goddess is to be released from the worship site, and her festival image is taken back to her shrine. The sponsor of the festival (Skt. *yajamāna*) is to give *dakṣiṇā* to the main priest, which ensures the Yajamāna's long life, health, power, splendour, and fame (*Īśvarasaṃhitā* 13.125–26; cf. *Śrīpraśnasaṃhitā* 48.56–59). In contemporary practice, the ninth day is celebrated elaborately. After the morning festival routine, both Varadarāja and Lakṣmī are taken in procession to the temple building that contains Lakṣmī's shrine.[5] A special feature on this occasion is the use of the temple's biggest umbrella during procession, which is twenty-two feet in diameter and weighs almost 390 pounds. I was told that this single huge umbrella symbolizes the union of Varadarāja and Lakṣmī. The deities climb the stairs leading up to the building with the Lakṣmī shrine. There, in the pavilion facing the shrine, Lakṣmī and Varadarāja, along with his two consorts Śrī and Bhū, are placed on a wooden platform facing the main stone image of Lakṣmī inside the shrine. The shrine's doors are kept open. After a public ablution of the festival images and another ablution (*ekānta abhiṣeka*) behind closed curtains, all deities are dressed in white clothes (Tam. *veḷḷai cāttupaṭi*), a special feature of the ninth day of Navarātri at this temple. In this attire, the divine couple proceeds to the hundred-pillar pavilion in the evening.[6] The huge umbrella is used again. The rest of the evening rituals are performed like those of the previous days, ending in the mirror hall. With this, the Navāhotsava is concluded.

The *Īśvarasaṃhitā* (13.127) then prescribes a festival called Mṛgayotsava (Skt.; hunting festival; cf. *Śrīpraśnasaṃhitā* 43.3–4) for the tenth day. This festival focusses entirely on the male god and secures the prosperity of the kingdom. The adorned god is mounted on a horse and provided with weapons. He is led to the shores of a river or lake. There the horse and the weapons are bathed and adorned with special garlands and cloth. They return to the temple in a stately procession through the village, where the horse and the weapons are worshipped again, each with its *mantra* (*Īśvarasaṃhitā* 13.128–32; cf. *Śrīpraśnasaṃhitā* 43.5–6). After the regular worship for the god, he is bathed with twenty-five pots in the *āsthānamaṇḍapa*, where he is also adorned and fed (*Īśvarasaṃhitā* 13.133–34). Then follows the deity's second procession on the horse, during which the god wears his hunting outfit. This procession leads the god and his retinue into the "big forest" (*Īśvarasaṃhitā* 13.135–136; cf. *Śrīpraśnasaṃhitā* 43.7–10). There he is worshipped by forest dwellers and ascetics and is led to a *vahni* tree (Skt. *śamī*, Tam. *vaṉṉi*). The god is placed on a splendid throne at the foot of the tree, where the *puṇyāha* ritual has been performed. The weapons are again worshipped (*Īśvarasaṃhitā* 13.137–39; cf. *Śrīpraśnasaṃhitā* 43.11–15). The priest is to place a leaf of the *śamī* tree on the god's head while reciting the "root-mantra" (Skt. *mūlamantra*) and is then to worship the god elaborately (*Īśvarasaṃhitā* 13.140). He then takes the bow and arrow and shoots four arrows in the four cardinal directions, and one arrow up, another down, while reciting the "weapon-mantra" (Skt. *astramantra*). Then he again worships the god with diverse offerings. According to the text, this is done to conquer all directions, to defeat all enemies, and for the prosperity of the kingdom (*Īśvarasaṃhitā* 13.141–43; cf. *Śrīpraśnasaṃhitā* 43.15–17). In the evening, the god is again placed on the horse and taken in a stately procession through the village back into the temple. There he receives another bath with nine pots, is reunited with his two consorts, and worshipped together with them. With this, the festival is concluded (*Īśvarasaṃhitā* 13.144–46; cf. *Śrīpraśnasaṃhitā* 43.18–23).

Compared to these textual prescriptions, the rituals today are performed in a rather condensed way. After the morning ablutions on the tenth day, Lakṣmī returns to her own shrine. Her part is over, and then only Varadarāja has a role to play. He stays on in the mirror hall from where he leaves the temple compound in the evening, mounted on his horse for the *mṛgayotsava*, the hunting festival. For this, he even leaves his consorts Śrī and Bhū behind.[7] He circumambulates the temple compound on his horse and then returns to the temple courtyard. There he is led on his horse to a space between the huge temple tank and the *śamī* tree (Tam. *vaṉṉimaram*) at the corner in the northwest of the temple building.[8] The tank stands for the water mentioned in the texts. Around the *vaṉṉi* tree's trunk a dhoti is tied. Now the priest declares the day auspicious (Skt. *puṇyāhavacana*). He takes a miniature silver bow and arrow, which he points at different parts of the tree. Then he plucks a leaf and places it at the god's feet, who then is carried on the horse back into the temple. This last part is called *vaṉṉimaram pārivēṭṭai* (Tam., *vaṉṉi* tree hunting festival). The older priests of the Varadarāja temple remember that this hunting expedition once went as far as Rājakulam, a small hamlet around six miles away. There the deity even stayed overnight when the *vaṉṉimaram pārivēṭṭai* was enacted. Since the pavilion in Rājakulam is not under the management of the temple administration anymore and is not properly maintained, this practice was given up.

The descriptions of the Navāhotsava festival in the relevant normative texts and the contemporary practice emphasize the importance of the goddess through her daily ablution, the evening processions, her public "holding court," special worship, and special ornamentation. Also in both text and practice, the tenth day is celebrated as "hunting festival" with the male god as sole actor. Both parts of the festival are today celebrated less elaborately than suggested in the textual prescriptions, but the performance recognizably mirrors the text.[9] The lower scale of the performance compared to the text is underlined by the fact that, despite its length, Navarātri does not count as one of the major festivals at the Varadarāja temple. Yet importantly, this "downscaling" of the festival does not go *against* the texts, as these mention the possibility to perform the festival for less than nine days (*Īśvarasaṃhitā* 13.97–98).

As Rastelli (2015) shows in her investigation of the role of Śrī/Lakṣmī in the *Ahirbudhnyasaṃhitā* (ca. thirteenth century), the Pāñcarātrasaṃhitās only reluctantly integrated the worship of Lakṣmī in her own right into the Pāñcarātra ritual system.[10] It seems that the *Ahirbudhnyasaṃhitā*'s authors/redactors saw the need to tie royal circles to Pāñcarātra ritual specialists by integrating a pre-existing Mahālakṣmī worship popular among kings (Rastelli 2015, 349). The integration of Navarātri into the Pāñcarātra ritual program, as shown here, is another such reluctant compromise, reaching out to royal ritual sponsors but not fully embracing the worship of Lakṣmī in her own right. This is also reflected in the contemporary perception. I was repeatedly told that one special feature of Navarātri at the Varadarāja temple is that *the goddess is always united with Varadarāja* during the nine days of the Navarātri festival. During these nine days, Lakṣmī's active involvement is minimal. Her subdued role is in line with her general representation at the Varadarāja temple as a beautiful and peaceful yet passive goddess, as the exemplary subdued, peaceful Brahmin wife. Moreover, Lakṣmī leaves the scene entirely at the end of the nine days, when the male god takes center stage again. Since I had witnessed the Navarātri celebrations in the Kāmākṣī temple, where the goddess herself fights and kills a demon, I asked the Vaiṣṇava priest, Sampatkumāra Bhaṭṭar, why Lakṣmī is not involved in the hunting festival. He explained:

> The goddess does not do it herself because a lady cannot do it. So it is done by Perumāḷ [Varadarāja]. In other places it is Mahiṣāsuramardiṇī [the goddess as slayer of the buffalo demon], *there* Kālī herself does it. *Here* Perumāḷ kills the demon. Tāyār [Lakṣmī] undertakes a vow [*vratam*] for nine days. Tāyār does *tapas* [asceticism] to destroy the demon. The destruction of the demon is also called *vaṉṉimaram pārivēṭṭai* [*vaṉṉi* tree hunting festival]. But since she is a Tāyār [Lakṣmī as mother], whatever mistakes one does she will not have the mentality to kill the person. She is a kindhearted person. So instead of her, it is Perumāḷ who kills the demon. On behalf of the goddess, Perumāḷ kills him. This is called *vīralakṣmyutsavam*. In all Vaiṣṇava temples this is also called *vaṉṉimaram pārivēṭṭai*.[11]

This gendered distribution of roles is one reason why the first nine days of the festival in the Varadarāja temple are rather unimportant from the priests' perspective, while in the famous goddess temple in Kāñcipuram, the Kāmākṣī temple, Navarātri is one of its two major festivals and constitutes one of the two annual occasions that requires a priest to tie the *rakṣabandha* (Tam. *kāppu*).[12] There is a further noteworthy difference between the two temples, demonstrating the different emphasis placed on the Navarātri festival as a celebration of the goddess: In stark contrast to other festivals celebrated at the Varadarāja temple, which abound in references to local history and mythology (see for example Hüsken 2013), during the Navāhotsava one encounters is no explicit reference to local or to transregional Vaiṣṇava mythology. In contrast, Navarātri at the Kāmākṣī temple is closely connected to both, the mythological fight between the goddess and the demon Mahiṣāsura as narrated in the *Devī Māhātmya*, and to the local version of this myth, where Kāmākṣī as a prepubescent girl fights against the demon Bandhāsura (see Ilkama, this volume). No such narrative appropriation of the festival takes place in the Varadarāja temple. Neither in the ritual texts nor in oral narratives are the relevant passages in the *Mahābhārata* and *Rāmāyaṇa* explicitly referred to (cf. Biardeau 1981).

Kāmākṣī's Ambivalence and Navarātri

In contrast to Lakṣmī in the Varadarāja temple, Kāmākṣī assumes a very active role during the Navarātri celebrations. Most importantly, she herself attacks the demon every evening and finally kills him, even though she is generally presented as a benevolent and peaceful deity.[13] The different roles Lakṣmī and Kāmākṣī assume are closely related to their marital status. While Lakṣmī is undoubtedly a married and auspicious woman,

Kāmākṣī's status is more ambivalent, reflected in her calm and peaceful form on the one hand, and her fight with and killing of the demon on the other. Her ambivalent position is the result of specific historical developments in Kāñcipuram, which allowed Kāmākṣī to retain some of her power as unmarried goddess. Legend has it that the philosopher Śaṅkara (eighth century) subdued and tamed the originally fierce goddess Kāmākṣī by installing a Śrīcakra *yantra* (geometric representation of the goddess) in front of her and by establishing *vaidika* (literally, "Vedic") worship in her temple. The taming of a wild goddess often goes hand in hand with her wedding to a male god of the Sanskrit tradition. And in fact, according to local mythological texts (*māhātmya*), Kāmākṣī is Śiva's bride in the marriage myth of Ekāmranātha, an important form of Śiva in Kāñcipuram (see Schier 2012, chapter 4). Their wedding is enacted during Ekāmranātha's annual Paṅkuṉi Uttiram festival, on the day that falls under the auspicious star *uttiram* in the Tamil month of *paṅkuṉi*.[14] For this celebration, Kāmākṣī's original festival image, Baṅgāru Kāmākṣī (golden Kāmākṣī), had been brought to the Ekāmranātha temple, to participate as his bride in the festival procedures. However, at the end of the seventeenth century, Kāmākṣī's golden festival image was taken to Udayarpalayam (south of Kāñcipuram) to safeguard it from a military expedition of the troops of the Muslim ruler Aurangzeb. Thereafter, Kāmākṣī's golden festival image never returned to Kāñcipuram. Today, Baṅgāru Kāmākṣī is enshrined in a temple in Thanjāvūr (Tanjore). With the removal of Kāmākṣī's golden festival image from Kāñcipuram, the goddess Ēlavārkuḻali, who has a small shrine in the Ekāmranātha temple, took Kāmākṣī's place as the bride in Ekāmranātha's wedding celebrations, and the current festival image of Kāmākṣī serves as a bridesmaid. Despite this, the festival is advertised and understood by most people as the wedding of Ekāmranātha and Kāmākṣī. In contrast to this public perception, Kāmākṣī's priests insist on her independent status and vehemently emphasize that Kāmākṣī is and remains an unmarried goddess. This ambivalent situation with Kāmākṣī as tamed goddess and bride of Ekāmranātha on the one hand, and with Kāmākṣī as an independent and unmarried goddess on the other accounts for her ambivalent role during Navarātri. She is a benevolent and peaceful goddess who at the same time can be the fierce slayer of a demon, activating the power connected to her *unmarried* status and killing the demon herself.

Royal Aspects of Navarātri

While the Varadarāja temple's Navarātri festival emphasizes the goddess in her calm, beautiful, and perfectly subdued form, in text and performance, we see a strong focus on those aspects that reconfirm and celebrate royal power—indicating that this festival in the Pāñcarātra tradition was primarily aimed at royal clients of the priests. These royal aspects are the courts of Varadarāja and Lakṣmī, the recitation of specific verses in Tamil (*pattiyeṟṟam*) in honor of the god-king's deeds, the hunting excursion of the male god outside the temple compound to the *vaṉṉi* tree, his shooting of arrows in the direction of the enemies, and the display of wealth on the bodies of the attending women.[15] We do not know how old these practices at this temple are, but the Varadarāja temple was closely tied to the Vijayanagara kings, and the general pattern of this celebration goes back to their time.[16] The Navarātri festival at the court of the Vijayanagara kings was described by foreign guests, the testimony of whom suggests strong focus on the king and on the revitalization of his kingship as its main message.[17] Portuguese horse dealer Domingo Paes, who witnessed the festival in 1520, reported that the king and his closest acquaintances and relatives sat high up on a platform along with a cloth-covered shrine (chamber) with the king's deity inside. Sometimes, the flower-decorated deity was brought from its temple inside the palace and placed on the king's throne. The flowers were then used by the king to honor his elephants and horses. Buffaloes were sacrificed in front of the deity.[18] When horses were brought in front of the deity and the king, women circumambulated the horses, carrying pots containing lights (Brückner 2014, 93–94). Paes was especially impressed by the ornamentation and jewelry of the king's wives. Paes's description of the presence and roles of women during the Navarātri festival (Brückner 2014, 95) corresponds to the contemporary Navarātri scene in the Varadarāja temple. There, many well-dressed Vaiṣṇava women (mostly the wives of the temple priests) gather in front of the hundred-pillar pavilion, while Varadarāja and Lakṣmī hold court there, mirroring Paes's observations of the king's bejewelled wives. Horse dealer Nuniz, who witnessed Navarātri in 1535, mentions that the Vijayanagara king during a display of troops outside the city limits shot three arrows in the direction of his enemies' territories (Kane 1958, 191ff.). As described above, the god Varadarāja performs this ritual action outside the temple building, on the last day of the festival. While Sarkar (2017, 211–12 and 261ff.) rightly points out that the visitors to the Vijayanagara court did not witness and therefore did not report on the Tantric rituals from which the public was excluded, at the Varadarāja temple such rituals are neither proscribed by the ritual texts, nor are they part of the Vaiṣṇava ritual program today.

We could thus see that in the celebrations of Navāhotsava at the Varadarāja temple, the role of the king is enacted by the "gift-bestowing king," Varadarāja. Similarly, also in Hampi (the site of the former capital of the Vijayanagara empire), the male god Virūpākṣa is equated with the king when the celebrations of the Vijayanagara kings are performatively remembered. In Hampi, the goddess Pampā is the most important goddess (like Kāmākṣī in Kāñcipuram). Like Kāmākṣī, Pampā was integrated into Śaivism through marriage to Virūpākṣa, the state deity of the early Vijayanagara rulers (Brückner 2014, 98, 105). Today the wedding of Pampā and Virūpākṣa is celebrated in Hampi during the spring Navarātri, whereas during the autumnal Navarātri the fierce aspects of a Pampā as a standalone goddess are emphasized. Thus, in contemporary Hampi, Pampā is not confined to the temple area (Brückner 2014, 99f.). She accompanies her husband Virūpākṣa to the *śamī* tree. In Kāñcipuram, however, Kāmākṣī resists the alliance with Ekāmranātha and continues to be presented as an unmarried yet benevolent goddess, who resumes her fierce form only when killing the demon.

Although the unmarried fierce goddess who slays the demon and the victorious king who renews his royal power are enacted separately in different temples in Kāñcipuram, by Kāmākṣī and Varadarāja respectively, through comparison with contemporary practice in Hampi, we can see that they are *actually* two complementary parts of one unit. Kāmākṣī as the local warrior goddess and former tutelary deity of the royal lineage,[19] complements the royal *avatāra* of Viṣṇu.[20] Here we encounter a "division of labor" between Kāmākṣī and Varadarāja, the one representing the goddess's role and the other the role of the king, which only together make a "complete" Navarātri.[21]

Similarity, Difference, and Complementarity

Even though three powerful Hindu traditions and their temples share the limited space of the small temple town, a casual observer would notice very little *direct* interaction between the main deities in Kāñcipuram during the annual ritual calendar. Yet Navarātri is one important occasion temporarily defining the sacred space of Kāñcipuram as *one* ritual arena, in which only Kāmākṣī's and Varadarāja's performances seen *together* constitute important aspects of the festival, thus reinforcing the idea of Kāñcipuram as *one* sacred space (named for example *satyavratakṣetra*), as it is consistently represented in the diverse Māhātmyams.

In addition, we need to acknowledge a shared cultural imagination relating to goddess veneration, which is expressed first and foremost in the domestic Navarātri celebrations, which are very similar and independent from the houses' sectarian affiliation (see Ilkama and Shivakumar in this volume).[22] In the temples, this overlap is most obvious in the ritual sequences associated with the *vaṉṉi* tree. Varadarāja's senior priest Sampatkumāra Bhaṭṭar explained the events as follows (20.9.2006):

> On the day of Vijayadaśamī, a demon is killed. It is a *pārivēṭṭai* [hunting] festival. In the evening, he [Varadarāja] goes on the

> horse for *pārivēṭṭai* and comes back . . . The tree is considered to be the demon. We will tie a *vastram* [a white cloth] to the tree and consider the tree the demon. Then in eight directions eight arrows are shown, and then follows a shot at the tree. With this the demon is killed. On that day the *vaṉṉi* tree treated as demon and Perumāḷ [Varadarāja] shoots several arrows and kills the demon.

He also explained that the leaf of the *vaṉṉi* tree that is placed at the god's feet signifies this demon's defeat. While no demon is mentioned in the ritual texts of the Varadarāja temple, the motif of a demon who is to be killed is prominent in the Navarātri celebrations of goddess temples. In the Kāmākṣī temple, the goddess publicly fights with a demon, whom she finally defeats on the last evening of the festival. In contrast to the priest's interpretation, the *Īśvarasaṃhitā* (13.141–43) equates this ritual act not with the killing of a demon but with the conquering of all directions, symbolizing the defeat of all the king's enemies and securing the prosperity of the kingdom. The priest's explanation thus implicitly links the performance at the Varadarāja temple to the performances at the goddess temples in town, rather than reflecting his own tradition's textual norms. Biardeau (2004) shows that the *vaṉṉi* tree is closely related to the Vedic sacrificial post, to which the sacrificial animal (a buffalo) is tied, and that the tree's wood is the container of the sacrificial fire. The connection of the tree, the post, the sacrificial fire, the animal, and the killing of this animal (understood as a minor god or demon) is thus alive in the priest's interpretation of the rituals, even though this tradition's normative texts do not insinuate any of this.

When focusing on the actual performances—rather than starting from the textual norms—we detect even more ritual overlap between the two traditions, expressive of shared cultural values informing the festival performances independent from sectarian affiliation. In the Kāmākṣī temple, the daily worship (*pūjā*) of prepubescent girls (*kanyā*) and of auspicious married women (*suvāsinī*) is performed. *Kanyās* and *suvāsinīs* are defined in terms of their state in the reproductive cycle: prepubescent girls are potentially fertile but have not realized their fertility (and are therefore also potentially dangerous), and *suvāsinīs* have enacted their fertility and are therefore highly auspicious. Rodrigues (2009, 275) convincingly interprets the *kanyā pūjā* as a ritual that serves to provoke the *kanyā's* menarche and thus to turn her into a fertile woman. Similarly, also at the Varadarāja temple there exist references to female fertility, even though these are not as obvious. Yet I argue that the Navarātri *viśvarūpadarśaṇa* ritual at the Varadarāja temple might also be interpreted in these terms. During this ritual, the reproductive parts of a milk-giving cow with her calf and the divine couple face each other; they are venerated together, and the offering of the predominantly female devotees is milk. The *kanyā pūjā* and the *suvāsinī pūjā* of the Kāmākṣī temple thus implicitly resonate with the elaborate form of the *viśvarūpadarśaṇa* ritual of the Varadarāja temple. While this aspect of the festival is much more hidden in the Varadarāja temple than the *suvāsinī* and *kanyā pūjās* of the Kāmākṣī temple, the rituals at both temples following Brahmin ritual norms point toward a celebration of female fertility and maybe even toward attempts to manipulate fertility.[23]

The Navarātri festivals at the Brahmin temples in Kāñcipuram are enactments of normative ritual prescriptions based on the agenda of those who promote them. Yet there is more to Navarātri. Overlaps of interpretation and performance, which are not confirmed by the textual norms, are based on the physical proximity of the temples, on the shared social setting and norms of the celebrants, and on the shared cultural frame of reference of the traditions. The festival is important to the performers, participants, and spectators as an event that displays and negotiates cultural values relevant to them. This shows that the elements of successful festivals need to be open to different interpretations by different participants. A *vaṉṉi* tree can thus be fire, the king's enemy, a buffalo or the residence of a demon; the goddess can be married, unmarried, ferocious or subdued. It all depends on whom you ask. Yet importantly, while Navarātri is celebrated and understood in very different ways, it remains *one* festival.

Notes

I wish to thank Ina Ilkama, Moumita Sen, Caleb Simmons, Jenn Wilson, and Brigitte Luchesi for their input on earlier versions of this chapter.

1. The *Īśvarasaṃhitā* also allows for a shorter duration (from three to nine days), yet today the festival always is celebrated for nine days, followed by special rituals on the tenth day. The duration of the festival determines the outcome for the performer (*Īśvarasaṃhitā* 13.97–98). Only the nine-day *vaiṣṇava* festival is said to bring both *bhukti* and *mukti* (*Īśvarasaṃhitā* 13.93–94). The *Puruṣottamasaṃhitā* (27.22–30) similarly describes the *vīralakṣmyutsava*; see Smith and Venkatachari (1980, s.v.). See also *Tithitattva* as quoted by Kane (1958, 154).

2. Today, no *rakṣabandha* is tied by the performing priests. The acting priests of the festival days are those whose turn it is to serve the Lakṣmī shrine on that day. Yet the goddess does in fact have a *rakṣabandha* tied around her left wrist during the Navarātri festival. The worship described there, which includes the invocation of the goddess in *kumbha, maṇḍala, bimba* and *vahni*, is performed in the Varadarāja temple only during Pavitrotsava (see Hüsken 2006) and only for the male deity Varadarāja.

3. While *viśvarūpadarśaṇa* is supposed to take place daily with a cow and calf, at the Varadarāja temple, such elaborate public *viśvarūpadarśaṇa* is performed only during the mornings of the Navarātri festival.

4. In the local Vaiṣṇava Brahmanic tradition, women, and by extension the goddess, are ideally confined to the house. All processions of the goddess take place only within the temple compound. *Śrīpraśnasaṃhitā* (48.50–55) replaces "village" with "house" in the corresponding passage and thus is closer than *Īśvarasaṃhitā* to the actual practice at the Varadarāja temple.

5. They first briefly step out of the temple and pay a visit to the Vedānta Deśika shrine close to the entrance of the temple building, since his birth *nakṣatra* is celebrated on that day. Both local groups of Vaiṣṇavas (Teṉkalai and Vaṭakalai) start their recitation (*ghoṣṭi*) after Vedānta Deśika has greeted the deities.

6. On their way to the hundred-pillar pavilion in the evening, as the deities are taken down the steps of the Lakṣmī shrine, *pattiyeṟṟam* is recited.

7. Also during the other hunting festival celebrated at the Varadarāja temple (the Palayacīvaram *pārivēṭṭai*, performed on January 16 every year) the god leaves the temple without his female consorts.

8. This *vaṉṉi* tree in the Varadarāja temple was planted in the late 1990s. Before this tree had been planted, a branch of a *vaṉṉi* tree was brought to the same spot and tied to a banana tree trunk that was set up there for the occasion. Biardeau and others have repeatedly described how branches of *vaṉṉi* trees are tied to other trees.

9. In contemporary practice, Navarātri is overshadowed by the celebration of the birth *nakṣatra* of Vedānta Deśika of the Viḷakkoli temple in Tūppūl (Kāñcipuram). This coincides either with the last day of Navarātri or with Vijayadaśamī.

10. The only Pancarātra text assigning a central role to Śrī/Lakṣmī is the *Lakṣmītantra* (Rastelli 2015, 327).

11. However, I was told that in the Pāñcarātra Pārthasārathi temple in Triplicane (Chennai) no *vaṉṉimaram pārivēṭṭai* takes place, since this killing of a demon is considered "folklore."

12. *Rakṣabanda* is shared between three hereditary priestly families at the Kāmākṣī temple. The families take turns each year with the responsibility for the two major festivals, Navarātri and Mahotsava. Like Mahotsava, Navarātri includes for example a daily *śrīvidyāhoma* and an *avabhṛtasnāna* at the end.

13. The role of Kāmākṣī during the defeat of the demon is slightly ambivalent, since Durgā accompanies her for the final fight during the last evening. This reflects a distancing of the goddess from the act of killing, not unlike Caṇḍī in the *Devī Māhātmya*, who creates Kālī for those tasks "that appear too impure for her to do it herself" (Biardeau 2004, 311).

14. The first literary references to festivals at the Ekāmranātha temple are from the fourteenth century, yet none of them mentions the marriage festival specifically (Schier 2012, 50). However, one inscription from 1312 CE in the Kāmākṣī temple explicitly refers to the Paṅkuṉi Uttiram festival (Schier 2012, 53).

15. Stein (1983) refers to the fact women from important temples in the king's realm came to perform in front of the king, just like they would perform in front of the god. Interestingly, the ninth (and most elaborate) day of Navarātri in the Varadarāja temple is sponsored by descendants of the temple's former *devadāsīs*.

16. For details, see Varada Tatacharya (1978). The earliest inscription referring to a festival celebrated in Puraṭṭāci is from the thirteenth century. K. V. Raman (1975, 105 fn 45: 432 of 1919) suspects that this inscription refers to Navarātri, though the name of the festival is not given therein. Another epigraph dated

1530 CE refers to a Mahālakṣmī festival in Puraṭṭāci 1530 (1983). The *vaṉṉi*-tree festival is also mentioned in this record of 1530 (1975, 105; fn 47: SITI No. 378).

17. This annual ceremony as celebrated by Vijayanagara kings subsequently became known in many parts of South India, until it was finally adopted by many minor royal houses. Brückner (2014, 96–98) shows that we find a surprising continuity in the celebration of the festival at the courts of later dynasties. She also emphasizes the appeal of these rituals also for contemporary Indian states (Brückner 2014, 105; cf. Sarkar 2017, 211, 261ff.).

18. In the temples following Brahmin ritual norms of Kāñcipuram today, there is no indication of *bali* (blood sacrifice) in the celebrations (cf. Kane 1958, 184); on the ritual texts demanding *bali* for Kāmākṣī, see Ilkama in this volume.

19. It is certainly no coincidence that the Kāmākṣī temple is in the area where the royal palace might have stood and that the only animal sacrifice for the (vegetarian) male god Varadarāja takes place at the border between the Kāmākṣī's and Varadarāja's spheres, today Viṣṇu Kāñci and Śiva Kāñci, respectively.

20. Importantly, Varadarāja's local form emerges from the god Brahma's *aśvamedha*, the prototype of a royal sacrifice.

21. Fuller implicitly points to such a division of labor, stating that from the viewpoint of the "high" Brahmanic tradition, the goddess's slaying of the buffalo demon signals the end of demonic supremacy and the recreation of a kingly order (Fuller 2004, 108–9).

22. In the temple, male priests are the main agents, but in the homes of priestly families related to the Kāmākṣī and the Varadarāja temples, women oversee the ritual proceedings, and women and children are the main participants. While in the homes of the Kāmākṣī temple priests *kanyā pūjā* is also performed on a regular basis, this is not the case in the homes of the priests of the Varadarāja temple.

23. Many medieval ritual texts describe the honoring of *kanyās* or *suvāsinīs* (see Kane 1958, 191). For the people connected to the Varadarāja temple, the honoring of girls and women is confined to the domestic setting, where the women visit each other and admire and worship the *kolus* set up there (see Ilkama and Shivakumar in this volume).

References

Primary Sources

Īśvarasaṃhitā. Prativādibhayaṅkarānantācāryais saṃśodhita (Śāstramuktāvaḷi 45). Kāñcī, 1923.

Jayākhyasaṃhitā. Crit. ed. with an Introduction in Sanskrit, Indices etc. by Embar Krishnamacharya (Gaekwad's Oriental Series 54), Baroda, 1931.

Pādmasaṃhitā. Padma Samhita. (Part I): crit. ed. by Seetha Padmanabhan and R. N. Sampath; (Part II): Crit. ed. by Seetha Padmanabhan and V. Varadachari (Pancaratra Parisodhana Parisad Series 3 & 4). Madras, 1974, 1982.

Śrīpraśnasaṃhitā. Śrīpraśna Saṃhitā. Ed. by Seetha Padmanabhan with the foreword of V. Raghavan (Kendrīyasaṃskṛtavidyāpīṭhagranthamālā 12), Tirupati, 1969.

Secondary Sources

Biardeau, Madeleine. 2004. *Stories about Posts: Vedic Variations around the Hindu Goddess*. Translated by Alf Hiltebeitel, Marie-Louise Reiniche, and James Walker. Chicago: University of Chicago Press.

———. 1981. "L'Arbre *śamī* et le buffle sacrificiel." In *Autour de la déesse hindoue*, edited by Madeleine Biardeau, 215–43. Paris: Éditions de l'École des Hautes Études en Sciences Sociales.

Brückner, Heidrun. 2014. "Sakrales Königtum? Bildliche, literarische und performative Hinweise auf die Rolle des Königs in der Festkultur Vijayanagaras." In *Wege zum Heil(igen)? Sakralität und Sakralisierung in hinduistischen Traditionen*, edited by Karin Steiner, 91–118. Wiesbaden: Harrassowitz.

Colas, Gérard. 2013. "Vaiṣṇava Saṃhitās." In *Brill's Encyclopedia of Hinduism*, edited by Knut A. Jacobsen, Helene Basu, Angelika Malinar, and Vasudha Narayanan. Brill Online.

Fuller, Christopher J. 2004. *The Camphor Flame: Popular Hinduism and Society in India*. Rev. and expanded edition. Oxford: Princeton University Press.

Hüsken, Ute. Forthcoming. "Vaiṣṇava Temple Traditions: Vaikhānasa and Pāñcarātra." In *Many Vaiṣṇavisms: Histories of the Worship of Viṣṇu*, edited by Archana Venkatesan. Oxford: Oxford University Press.

———. 2006. "Pavitrotsava: Rectifying Ritual Lapses." In *Jaina-Itihāsa-Ratna. Festschrift für Gustav Roth zum 90. Geburtstag*, edited by Ute Hüsken, Petra Kieffer-Pülz, and Anne Peters (Indica et Tibetica 47), 265–81. Marburg: Indica et Tibetica.

———. 2013. "Flag and Drum: Managing Conflicts in a South Indian Temple." In *South Asian Festivals on the Move*, edited by Ute Hüsken and Axel Michaels, 99–135. Wiesbaden: Harrassowitz.

Kane, P. V. 1958. *History of Dharmaśāstra (Ancient and Mediaeval Religious and Civil Law)*. Vol. 5.1, *Government Oriental Series*. Poona: Bhandarkar Oriental Research Institute.

Raman, K. V. 1975. *Śrī Varadarājaswāmi Temple, Kānchi: A Study of Its History, Art and Architecture*. New Delhi: Abhinav.

Rastelli, Marion. 2015. "Mahālakṣmī: Integrating a Goddess into the Ahirbudhnyasaṃhitā." *Indo Iranian Journal* 58: 325–56.

———. 2013. "Pāñcarātra." In *Brill's Encyclopedia of Hinduism*, edited by Knut A. Jacobsen, Helene Basu, Angelika Malinar, and Vasudha Narayanan. Brill Online.

Rodrigues, Hillary Peter. 2009. "Fluid Control: Orchestrating Blood Flow in the Durgā Pūjā." *Studies in Religion / Sciences Religieuses* 38 (2): 264–92.

Sanderson, Alexis. 2009. "The Śaiva Age—The Rise and Dominance of Śaivism during the Early Medieval Period." In *Genesis and Development of Tantrism*, edited by Shingo Einoo, 41–349. Institute of Oriental Culture, University of Tokyo.

Sarkar, Bihani. 2017. *Heroic Shāktism: The Cult of Durgā in Ancient Indian Kingship*. Oxford: Oxford University Press.

Schier, Kerstin. 2012. "The Goddess's Embrace: Multifaceted Relations at the Ekāmranātha Temple Festival, Kanchipuram." PhD thesis, IKOS, Oslo University.

Schwarz Linder, Silvia 2014. *The Philosophical and Theological Teachings of the Pādmasaṃhitā*. Vol. 853, *Beiträge zur Kultur- und Geistesgeschichte Asiens*. Wien: Österreichische Akademie der Wissenschaften, Philosophisch-Historische Klasse.

Smith, H. Daniel, and K. K. A. Venkatachari. 1980. *A Descriptive Bibliography of the Printed Texts of the Pāñcarātrāgama, Vol. II. An Annotated Index to Selected Topics*. Vol. 168, *Gaeckward's Oriental Series*. Baroda: Baroda: Oriental Institute.

Stein, Burton. 1983. "Mahanavami: Medieval and Modern Kingly Ritual in South Indian History." In *Essays on Gupta Culture*, edited by Bardwell Smith, 3–51. Durham: Duke University Press.

Varada Tatacharya, R. 1978. *The Temple of Lord Varadaraja, Kanchi: A Critical Survey of Dr. K. V. Raman's Sri Varadarajaswami Temple, Kanchi*. 1st ed. Kanchi / Madras: Sri Tatadesika Tiruvamsastar Sabha.

NAVARĀTRI INSIDE

10

Bengali Durgā Pūjā

Procedures and Symbolism

HILLARY RODRIGUES

The Durgā Pūjā is a complex series of devotional rites to worship the Great Goddess, who is generally referred to as Devī, Mā, or Durgā. The rite typically takes place during the *śāradiya* Navarātra (or Navarātri), which occurs during the first nine days of the waxing fortnight (*śukla pakṣa*) of the autumn month of Āśvina. Throughout India there is a palpable excitement in the air as Navarātra approaches. In large cities where the Durgā Pūjā will be celebrated, such as Kolkata (Calcutta) and Benares, boys' clubs solicit money to arrange communal performances, and dozens of images of Durgā and her attendant deities are fabricated in the workshops in the artisanal quarters.

Pūjā is a process through which a deity is invoked and established into a particular place and form, such as an image (*mūrti*), rendered veneration, often through service and offerings, known as *upacāra*, and finally dismissed. Simple five-part *pūjās* or *pañcopacāra pūjā* mostly center on five typical offerings (*gandha* [fragrant anointing], *puṣpa* [fresh flowers], *dhūpa* [fragrant incense], *dīpa* [a flame], and *naivedya* [an edible]), which are rendered to a deity that has already been established in a home shrine or temple. The invocation and dismissal rites are naturally absent in those settings. Whereas a simple *pūjā* to an already established deity may take a few minutes, the Durgā Pūjā has a duration of several days and appears dazzling in its complexity. Some of the Durgā Pūjā's complexity derives from the lengthy processes of invoking and installing the Goddess into a plethora of forms but also from the wide assortment of services and offerings that are then rendered to her. Anyone in attendance watches how, with great dexterity and clear purpose, the ritualist (*purohita*) ministers to a colorful tableau of the goddess Durgā slaying the buffalo demon Mahiṣa that stands before him. For days, he will manipulate flowers, foods, oils, pastes, waters, and unusual implements. He will perform an assortment of *mudrās* (ritual gestures) and draw a variety of *yantras* (ritual diagrams), while uttering a lengthy litany of prayers and sacred utterances (*mantra*). There are many types of Durgā Pūjā celebrated and practiced in India and abroad, but my focus is on the Bengali style where Tantric variants may be substituted for Vedic prayers. The Bengali style is not regionally marginal, or minor, because it has influenced the widespread community Durgā Pūjās that entail setting up temporary public shrines (*paṇḍal*) and establishing the Goddess in a polychrome unbaked clay image group. The group consists of Durgā and her lion, Mahāsiṅgha, slaying the buffalo demon, Mahiṣa, which often form a triad, along with four accompanying deities, namely, the goddesses Sarasvatī and Lakṣmī, and the gods Gaṇeśa and Kārttikeya (cf., previous scholarly studies of the Durgā Pūjā by Ghosha [1871] and Östör [1980]).

The description of the Durgā Pūjā provided here summarizes material presented in my detailed study (Rodrigues 2003). It is based on close observations of the rite in 1990 and 1991, performed in Benares by the master ritualist Pandit Nitai Bhattacharyya at the home of Manindra Lahiri. Mr. Lahiri was a Bengali *zamīndār*, a hereditary landlord from Rangpur, in east Bengal, whose family had lost their landholdings when the region was partitioned into east Pakistan in 1947. He eventually retired to the home that his family kept in Benares, where his ancestors had been celebrating the Durgā Pūjā since the 1890s. The Lahiris had always conducted an elaborate Durgā Pūjā in their home, even in Rangpur, and there was a bit of an open-door policy for friends and neighbours to join in the celebrations on Saptamī, Aṣṭamī, and Navamī, the seventh, eighth, and ninth days of Navarātra. Theirs was one of the few traditional Durgā Pūjās to endure in a domestic setting, because only communities and organizations now seem able to afford the growing costs. I spent the intervening year between the two iterations in 1990 and 1991 and subsequent years accumulating information on the sequence of ritual actions, the actions themselves, such as the performance of *mudrās* and *yantra* construction, the invocation verses and *mantras* of worship, and a host of other details by studying with Pandit Hemendranath Chakravarty. Pandit Chakravarty had been a student of the renowned Tantric scholar, Gopinath Kaviraj, and much of what I know about the Durgā Pūjā derives from his enormous corpus of knowledge on the ritual, which he had both studied and performed dozens of times. I also extracted symbolic meanings applied to the rite through informal conversations and interviews with him, members of the Lahiri family, and scores of others in Benares during my visits to the city and when observing other iterations of the Durgā Pūjā in India and abroad.

It may be an oversimplification to speak of *the* Bengali Durgā Pūjā, because there are variations even among these, based on the prescribed sources from which their forms had developed. Such prescriptions are found in certain Purānas, such as the *Kālikā, Devī,* or *Bṛhannandikeśvara.* They may also derive from various *nibandhas* (*dharmaśāstra* digests), some of which were quite Tantricized, such Raghunandana Bhaṭṭācārya's *Durgāpūjātattva,* composed in the sixteenth century CE (Sarkar 2012). The Lahiri family's Durgā Pūjā tradition was apparently influenced by the *Durgābhaktitaraṅgiṇī* (*Waves of Devotion to Durgā*), attributed to Vidyāpatī, a fifteenth-century poet from Mithilā in northeast India. The priest's ritual style aligned with prescriptions found in the *Purohita Darpaṇa* (*Mirror for the Priest*), which is a popular, comprehensive manual (*paddhati*) among contemporary Bengali ritualists for all types of *pūjās* (see S. Bhattacharya 1973–74). Despite these variations, there are core features shared by most of the Bengali Durgā Pūjās.

It is crucial to recognize at the outset that the realities of rituals differ markedly from generic descriptions and prescriptions in ritual manuals, and even shift from year to year. Every iteration of a *pūjā* is unique. Ronald Grimes (2014, 308) makes this point when distinguishing between ritual performance and competence. He indicates that ritual performance, which is what people do, is like speech in that it can be culturally malleable. However, competence, which is more deeply rooted, and somewhat akin to grammar (as opposed to speaking), is far less malleable. So, variations in competence may be evaluated against some standard, whereas variations in types of performances may not. My discussion here pertains to performance more than competence. It is also worth remembering that just as ritual is malleable, so are the meanings ascribed to ritual action. Frits Staal (1989) argued, somewhat extremely, that humanity's rituals, particularly ancient Vedic ones, are rule-based activities without meaning and perhaps derive from our prerational instinctive predispositions. While he may be correct about the origins of humanity's ritualistic propensities, it is evident that as our rational faculties developed, we began to create symbols and ascribe meanings to them and to seek meanings in what we perceive as symbols. And thus, our ritual lives enact a somewhat mysterious interplay between symbols and meaning.[1]

By mysterious interplay, I mean that certain symbols can yield to exegesis, or the elucidation of the meanings associated with them, while others may be magnets for eisegesis, attracting to themselves an overlaying of meanings that were never originally there. The ninth day of the waxing lunar fortnight in the autumn month of Āśvina may never have originally meant anything, but over time it has come to mean, among other things, the great day of the Great Goddess. While a scholar of religion should not engage in eisegesis, it is not an uncommon practice for religious "insiders" to do so. But when insiders engage in eisegesis and superimpose new meanings onto symbols that had no meaning or different meanings up to that point in time, these new meanings now become valid objects for a scholar's exegesis. So, ritual is alive, not only thorough the transformations wrought by the ritualist but within the hearts and minds of all in attendance who participate in the life of the rite. With that short prelude, let us examine some of the key procedures of the Bengali style of Durgā Pūjā and exegete some of the symbols within its vibrantly living ritual actions. Given the complexity and symbolic richness of the rite, there are no pretensions that the discussion here is in any way comprehensive.

Procedures of the Durgā Pūjā

The Durgā Pūjā typically begins with the *bodhana* (awakening rite) and ideally takes place in the vicinity of a *bilva* (wood-apple) tree. This normally occurs on the sixth day of Navarātra, or on the evening of the fifth day (*pañcamī*) if the sixth lunar day (*ṣaṣṭhī tithi*) will end before four p.m. Since the Durgā Pūjā takes place in autumn, when the gods are generally regarded as sleeping, this rite is often called an *akāla bodhana* (untimely awakening). The term relates to a myth best known through the Bengali *Rāmāyaṇa* by Kṛttivāsa (c. fifteenth century CE), in which the desperate prince Rāma wakes up the Goddess, unseasonably, to enlist her help in defeating his demon adversary, Rāvaṇa.[2] The liturgical procedures and complete litany of Sanskrit prayers with their translations are found in my 2003 study (Rodrigues 2003, 84–120). I will hereafter refer to sections of that study, from which I derive the relevant summary descriptions that follow. The Goddess is first awakened in the *bilva* (wood-apple) tree, and from there, she is established in a jar or pot effigy, referred to as the *ghaṭa* or *kalaśa*. If there is no *bilva* tree present, a branch from the tree, ideally possessing two pieces of fruit symbolizing the Devī's breasts, is ritually severed, "planted" in a pot, and taken to the ritual space (*pūjālaya*).

The *purohita* then draws a sacred diagram (*yantra*) upon the ground. This may be a simple downward pointing triangle or the more elaborate *sarvatobhadra maṇḍala*, into which the Goddess will be more formally established on the eighth day. Onto this *yantra*, a low altar of soil is constructed, identified as Aditi, the mother of the gods, and as the goddess Earth, supporter of the world. The *purohita* sows five types of grain into the altar and places a narrow-necked, wide-bodied jar atop it. The earthen or metal jar is filled with water, has five types of leaf-bearing twigs placed in its mouth, and is topped, ideally, with a twig-bearing green coconut, a symbol of fertility. It is shrouded with a scarf until it resembles a pregnant or squatting woman wearing a sari. The Devī, as Śrī, the goddess associated with grace and bounty, is invoked into the jar. This brimming jar, the *pūrṇa kalaśa,* the Asian equivalent of the cornucopia, is an ancient symbol of fertility and abundance often found in iconographic contexts with Lakṣmī and the lotus. In the Bengali rite, if the period of auspicious time is short, the priest may opt to use the Tantric method of installing the jar (*ghaṭasthāpana*) by uttering simple seed syllables such as Strīṃ, or Huṃ at each phase, instead of lengthy Vedic verses. When the jar is being filled with pure water, the priest invokes all rivers, beginning with the Gaṅgā, to abide in it. Thus, the element (*bhūta*) of water (through all the riverine goddesses), along with the earth element (in the earthen altar and clay jar), and the vital essence of life (in the seeds, the leaf-bearing twigs, the green coconut, and a fruit-bearing *bilva* tree branch) are all present at the very inception of the Durgā Pūjā. These motifs, of the amalgamation of the constituent elements of the cosmos, will recur repeatedly.

Figure 10.1. Devī embodied in a jar atop the Sarvatobhadra Maṇḍala.

For most devotees, the Durgā Pūjā proper begins on Mahāsaptamī, the so-called Great Seventh day of Navarātra. However, as we have seen, the crucial *bodhana* rites actually begin on the sixth or even the fifth day. A significant rite of the sixth day is the *adhivāsanam* (or *adhivāsa*), or perfuming (see Rodrigues 2003, 120–32). During the *adhivāsa*, as many as twenty items are offered to the jar and the *bilva* tree, and then to all the other abodes into which the Devī will subsequently be invoked, such as the Navapattrikā (a cluster of nine leaves or plants), the sacrificial sword or mirror, and the clay images. The items offered in this perfuming rite include sandalwood paste (*gandha*), soil, a small stone, rice, flowers, *dūrvā* grass, collyrium, cow bile, yellow mustard, precious metals, a mirror, and a fly whisk (*cāmara*). Again, I note the many elemental substances that are offered, as well as items pertaining to royalty. If the *bodhana* was the awakening rite, one could imagine the *adhivāsa* as a sort of "getting up" process, because as the abodes of the goddess are anointed with each item, the *purohita* continuously rings a bell. A *dhāk* drum may also be sounded continuously. The sounds not only symbolically arouse the Devī; they enliven the worshippers in the household and community, who begin to feel the intensifying presence of the arrival of the Goddess.

The extensive rituals of the following day, the Great Seventh include the official appointment of the *purohita* and his commitment to perform the entire sequence of rites over the course of subsequent days (on Saptamī rites, see Rodrigues 2003, 132–94). One of the day's first set of activities is an extensive series of bathings and anointings of the nine plants of the Navapattrikā. The shape of the Navapattrikā is derived primarily from a plantain sapling, to which the *bilva* branch with two pieces of fruit is attached, along with seven other plants. The items used for the bathing/anointing include the five products of the cow (urine, dung, milk, curd, and *ghī*), five nectars (sugar, honey, curd, milk, and *ghī*), various kinds of water (from a tank, hot water, dew, water mixed with flour, water with powered herbs, ocean water, water with oil, water from the Gaṅgā, rainwater, from a waterfall, and so on). Each of the waters and ointments must first be purified and then applied to the plant effigy of the Goddess. Then the clay image cluster is bathed in the same way. However, because it is impractical to pour so much water onto the unbaked clay *mūrti*, the ministrations are performed to the image's reflection in a mirror. In more martially oriented celebrations of the Durgā Pūjā, the shining surface of the sacrificial sword's blade captures the Devī's reflection. However, the mirror is now a substitute that orients the *pūjā* toward adoration of the Goddess and her feminine beauty and away from original, militaristic notions that the Devī's essence enters into the sword, which will eventually taste the blood of the sacrificial offering.

Although the bathing and anointing items are roughly similar and as extensive as were used for the Navapattrikā, the *purohita* uses ritual implements associated with royal consecrations for bathing the clay image in the mirror. During the Great Bath or Mahāsnāna rite, he bathes the Goddess with water from a *bhṛṅgāra* (a golden pitcher), a conch shell, and a *sahasradhārā* (a type of millifluent sieve with numerous openings), all implements associated with royal consecrations. After also installing Gaṇeśa into an earthen pot (*ghaṭa*), the priest moves to invoke Durgā into the clay image. After performing many self-transformation rites, such as the *bhūta śuddhi* and various types of *nyāsas* or imprintments, through a series of visualizations, in concert with the utterance of meditative verses (*dhyāna śloka*), he invites the Goddess to take up her abode in the clay image. The great lion mount of Durgā, Mahāsiṅgha, and Mahiṣāsura, are also invoked into their images at this time. The high point is when the images are brought to life through the rites to open the Devī's three eyes (*cakṣur dāna*) and install vital energy (*prāṇa pratiṣṭhā*) in the deities. Now that this is done, the Goddess is rendered worship. Unlike the common five-part *pūjā,* Durgā is worshipped with dozens of offerings, including clothes, sweets, and adornments. The other deities are also invoked to preside at the ritual. Nine goddesses are invoked into the nine plants of the Navapattrikā, and Gaṇeśa, Kārttikeya, Lakṣmī, and Sarasvatī, who are often thought of by worshippers as Durgā's family, are invoked into their images and rendered worship. The lion mount and Mahiṣāsura are rendered homage. The Navapattrikā, which takes its lithe form from the plantain tree, is draped in a sari and placed next to Gaṇeśa. In a telling example of the fuzziness inherent in the exegesis/eisegesis distinction, most devotees call the Navapattrikā the *kalā bau* (banana-plant wife), regarding her as the wife of Gaṇeśa. However, the litany, which is not understood by most devotees, is explicit in identifying the Navapattrikā as the Great Goddess. Such interpretive inconsistencies are quite common. For instance, many devotees identify the Goddess with Pārvatī, the spouse of Śiva, and as the mother of Gaṇeśa. But they simultaneously regard the Goddess as a virgin.

Now that all the deities are present and enlivened, the priest again worships Durgā by repeating her *mantra "Om duṃ durgāyai namaḥ"* at least ten times. After the flame worship and a recitation of a hymn of praise, such as the "Durgā Stava" from the *Mahābhārata,* devotees in the audience may participate in a nominal act of worship. The worshippers are first purified by the priest and may then shower the Goddess with flowers in what is known as the *puṣpāñjali* (adoration with flowers). The rites of Mahāsaptamī conclude with the collective recitation of the famous *namaskāra mantra,* found within the *Devī Māhātmya* (11.9).

> sarva maṅgala maṅgalye śive sarvārtha sādhike/
> śaraṇye tryambake gauri nārāyaṇi namo 'stute//[3]
> O auspicious one, blessed with every blessing, who fulfils every aim;
> O three-eyed Gaurī, who are a refuge, O Nārāyaṇī, praise be to you. (My translation)

The ritual sequences on each of the days of Durgā Pūjā, like *rāgas* in Indian classical music, are repeated patterns with distinctive variations, which build up to a great climax. The repeated patterns in the Durgā Pūjā include the many purifications of the ritual space and the offerings to be made and the general worship of the many deities that have now come to reside in the ritual space. On a related note, I could not easily distinguish between Mr. and Mrs. Lahiris' joy at the reunion of their four married daughters and their families to the ancestral home in Benares for the Durgā Pūjā celebrations and the invoked presence of the Goddess and all the other deities now within their home. The emotional energies of all their presences seemed mutually intertwined. While the key ritual variation of the Durga Pūjā rituals on Mahāsaptamī was the invocation of the deities into the Navapattrikā and the clay image cluster, on Mahāṣṭamī it is the installation and worship of Durgā in the yantric form of the Sarvatobhadra Maṇḍala, the Sphere of All-directional Auspiciousness (on Mahāṣṭamī rites, see Rodrigues 2003, 194–210). If the *purohita* is extremely adept or has enough time, he may draw the *maṇḍala* while engaged in its worship. Otherwise, he will construct it earlier for use on Mahāṣṭamī. Durgā and her eight accompanying *śaktis* (goddesses) are invoked into this *maṇḍala*, along with the sixty-four Yoginīs (Tantric goddesses of "yoga"), the Mātṛs (Mothers), and all other gods and goddesses, including Baṭukas (boy forms of Śiva), Kṣetrapālas (guardians of the field), and Bhairavas (fierce forms of Śiva), each of which is placed into an appropriate segment of the diagram. The Devī's weapons and ornaments, which in this case are simply made out of tin, are also worshipped. In appropriate militaristic contexts, actual weapons would be worshipped at this time. In certain temple settings, persons may bring their weapons to the Devī on Mahāṣṭamī for them to be blessed.

In the Bengali tradition, the *sandhi* or juncture between the eighth and ninth lunar days (*tithi*s) is crucial (on *sandhi* rites, see Rodrigues 2003, 210–24). The key event during this forty-eight-minute period, when Durgā is invoked in her fierce form as Cāmuṇḍā, is the offering of a blood sacrifice. In the Lahiris' Durgā Pūjā, a *kūṣmāṇḍā* melon is a substitute, "sacrificed" by the men and prepared into *bhog* (cooked food offering) by the women.[4] The *bhog* is one of the most important blessings (*prasada*) to be handed out to participants and consumed. While the priest is conducting rituals in the *pūjālaya*, the kitchen is another hidden ritual arena, where initiated postmenopausal women, often widows, are engaged in food preparation. As part of the *ārati* segment of worship, 108 lamps are lit, perhaps evoking the tale in Kṛttivāsa's *Rāmāyaṇa*, where Rāma must offer 108 blue lotuses to the Devī. The Goddess tests his devotion by hiding one of the flowers and only appears to him when he is about to pluck out one of his own lotus eyes as a substitute (Bose and Bose 2013, 109). Virgin worship is also recommended to be performed during this short period of sacred time, a conjunction with the blood sacrifice calling out for exegesis. However, because of the logistics involved, the *kumārī pūjā* now often takes place on Mahānavamī. In the *kumārī pūjā*, one, nine, seventeen, 108 or more prepubescent, virgin girls are worshipped as living forms of the goddess. At the most basic level of interpretation, this *sandhi* is a highly auspicious astrological time. As the result of all the prior worship, which culminates in the dramatic 108-lamp *ārati* and the blood sacrifice, the Devī's grace is thought to be most available at this juncture. She manifests in the living form of the *kūmārī* and in the sword that beheads the symbolic demon. She has made herself manifest in multiple forms and abodes through which ardent votaries may apprehend her presence and avail themselves of her grace. If ever one were going to "perceive" the Goddess, it might be then, at this climax of the *pūjā*.

Figure 10.2. The *purohita* prepares an *argha* offering to the Devī during the Durgā Pūjā.

The key variant ritual on Mahānavamī, apart from the *kumārī pūjā* if it is performed on this day, is the *homa* or fire oblation (see Rodrigues 2003, 224–36). One hundred and eight unblemished, tripartite *bilva* leaves are offered into the fire, with the mantra: *durge durge rakṣaṇi svāhā*. The *purohita* also receives his platter of offerings and performs the final oblation. The ashes may be used to anoint one's head, throat, shoulders, and heart. Navarātra has come to an end, but the Durgā Pūjā has not, for there are several rites on the following day, known as Vijayā Daśamī (Tenth for Victory) (see Rodrigues 2003, 236–47). With various *mantras*, the priest dislodges the *ghaṭa* and the *pratimā*, the clay image cluster. He worships the Goddess in the cast-off remnants of the *pūjā*, the old flowers and debris from the worship. He sends her on her way but asks her to remain in the earth, the water, and the home. Although the following rite is skipped in most homes and public *pūjās*, the Lahiris still perform the worship of the goddess Aparājitā (She Who Is Invincible). In this ritual, the *Clitoria ternata* creeper, with its deep indigo flowers that resemble the female reproductive organ, which was used to bind the Navapattrikā, is worshipped and embedded into an amulet to be worn on the body for protection. One can imagine the enormous value of receiving and wearing such an amulet in the martial contexts of the Durgā Pūjā, which takes place at the end of the monsoons, just as the traditional period of warfare begins. Finally, the images, from which the deities have already departed, are carried to the river for immersion. It is a bittersweet event, because not only is the Devī thought to be departing to her distant abode, but the family too will disperse, and the married daughters will return to their husbands' homes. The atmosphere at the riverbank is raucous. The air is full of incense smoke, and the rhythmic beat of the *dhāk* drums fills one's ears. The festive atmosphere is but a shadow of what is prescribed in the *Kālikā Purāṇa*, which insists that the Goddess is angered by those who do not carouse and address each other with highly explicit sexual language (Kane 1958, vol. 5, 177).

Symbols and Meanings within the Durgā Pūjā

Although the foregoing description may have seemed overly detailed, it is a very abbreviated description of the actual procedures of the Bengali Durgā Pūjā. The previous section offered some measure of the rite's intricacies and touched briefly upon interpretations of some of its symbols. Here we press further into extracting other meanings from the *pūjā*.

One may reasonably infer that as a grand devotional rite to the Great Goddess that takes place annually, the entire scale of the devotional services rendered should be magnified, in comparison to other more minor *pūjās*, and this is certainly the case. However, one wonders why the rite of bathing the Devī is so extensive. We know that temple deities are routinely bathed and the sanctified water handed out to devotees as a blessing (*prasāda*). Since *pūjā* mirrors the services offered to honored guests, who are offered a cleansing bath to refresh themselves after their journey, it is natural that the arrival of the Devī necessitates lengthy bathing. She has traveled from afar and has been awakened in the midst of her slumber. But the bathing rite also clearly evokes royal rejuvenations of the sort found in the Vedic *rājasūya* ceremony (Heesterman 1957) and the royal consecrations as described in the *Viṣṇudharmottara Purāṇa* (2.21). The Goddess is the supreme queen (*maheśvarī*), and the Durgā Pūjā is the ultimate royal rejuvenation and consecration. It is sometimes compared to the ancient Vedic *aśvamedha*, the horse sacrifice that established a king as an emperor and engendered offspring in his wives. The Durgā Pūjā, too, holds out the promise of expanded or successful sovereignty, as well as auspicious beneficence and fertility for the patron, and for one's kingdom or community.

Even so, the Durgā Pūjā actually serves more than this-worldly needs. Over a thousand years ago, in the *Parā Pūjā*, a short poem attributed to him, Śaṅkara asked a series of rhetorical questions concerning the seeming contradictions in the acts of *pūjā*. "Why a bath to one free from blemish?" he asks, along with other such questions (Gussner, 1973, 202–4). Śaṅkara determines that upon realizing the omnipresence of divinity, one knows that whatever one does is, in fact, *pūjā*. This, of course, is consistent with the perspective of non-dual Vedānta. However, it also offers us a certain metaphysical logic behind the actions of *pūjā* for those who have not yet attained the highest realization. In the symbolic actions that bring the Goddess into one's home and by rendering her worship, one is actually engaged in an act of self-transformation, purifying the constituents of one's own body and psyche so that one may perceive the highest divinity, symbolized by the Great Goddess. Just as the Goddess is symbolically bathed in a mirror, worshippers are themselves reflected and cleansed in the symbolic mirror that is the *pūjā* itself, regardless of whether their notions of divinity are polytheistic, monotheistic, dualistic, or monistic.

One notes that the *purohita* is a crucial conduit in this process of divine manifestation. To cause deities to take up their presence in various abodes, the *purohita* performs a series of self-transforming acts. In the *bhūta śuddhi* rite, which he performs before attempting any invocation, with the aid of *prāṇāyāma* and various *mantras*, he awakens the dormant *kuṇḍalinī* energy to move up the *suṣumnā* or central energy channel to unite his limited self (*jīvaśiva*) with his supreme self (*paramaśiva*). He thereby purifies (*śuddhi*) the constituent elements (*bhūta*) of his body (for details of this procedure, see Rodrigues 2003, 96–98). Next, through an extensive variety of *nyāsas* (imprintments), he transforms his entire body into the vibrational body of the Goddess herself (for details, see Rodrigues

2003, 98–109). Through the *mātṛkā nyāsa* he unleashes the power of the vowels and consonants and imprints them onto his entire body. With the *kara* and *aṅga nyāsa* he imprints his hands and limbs. With other *nyāsas* he visualizes the goddess of speech (*vāgdevatā*) and enfolds her body as well as her *pīṭhas* (seats or abodes) into his own. To bring other deities into manifestation into his own body, he, as the goddess of speech, now fuses sacred word, thought, and action. The *purohita* first holds a flower within his hand in the *dhyāna* or *yoni mudrā*, while performing a meditative visualization as described in the meditative verses (*dhyāna śloka*) of the deity. He then places the flower upon his head, symbolically transforming himself into the deity itself. He may render it/him devotional service through creative visualizations (*mānasa upacāra*). Finally, he transfers the flower to the place where the deity will be installed, and repeats the meditative verses and visualizations. This feature, in which the *purohita* himself becomes an independent locus for the manifestation of the deity, distinguishes Tantric *pūjās* from Vedic methods. In this Tantric form, there is both self-identification with divinity, and self-differentiation from divinity in this process.

When we look back at the overall scheme of the Durgā Pūjā, we note that it is a complicated braiding of diverse conceptual, mythological, and methodological schemes. Tantric variants may replace Vedic ones at times, although Tantric elements are fundamental in the processes through which the Goddess manifests. A vegetable sacrifice may symbolically replace a blood sacrifice, and virgin girls may be worshipped at a time other than during the *sandhi* juncture. What is quite apparent is that the Goddess is very overtly regarded as closely tied to the earth, water, and life. She is all the gross and subtle elements in creation, as well as the senses that perceive them. She is also explicitly embodied in the virgin girls worshipped during the *kumārī pūjā*, but implicitly in all women, such as the married daughters who have returned to their parents' home, and the post-menopausal widows who prepare the food offerings. One would be short-sighted to imagine that women are not identified with Durgā during the Pūjā.[5] A detailed discussion of the role and symbolic presence of women in the Durgā Pūjā is found in Rodrigues (2005).

The Goddess appears to be invoked both explicitly and implicitly within all of creation (she is Prakṛti, as it were, including gross and subtle elements, the senses, and the inner faculties of mind). Moreover, the Durgā Pūjā abounds with symbols of the *yoni*, the female reproductive organ, which are the portals through which she manifests. At the very beginning of the *pūjā*, the earthen altar upon which the jar form of the Goddess is established is set upon a *yantra*. While this may be the more elaborate Sarvatobhadra Maṇḍala, the *purohita* may simply draw an inverted triangle, the symbol of the *yoni*. There are repeated *argha* offerings made to the Goddess throughout the Durgā Pūjā. *Argha* is an unusual term, which the *Amarakośa*, an early Sanskrit thesaurus, defines simply as an offering of flowers and water. The Goddess proclaims that she delights in these offerings in the *Devī Māhātmya* (12.19). However, the *argha* is also regarded as a synonym for the *yoni* and refers to a boat or cup shaped container within which *liṅgas* are seated or offerings made (Garg 1992, 602). The *kośa* and *kuśi* are both *yoni*-shaped ritual implements, and *argha* offerings are placed within them. It does not take much imagination to see in shape and preparation of the *argha*, with its sandalwood paste and hibiscus flower, a symbolic representation of the *yoni*. Indeed, all the flowers could be viewed as symbols of the orifice through which the creation blossoms. A more explicit connection between flowers and the *yoni* is the flower of the Aparājitā creeper, specifically chosen because of its appearance. There are innumerable tripartite or triangular items implicitly or explicitly identified as *yonis*, or the triadic nature of Śakti. These include tripods, triangular supports, and, of course, the *yoni mudrā*, which is vital for every manifestation of every deity.

Figure 10.3. The *kośa* and *kuśi* (*yoni*-shaped ritual implements) are visible as the *purohita* performs *mudrās* during the Durgā Pūjā.

Although I have not encountered written sources that explicitly offer some of the foregoing or following symbolic interpretations of the Pūjā's elements, it is doubtful that Śākta Tantrism was oblivious to such meanings being extracted from the Durgā Pūjā's symbolism. Several such interpretive ideas were indeed offered by ritual specialists and ordinary devotees, who also offered other uncommon meanings regarding the nature of the demon and of blood sacrifice. Is it useful to restrict interpretation only to mainstream perspectives, rather than seek out less common symbolic meanings? Critical voices may ask: How useful is a votary's Marxist interpretation that the demon Mahiṣa represents the arrogance of corrupt power and ill-gotten wealth? Or, is it valuable to wonder if the sacrificial animal may be thought of as the devotee's self-sacrifice? What about the unusual interpretation that the Goddess sacrifices herself? I contend that such expressed interpretations, although not widespread among the populace, find ample support in various aspects of Śākta and Tantric systems. They do tell us about Hinduism's creativity and that of human beings generally, when faced with symbols that cry out for interpretation. They may be marginal, but they are far from useless. For instance, Mahiṣa's arrogance is a trope throughout the Purāṇas, and anyone who has viewed the inventive portrayals of Mahiṣa in community *paṇḍals* would not find a Marxist interpretation of the demon among some Bengalis to be unusual, or even marginal. After all, the demon is not just a buffalo. Even mythically, he undergoes many transformations, into a lion, a buffalo, and a person. Both the buffalo and the demon are symbols. Moreover, they are multivocal symbols. The interpretations that currently hold hegemony are not the only ones of value when attempting to understand meaning. As Clifford Geertz (1973, 3–30) had pointed out long ago, there is a world of difference between a blink and a wink, and many layers of assorted meanings within the various types of winks that we wink. The blood sacrifice does not mean just one thing. It can mean different things to different people and disparate things to the same person, simultaneously.

In the *Devī Māhātmya* (11.42–46), the Goddess explicitly states that in a particular incarnation, during a terrible drought, she will support the world with life-sustaining vegetables from her own body. Kūṣmāṇḍā, a type of melon (ash gourd), which is frequently used as a sacrificial substitute, is another name for Durgā. The fourth member of the popular cluster of Nine Durgās mentioned in the "Devī Kavaca," a well-known appendage of the *Devī Māhātmya,* is Kūṣmāṇḍā Devī. In Benares, Kūṣmāṇḍā Devī is identified as the Durgā of Durgā Kuṇḍa temple. The common interpretation is that the Goddess is so named because she receives such melons as offerings. However, it is hardly a stretch to interpret the sacrificial offering as also potentially representing the Devī herself, who shares her name with the melon that is symbolically "sacrificed" and consumed as *bhog*. Neither is it overinterpretation to recognize the possibility that the sacrificial animal may represent the devotee, enacting deep devotional commitment. We know that king Suratha and the merchant Samādhi from the *Devī Māhātmya* narrative made offerings to the Goddess sprinkled with blood from their own limbs (13.9). And we have iconographic depictions in the region of the Pallava empire of devotees extracting blood or severing their own necks (Vogel 1930–32). It is perhaps too sanguine a note on which to end this chapter, but the Goddess does have a very close relationship to blood, which is the sap of life (Rodrigues 2009). Her myths and rites of worship are replete with symbols, and her devotees continue to extract and attach personally valuable meanings to these. I have written elsewhere about interpretations of the juxtaposition of the blood sacrifice and the worship of the pre-menstrual virgin girl during the climax of the Durgā Pūjā (Rodrigues 2009). And Durgā Pūjā's roles in self-, communal, and sovereign empowerment have also been discussed elsewhere (Östör 1980; Rodrigues 2003; McDermott 2011), so I offer something else by way of conclusion.

The Durgā Pūjā, in part, precisely tries to illustrate to devotees that the Devī's presence is ubiquitous. She is everywhere and in everything. She is in the earth, in water, in living things, and in the home. She is in speech, in blood, in fire, and in ash. Likewise, she is in rituals of worship and in the cast-off remnants of existence as well. She is in women and the gods. She is both life and death. A line from the "Nārāyaṇī Stuti" a well-known hymn of praise within the *Devī-Māhātmya* (11.5), states:

> sarvabhūtā yadā devī svargamuktipradāyinī/
> tvaṃ stutā stutaye kā vā bhavantu paramoktayaḥ//
> O Goddess, when you, the granter of heaven and supreme liberation, who are everything (*sarvabhūtā*), are glorified (*stutā*), what could be the words exquisite enough to exalt you? (My translation)

In a similar vein, the Durgā Pūjā implies, "What rites of worship would be adequate to do you justice? What substances can we offer that are not already from you? What words can we utter that are not also from you? And yet, ultimately we shall try." And by doing so, every year, devotees, communities, kings, kingdoms, even the entire cosmos are intrinsically revitalized, reinvigorated, even reborn through the awakened and consecrated presence of the Great Goddess by and within her own creation.

Notes

1. I include symbolic action in the broad concept of what I mean by a symbol. More details on theoretical orientations to the Durgā Pūjā "as ritual" are found in Rodrigues (2003, 303–12), particularly in notes 40–67.

2. Kṛttivāsa's *Rāmāyaṇa* did not introduce this myth, which is found in the *Bṛhaddharma* (1.18–22, according to Kinsley [1986, 109, 234]), the *Kālikā* (60.25–31), and *Mahābhāgavata Purāṇas* (36–48), which tell how Hanumān convinces Devī to withdraw protection from Laṅkā if Rāma performs the Durgā Pūjā in autumn. In Vālmiki's *Rāmāyaṇa* (VI.106), the *ṛṣi* Agastya advises Rāma to worship Aditya to vanquish Rāvaṇa.

3. This verse is found on line 11 of the famous Dadhimatī Mātā inscription, which some date at 608 CE, but is more persuasively dated by Mirashi (1964, 186) as c. 813 CE. Although the *Devī Māhātmya* was probably composed earlier if one of its verses was selected for use in an inscription, it was quite likely not composed later than 813 CE. The recitation of that well-known verse even today by nonspecialist devotees makes us wonder if it was being used in a similar manner in the worship of Durgā in the ninth century.

4. In conversations in June 2017 with organizers of the Durgotsava Sammilini, the oldest communal Durgā Pūjā in Benares, I was informed that in their celebration the priest performs the sacrifice of the melon. He must sever it with a single stroke, and it is ignored while the *bhog* is prepared from other vegetables.

5. For this view, see Ferro-Luzzi (2004, 674). In the so-called Nārāyaṇī Stuti of the *Devī Māhātmya* (11.5), which is well known to most worshippers, the gods praise the Goddess, saying that she is "*striyaḥ samastāḥ sakalā jagatsu*" (every woman in all the worlds).

References

Agrawala, Vasudeva S., trans. 1963. *Devī-Māhātmya: The Glorification of the Great Goddess*. Varanasi: All-India Kashiraj Trust.

Bhattacharya, Surendramohana, ed. 1973–74. *Purohita darpaṇa*. Revised by Yogendracandra Vyākaraṇatīrtha. Calcutta: Satyanārāyaṇa Library.

Bose, Mandakranta, and Sarika Priyadarshini Bose. 2013. *A Woman's Rāmāyaṇa: Candrāvatī's Bengali Epic*. New York: Routledge.

Coburn, Thomas B. 1991. *Encountering the Goddess: A Translation of the Devī-Māhātmya and a Study of Its Interpretation*. Albany: State University of New York Press.

Devī-purāṇa. 1973. Edited by Pushpendra Kumar Sharma. New Delhi: Kendriya Sanskrit Vidyapeeth.

Ferro-Luzzi, Gabriella Eichinger. 2004. *Review of Ritual Worship of the Great Goddess: The Liturgy of the Durgā Pūjā with Interpretations*, by Hillary P. Rodrigues. *Anthropos*, Bd. 99, H. 2, 674–75.

Garg, Ganga Ram. 1992. "Argha (Yoni)." In *Encyclopedia of the Hindu World, Vol. 3*, edited by Ganga Ram Garg, 602. New Delhi: Concept.

Geertz, Clifford. 1973. *The Interpretation of Cultures: Selected Essays*. New York: Basic Books.

Ghosha, Pratapchandra. 1871. *Durga Puja, with Notes and Illustrations*. Calcutta: Hindoo Patriot.

Grimes, Ronald, L. 2014. *The Craft of Ritual Studies*. New York: Oxford University Press.

Gussner, R. E. 1973. "Hymns of Praise: A Textual-Critical Analysis of Selected Vedantic Stotras attributed to Sankara with Reference to the Question of Authenticity." Dissertation, Cambridge, MA, Harvard University.

Heesterman, J. C. 1957. *The Ancient Indian Royal Consecration*. The Hague: Mouton.
Kālikā-purāṇa. 1891. Bombay: Veṅkaṭeśvara.
Kane, Pandurang Vaman. 1930–62. *History of Dharmaśāstra (Ancient and Medieval Religious and Civil Law)*. 5 vols. Poona: Bhandarkar Oriental Research Institute.
Kinsley, David R. 1986. *Hindu Goddesses: Visions of the Divine Feminine in the Hindu Religious Tradition*. Berkeley: University of California Press.
Mahābhāgavata-purāṇa. 1913. Bombay: Manilal Itcharam Desai.
McDermott, Rachel F. 2011. *Revelry, Rivalry, and Longing for the Goddesses of Bengal: The Fortunes of Hindu Festivals*. New York: Columbia University Press.
Mirashi, V. V. 1964. "A Lower Limit for the Date of the Devī-Māhātmya." *Purāṇa* 6:181–86.
Östör, Ákos. 1980. *Play of the Gods: Locality, Ideology, and Time in the Festivals of a Bengali Town*. Chicago: University of Chicago Press.
Rodrigues, Hillary. 2009. "Fluid Control: Orchestrating Blood Flow in the Durgā Pūjā." *Studies in Religion/Science Religieuses* 38 (2): 263–92.
———. 2005. "Women in the Worship of the Great Goddess." In *Goddesses and Women in the Indic Religious Tradition*, edited by A. Sharma, 72–104. Leiden: Brill.
———. 2003. *Ritual Worship of the Great Goddess: The Liturgy of the Durgā Pūjā with Interpretations*. Albany: State University of New York Press.
Sarkar, Bihani. 2012. "The Rite of Durgā in Medieval Bengal: An Introductory Study of Raghunandana's Durgāpūjātattva with Text and Translations of the Principal Rites." *Journal of the Royal Asiatic Society* 22 (2): 325–90.
Staal, Frits. 1989. *Rules without Meaning: Ritual, Mantras and the Human Sciences*. Bern: Peter Lang.
Viṣṇudharmottara-purāṇa. 1938. Bombay: Venkateśvara Steam.
Vogel, J. Ph. 1930–32. "The Head-Offering to the Goddess in Pallava Sculpture." *Bulletin of the School of Oriental Studies* 6:538–43.

11

The Internal Navarātri

Sarkar Baba of Benares and the Goddess Within

JISHNU SHANKAR

In this chapter, I provide a closer look at the expressions of the personal-spiritual element inherent in the celebration of the Navarātri festival, especially as conceptualized within the Aghor tradition of ascetics and devotees. While participants in the social world might be propitiating a beautiful idol of the goddess or exulting with song and dance, I am interested in how the practitioners of the Aghor tradition transform themselves physically (making the body sacred through the application of ash) as well as mentally (incubating the goddess within) during the nine nights. Such Aghor practices may seem austere, but for the practitioner, they produce the company of the goddess, the goal of their ascetic path. The basis for my study is the advice given by Aghoreshwar Mahaprabhu Baba Bhagwan Ram ji (also known as Sarkar Baba to his devotees) to individual practitioners for these nine days, whether it be the *vasant* (spring) Navarātri (celebrated during the Hindu month of *Caitra* [March–April]) or the *śarad* (fall) Navarātri (celebrated during the Hindu month of Āśvin [September–October]). In this vein, this chapter is what has been called a "descriptive microstudy" (White 2009). As such, it is a close examination of a single institution in Benares (Vārāṇasī): Shri Sarveshwari Samooh Kusht Sewa ashram and its leprosy hospital, initiated by Sarkar Baba formally in 1961. My study is based on the institution's Hindi language newsletter and books and my own participant observation. Such a microstudy is indispensable for gaining a fuller picture of and range of expressions that exist within the festival of Navarātri. Since most of the literature available from Shri Sarveshwari Samooh is in Hindi, I have taken the liberty of translating freely the relevant passages quoted herein. My narrative is autoethnographical.

Sarkar Baba and His Approach to Ritual

Sarkar Baba was born in 1937 as a result of his parents receiving a blessing from a holy ascetic. He lost his father at the age of five, and by age of seven he left his home to reside in the groves and fields around his village, meditating and singing devotional songs with his childhood friends. Tradition holds that miracles began to happen around him, and soon he was recognized by the village people as a healer. His spiritual quest took him to the Bābā Kīnārām Sthal in Benaras, where he was initiated as a monk into the Aghor tradition. A little after his initiation, he commenced his period of austere penance as a mendicant wandering alongside the river Ganges, spending time in the cremation grounds along its shores, begging for food and meditating continuously. His severe austerities bore fruit, and at the age of fifteen, he attained enlightenment. Along with the miracles that occurred around him, people realized that if they followed his instruction on spiritual matters, they greatly benefited. This soon led to scores of devotees vying to be in his company at all times. To provide a structure and stability to this group of devotees, Sarkar Baba established Shri Sarveshwari Samooh, a social service organization.

Sarkar Baba's devotees referred to him as "Aghoreshwar," a title used to refer to a saint who has attained the highest pinnacle of the Aghor tradition, much like the Paramahaṃsa in other traditions. He was regarded as a *siddha* (perfected) saint, a walking embodiment of the Hindu deity Śiva. Some of his devotees also referred to him as "Ma-Guru," guru in the form of the Mother and the Goddess incarnate. Sarkar Baba talked of Śiva and the gods Viṣṇu and Brahmā with great respect, but I saw him perform only the Navarātri celebration.

The prominent deity in Sarkar Baba's ashram temples was Mother Kālī. Sarkar Baba was well versed in the intricacies of rituals. In fact, many prominent Brahmin scholars, pandits, and priests—including his devotee, the priest of the Kāśi-Viśvanāth temple—of Benares came and consulted with him regarding proper ritual performance. However, he never confined himself to what was written in books. Although Sarkar Baba never claimed so, his devotees felt he was in touch with another dimension of cognizance and therefore regarded his advice as the ultimate word. On occasion, he diverged from what was written in the manuals and provided alternatives to devotees when a certain ritual could not be performed as prescribed. Ever against perfunctory elaboration of rituals in devotion, he frequently simplified the ritual to make the devotee more at ease in communicating with the Goddess. To him, the right sentiment (*bhāva*) was the crucial element in propitiating the Goddess. All else was secondary, simply an expression of that sentiment.

Navarātri: As Explained by Sarkar Baba

For Sarkar Baba, Navarātri was a supreme occasion for experiencing the Goddess. He emphasized that such an experience is possible, but only *within* the seeker, because the Goddess is beyond all forms. For an experience of her, the seekers had to ready themselves to prepare the ground where she could arrive through the cultivation of their body-*yantra* (body-tool). Only then could her arrival be perceived by the seeker. He stressed:

> For the nine days of Navarātri, . . . with stable mind and heart, with pleasant feelings and thoughts, let us watch what happens within us. Let us understand what happens within this body-*yantra* (instrument) of ours. Once you know this *yantra*, understand it, hear it, nothing will be difficult for you. Everything will be available to you. (Ram 2007, 197)

This process of making one's mind and heart stable entails withdrawing from the normal worldly activities and letting the Goddess's vibrations take over. Sarkar Baba likened this process to a tortoise that withdraws its limbs inside its shell and remains there peacefully, content within itself, oblivious to the forces raging outside. With the right orientation, the seeker could then fully engage in Navarātri.

During the Navarātri festival, the residents of the Shri Sarveshwari Samooh ashram are to observe eleven austerities. The following are the official penances for the nine days:

1. Celibacy, sense control.
2. Silence.
3. Sleeping on the ground—to not sit or sleep on someone else's bed or let anyone else sit or sleep on theirs.
4. Eating once in twenty-four hours.
5. Recalling the mantra on the *mālā* (like a rosary).
6. Reading of the holy books.
7. Meditation.

8. Maintaining a mind free of desires and aspirations.
9. Eschewing negative acts.
10. Bowing to one's desired deity with the whole body in any direction.
11. Gentle behavior with everyone. (*Sarveshwari Times*, March 15, 1973, 4; Kumar 2001, 21)

However, the residents of the ashram observe these austerities in varying degrees: some fast during the day; some abstain from drinking water; and some sleep on the ground for the nine nights. Others let nature take over their body and stop shaving or pairing their nails, and yet others maintain a vow of silence for the entirety of the festival.

Even though Sarkar Baba himself fasted for all nine days of the festival, in his teachings, he did not endorse his devotees' observing austerity if their hearts and minds were not in tune with such discipline:

> Controlling our senses during Navarātri does not imply renouncing the world or its pleasures. The Mother Goddess provides both enjoyment (*bhukti*) as well as liberation (*mukti*). During her worship we receive both sensory gratification (*bhoga*) as well as *yoga*. But we are naturally inclined towards sensory gratification. The effort to become somewhat distant from it is *yoga*. Both *bhoga* and *yoga* are two wheels of the chariot of human life, both are necessary for it to continue. (*Sarveshwari Times*, October 15, 1972, 1)

For Sarkar Baba, sense control was not about mortification, but the Navarātri observances allow for the balance of gratification and indifference. He further explained that the vows (*vrata;* see Kane 1958, Vol. 5.1, chapter 1) were not intended to inflict the body with unnecessary austerities but were to be undertaken for the benefit and strength of the devotee.

> During our Navaratra *vrata* . . . we are forbidden from fasting, ejaculating in vain, and wandering without purpose . . . [W]hen we receive sanctified food (*prasād*) in the evening, we receive it [as if] an herb, a medication to generate vigor, to generate luster, to generate semen, to generate strength within us. We do not have anything named *vrata* amongst us. (*Sarveshwari Times*, March 30, 1972, 3).

Observances, then, allow the devotee the opportunity to act mindfully, becoming aware of both sides of the Goddess. When these two quotes are read together, I do not think the published observances for Navarātri mentioned above were ever meant to be rigid strictures but were suggested observances that could be undertaken by Sarkar Baba's devotees. However, following at least some of these suggestions could help his devotees who were householders set apart the period of Navarātri from the activities of their normal daily life. Navarātri provided Sarkar Baba's disciples an opportunity to turn away from fixations on the physical acts of austerity, and instead, to cultivate a relationship with the Goddess within themselves. Furthermore, he emphasized that this relationship was not manipulated by austere actions. In one striking example of this, he asked devotees if they were trying to "intimidate" the Goddess by going on a hunger-strike! He explained that Navarātri is a period of her appearance and presence and, therefore, ought to be a period of great joy for both her and the devotee. But the Mother, certainly, is not happy to see her children go hungry. Therefore, those who need to eat during the day should do so without any feeling of guilt, for the worship of the Mother happens within: in the mind, in the heart, and in the sentiments one holds for her.

Ashram Navarātri, the *Devī Māhātmya*, and the Incubation of the Goddess through Ritual

In general, the nine days of Navarātri in India are dedicated to the nine successive forms of *Devī* (the Goddess), one each day. These nine forms are derived from the *Mārkaṇḍeya Purāṇa's Devī Māhātmya*, which is also called the *Durgāsaptaśatī* (seven hundred verses dedicated to Durgā) within ritual contexts (See Singh 1983, 129–34). The nine forms of Devī, which preside over the festival starting on the first day of Navarātri successively are Śailaputrī, Brahmacāriṇī, Candraghaṇṭā, Kūṣmāṇḍā, Skandamātā, Kātyāyinī, Kālarātri, Mahāgaurī, and Siddhidātrī (Shankaranarayanan 1968, 81; Singh 1983, 159).[1] Although this list does not mention Durgā, all these forms of the Goddess are understood within the tradition to be her different emanations.[2] Textually, the *Navadurgā* concept of the nine Devīs occurs in the "*Devī kavaca*" section (v. 3–5) as part of the "method of reading" instructions included in independent ritual circulations of the *Devī Māhātmya*. In the general nine Devī conceptions of the *Navadurgā*, each form of Devī is regarded as a "level" of spiritual accomplishment or the specific boon-granting capacity of the Goddess according to her specific form. Additionally, these nine *Devīs* are believed to preside over the entire cosmos, which is divided into nine parts, each one presided over by one of the *Navadurgā* (*Sarveshwari Times* October 15, 1972, 3).

As with the adumbration of the ritual observances of Navarātri, Sarkar Baba's ashram reduces this nine-fold schema to just three visions of *Devī* with three distinct names. In this alternate conception, the first three days of the Navarātri are dedicated to Mahākālī, days four through six are dedicated to Mahālakṣmī, and the last three days are dedicated to Mahāsarasvatī (Kumar 2001, 13). In the alternate three Devī conceptions of the Goddess and Navarātri, these three forms of Devī are regarded as the three primary *guṇas* (traits; i.e. *tamas, rajas,* and *sattva,* respectively) of all that exists.[3] This interpretation of the forms of the Goddess is also found in the *Devī Māhātmya.* The tripartite Devī is discussed in *Durgāsaptaśatī's aṅga* (limb) texts "*Prādhānik*" and *Prākṛtik Rahasya,* which are used for performing the text's attendant rituals (see Shankaranarayanan 1968, 288; Singh 1983, 167–68).

The *Devī Māhātmya* and its limb texts not only describe the story of Devī's battles with fierce demons, but they also lay down the prescribed way of inviting and communing with the Goddess during these nine days through certain rituals. Sarkar Baba was part of the Aghor tradition, which is widely regarded as Tantric. Consequently, Navarātri ritual processes as observed in the ashram, or in the homes of its devotees, also reflect this element. In the ashram, this process involves establishing a *kalaśa* (pot) filled with water, which is placed over a sacred base upon which a *yantra* (a geometric design) would have been drawn and which would be infused with an appropriate *mantra* (sacred phoneme). The seeker then would ritually enliven the *kalaśa* by infusing it with the life-force (*prāṇa-pratishṭhā*) and imagining that a living Goddess was present in that vessel (see Einoo 1999). It is generally known that a *kalaśa* does not need to be established in a place where there already exists a ritually enlivened idol. For this reason, Sarkar Baba always had someone else establish the *kalaśa* in the ashram, but he would do it himself when traveling abroad or in the homes of his devotees, where the *yantra* or the idol of the Goddess was not present. Regardless, Sarkar Baba was sure to have the *kalaśa* ritual in the ashram to provide more affinity between his practice and the practice of many of his devotees. For them, Navarātri meant the establishment of a *kalaśa,* and without it the ritual might have seemed incomplete. Indeed, the establishment of the *kalaśa* with all the proper rites signals the invitation to the Goddess to arrive and stay for the nine days. Only one such *kalaśa* needs to be established, although there would be many Navarātri observers. Sarkar Baba's participation in this rite in the ashram, as well as while traveling abroad, made participants confident that the Goddess had indeed arrived to be with them.

Once the *kalaśa* was established, worship was initiated as devotees made vows (*saṃkalpa*) to perform a certain number of *japas* (recitations) by the evening of the eighth night. Then they would all commence their meditations, performing *ācamanī* (ritual sipping of water), *bhūtaśuddhi* (dissipating all negative forces), *digbandhana* (tying of the directions to keep evil spirits away), *prāṇāyāma* (breathing exercises), *dhyāna* (visualization, meditation), *japa*, and so on. This process of initiating worship in the ashram, however, is not exclusive to Navarātri. Lay as well as initiated devotees practice this every time they sit down to meditate. What *was* exclusive for Navarātri was that Sarkar Baba advised the application of ashes (*vibhūti*) for his devotees, advice that turned their ordinary worship into an ascetic's practice.

> For these nine days of worship we should smear *vibhūti* (ashes) on our body. Our body becomes a cremation ground, to which divinities come only because of these ashes . . . By smearing these ashes, by remembering these ashes, our cremation-ground-like body begins to seem pure and auspicious. It then looks beautiful, clean, and untainted. *Vibhūti* is the name of prosperity and glory. You wear this prosperity and glory. (Ram 2007, 197–98)

The observers who had access to the ashes applied them and then continued their worship of the Goddess through their recitations. There was no fixed time to perform *japa*. People did it whenever their time and physical constraints allowed. After dark and after the evening *āratī* (worship with flame-light), a bell would sound to indicate that everyone was invited to eat, and simple vegetarian food prepared in the ashram kitchen was distributed.

On the eighth night Mahāniśā Pūjan (worship of the grand night) was performed after all had finished their *japa*, with the performance of *havan* (offering oblations into the fire) around midnight. Prior to the *havan*, each observer had to prepare (*puraścaraṇa*). Without the *puraścaraṇa*, performance of *havan* was not possible because the process dictates that the seeker needed to perform *havan* with one-tenth of the number of *japa* they had vowed to perform. So, if a person had performed one hundred thousand *japa* that person would need to perform *havan* oblations ten thousand times—a truly daunting task for most! Therefore, as part of their *puraścaraṇa*, Sarkar Baba instructed the Navarātri observers to perform another *japa* that was equal in number to this one-tenth *havan*. Continuing our example from above, this meant that the devotee would do another ten thousand *japa*. Then the devotee would perform another *japa* sequence of one-tenth of this ten thousand and so on, until the seeker was left with just one *mālā* (rosary), 108 *japa*, to perform. This one *mālā* then constituted the number of oblations one would have to offer in the *havan* fire.

For his devotees who live abroad, in wooden houses, or in regions where strict fire codes prevent them from performing the *havan*, Sarkar Baba suggested a substitution. He asked them to perform *tarpaṇa* (putting oblations into water). In this case, the Navarātri observers place a vessel full of water before them and then, with rice and flowers as oblations, perform one hundred and eight oblations in water. This is a significant instance where Sarkar Baba changed the traditional ritual scheme. According to Sarkar Baba, this ritual satisfied the Goddess just as much as the traditional *havan*, although for the purists in India, this is somewhat unsatisfactory. This is because *tarpaṇa* already exists in the Hindu ritual cornucopia as a ritual performed to satisfy dead ancestors. Its association, then, with the Goddess seems odd to them. However, the larger meaning of *tarpaṇa* is not limited to propitiating one's ancestors and includes "satiating of the Gods and deceased persons" (Williams 2002). Once Sarkar Baba had mentioned this as a valid ritual, his devotees abroad had no problems performing it.

In the ashram, the *havan* ceremony culminated in a *bali* (sacrifice) usually signified by the breaking of a coconut or the slicing of a grapefruit, although many years ago a goat was sacrificed at the foot of the ashram's temple.[4] Sarkar Baba changed this practice because some devotees felt uncomfortable watching an animal being sacrificed. Sarkar Baba explained that when they break a coconut or slice a grapefruit as *bali*, it implies that they are offering the animal within themselves to the Goddess. He defined the animal within to be all the negative traits of a human personality such as jealousy, anger, impatience, greed, or infinite desires. In effect, Sarkar Baba's view of this sacrifice is a self-sacrifice, where the sacrificer offers portions of the self to the Goddess, in this case their own negativities leaving only the positives behind. Here Sarkar Baba's interpretation of the Navarātri sacrifice aligns with the scholarly interpretation by Axel Michaels, who writes, "The benefit of the sacrifice is based to a large extent on substantive and ritualistic identifications of the sacrificer with the sacrifice" (2003, 246).

After the *bali* was performed, people laughed and talked, satisfied at having successfully completed the difficult ritual process for eight days and nights. I interacted with the participants in the ashram during this period on several occasions. From what they talked about, and from their general demeanor, I could see they felt as if they had experienced some form of communication with the Goddess, depending upon how focused and attentive they had been during their meditations. I believe ending their austerities with such a happy experience was fulfilling for them.

On the ninth day, many people performed *kumārī pūjā* by feeding little girls as embodiments of the Goddess. Within the ashram precincts, there were usually families with young daughters. Devotees elsewhere in the city, however, had to go around their communities and invite parents and their young daughters to their homes for the ceremony. This usually became a social event enjoyed by the parents and their daughters, who did not always understand what the event was about. Finally, on the tenth day, the rite of *visarjana* (bidding farewell to the Goddess) was performed, and every material associated with this grand worship ceremony was ritually submerged in a body of water. With the Ganges only a short distance from the ashram, this was a simple though sad task.

Sarkar Baba likened the establishment of the ritual *kalaśa* as the bringing forth of an egg. After establishing the *kalaśa*, the seeker needs to give it the same warmth, affection, attention, care, and service that a bird provides an egg while incubating it. He described how the bird remains ever attentive to the egg so that no harm comes to it, constantly protecting and nurturing it, remaining focused on it. He said that if the seekers could emulate the focus of the attentive bird, their whole thought processes would become concentrated on the Goddess and her nature. Then their senses would also become automatically self-controlled, and concerns of the external world would dissipate as a dream. He emphasized that to incubate the Goddess in this manner, it was not necessary to establish an external *kalaśa* to worship. Seekers could simply invite the Goddess to be with them during this period. They could then focus on her internally, thus incubating the Goddess within with the same warm feeling and sentiment that a bird has for its egg. He said that this warm feeling and care needed to be reflected in all of one's actions during Navarātri.

For Sarkar Baba, focus and sentiment must exist simultaneously to produce the desired results. This becomes clear in his comparison of rituals and gathering flowers:

> Your mental state while acquiring and offering rice, leaves, flowers . . . to your divinity is important. While collecting flowers, become so absorbed . . . that even the cacophony of a passing army would not disturb you. Only then will you know the divinity of the *mantra*, the benefit and virtue of offering flowers to your divinity. But if your mental state is turbulent, if you are thinking about the deeds and misdeeds of people while collecting flowers, then you are not picking flowers, you are collecting little pouches of poison for yourself. You are collecting garbage that you will then throw on your divinity. (Ram 2007, 196)

If one's mind is not fixed on the task at hand all of the physical actions have deleterious results. In both the analogies, the practice requires a certain kind of mental discipline. Sarkar Baba emphasized the need for discipline by enumerating its benefits:

> You will have better interest in deep meditation, visualization and prayer only when you assume your proper posture (*āsana*), keep your vertebral column (*merudaṇḍa*) straight, and harmonize the flow of breath (*śvāsa*). [We] close our eyes lightly without applying too much pressure, we try that our ears may

> not pay attention to the sounds coming from elsewhere. We keep our attention focused on the vibrations of the *mantra* that keeps happening with our breath and the beat of our heart. Then what happens? That Goddess begins to affect your body. (*Sarveshwari Times*, May 15, 1972, 4)

Many Navarātri observers in the ashram mentioned that on occasion when they would become in-tune with their *mantra*, especially when they let the *mantra* resonate with their heart-beat or the flow of the breath, they lost track of time or even their body awareness. Those who experienced knee or back pain from sitting still for a long time explained that they did not even feel their bodies. For those who could maintain their absorption in the *mantra*, even in light of any external sound that might jar their senses, they claimed that their awareness seemed to expand indescribably. Incubating the Goddess through ritual awareness in such a manner appeared to have generated an altered kind of energy, a distinctive state of consciousness within the seeker.

Creating Space for and Surrendering to the Goddess

In Sarkar Baba's ashram, while some people recited the *Durgāsaptaśatī* during Navarātri, Sarkar Baba never made a prescription of it. For him, the Goddess was not limited to the words in a text but could be experienced firsthand. Therefore, he suggested that devotees not be limited by the ritualism or tied down with preconceptions about the Goddess presented in a text. He said, "We think, like a cartoon that the gods have four hands, ride tigers, ride elephants, ride horses. Friends, it is not so" (Ram 2007, 200).

For those who read the *Durgāsaptaśatī*, this is clearly a very different kind of view. Sarkar Baba's is quite unorthodox when he equates the lion-, tiger-, or elephant-riding gods with four or eight arms with cartoons. But such a view can be better understood if, in keeping with the generally understood Tantric principles, one thinks of the Goddess as an omnipresent principle. Similarly, the *mantra* is more than just a letter written on a surface, or just a syllable to be uttered; the *mantra* is regarded as the manifestation of cosmic vibration. Likewise, a *siddha* guru is believed to embody the power of God or *śakti* within; he is not just a person (See Gupta and Gombrich 1986). In effect, for the perceptive seeker, there is really no difference between the guru, the *mantra*, and the Goddess because they are three aspects of the same principle. The presence of a guru is viewed as the visible grace of God or Goddess. The *mantra* that the guru gives to the disciple is understood to be the vibrational principle through which power (*śakti*, or as Sarkar Baba called it, a constant and ever-present friend) is harnessed, and the Goddess, of course, is the epitome of such power. Fixating on the descriptions provided within a text can mask this principle of interrelation.

Moreover, going beyond textual descriptions and understanding this principle is believed to help create an internal climate where the presence of the Goddess may be felt. There exist many obstacles to the creation of such a climate, a primary one being the stressed and distracted nature of the human beings. Sarkar Baba stressed the human proclivity towards distraction for knowledge of the external world. Thoughts of friends, family, enemies, work, and business prove to be equally distracting. Sarkar Baba taught that those following the Navarātri observations should not remain focused on their mundane activities or consume the information continuously presented in the media, but instead should turn their senses inward. Even so, it is not simply enough to shut out the external world; the seeker must also work to not produce such a world internally or express it externally through the medium of words. The performers of such Navarātri practices are thus making their selves impervious to the external and internal influences that could disturb their tranquility and that of those around them. Such practice requires a degree of self-awareness and self-control to constantly observe one's own actions, physical as well as mental. By shutting out the external world of the senses and maintaining tranquility within, the devotee opens the door to the internal world creating space for the Goddess to arrive.

Sarkar Baba stated that at least during these nine days the Navarātri observers should try to see and feel the Goddess in her subtlety. She could be seen in the sunshine, in the air around them, in the happy sounds of children at play, in the space between the earth and the sky that seems to be empty, in the restful feeling of going to sleep at night without a care; it is all an expression of the Goddess. The observer simply needed to get in tune with her to perceive it so.

Becoming impervious to the influences of the world, however, is still a minor step in the direction of truly observing Navarātri.

> [I]f we so much as utter the word Sarveśvarī, who is the Goddess of all . . . And if we also add . . . that we are in your refuge, O mother Sarveśvarī, . . . then all my baggage, my load, the maintenance of my life, is not a matter of my own hands anymore. Now she is the one guiding everything. When she is handling this then my effort to obstruct it, to make intellectual arguments and counter-arguments . . . will only create sorrow. (Kumar 2001, 25–26)

What Sarkar Baba is emphasizing here is that merely speaking the Goddess's name is sufficient to give a practitioner a lot in life. But if with that utterance there is also a feeling of surrender to the Goddess—letting the Goddess manage one's life rather than obstructing the Goddess's management by exercising one's own intellect—then she takes over the practitioner's life. The practitioner, then, becomes free of the heavy burden of life and feels light.

Sarkar Baba then moves on to how this can be done. First, he points out the right time to try to connect with the Goddess:

> Great souls regard the state of sleeping as wakefulness, and the state of remaining preoccupied with myriad acts and inclinations as a state of sleeping. The night takes you into the state of *samādhi*, it fulfills you, through new dreams and thoughts it shows you new things and new universes. (*Sarveshwari Times* October 15, 1973, 4).

Sarkar Baba shows here the ease with which seekers can connect with the Goddess at night because their minds are not preoccupied by things that happened during the day, when their minds are not calm. Once one's mind is calm, one can begin to visualize the Goddess, but even that is not without special efforts to keep one's mind a blank slate.

> Friends, your *mantra* has the power, the strength, so that you can have present before you the forms [of the Goddess] that you want to meditate upon . . . and you can also make them speak in a way that you want them to. But even this is not good for you friends! . . . [I]t is not right that you should make them speak as you want, [because] it may not turn out beneficial for you. What is important is to realize what *she* wants. (Kumar 2001, 29–30, emphasis added)

Sarkar Baba asks the Navarātri observers who have created a space for the Goddess to arrive to visualize the Goddess as they wish to, but tells them that their *mantra* can act as a sculpting tool, like a chisel or a hammer, to help them do this. But then he also cautions that the Goddess ought to be free to reveal how she wants to appear. The *mantra* then becomes the presence of the Goddess within or, in the words of Gupta and Gombrich, "*mantra* is a *śakti*–in fact, it is power, the Goddess, in action" (Gupta and Gombrich 1986, 130).

The Goddess within requires the same attention as the egg to be incubated, focus with absolute sense-control. The effect of the absorption in the resonance of the *mantra* within the seeker can open doors of perception, diminishing attachment to the external senses during which the devotees are able to maintain this state without distraction. With these senses no longer distracting the self, the seekers are now privy to "senseless" perception. Their breathing becomes harmonized; their minds become calm; the internal processes within their bodies become more evident; and the existence of the Goddess becomes increasingly more discernible (Kumar 2001, 78). With the warmth, affection, and attention that the seekers have been providing to her, now there can be perceived stirrings of life in the egg, the Goddess within.

> We perceive God, our dear deity only through the medium of our thoughts, not with our physical eyes . . . At the time of activating your thoughts you put your hands in God's hands. You kiss the feet of that God. You kiss her forehead. You embrace her. She also embraces you . . . Happily, she puts her hand on your head, the hand which opens the eyes of the heart. She touches that body part which unlocks the knots of your speech. She puts that garland around [the seeker's] neck, which makes the mind and heart joyful . . . It is through the medium of that thought we see her in a bright flame in the sky, and perceive that flame to have infinite depth. (*Sarveshwari Times,* April 15, 1972, 2)

To the casual observer or skeptic, this may sound like a process of self-hypnosis. I am sure Sarkar Baba was aware of this. Sometimes while describing the process of meditation, he would quote a popular colloquialism: "(most) make a play of it, for real it happens; for real plays but one in a million."[5] This quote implies that a devoted act performed even in play can turn out to be real, but alas, there are very few who are able to perform so in reality! That is to say that even though you are imagining the deity, it is through this "practice" that the deity can become realized. As Hüsken has illustrated in a different but related context that even when children play at worshipping their gods they simultaneously learn to enact the right practices generating the right mental and emotional attitude to "real" worship (2012). Thus, by imagining the Goddess within one's mind the devotee makes it possible to see the Goddess. Sarkar Baba emphasized it is not possible to see the Goddess with our physical eyes. She can only be seen with the mental and the emotional eye, the experience. Only that eye is needed here. By cultivating the practice Sarkar Baba asks them to perform, the devotees then begin to perceive the presence of the Goddess.

The Presence of the Goddess

The natural question that arises: Is this all imaginary? Does the seeker simply make-believe that there exists a Goddess and that the Goddess arrives during meditation and interacts with the seeker? Or is there a Goddess that exists outside of the meditative state? This might be a question less for a believer or a mystic and more for an academic, although the answer may be equally relevant to both in markedly different ways. During fieldwork, devotees in the ashram narrated many stories about their belief in the presence of the Goddess, stories that strengthen the devotees' belief that the Goddess does, indeed, exist. Here, for purposes of illustration I paraphrase only two: one from Kedar Sav, a businessman and longtime devotee of Sarkar Baba from Mirzapur; and the second, from Ghasi Ram Ji, a mason from Raigarh, Chhattisgarh. From the believer's point of view, they portray the feeling of faith and devotion in the genuineness of the experience related to the Goddess. For the academic, such practices may represent the cultivation of a specific set of mental attitudes charged by emotion that lead to a state like autohypnosis.

Kedar Sav's Story

One morning during Navarātri, Kedar Sav and his friend Babaguru were preparing for their day in the fields and discussing how Sarkar Baba should give them a real live *darśan* (divine vision) of the Goddess. Even as they spoke, a woman wearing a red sari appeared out of nowhere, walked deliberately past them, and disappeared in the fields. They thought nothing of it. Sarkar Baba later asked them, "Isn't this a direct *darśan* of the Goddess?" Kedar Sav and Babaguru were amazed.

This is clearly a story of faith. The woman in the red sari could have been anyone. But when their guru told them about it, the episode took on a mystical color. As Sarkar Baba said after this episode, "She is everywhere. She can be found everywhere" (see Ram 2003, chapter 9).

Ghasi Ram Ji's Story

During the festival of *Gurupūrṇimā,* Ghasi Ram Ji mentioned to Sarkar Baba that he wanted to go to Vindhyācal for a *darśan* of Mother Vindhyavāsinī (the goddess who dwells in the Vindhya mountains). Baba laughed and said, "Have *darśan* to your heart's content." With this blessing, Ghasi Ram Ji started on his journey and encountered a series of happy coincidences where all his travel problems were immediately and miraculously solved. When he reached the temple of Mother Vindhyavāsinī and had her *darśan,* he felt so moved that he lost consciousness. When he regained consciousness, someone asked him, "How was the *darśan*?" Ghasi Ram Ji then gave the questioner a vivid description of the room where he had seen the Goddess. His description surprised the questioner, who had long been tending the idols in the temple, because he had never seen the room which Ghasi Ram Ji described. It was as if he had a *darśan* in a completely different realm (see Ram 2003, chapter 10).

Although this story is set during Gurupūrṇimā and not Navarātri, it clearly portrays Ghasi Ram Ji's experiences of the Goddess. For him, there was without a doubt a Goddess, and she was graceful enough to give him her *darśan*. This story is different from Kedar Sav's story in its sense of adventure. Ghasi Ram Ji does not know much about the Goddess, and he does not expect much from his journey. However, through a series of coincidences that appear miraculous to him, his trip turns into a journey of the Mother's grace. He gets to see her in forms that even those who are intimately associated with her temple complex have never seen. He also has a trancelike experience before the Goddess. As skeptics, we may argue that Ghasi Ram Ji was already in an emotionally charged state, and therefore his mind might have played tricks on him. But for Ghasi Ram Ji, it was all undoubtedly very real, especially when corroborated by the gentleman associated with her temple complex.

Becoming (like) the Goddess

Once the Goddess becomes visualized as if present before the observer, Sarkar Baba exhorts seekers not to allow their intellect to interfere in the form that she takes to manifest herself. At this moment, devotees should carefully ask the Goddess to manifest in the form in which *she* wishes to appear; otherwise it will not be an act of absolute surrender. This is because on seeing her, human thoughts, mediated by the limitations of the senses, may commit the mistake of asking her for something that may be potentially harmful. Therefore, the effort here is to develop one's intellect to become like that of the Goddess. But how can one become like the Goddess? Sarkar Baba explains:

> [W]e pray to her. O my Mother please give me such inspiration that I become blemish-free, cunning-free . . . *Let your nature enter into my nature*. Then what will happen to me? I will experience joy, I will experience affection, I will have love for others, and I will know of your arrival, that you have now entered my body. When you enter my body my mind, intellect, heart, will become very peaceful, and with this peace I will begin to be amongst those human beings who are divine souls, holy souls, beautiful souls. (Kumar 2001, 31–32, emphasis added)

Here, Sarkar Baba completes the process of internalizing the Goddess as she takes over the body of the practitioner, resonating within the devotee with the vibrations of the *mantra*, transforming her own nature, her own peace and joy into their nature, their peace, their joy. The egg that was incubating within now turns out to be the very being, the very self of the seeker. Through the process of this incubation, the devotee's self is transformed into the nature of the Goddess herself. The seeker achieves the company of the Goddess, and here, only peace and joy exist. Through Navarātri practices the seekers in the ashram make the Goddess their own, and in turn, they become hers.

Conclusion

To recap, the process began with the invitation to the Goddess through the installation of the *kalaśa* bringing the egg forth. The egg is tended to and incubated through the festival observances including the *japa* performed by the devotee. With the sacrifice, that incubating egg hatches and brings the Goddess back into the world worshiped as a "daughter" and visible as young girls who are worshipped as the Goddess's embodiment. If the *kalaśa* represents bringing forth an egg, this *kumārī pūjā* is the recognition of the new life form of the Goddess with all its creative potential. The process of incubating the Goddess within then begins as the seekers invite the Goddess within them through the body *yantra*. During the process of inviting the Goddess to be with them, the seekers now address her as the "Mother." This process, which can be visualized in the diagram below (figure 11.1), culminates in the devotees becoming one with the Goddess.

Sarkar Baba asked his followers to observe the festival of Navarātri through austerities, meditation, and one-sighted focus. This picture is quite

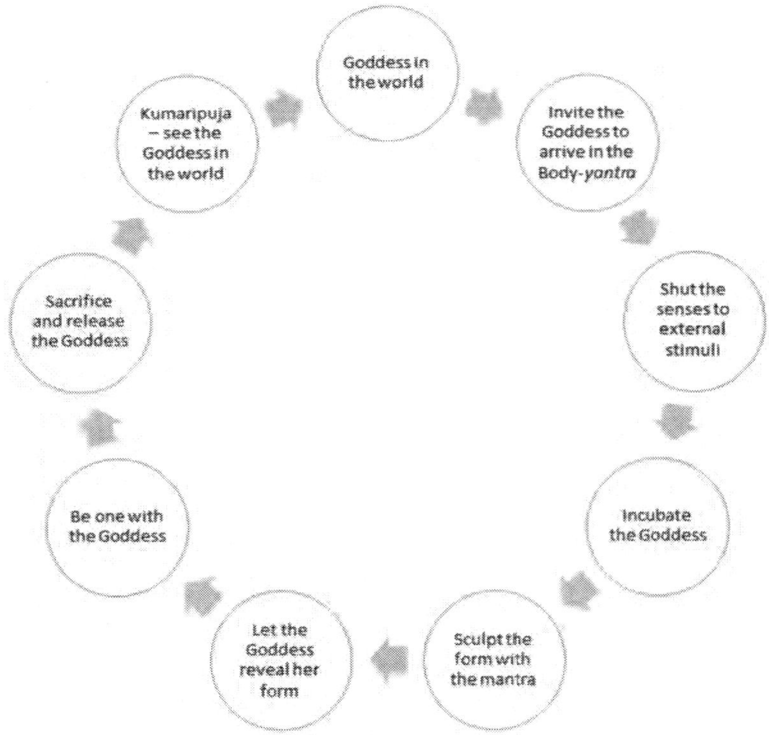

Figure 11.1. The process of internalizing and releasing the Goddess during Navarātri.

different from the music, dance, aromatic food, and throngs of people that characterize many of the public and domestic observance of this festival described in this volume. Sarkar Baba's Navarātri is about a very personal and emotionally charged relationship that a seeker establishes with the Goddess. Having established this relationship, instead of asking for wealth, or power, or other types of worldly boons, the Navarātri observer seeks to acquire and retain the essence, and hence the power, the *śakti*, of the Goddess within them.

Sarkar Baba wanted his followers to experience the joy of celebrating the Goddess. However, his focus was on first experiencing the Goddess by becoming the vessel where she could arrive, take abode, and infuse her grace. When viewed through that experience, everything that exists is inseparable from the grace of the Goddess. The joy of Navarātri, then, becomes permanent and infuses all parts of the seekers' lives.

Notes

1. Contrary to expectation, we do not see the name Durgā mentioned in this list, although Kaviraj does mention a list where this name exists: Hṛllekhā, Gaganā, Raktā, Mahocchuṣmā, Karālikā, Icchā, Jnāna, Kriyā, and Durgā (Kaviraj 1966, 240). Another common name for this text is *Candī Saptaśatī* (Singh 1983, 5). Some people contend that the name of this text should be "Saptasatī" because the *Māhātmya* deals with the story of seven satis. But there exists, again, a difference of opinion about who these seven satis are—the seven mothers, Brāhmī, Māheśvarī, Kaumārī, Vaishṇavī, Vārāhī, Indrāṇī, and Cāmundā—or the seven incarnations of the Mother—Nandā, Śākambharī, Bhīmā, Raktadantikā, Durgā, Bhrāmarī and Śatākṣī (Shankaranarayanan 1968, 7).

2. According to Shankaranarayanan, "Some Tantras enumerate the names of the nine Durgas as the Vanadurga, Jaladurga, Agnidurga, Sthaladurga, Viṣṇu durga, Brahmadurga, Rudradurga, Mahadurga and Shulinidurga" (1968, 81).

3. Gaurinath Sastri explains, "The Mārkaṇḍeya Purāṇa describes that prior to the first creation there was Caṇḍikā or śakti alone . . . In the beginning of creation Caṇḍikā came to be looked upon as Mahālakṣmī, the First Creator. In her we find the transcendent conception of Caṇḍikā first transformed into an immanent one. But there is no radical difference between the two conceptions. Looked at from the empirical standpoint She is regarded as Mahālakṣmī, the creator. Mahālakṣmī as non-different from Caṇḍikā is regarded as the equilibrium of the three guṇas and serves as the background of all further evolution . . . In the beginning of a cycle of creation Mahālakṣmī found herself all alone and wished to multiply herself. Then from her proceeded a new emanation named Mahākālī as a consequence of the preponderance of the element of *tamas* in her. Thus, Mahākālī is neither made nor created nor begotten from Mahālakṣmī but she proceeds from the latter according to the operation of divine inertia . . . After this second emanation there was yet another disturbance of the equilibrium in the divine nature of the Great Goddess. This time the *sattva* element in her temporarily foredominated and Mahāsarasvatī, the third Divine Female of the Blessed Trinity, proceeded

from Mahālakṣmī by the operation of divine intelligence (Singh 1983, 9–11). For a discussion of the various traditions that seem to be reflected in the persona of the Goddess in the *Devīmāhātmya*, see Kinsley 1978.

4. Sarkar notes from Raghunandana's *Durgāpūjātattva*, "For the more orthodox, Raghunandana provides the default option of using certain vegetables as substitutes such as the pumpkin and the sugar cane along with spirits, the offering of which is said to be as fruitful as the offering of a goat" (2012, 354).

5. Jhuṭhmuṭh khēlai sacmuc hoi, sacmuc khēlai Biralai koi.

References

Primary Sources

Kumar, Anjani. 2001. *Navarātri Talks Series (Navarātri Pravacana Mālā)*. Varanasi, UP: Aghor Shodh Evam Sewa Sansthan, Baba Kinaram Sthal.

Sarveshwari Times. 1972. Parao, Varanasi, UP: Shri Sarveshwari Samooh. March 30; April 15; May 15.

———. 1973. March 15.

———. 1976. September 30; October 15

———. 1977. April 15.

Ram, Akinchan. 2003. *The Ambrosia of the Play of Bhagawan Ram (Bhagawānarāmalīlāmrit)*. Banora, Raigarh, Chhattisgarh: Aghor Guru Peeth Trust.

Singh, Satyavrat, ed. 1983. *Śrī Durgāsaptaśatī* (with Hindi Commentary). With a Foreword by Gaurinath Sastri. Naimisharanya, Sitapur: Institute for Pauranic and Vedic Studies and Research.

Secondary Sources

Biardeau, Madeleine. 1984. "The Sami Tree and the Sacrificial Buffalo." *Contributions to Indian Sociology* 18:1.

Crooke, William. 1915. "The Dasahra: An Autumn Festival of the Hindus." *Folklore* 26 (1) (March 31): 28–59.

Einoo, Shingo. 1999. "The Autumn Goddess Festival: Described in the Purāṇas." In *Living with Śakti: Gender, Sexuality and Religion in South Asia*, edited by Masakazu Tanaka, Musashi Tachikawa, and Kokuritsu Minzokugaku Hakubutsukan, 33–70. Osaka: National Museum of Ethnology.

Fuller, C. J. [1994] 2004. *The Camphor Flame: Popular Hinduism and Society in India*. Princeton, NJ: Princeton University Press.

Gell, Alfred. 1997. "Exalting the King and Obstructing the State: A Political Interpretation of Royal Ritual in Bastar District, Central India." *The Journal of the Royal Anthropological Institute* 3 (3) (September 1997): 433–50.

Gupta, Sanjukta, and Richard Gombrich. 1986. "Kings, Power and the Goddess." *South Asia Research* 6 (2) (November).

Hüesken, Ute. 2012. "Training, Play and Blurred Distinctions: On Imitation and "Real" Ritual." In *Religions in Play: Games, Rituals, and Virtual Worlds*, edited by Maya Burger and Philippe Bornet, 177–96. (CultuRel 2), Zürich: Pano.

Kane, Mahāmahopādhyāya P. V. 1958. *History of Dharmaśāstra*, 5, Pt-1. Government Oriental Series Class B, no. 6. Poona: Bhandarkar Oriental Research Institute.

Kaviraj, Mahāmahopādhyāya Gopinath. 1966. *Aspects of Indian Thought*. Burdwan: University of Burdwan.

Kinsley, David. 1978. "The Portrait of the Goddess in the Devī-māhātmya." *Journal of the American Academy of Religion* 46 (4) (December): 489–506.

Michaels, Axel. 2003. *Hinduism: Past and Present*. Trans. Barbara Harshav. Princeton, NJ: Princeton University Press.

Monier-Williams, Monier. 2002. *Sanskrit-English Dictionary*. Delhi: Motilal Banarsidass Books.

Ram, Baba Bhagwan. 2007. *The Book of Aghor Wisdom: Aghoracharya Baba Kinaram Aghor Shodh Evam Seva Sansthan*. Varanasi: Indica Books.

Sarkar, Bihani. 2012. "The Rite of Durgā in Medieval Bengal: An Introductory Study of Raghunandana's *Durgāpūjātattva* with Text and Translation of the Principal Rites." *Journal of the Royal Asiatic Society* 22: 325–90. doi:10.1017/S1356186312000181.

Shankaranarayanan, S. 1968. *Glory of the Divine Mother (Devī mahatmyam)*. Pondicherry: Dipti.

Vahia, Mayank. 2014. Electronic Document, "Why Do We Celebrate Makar Sankranti on January 14 Every Year?" Sunday, March 9. http://www.dnaindia.com/analysis/standpoint-why-do-we-celebrate-makar-sankranti-on-january-14-every-year-1968036.

White, David Gordon. 2006. "Digging Wells While Houses Burn? Writing Histories of Hinduism in a Time of Identity Politics." *History and Theory* 45 (4): 104–31.

NAVARĀTRI AT HOME

12

Kolus, Caste, and Class

Navarātri as a Site for Ritual and Social Change in Urban South India

NICOLE A. WILSON

It was the first day of the nine-night Hindu festival known as Navarātri. Along with other female neighbors, I had been invited to Jayanthi's house for a celebratory *pūjā*/singing event. Later in the evening, Jayanthi and a few other female community members would meet at the Śrī Maṅkala Vināyakar temple to decorate for the ensuing evenings of worship. But for the moment, I was happily exploring Jayanthi's *pūjā* room and waiting for the other neighbors to arrive. In my explorations, I was struck by a large decorated altar dedicated to Lakṣmī that Jayanthi had fashioned in an adjoining room. In yet another room, she had arranged small cups full of coffee and tea, as well as silk-screened canvas bags packed with items of feminine toilette, a banana, and a betel nut. The altar and gifts were not striking to me because Jayanthi was irreligious or lacked generosity in normal circumstances but because she was of a lower caste, one that is not historically known to mark Navarātri with such décor and gifts. Indeed, in my previous experiences during Navarātri, I found myself only in Brahmin and Chettiyar (higher caste) homes, viewing a traditional ritual doll display (*kolu*) and receiving a simple, small packet of cooked beans as a parting gift.

Jayanthi's celebration of Navarātri takes place during a time in contemporary Indian history when distinct caste markers are not only identifiers of caste culture but also influence class identifications, as class continually gains ground as an identity category. This event at Jayanthi's house would not only mark the beginning of Navarātri that year, but it also marked the beginning of my reeducation about how Navarātri was celebrated and how caste and class were negotiated with respect to Hindu ritual and community in contemporary South India.

Urban Religious Festivals, Class, and Caste

Religious Festivals and Urbanization

As devices of identity construction and communication, religious festivals are often used to display wealth, knowledge, authority, and other markers of social status (Welbon and Yocum 1982; Trouillet 2008). The use of religious celebrations in this way is heightened by their locations in urban environments, locales that frequently imply a mixing of social groupings and the necessary mediation of differences between these social groupings. Many of the women in Jayanthi's middle-class community grew up in rural environments where caste distinctions were more spatially enacted. They have now moved to urban environments where they are in close proximity to neighbors of differing castes, necessitating a renegotiation of caste barriers and social interaction. This proximity has affected the women's perceptions of community and religious participation in many respects, including the ways that annual Hindu festivals and their associated rituals are celebrated and how they are used to reconfigure social distinctions.

Navarātri, in an urban context, is one religious festival that seems to have undergone several of the modifications discussed above. In focusing on its local manifestation in Madurai, Tamil Nadu, I have found that while rituals associated with Navarātri have historically been reserved for particular groups of people (i.e., caste groups), changes relating to social mobility and socioeconomic status in urban living environments have affected how Navarātri rituals are carried out.

Middle Classness

Scholars who study the growing middle class in India have argued that over the past few decades, the country has experienced a "bourgeois revolution," which has created an influx of middle-class desires, sensibilities, and identifications (Stern 2003, 3). However, the practices signifying these desires and identifications are a contested subject in research on South Asia. Still, most maintain that middle-class identity is not merely a function of economics but is also culturally constructed (Fernandes 2000). Most studies indicate that a middle-class Indian family is classified not only according to their household income, but also by how they utilize that income to perpetuate certain values and a particular worldview. Subsequently, we have come to identify specific objective and categorical "markers" of middle-class identity that articulate both access to and consumption of particular goods (televisions, motorbikes, refrigerators, and cellphones [Lakha 1999] or domestic servants [Dickey 2000]) which constitute symbolic capital within a community as well as cultural values (e.g., valuation of higher education [Dickey 2000; Donner 2008; Gilbertson 2014a; Fuller and Narasimhan 2014], vegetarianism [Malhotra 2002; Donner 2008], "decency" and neatness in self-presentation [Dickey 2012, Gilbertson 2014a], democracy [Ahmad and Reifeld 2001], altruistic community service work [Waghorne 2004], guru-centered movements [Warrier 2003, 2005], and the current growing Hindu nationalist movement [Hancock 1995; Hansen 1999; Mankekar 1999; Fernandes 2000]).

These values and worldviews are intricately tied to the historical relationship between caste and class identities in India. For instance, there is a distinction between what is known as the "old middle class" and the "new middle class" (Sheth 1999; Fernandes 2000). The "old middle class" is described as those upper-caste individuals (mostly Brahmins) who, under British colonial rule and immediately after independence, had primary access to higher (read: English) education and better employment opportunities (Chatterjee 1992; Fernandes 2000; Fuller and Narasimhan 2014). This access allowed these higher castes to obtain the income necessary to identify as middle class. The "new middle class" is characterized as a population that is increasingly lower in caste (but also includes those of higher-caste communities) and has benefited from education and employment reservations that had resulted from the Mandal Commission of the 1980s. These reservations, in combination with the liberalization of the Indian economy in 1991 (Saavala 2003; Nanda 2009), have allowed a "new" set of individuals to attain a middle-class status (Sheth 1999). The caste affiliations that have become politicized through the reservation system are interacting with India's fast-paced economic growth and the subsequent formation of socioeconomic class divisions. This creates an environment where class associations are uniquely positioned in relation to modern interpretations of caste culture. As we will see in our exploration of Navarātri celebrations by the middle-class, multicaste residents of Jayanthi's neighborhood, this interaction between caste and class manifests itself in a challenging of caste stereotypes and practices and in the construction of class identities.

Sanskritization and Brahminization

Examinations of social mobility and variations in caste identity in India have long been a part of South Asian studies (Singer 1972; Mines 2005).

A classic case study of these issues is seen in the work of M. N. Srinivas. Studying among the Coorgs in south India, Srinivas provided a detailed picture of village life, caste structures, and social mobility (Srinivas 1952). In this work, he described the phenomenon of "Sanskritization," a process by which members of lower castes could achieve social mobility through the emulation of higher caste practices (Srinivas 1956). While Sanskritization was certainly a viable interpretation for the time, I would argue that today social mobility in India is much more a consequence of socioeconomics than in previous decades.

Following Srinivas's attempts to explain social mobility and transformation, Karin Kapadia (1995) has offered her own ruminations about social change in India. In her theory of "Brahminization," Kapadia highlights the relationship between perceptions of caste and class. She maintains that ideas of sophistication, modernity, and other Indian middle-class ideals are intricately connected to Brahmin values and social practices. This concept of Brahminization is quite prevalent in the social milieu of Tamil Nadu.

Brahmins in Tamil Nadu

The Brahmin association with the middle- and upper-class values is a widespread local assumption in both urban and rural areas. This is related to a variety of factors and curiously conflicts with a good deal of academic literature that conflates the social influence of Brahmins and their percentage of representation among the Tamil population (approximately 3 percent).[1] Using this model, the literature argues for a decreasing Brahmin influence due to the local Dravidian political history and its anti-Brahmin rhetoric (Ramaswamy 1997 and 1998; Fuller 2003; Kolenda 2003; Pandian 2007). C. J. Fuller has refuted this assertion, arguing that "the decline of the Tamil Brahmins has in fact been exaggerated in the scholarly literature—as well as in much commentary within Tamil Nadu itself—by a tendency to over-emphasize the political campaign against them" (Fuller 1999, 32). Fuller goes on to note that rural Brahmins have continuously had a high rate of migration to cities, which, in combination with monies collected as village landlords, has given them an advantage in comparison to other castes living in urban areas. Many of the first migrants from rural to urban areas in Tamil Nadu were Brahmins, as they could afford education and bribes necessary for entrance into government jobs (Fuller 1999, 33; see also Fuller and Narasimhan 2014). With this link to higher education and wealth, Brahmin status not only has come to represent higher-caste Hindu ritual practice but has become a common indicator of higher socioeconomic class. In fact, Fuller makes the argument that in urban Tamil Nadu, "there is a consistent tendency to identify Sanskritic Brahminical culture as the core of Tamil 'civilized,' high culture, which in many respects is deemed Brahminical because it is high, rather than high because it is Brahminical" (Fuller 1999, 36). He observes that in Tamil urban settings, "members of the mainly urban socio-economic elite, both Brahmin and non-Brahmin, are predisposed to identify their own cultural values as Brahminical, and upwardly mobile non-Brahmins are attracted to those values" (Fuller 1999, 36). The following ethnographic material will illustrate how the complex association between perceived Brahmin ritual practice and higher socioeconomic status is enacted on a local scale, during celebrations of Navarātri in the suburban neighborhood surrounding the Śrī Maṅkala Vināyakar (SMV) temple in Madurai.

Navarātri in South India

Navarātri (Tamil: Navarāttiri) is a nine-night festival that is specified according to the lunar calendar and takes place in the Tamil month of Puraṭṭāci (mid-September to mid-October) (Fuller 1980). The festival marks an astrologically auspicious time to worship the Goddess in several forms and is primarily associated with the Hindu epic *Devī Māhātmyam* from the *Mārkaṇḍeya Purāṇa* in which the goddess Durgā is embroiled in a great battle with the demon Makiṣāsuraṉ (Sanskrit: Mahiṣāsura) and his army (*Devī Māhātmya* chapter 3). After Durgā has defeated his army, she spears Makiṣāsuraṉ and cuts off his head.

Historically, Navarātri in south India was a ritual relating to kingship (see Balkaran and Simmons, this volume). During the Vijayanagar period (thirteenth–sixteenth centuries CE) it was recognized as a time to renew royal sovereignty (Stein 1980; Fuller and Logan 1985). However, it has been argued that while most temples celebrate the festival in some way, Navarātri in contemporary south India has also become an occasion for heightened domestic ritual (Fuller and Logan 1985).

In general, the nine nights of Navarātri are organized into three sections, the first three days reserved for Durgā, the next three days reserved for Lakṣmī, and the final days reserved for Sarasvatī (Tanaka 1999).[2] The final day of Navarātri in Tamil Nadu is known as "Sarasvatī Pūjā" or "Vijayadaśamī" (the victorious tenth day). In Tamil Nadu, Sarasvatī Pūjā is the most popular day for celebration (i.e., by all genders and a wider assortment of castes and socioeconomic classes) and is marked across the state through the adornment of anything from books to motorbikes with sandalwood paste and vermilion powder as a mark of the Goddess's blessing. According to one account, this adornment reflects the idea that Sarasvatī Pūjā "is considered to be an auspicious time to worship tools used to earn an income" due to an association with Arjuna's retrieval of his weapons in the *Mahābharata* on the last day of Navarātri (Krishna 2008, 1). In addition to the decoration of specific items, families often have special meals on this day.

As articulated above, at the heart of most Navarātri celebrations is the recognition of the goddess Durgā as the destroyer of evil. However, Durgā's positioning in the Hindu realm is undergoing transformation. Early work on Durgā in south India focused on her threshold position in the Hindu pantheon, a liminality based on her unmarried status and "untamed sexual energy" (Kinsley 1986, 115). This unmarried status often results in the Goddess being represented alone within Tamil temple settings, which, Fuller (1984) argues, attributes a fiercer and more vengeful attitude to the Goddess. Yet, this attitude is also said to contribute to Durgā's popularity in contemporary Tamil Nadu and Kerala, as she is "thought to be very effective in dealing with the vexations of society and the economy today" (Fuller 2004, 273; see also Osella and Osella 2000, 167–68; Waghorne 2004, 134).

Recent studies in north Indian contexts suggest that some worshipers of this "wild" goddess have transformed her into a protective and caring mother figure (Wadley 2004, McDermott 2011). This supposed transformation is said to be a product of Durgā's association with "Vaishanvaite traditions" (Wadley 2004, 103; see also Shanmugalingam 1997) such that the goddess, who is considered to be "a late feature of Vaishnavism" (Wadley 2004, 101; see also Hume 1990, 147), can now "easily fit into the devotional traditions of bhakti [sic] as a 'naturally forgiving and . . . kind mother'" (Wadley 2004, 103; see also Hume 1990, 433). Associated with *bhakti* devotionalism, Durgā and her other forms can "be represented as perfect wives or other ideal role models for Hindu women" (Fuller 2004, 277). A song sung in Tamil Hindu temples to Durgā reflects the dual personality that the goddess seems to have acquired.[3] In it, we recognize the motherly protector and forgiver and the fierce adversary of Makiṣāsuraṉ:

> You are in my heart, I am in your heart,
> Tell me Durgā, who is whose relative?
> You rescue me from the forest and show me the way to get out.
> Take care of me in danger, forest-ruling Durgā—you . . .
>
> Victory Durgā, with your trident you ripped the force of anger from the lion.
> With your legs you stamped on the sluggish Makiṣāsuraṉ.
> You have given relief, peaceful Durgā—you . . .
>
> Wherever I go you follow me.
> There is no boundary or price for love.
> Please forgive me if I make any mistakes.
> No other companion is there to give prosperity/life—you . . .

In sum, while her devotees in Madurai, Tamil Nadu, are negotiating the caste and class axes of their identities, Durgā, based on worship context, is continually undergoing her own identity shifts.

Navarātri in the Śrī Maṅkala Vināyakar Temple

Every day at approximately four o'clock in the evening during Navarātri, the middle-class women of Jayanthi's neighborhood congregate at the local Śrī Maṅkala Vināyakar temple. They complete their usual circumambulations of the temple and then proceed to organize small cardboard place settings that include two small bowls, one empty and one filled with vermilion powder (*kuṅkumam*). These bowls are then handed to willing female participants who recite the 108 names of the goddess while counting pinches of the red powder in a practice known as *kuṅkumam arccaṉai.* After the *kuṅkumam arccaṉai* is complete, the red powder that has been transferred during the name recitation is combined and given to the temple priest. He then places the bowl of vermilion powder in front of the goddess statue and will later use it to mark the foreheads of devotees.

The decorations in the Śrī Maṅkala Vināyakar temple are primarily organized by local female devotees who draw elaborate rice-flour designs (*kōlaṅkaḷ*) at the front entrance to the temple. These devotees also purchase the fabric and props that adorn each form of the goddess. Each night of Navarātri is also associated with a particular color with which women often adorn themselves when going to the temple on the corresponding evening. The forms of the Goddess and the order in which they are worshipped vary according to region and by temple. This is exemplified in the list of goddesses worshipped at the Śrī Maṅkala Vināyakar temple:

1. Rājārajeśvarī (red)
2. Āṇḍāḷ (purple)
3. Mīnākṣī (green)
4. Kāmākṣī (yellow)
5. Aṇṇapurnī (orange)
6. Bhūvaneśvarī (white)
7. Pū Pāvāṭai (flower skirt) (blue)
8. Lakṣmī (pink)
9. Sarasvātī (purple)

The eighth day is reserved for Lakṣmī. According to the wider tradition, the final three days are to be reserved for Sarasvatī (Tanaka 1999). Moreover, purple is specified twice, and "*Pū Pāvāṭai*" (flower skirt) is a form that has only been noted in one other examination of Navarātri (Fuller and Logan 1985, 2).[4]

One can also purchase special tickets to have a blessing made for a loved one during the time of Navarātri. These cost Rs. 100 (approximately US$2.00, quite expensive if you are not at least middle class), and you are asked for the name of the person you wish to be blessed and their birth star. Near the end of the *pūjā*, the priest will recite Sanskrit *mantras* and add in each person's name and birth star. He will then crack a coconut and return it with the ritual food offering as *prasāda* (blessed food) at the end of the evening's event. Occasionally, the devotees (mainly lower caste) in the temple will not know the birth star of the person they wish to have blessed. In these instances, the priest will use a generic saying to bless the person.

The community involvement I witnessed during the celebration of Navarātri at the Śrī Maṅkala Vināyakar temple was not at all ubiquitous. On several occasions, I visited other neighborhood temples of the same size and observed that elements of community *arccaṉai* (*kuṅkumam* bowl ritual) and even devotees singing were noticeably absent. Instead, these other temples had constructed very elaborate higher caste ritual displays (i.e., *kolu*, see below), perhaps as a mode through which to communicate a higher form (read: authentic/proper) of Hindu religiosity and deter adoption of privileged religious knowledge (associated with Brahmin religious practices). This is not out of the ordinary in many south Indian Hindu temples, as is exemplified by the strategic adornment of deities on ritual occasions. Many temples that wish to demonstrate what they consider to be a higher form of religiosity will dress a female deity in a nine-yard sari, a type of sari usually reserved for Brahmin women. This decoration of female deities acts as a symbol of how temple priests and trustees would like the temple to be perceived.

After the formal celebration of the Goddess and the dispersal of the day's food offering, it is common for some devotees to invite female temple-goers to view their *kolu*, a common element of the Navarātri festival. Below, I describe the *kolu* in detail and discuss how caste and class are integrated into the construction and viewing of this ritualized component.

Kolu Viewing at Navarātri

A *kolu* is a tiered display of clay/porcelain/plastic three-dimensional images/dolls of gods and goddesses, political figures (e.g., Gandhi and Nehru), cultural scenes (such as weddings and temple festivals), and food items (figure 12.1). According to many devotees, the items included

Figure 12.1. An elaborate *kolu* constructed at the home of a middle-class Chettiyar family in Madurai, Tamil Nadu.

in the *kolu* are arranged according to intricate Sanskrit instructions, and to construct a proper *kolu*, the items must be placed on the steps while reciting specific *mantras*. There are several interpretations of the *kolu* structure. Some consider the *kolu* to be a representation of "the cosmos, inhabited by beings divine, human, and animal" (Ramnarayan 2013, 1). Others maintain that the term *kolu* refers to "a sovereign sitting in his royal darbar" and that the arrangement of the dolls recalls the goddess Durgā "sitting in her *golu*, prior to the slaying of the demon Mahisasura" (Krishna 2008, 1). In her research on Navarātri celebrations in the Tamil town of Chidambaram, Tanaka notes that the *kolu* ideally consists of nine tiers, to correspond with the nine nights of the festival. If the use of nine tiers is not feasible, one should pay heed to the auspiciousness accorded to odd numbers in Indian culture, as well as the fact that it is necessary to have a minimum of three tiers for the worship of the Goddess (1999, 124).

In an influential article on Navarātri in the city of Madurai, Fuller and Logan (1985) comment in depth on the religious significance of the *kolu*. Attending to the notion that Navarātri is a time to celebrate the goddess's defeat of the demon Makiṣāsuraṉ, they argue that *kolus* "display the harmony that is threatened by Makiṣāsuraṉ, for they represent the world in its creative, beneficent, hierarchically-ordered aspect" (Fuller and Logan 1985, 97). Fuller and Logan also address the significance of ritual time with respect to *kolu* symbolism and construction. They comment, "[T]he kolus represent the converse of the evil disorder that those agents [demons] bring; they are honoured at night, the time associated with evil forces, but they are illuminated, to suggest perhaps that those forces have been dispelled" (Fuller and Logan 1985, 97). The factors of illumination and the dispelling of evil forces is particularly interesting considering the frequent visiting of homes with *kolus* by females, members of society who ordinarily are socioculturally limited in their movements at night.

As alluded to earlier, the showing of a *kolu* during Navarātri is predominantly practiced in higher-caste (Brahmin and Chettiyar) homes and many non-Brahmins both within and outside the neighborhood located the showing or keeping (*vai*) of a *kolu* as a particularly Brahmin practice. Still, a few non-Brahmins, mostly high to middle in the local caste hierarchy (e.g., Saiva Pillais, Mudaliyars) argued that they did not build and show a *kolu* because they did not have female children who could help them with the work inherent in its construction. *Kolus,* according to members of these communities, as well as many of their neighbors, were understood as connected with women's/domestic work. It was also argued that for the practice of showing a *kolu* to be socially respected, it had to be performed every year without fail (an exception being the presence of ritual death pollution in the home during the time of the festival). Hence, many non-Brahmins, instead of asserting that *kolu*-keeping was a caste-specific practice and locating this as the reason for their participatory abstinence, maintained that they either did not have female children to help them and/or they were not prepared to take on the long-term commitment involved in the practice. Brahmins who did not show *kolus* rarely used these justifications, instead, simply stating that it was not their habit (*paḻakkam illai*).

Although this section focuses specifically on the place of *kolu* construction in shifting perceptions of caste and class, *kolus* are also involved in the changing south Indian socio-cultural landscape in other ways. For example, in a recent Chennai magazine article, Shobha Warrier discusses the making of *kolu* dolls and the practicing of *kolu* construction by those other faiths, noting that "the artisans say they have also started preparing dolls based on biblical characters because the Christian community has adopted the tradition for Christmas" (Warrier 2013, 2). Furthermore, *kolus,* as they are considered conversation pieces during viewers' visits, sometimes reflect changes in Indian history, from the replacement of Sarasvatī's *veena* (traditional Indian lute) to the more modern violin under the British raj or the more current depictions of women's rights, child labor, and shopping malls (Ramnarayan 2013, 1). Here, we might consider *kolus* to be rather personal expressions that also provide social commentary (see also Hancock 2001), like the *pandals* of Durgā Pūjā (McDermott 2011; see also Sen in this volume) and the Mithila art studied by Susan Wadley (2013).

Visiting the *Kolu*

If the invited women accept the invitation to view someone's *kolu*, they are shown into the house, asked about the quality of the respective *kolu*, possibly asked to sing a religious song at the base of the *kolu*, and then given gifts such as plastic mirrors and storage containers and bananas and a betel nut. This phenomenon agrees with the work of Mary Hancock who researched Navarātri in Chennai in the early 1990s. She claimed that the gifts "were considered emblems of feminine beauty and domesticity" (Hancock 1999, 3). However, earlier research on Navarātri gifts (see Logan 1980) indicates that the gifting of plastic containers and more elaborate feminine items than vermilion powder and sandalwood paste is a more recent occurrence (i.e., past three decades). In all respects, the gift giving and receiving at domestic *kolu* viewings are located within women's realm. During my own experiences in suburban Madurai, I noticed that (with the exception of myself) the gifts were not presented to the children who accompanied their mothers to the viewing but only to the auspiciously married female *kolu* admirers, themselves the archetype of Tamil beauty and domesticity.

Gift giving and *kolu* viewing more broadly are avenues through which middle-class identity and socioeconomic standing are communicated. Like the conspicuous consumption found in middle-class Tamil Hindu weddings (Wilson 2013), *kolu* viewing in suburban Madurai is also known as a time when upper- and middle-caste/class families can more overtly highlight their expendable wealth in front of neighbors and friends. This wealth is manifested in the number and quality of the dolls constructing the *kolu* and the amount and value of gifts given to each viewer. With respect to doll quality, an assessment is made based on tangible qualities, such as the material out of which the dolls are made, but also includes the dolls' associations with foreign cultures. Today, many *kolus* include Barbie dolls, which signal higher quality due to their connection with the West. In contrast, dolls that are said to come from China are considered cheap and of lower quality (Ramnarayan 2013, 1). The gifts given to *kolu* viewers are taken home and shown to other family members (especially males) who did not attend the viewing but can also draw conclusions about a family's class status and wealth.

In a variety of religious communities, gift giving is perceived as a mode that communicates social status. However, gift giving can also be said to spread ritual pollution (Raheja 1988; Shuman 2000). Through the giving of standard Navarātri gifts such as plastic containers and food packets, one could potentially be passing on ritual pollution as ascribed by one's caste. Although some higher castes do often accept food gifts made in lower-caste homes and then discard them, in today's India there seems to be a change in focus from gift giving as an event that emphasizes caste distinctions and ritual pollution to an occasion during which a multitude of castes can express socioeconomic mobility and emphasize class community-building.

It is in the context of gift giving and urban community building that I find Jayanthi's altar and gifts described previously to be particularly interesting. While traditionally *kolu* constructing and viewing has been a higher caste practice, those of the middle class but of perhaps lower castes, like Jayanthi, are now locating the festival of Navarātri as a time during which their socioeconomic mobility affords them the ability to negotiate more rigid caste rituals and identities. In the following sections, I utilize my experiences with Jayanthi's middle-class neighbors to demonstrate how the Navarātri festival, along with its associated domestic rituals, is a crucial site of social change in South India.

Innovating Ritual in the Śrī Maṅkala Vināyakar Temple Community

A Lecture at the Śrī Maṅkala Vināyakar Temple

During my second Navarātri at the Śrī Maṅkala Vināyakar temple, it was announced that a Brahmin woman had been asked to come and give the devotees a lecture about Navarātri and why it is celebrated. She arrived after the formal rituals had taken place, and many of the female devotees stayed to listen to her presentation. She began the lecture by introducing herself and then singing a song to Vināyakar (perhaps because he is the main deity of the temple). She then spoke of difficulties one encounters in life and the Goddess's place in resolving these issues:

> Who can say, "For me there are no difficulties. I am always content and peaceful?" Who can say that? Certainly no one can say that. But going along with you is Śakti, going along with you is power. Ampāḷ (the Goddess) is there.

In response, many of the women in the temple nodded their heads in agreement. Meenakshi Amma, the lecturer, continued by speaking about the importance of the Navarātri festival as a time reserved for women in particular. She also spoke of the conflicts and confluences between tradition and modernity, arguing that while "we need modern techniques, we should not forget tradition." With respect to this she lamented that many women are no longer taught the specific details of Navarātri *pūjā*, and many use the excuses of work and other aspects of modern life in their explanations of why they do not follow the traditions that are deemed their responsibility as Hindu women. She commented that today women must be shown and reminded of the proper ways to follow tradition, hence her visit to the Śrī Maṅkala Vināyakar temple. The lecture was then concluded with a song that Meenakshi encourages the other devotees to sing with her.

While there are often public lectures held in larger temples, this event was unique in that it took place in a small neighborhood temple and was not focused on the details and history of a particular deity or religious epic, such as the *Rāmāyana* or the *Mahābhārata*. Furthermore, in all of my experiences at the Śrī Maṅkala Vināyakar temple, I did not witness a lecture like this either before or after this Navarātri-related event. Notably, Meenakshi Amma's lecture was a kind of social analysis, directed at the middle-class worshippers in the temple, about interpretations of tradition and modernity as they appear in the everyday lives of women in suburban Madurai. This corresponds to recent studies of how gender and modernity are implicated in middle-class identity formation (Donner 2008; Gilbertson 2014a, 2014b; Lahiri-Dutt and Sil 2014). In her study of fashion and respectability in Hyderabad, Amanda Gilbertson (2014a) argues that middle-class Indian women, in particular, are placed in a precarious cultural and social position in which they must intricately balance conceptions of tradition with status-increasing but "acceptable" forms of modernity. These middle-class women's social positions are contrasted with those of elite women in Hyderabad who Gilbertson's interlocutors claim are "overly Westernized . . . [and] lack proper Indian family values" as well as "a middle-class concern for the opinion of others" (Gilbertson 2014a, 130).

The lecture also reinforced social distinctions in that Meenakshi Amma, a middle-class Brahmin housewife living in a part of the city that was once an area reserved only for Brahmins, was sharing her religious knowledge (supposedly worthy of a public temple lecture) with other female devotees who either conceived of themselves or were conceived by their neighbors as needing enlightenment with respect to proper ritual and religiosity. Meenakshi Amma's Brahmin identity was communicated through her speech (she used a socially recognized Brahmin dialect of Tamil) and through her knowledge of Hindu cosmology and astrology, topics that in the past were reserved for those of the Brahmin caste.

This phenomenon of a public lecture concerning modern life and the practicing of traditional religious ritual by women was an event that was certainly distinctive in my experiences of middle-class India. This event exposed devotees to a discourse concerning modern religiosity and the place of women within it. But why was this lecture seen as necessary by temple trustees? This moment in India is recognized, specifically by the middle classes, as a time when tradition and modernity are under constant scrutiny and negotiation in a multitude of circumstances, including those in which religiosities and social structures are being reevaluated and reformulated (see also Wilson forthcoming). In her effort to join modernity with tradition with respect to the rituals of Navarātri, Meenakshi Amma combined a more "traditional" understanding of women as ritual practitioners, while also responding to their attraction to the "techniques" of modern life and the daily changes that have arisen from them.

Jayanti's Novel Navarātri

As presented at the outset of this chapter, Jayanthi, a middle-class and lower-caste woman living in a Madurai suburb, had elaborately decorated an altar for Lakṣmī. She also had prepared gifts for the visitors that would attend her home on the first day of Navarātri. Each visitor was offered a silk-screened bag filled with items one might receive at a *kolu*-viewing, such as vermilion powder, a banana, a package of cooked beans, and a one-rupee coin. In addition, Jayanthi included a coconut, a pair of plastic red bangles, and a packet of red *poṭṭukaḷ* (round red stickers) for the women's foreheads (totaling approximately Rs. 70 or US$1.50 per guest). Although Jayanthi's altar was certainly quite different from a *kolu*, the viewing of the altar, the singing in front of it, and the presentation of gifts were quite reminiscent of a traditional *kolu* viewing at a higher-caste home.

Curious about the potential connection to my other *kolu*-viewing experiences, I asked Jayanthi how her Navarātri function came about. She told me that it was something she had created, having been inspired by Brahmin members of her community. She was also adamant that *kolus* were originally caste-specific. She said,

> It's new. I watched Brahmins and learned. Now any caste will keep a *kolu*, but mainly they are Brahmins. Other people only do it after seeing Brahmins keep them. The Brahmins know the rules for how to make the *kolu* [i.e., what needs to go on what step].

Although Jayanthi locates the Brahmin *kolu* as inspiration for her Navarātri altar invention, the physical alterations in marking Navarātri, particularly the lack of a formal *kolu*, may have also been part of a trend that I began to see among other more socioeconomically well-off Hindus in

Madurai. For example, a Brahmin woman named Nitya, who by Madurai standards would have been considered upper middle class, also chose not to construct a *kolu* but instead held a singing event like that which Jayanthi sponsored at her home. Approximately thirty guests attended the event and were later given gifts that would be considered of higher quality (e.g., plastic items, fresh flowers) compared to others that one might receive over the nine-night period.

Selvi and the Status-Raising *Kolu*

Although it was recognized by many in the community that Jayanthi and Nitya were relatively well-off, and, hence, able to celebrate Navarātri in an accentuated fashion, this could not be said for Selvi, another neighborhood woman, who was also of a lower caste but with much less disposable income. That said, Selvi seemed to take up the Navarātri festival and the associated *kolu* viewing as a time when she might be able to further build her status as middle class, particularly via the construction of a *kolu* and the conspicuous consumption related to it.

One evening during the Navarātri festival, Selvi decided to invite a few neighborhood women to view and sing in front of her *kolu*. After singing a few songs in her modest living area and paying respects to the gods and goddesses located in her *pūjā* room, the women were led upstairs to a small room on the roof. From top to bottom, this room was filled with *kolus*, including both a traditional staircase display and miniature depictions of familiar cultural scenes, such as "the village" and the performance of Tiruviḷakku Pūjā, a form of goddess worship in which the main participants are female devotees. Selvi also drew our attention to a scene depicting the lifestyle of the Chettiyar caste. It was important that we saw how elaborately she had decorated and how cognizant she was of higher caste (here also, class) modes of living.

The case of Selvi and her *kolu* is interesting not only because of her lower positioning in the caste hierarchy but also because of her socioeconomic position. In contrast to other members of her community, Selvi's husband runs a tea stall, hardly considered a middle-class occupation. In addition, according to her close friend, Selvi has only a second standard education, which not only indicates lower-class status but also hinders Selvi from reciting the supposedly necessary Sanskrit *mantras* during the construction of a *kolu*. Through her *kolu* and her invitation to view it, Selvi was attempting to engage in the community of her middle-class peers and raise her social status in the neighborhood. The display of conspicuous consumption that *kolu* construction provided was meant to erase Selvi's lack of other emically agreed-upon middle-class characteristics, such as literacy and white-collar employment. While not overtly expressed to me, I suspect that Selvi and her family spent much more money than their budget allowed to construct the *kolu* and present so many guests with gifts and afternoon snacks.

Conclusion

I close with a question about the relationships between social status and religious festivals in contemporary South Asia. While it has been argued that urban religious festivals are often considered locations where social identities can be evaluated and reformulated, is there something about the festival of Navarātri in particular that lends itself to the assertion of middle-class status in today's India?

First, one could argue that Navarātri is a festival that encourages the display of conspicuous consumption, particularly with respect to *kolu* construction, and therefore dovetails with assertions of socioeconomic class status. However, there are many other Hindu religious festivals that incorporate conspicuous consumption, including Dīpāvalī (Hindi: Dīvālī) and Gaṇeśa Caturthī. Across India, Dīpāvalī is celebrated with the purchase of new clothing, fireworks, and special food. In some parts of India, Gaṇeśa Caturthī requires the costly construction of massive, elaborate recreations of the god Gaṇeśa, which are destroyed by immersion in water. So, we could argue that Navarātri's relationship with middle-class identity is not unique in this way.

Perhaps Navarātri is unique in that it embraces women allowing more freedom with respect to movement, as women visit homes with *kolus* during the evening hours. But this assertion is in contention with a middle-class worldview in India that is much more conservative with respect to women's freedoms and responsibilities. In fact, my middle-class interlocutors have continually explained to me how both the upper classes and lower classes are less restrictive when it comes to women's exposure to the outside world. The upper classes are quite progressive in their interpretations of the maintenance of a woman's reputation, and the lower classes have no choice but to allow women to move outside of the home because their livelihood depends on it. Therefore, we can rule out Navarātri as a festival that conveys middle-class status via women's freedom of movement.

So, what if the uniqueness of Navarātri as a mode through which to communicate and negotiate middle-class status can be found in the geographical particularities of its celebration? This chapter has specifically addressed the celebrations of Navarātri in suburban Madurai, a city located in the south Indian state of Tamil Nadu, and therefore a part of India that is often referred to as the "religious South." This moniker, along with Madurai's nickname "Temple City" (as home to the famous Mīnākṣī Sundareśvara temple) depicts this region of India as particularly conservative, both with respect to religious and cultural customs. Perhaps, due to its association with proper domesticity, but also the occasional acceptance of its modern incarnations, Navarātri in suburban middle-class Madurai presents a more appropriate mode through which to assert one's class status—through a gendered religious lens. Moreover, as previously mentioned, the depiction of Durgā is undergoing an identity shift to a more motherly role only solidifies the crucial gendered aspect in this scenario. Although the basis for the Navarātri celebration certainly emphasizes the fierceness of the Goddess, this nuanced dual personality can certainly help us think through how Navarātri has become a site for ritual and social change among Tamil Nadu's middle classes.

In this chapter I have shown that during this time in Indian history, conceptions of class, caste, tradition, and modernity are in flux. The experiences of Jayanthi, Selvi, and other female temple-goers in the Śrī Maṅkala Vināyakar temple neighborhood during Navarātri illustrate how these identifications and cultural concepts are being reevaluated and reformulated through ritual innovation, contestation, and conversation. Indeed, *kolus*, caste, and class, along with feminine ritual roles, appear to be at the heart of how Navarātri motivates social change in urban South India.

Notes

1. This is based on the census of 1931, as it was the last to contain Brahmin caste-related data in India. In 2011, the Socio Economic and Caste Census (SECC) was carried out across India; however, data specifically regarding Brahmin populations was not disclosed.

2. Fuller and Logan (1985, 98) argue that domestic ritual during Navarātri in Madurai revolves around the worship of Śakti and not specific forms of the goddess such as Durgā or Lakṣmī. Moreover, Tanaka (1999) found that in Chidambaram, Tamil Nadu, Lakṣmī was left out of Navarātri worship all together. During my experiences of Navarātri in suburban Madurai, the three forms of the Goddess were worshipped and given equal authority.

3. Sheela Chavan, Laurah Klepinger, and I translated this song from Tamil to English in January 2009.

4. Although my interlocutors did not overtly express it, the association between a festival day and a particular color may be related to colors as they correspond to the *navagraha*, the nine planets worshipped by Hindus, which also correspond with particular colors (e.g., Surya with the color red) (Balkaran 2015).

Bibliography

Ahmad, Imtiaz, and Helmut Reifeld. 2001. "Introduction." In *Middle Class Values in India and Western Europe*, edited by Ahmad and H. Reifeld, 1–17. New Delhi: Social Science Press.

Balkaran, Raj. 2015. Personal Communication. August 23, 2015.
Chatterjee, Partha. 1992. "A Religion of Urban Domesticity: Sri Ramakrishna and the Calcutta Middle Class." In *Subaltern Studies VII: Writings on South Asian History and Society*, edited by P. Chatterjee and G. Pandey, 40–68. New Delhi: Oxford University Press.
Dickey, Sara. 2000. "Permeable Homes: Domestic Service, Household Spaces, and the Vulnerability of Class Boundaries in Urban India." *American Ethnologist* 27 (2): 462–89.
———. 2012. "The Pleasures and Anxieties of Being in the Middle: Emerging Middle-Class Identities in Urban South India." *Modern Asian Studies* 46 (3): 559–99.
Donner, Henrike. 2008. *Domestic Goddesses: Maternity, Globalization and Middle-class Identity in Contemporary India*. Hampshire and Burlington: Ashgate.
Fernandes, Leela. 2000. Restructuring the New Middle Class in Liberalizing India. *Comparative Studies of South Asia* 20 (1–2): 88–112.
Fuller, C. J. 2004. *The Camphor Flame: Popular Hinduism and Society in India*. Princeton: Princeton University Press.
———. 2003. *Renewal of the Priesthood: Modernity and Traditionalism in a South Indian Temple*. Princeton: Princeton University Press.
———. 1999. "The Brahmins and Brahminical Values in Modern Tamil Nadu." In *Institutions and Inequalities: Essays in Honour of Andre Beteille*, edited by R. Guha and J. Parry, 30–55. Delhi: Oxford University Press.
———. 1984. *Servants of the Goddess: The Priests of a South Indian Temple*. Cambridge: Cambridge University Press.
———. 1980. The Divine Couple's Relationship in a South India Temple: Minakshi and Sundareswara at Madurai. *History of Religions* 19:321–48.
Fuller, C. J., and Haripriya Narasimhan. 2014. *Tamil Brahmins: The Making of a Middle-Class Caste*. Chicago and London: University of Chicago Press.
Fuller, C. J., and Penelope Logan. 1985. "The Navaratri Festival in Madurai." *Bulletin of the School of Oriental and African Studies, University of London* 48 (1): 79–105.
Gilbertson, Amanda. 2014a. "A Fine Balance: Negotiating Fashion and Respectable Femininity in Middle-Class Hyderabad, India." *Modern Asian Studies* 48 (1): 120–58.
———. 2014b. "From Respect to Friendship? Companionate Marriage and Conjugal Power Negotiation in Middle-Class Hyderabad." *South Asia: Journal of South Asian Studies* 37 (2): 225–38.
Hancock, Mary. 2001. "Festivity and Popular Memory in Southern India." *South Asia Research* 21 (1): 1–21.
———. 1999. *Womanhood in the Making: Domestic Ritual and Public Culture in Urban South India*. Boulder, Colorado: Westview.
———.1995. "Hindu Culture for an Indian Nation." *American Ethnologist* 22:907–26.
Hansen, Thomas Blom. 1999. *The Saffron Wave: Democracy and Hindu Nationalism in Modern India*. Princeton: Princeton University Press.
Hume, Cynthia. 1990. *The Text and Temple of the Great Goddess: The Devi-Mahatmya and the Vidhyacal Temple of Mirzapur*. Vol. 2. Iowa City: University of Iowa Press.
Kapadia, Karin. 1995. *Siva and Her Sisters: Gender, Caste, and Class in Rural South India*. Boulder, CO: Westview.
Kinsley, David. 1978. "The Portrait of the Goddess in the *Devī-Māhātmya*." *Journal of the American Academy of Religion* 46 (4): 489–506.

Klostermaier, Klaus. 1994. *A Survey of Hinduism, 2nd Edition*. New York: State University of New York Press.

Kolenda, Pauline. 2003. "Memories of a Brahman *Agraharam* in Travancore." In *Caste, Marriage and Inequality: Essays on North and South India*, 125–64 Jaipur: Rawat.

Krishna, R. 2008. "Nine Nights of Shakti. Daily News and Analysis." DnaIndia, October 5. http://www.dnaindia.com/india/report-nine-nights-of-shakti-1195608.

Lahiri-Dutt, Kuntala, and Pallabi Sil. 2014. "Women's 'Double Day' in Middle-Class Homes in Small-Town India." *Contemporary South Asia* 22 (4): 389–405.

Lakha, Salim. 1999. "The State, Globalisation, and Indian Middle-Class Identity." In *Culture and Privilege in Capitalist Asia*, edited by M. Pinches, 251–74. London: Routledge.

Logan, Penelope. "Domestic Worship and the Festival Cycle in the South Indian City of Madurai." PhD diss., University of Manchester, 1980.

Malhotra, Anshu. 2002. *Gender, Caste, and Religious Identities: Restructuring Class in Colonial Punjab*. Delhi: Oxford University Press.

Mankekar, Purnima.1999. *Screening Culture, Viewing Politics: An Ethnography of Television, Womanhood, and Nation in Postcolonial India*. Durham: Duke University Press.

McDermott, Rachel Fell. 2011. *Revelry, Rivalry, and Longing for the Goddess of Bengal: The Fortunes of Hindu Festivals*. New York: Columbia University Press.

Mines, Diane. 2005. *Fierce Gods: Inequality, Ritual, and the Politics of Dignity in a South Indian Village*. Bloomington: Indiana University Press.

Nanda, Meera. 2009. *The God Market: How Globalization Is Making India More Hindu*. New York: Monthly Review.

Osella, F., and C. Osella. 2000. *Social Mobility in Kerala: Modernity and Identity in Conflict*. Princeton: Princeton University Press.

Pandian, M. S. S. 2007. *Brahmin and Non-Brahmin: Genealogies of the Tamil Political Present*. Delhi: Permanent Black.

Raheja, Gloria. 1988. *The Poison in the Gift: Ritual, Prestation and the Dominant Caste in a North Indian Village*. Chicago: University of Chicago Press.

Ramaswamy, Sumathi. 1998. "The Language of the People in the World of Gods: Ideologies of Tamil Before the Nation." *Journal of Asian Studies* 57 (1): 66–92.

———.1997. *Passions of the Tongue: Language Devotion in Tamil India, 1891–1970*. Berkeley: University of California Press.

Ramnarayan, Gowri. 2013. "The Story of 'Kolus': Many Themes and Transformations." *Daily News and Analysis*, October 11, 2013. http://www.dnaindia.com/analysis/column-the-story-of-kolus-many-themes-and transformations-1901992.

Saavala, Minna. 2003. "Auspicious Hindu Houses. The New Middle Classes in Hyderabad, India." *Social Anthropology* 11 (2): 231–47.

Shanmugalingam, N. 1997. "A New Face of Durga: Religious and Social Change in Present Day Jaffna." University of Jaffna, unpublished doctoral dissertation.

Sheth, D. L. 1999. "Secularisation of Caste and Making of New Middle Class." *Economic and Political Weekly* 34 (34/35): 2502–10.

Shuman, Amy. 2000. "Food Gifts: Ritual Exchange and the Production of Excess Meaning." *The Journal of American Folklore* 113 (450): 495–508.

Singer, Milton.1972. *When a Great Tradition Modernizes: An Anthropological Approach to Indian Civilization*. New York, Washington, London: Praeger.

Srinivas, M. N. 1956. "A Note on Sanskritization and Westernization." *The Journal of Asian Studies* 15 (4): 481–96.
———. 1952. *Religion and Society among the Coorgs of South India*. Oxford: Clarendon.
Stein, Burton. 1980. *Peasant, State and Society in Medieval South India*. Delhi: Oxford University Press.
Stern, Robert. 2003 [1993]. *Changing India: Bourgeois Revolution on the Subcontinent*. New York: Cambridge University Press.
Tanaka, Masakazu. 1999. "The *Navarātri* Festival in Chidambaram, South India." In *Living with Sakti: Gender, Sexuality and Religion in South Asia*, edited by M. Tanaka and M. Tachikawa, 117–36. Osaka: National Museum of Ethnology.
Trouillet, Pierre-Yves. 2008. "Mapping the Management of Threatening Gods and Social Conflict: A Territorial Approach to Processions in a South Indian Village (Tamil Nadu)." In *South Asian Religions on Display: Religious Processions in South Asia and in the Diaspora*, edited by K. Jacobsen, 45–62. New York: Routledge.
Wadley, Susan Snow. 2013. "Painting Women's Lives in Rural Northern India." In *South Asia in the World: An Introduction*, edited by S. Wadley, 241–260. Armonk: M. E. Sharpe.
———. 2004. *Raja Nal and the Goddess: The North Indian Epic Dhola in Performance*. Bloomington: Indiana University Press.
Waghorne, Joanne. 2004. *Diaspora of the Gods: Modern Hindu Temples in an Urban Middle-Class World*. Oxford and New York: Oxford University Press.
Warrier, Maya. 2005. *Hindu Selves in a Modern World: Guru faith in the Mata Amritanandamayi Mission*. London and New York: Routledge Curzon.
———. 2003. "Guru Choice and Spiritual Seeking in Contemporary India." *International Journal of Hindu Studies* 7 (1–3): 31–54.
Warrier, Shobha. "Navratri Kolu: A Peek into the Life of the Doll Makers of Tamil Nadu." *Rediff.com*, October 10, 2013. http://www.rediff.com/getahead/report/slide-show-1-specials-dying-a-slow-death-a-peek-into-the-life-of-kolu-doll-makers/20131009.htm#1.
Welbon, Guy, and Glenn Yocum.1982. *Religious Festivals in South India and Sri Lanka*. New Delhi: Manohar.
Wilson, Nicole. Forthcoming. "The Śrī Maṅkala Vināyakar Satsang Group: Religious Practice and Middle-Class Status in Tamil Nadu, South India." *International Journal of Hindu Studies*, 23 (1).
———. 2013. "Confrontation and Compromise: Middle-Class Matchmaking in Twenty-First Century South India." *Asian Ethnology* 72 (1): 33–53.

13

Display Shows, Display Tells

The Aesthetics of Memory during Pommai Kolu

DEEKSHA SIVAKUMAR

On the eve of Navarātri, the household murmurs with the sounds of men and women running errands, buying last-minute festival comportments. Lalitha, the oldest wife of three brothers, brings us a steaming cup of her best coffee in her daughter Shriya's bedroom. With the balcony windows open, we unwrap dolls and place them upon the *kolu*. Family dolls especially made and purchased for Pommai Kolu (literally "dolls holding court") are only unpacked once a year and assembled into dioramas on these triangular and tiered displays. Lalitha arranges the dolls carefully while putting away the boxes that have held them during the year. Earlier that evening, Sridhar, Lalitha's husband, had helped her arrange the *kolu* space by assembling the steps with tables and benches in their home. Upon this structure, a white cloth or brightly colored sari was draped to offer a clean canvas upon which to begin displaying the dolls.

This chapter will explore how homes and their possessions function like museums during Pommai Kolu, preserving personal and religious memories through aesthetic arrangement. These memories are represented through material artifacts accumulated over several years and passed down from mothers to their daughters. Motivated by aesthetic choices, as well as social, economic, and cultural limitations, a *kolu* can display prosperity beyond the monetary value of the dolls housed within it. Displaying order, life histories, and prosperity, a *kolu* showcases one's memory materially through aesthetically pleasing arrangements. By visually marking one's native place, travel history, and social class, a *kolu* allows for conversations with memories using aesthetics, challenging the "situatedness" of the self and other in the larger world.

This chapter will examine Pommai Kolu in Chennai, India, and San Francisco Bay, California. Within these two areas, I primarily focus upon the suburbs of Mylapore and Sunnyvale, respectively, because of their sociocultural demographic. Mylapore is a famous suburb in Chennai, and some say its history as a trading post predates Marco Polo.[1] Today it is home to many of the first Brahmin settlers in Madras, and it is a marketplace, aside from vegetables and fruits, known for religious ritual objects and materials. Sunnyvale, a suburb near San Francisco, is home to many Tamil Brahmin American families who immigrated to the United States, beginning in the early 1970s and is also a shopping destination for ritual wares among South Asian immigrants and Tamil Brahmins. The latter often speak fondly of their visits to the Bay Area to see relatives, eating *dosas* (rice/lentil crêpes) at the famous Chennai fast-food chain Saravanaa Bhavan and the "full-meals" at Komalavilas, a small restaurant that sells *kolu* dolls.[2] While immigrants from other Indian states or caste communities may not find it as familiar, Tamil Brahmins love Sunnyvale and find it a "home-away-from-home." This chapter will also cover three spatial contexts for Pommai Kolu: a traditional and Brahmin domestic context in India, presumably where the festival has roots; a diasporic context where it comes to be innovated and experienced by first-time participants and viewers; and a public context where members of an organization promoting arts and culture seek to restore what they believe to be ancient religious practices. These contexts are connected through their celebration of religious and ethnic identity, and they will provide enough material for discussing the various ways in which life histories, prosperity, and order come to be exhibited and created during the nine nights of Navarātri for the upcoming year.

The transition from summer into monsoon season is rather lengthy and occurs over two or three months, when the rain gods bless the land with abundant showers. In the Tamil month of Puraṭṭasi (September–October), there is a second harvest season, sometimes called "postmonsoon" for its unpredictable weather and occasional heavy rains that prolong the monsoon. Also called Sharad Ṛtu (autumn season) in north India, Puraṭṭasi is an especially auspicious time of the year to worship ancestors and celebrate Durgā Pūjā before the coming of the Dīwāli/ Dīpāvali. However, during the auspicious time, there occurs a volatile period between the waxing of the full moon and the waning of the new moon, a period of fasting and rituals. Pommai Kolu (also called Navarātri) commences on the day after the *āmāvāsya* (new moon), a nine-day period of celebration and rituals to the goddess through a tiered arrangement of dolls. Pommai Kolu also marks the very important autumnal equinox. The long evening hours are spent visiting one another's homes, viewing *kolus* and partaking in *sundal* or sautéed sprouted lentil offerings (a direct result of the harvest season). The tenth day after *āmāvāsya*, called Vijayadaśmi, marks the victory of good over evil: Rāma defeating Rāvaṇa and Durgā vanquishing Mahiṣāsura.

Memories of *Kolu*

Modern psychologists have observed that there are many ways one can free-associate to store and retrieve memories of one's past. When a householder is asked about the display, she immediately resorts to a personal memory, either a time when she purchased the doll, or perhaps a person who presented her with the doll. At other times, she will resort to a story about the doll, the material used to make the doll, or the character that is depicted as a doll. In these ways, the dolls and the materials displayed for Pommai Kolu become triggers of personal and communal life histories, showcasing the variety of memories experienced by the participants who keep a *kolu*. Some dioramas tell a story of a native place, its people, and their way of life. Other dioramas tell stories of important characters who lived among us, gods and legends, whose lives serve as moral lessons to the modern world. Within this discussion, Pommai Kolu and one's participation in this festival will illuminate important ways in which our religious and communal selves are shaped by our cultural and familial worlds. It was in this milieu that I found three different but similar displays, each telling its own story, trying to materially call to mind its personal, social, and religious past while actively creating tradition for the community's gaze.

Mrs. Seshadri's *Kolu*

Mrs. Seshadri's *kolu* is hardly atypical but is one of the largest private home displays in the San Fransisco Bay Area. Many women I spoke to the weekend before stressed the importance of visiting her *kolu* because of its sheer size and the abundance of dolls and dioramas. Those women, however, did not explicitly mention the lively discussion that would take place in Mrs. Seshadri's home due to her guests and their interests. Mrs. Seshadri was one of the oldest residents in the mainly Indian American neighborhood of Sunnyvale, California. She had immigrated with her husband in 1982 and had been conducting *kolus* since her marriage the year before. Mrs. Seshadri and her husband had one son, a consulting software engineer who lived in New York.

Most of the dolls in Mrs. Seshadri's *kolu* were souvenirs her son had brought home from his trips abroad. He knew how much his mother enjoyed the festival, so he brought her sets of dolls, scenes, and dioramas. In 2014, when I met Mrs. Seshadri, her son had recently visited Peru and brought back several dolls. She had made a replica of Machu Picchu and recreated all the shops and their wares in elaborate detail. When I asked her about the diorama, she described the places in detail, as if she had visited them herself. She was reliving not just her son's experience, but her memory of hearing her son's experiences. Alongside the Peruvian landscape, there were two porcelain dolls depicting Laurel and Hardy. Before I could ask about them, Mrs. Seshadri's close friend Uma, who was also observing the *kolu,* explained that these were a familiar sight. She remarked that Mrs. Seshadri had purchased them on a trip to London with her son and husband in the early nighties, and since then she had seen them on display every year. So, while some dolls changed, such as the souvenirs Mrs. Seshadri's son brought home, some dolls, like the Laurel and Hardy set and a fountain Gaṇeśa, were displayed every year. Mrs. Seshadri had sentimental value for her display, so she chose certain dolls over others repeatedly. Uma, too, recalled these dolls and looked out for the commonalities and differences in her close friend's *kolu.*

Both the householder and the participants formed memories of not just one *kolu,* but every *kolu* they had ever seen by one person in relation to the *kolus* elsewhere. The creation of a *kolu* archive in the participants' memory is enhanced with today's technology and the preservation or circulation of photographs. Very few families have photos of Pommai Kolu before 1950, but today there are millions of pictures being circulated every Navarātri on the internet by many families. These photographs make recall easier, allowing for women to be inspired by one another's collections. Some may even ask their friends to purchase dolls on their behalf. The sharing of *kolu* resources has improved in recent times. *Kolu* resources were discussed at length at Mrs. Seshadri's *kolu* and other Pommai Kolu celebrations I witnessed.

At Mrs. Seshadri's home, while the women sat down to discuss *kolus,* everyone whipped out their iPhones to show and share pictures, exchange doll makers and shop names, and recollect displays that were adorned well. Other kinds of sharing occurred on blogging platforms, such as Flickr, and query-based sites, such as Indusladies and Askmaami.

Mrs. Seshadri's *kolu* was notable for its depiction of familial relationships and travel experiences. Her family's global exposure was made apparent by the materials and dolls within the *kolu,* as well as the discussions surrounding their display. Prosperity was emblematized by the dolls important to her son (a birth after several years of trying) and the abundance of their international trips. Moreover, we also saw that Mrs. Seshadri aesthetically played with her display, showing some dolls repeatedly, while changing up others. In this way, she was able to innovate in her display, telling a story, keeping a frame narrative while improvising within it.

The Mylapore Trio's *Kolu*

The Mylapore Trio, made up of two brothers and one sister, are a self-made organization, supported by the Sri Sumukhi Rajasekharan Foundation, created to promote arts and culture in Chennai. The oldest sibling, Surendranath, is a dance teacher for the Kala Academy, and his brother, Amarnath, is a history professor at Madras University. Their sister, Aparna, is the treasurer and a financial advisor for the Indian government via ICICI bank. The Trio gained popularity by creating an outstanding *kolu* covered by the local news channels and the *Mylapore Times*. Their popularity was triggered by public appreciation for their five-room *kolu*. Since 1991 they have been hosting workshops and organizing and judging *kolu* competitions around the city. Today they travel to Madurai and Trichy to host Pommai Kolu in temple contexts and invite new participants to the festival via their presentations and workshops. Their life history goes along with their established goals of providing a public service to the community. In their eyes, Pommai Kolu is a disappearing religious festival that requires revival from passionate artists within the society.

The deceased founders of the primary donors of the Sri Sumukhi Rajasekharan Foundation, Sumukhi and Rajasekharan adopted and raised the Trio with deeply traditional and Brahmin roots. Local freedom fighters and owners of a small textbook publishing house, the couple provided financial support and boarding and lodging to several poor families, believing in raising an Indian community that was free of caste and economic distinctions. The Trio thus also joined the Chennai Kala (Arts) Academy fairly young and learned Bharatanaṭyam (a form of Indian dance) and classical Carnatic music in their upkeep of traditional Brahmin household rituals and festivals. Their usual household visitors included Rukumani Arundale and several famous Kala academy dancers.[3]

The Trio keeps an elaborate *kolu* spread over five rooms in their traditional home in Mylapore. Given their social standing, most families who couldn't keep *kolus* or those who felt the organization was preserving an old tradition donated their unique and old dolls to the Trio for safekeeping. Some also donated highly valued vintage brass lamps. Maintaining their ever-growing collection seemed to be a huge concern for the Trio. They lamented that no one else did as good a job of seeing that the dolls and lamps received a proper home. Preserving tradition within an irreverent modern present necessitated the Trio's Pommai Kolu displays. Their themes are religious and based in various mythological texts and local narratives about Viṣṇu, Śiva, Murukaṉ, and Ammaṉ. Their personal life history narrative repeatedly found its way into our discussions about *kolus*. They were thankful for all the rituals that Sumukhi and Rajasekharan had taught them, and they dissuaded people from following wayward pop culture trends while ignoring their cultural and religious heritage. They filled up to capacity their routine workshops held in a variety of Mylapore venues for theological discussions and instructions on how to perform various *pūjās*. It was through their public persona that I came to learn of their *kolu* and visited their home on several occasions to hear about it.

One of the most distinct features of their multiroom *kolu* is a large picture of Sumukhi and Rjasekaharan, which sits centrally on the living room display shelf, adorned by fresh flowers, a small lamp sitting in front of it. The picture is treated with reverence. Guests often ask about it as it is unusual to see pictures of dead relatives upon a *kolu*. Amarnath responds apologetically, saying that although it is unusual, the Trio hold "tremendous respect" for their adopted parents and their way of life.

Prosperity is showcased in the Trio's *kolu* by the sheer magnitude of religious narratives and figurines displayed. Aesthetically, no one family can acquire the depth and range of designs and materials that are shown by this one organization. The Mylapore Trio's *kolu* is also an example of how communal values about nationhood and economic and caste equality emerge from practices within a home, although their home was a unique shelter of sorts for engaging with these discussions during their youth. Their reverence for their adopted parents and central placement within their *kolu* also spoke volumes about the deified or legendary status they had thus been awarded, memorializing them within the current Mylaporean community.

Sarasvati's *Kolu*

Sarasvati has one of the largest and oldest personal collections of dolls I have ever seen. Although her *kolu* only occupied in one room, it was nine feet tall and extended in two feet on either side of the triangular, tiered display. Her dolls ranged in height from one foot to four feet, all painted in natural vegetable dyes and made of alluvial clay. She also had a large collection of brass floor lamps; brass birds, wild animals, and religious characters; a traditional brass miniature kitchen set; and copper and bronze display plates of various sizes with insignia. Sarasvati lives in a Brahmin joint family and has been keeping a *kolu* since she was a little girl in her parents' home, and she continues in her in-laws' home. Her passion for *kolus* emerges from her love for dolls and her interest in depicting mythological themes for her family and friends. She lives with her husband, parents-in-law, her older son and his wife, and their son and daughter in a spacious five-bedroom house in Mylapore. They are far wealthier than their neighbors, and many of the ladies' club members, through whom I was introduced, often exalted Sarasvati's Pommai Kolu celebrations and praised her benevolent and charitable offerings. Sarasvati's marital home was steeped in colonial and Brahmin traditions. Her father-in-law mingled with British officers in the navy, and her husband is a high court judge. They value certain aspects of British rule while applauding Indian culture and "Hindu" religion for its merit and uniqueness. The coexistence of Indian and Western philosophy is quite common among Tamil Brahmins in Mylapore, especially those who worked in high-ranking positions during the early nineteenth century.

The evening of Pommai Kolu I spent with Sarasvati was colorful, with musical performances and several guests streaming in and out, children rushing around with their hands and mouths filled with *sundal* and sweets, and older men chit-chatting in the living room beside the *kolu*, drinking steaming cups of coffee and eating hot fried dough. Sarasvati was rather quiet around her husband and parents, but her persona completely changed around women and children. Beside her *kolu*, she took charge, pointing out the various stories to her guests and staying attentive to everyone who was in her home. She had a story about each one of her dolls, and her collection spanned several decades. Many of her dolls are no longer available in the *kolu* markets, and she takes special care to restore any chips and dings they may have accrued.

Sarasvati is a perfect example of an urban Chennai Brahmin householder who has seen *kolus* in two generations. In her natal home, she participated in keeping *kolus* with her mother, and now she re-creates the tradition in her married home, having added to the small collection she was gifted in her wedding trousseau. She isn't middle-class, and neither is her *kolu*. The dolls in her display and household collection are materially valuable as well as rich with tradition. Her antique dolls are no longer made and are comparable only to the Trio's vast collection. When I was there, she narrated a history of each of her dolls, especially the ones she purchased with her mother when she was a child. A pair of Madras Police dolls stood out to us because of their attire. She excitedly told me that she enjoyed watching the policemen dressed in their funny turbans and was sad to see that they don't wear such costumes nowadays. Her *Tiruvilayādal* (lit: *The Games of Śiva*, a Tamil text about Śiva's life as a householder c. fifteenth century) diorama is a unique set from the 1960s. After the popularity of the Shivaji Ganeshan movie on this devotional text, such sets became ubiquitous among doll markets and women who collected from that era. The diorama contained a Śiva (third eye closed, dressed in deer skin with a snake around his blue neck, and a dreadlock top knot) and Pārvatī (with long flowing hair, dressed in a sari and a crown, and adorned with jewels) dolls seated upon ornate gold thrones with the backdrop of Kailaśa mountains and a young Gaṇapati (seated upon his mother's lap wearing a *dhoti* [traditional Indian male clothing] and sacred thread) while Murukaṉ stood beside his parents (youthful, with a bob haircut, wearing a yellow *dhoti* with one arm resting upon a peacock). This doll set has gone through several iconographic changes in the doll market, but her particular diorama retains the style that was popular in the 1960s. Sarasvati's artistic talent was evident as she had restored these old dolls and added features to the display and dolls' costumes. Murukaṉ and Gaṇapati had received delicate foil crowns, Pārvatī had an added gold necklace and yellow thread, while she had constructed the rest of the court around them and populated it with Nandi and several attendants. Sarasvati's *marappaci* (red sandalwood husband-wife couple) dolls were equally well dressed, with hand-sewn sari and jewels. She had added her own details to every doll and diorama. The merchant couple dolls sat beside a large collection of brass kitchen items over-flowing with lentils and rice, and near the merchant's wife was a little lock box, which Sarasvati encouraged the children to open—it contained copper coins and a few keys! It wasn't surprising to see why the children and women alike enjoyed observing every detail of her *kolu* display.

Sarasvati's *kolu* depicts prosperity in one of the most traditionally understood ways. Her family is materially wealthy in Mylapore. They are also well known in her community for their charitable ways and honorable professions. Sarasvati's *kolu* also exhibits some of the dolls and objects considered most aesthetically Tamil and Brahmin. These same objects can be seen in many other Tamil Brahmin homes in the country and beyond weaving together the identity of the displayers as well as the viewers. The communal memories shared by the Tamil Brahmin community, the legends, the nationalist figures they found remarkable, and even the moral teachings they valued from the plethora of religious texts available to them are only conceivable for the observer looking in from the outside. There are recognizable patterns that situate Sarasvati and her family's identity in relation to the various other communities, families, and castes living around them.

Every year, these householders, whether they are in Chennai or Sunnyvale prepare an assembly of dolls to invite their favorite householders home. This could be comparable to a city's art walk evening. Instead of wine and appetizers, these houses dish out smooth and silky, frothy Kumbakonam coffees and savory and sweet warm treats. Instead of art critics, they are distinguished householders known for their keen aesthetic eye. What is worth preserving often changes from person to person. Some would like to preserve the traditional and "religious" nature of the ritual by making sure to invite guests home; do *pūjā* with food, lamp, and devotional songs to the *kolu*; and send their guests home satiated on *sundal* with a few small trinkets as a return gift. Some others value innovation and challenge themselves and their viewers with complex themes and dioramas depicting nonreligious narratives, souvenirs from global travels, and re-purposing unique objects as decorations. They visit each other's homes, too, as visiting is as important as inviting. Their full participation includes critiquing and commending one another's displays and keeping an eye out for unique representations for inspiration in the coming years. Just as display begets reflexivity on the part of the householder, who keeps a *kolu*, *kolu* displays also invite a critical gaze from the audience.

Comparing *Kolu* Displays

All three *kolu* displays serve a functional purpose. They all contain the *kolu* makers' personal life and experiences; their families and their habits; and their favorite religious characters, stories, places, and objects, all in the form of dolls or materials. These materials are assembled using personal aesthetic discretion. The dolls are part of larger dioramas, and artistic additions like costumes, jewels, and make-up have been added to enhance their appearance and create associations for the viewers. Seeing a *marappaci* doll dressed in wedding attire versus seeing one dressed in a royal costume sends different messages. Seeing Rāma and Sītā sitting upon a throne wearing crowns is quite different from them dressed in bark cloth wandering the forest with deer. Each diorama depicts not just a story but also how the *kolu* maker views the characters within the story. Moreover, *kolus* are all constructed to evoke responses from the guests: the Trio placed a picture of their adopted parents upon the central step of the main room beside religious objects of significance; Sarasvati hid coins and keys inside the merchant wife's lockbox; and Mrs. Seshadri annually displays her Laurel and Hardy figurines.

Kolus represent the life histories of the communities who keep this festival. Most of the dolls vary from family to family whose traditional collections are passed down in bridal trousseaus between mothers/mothers-in-law and daughters. On her wedding day, a householder is presented with a plate arranged with a pair of red sandalwood dolls (*marappaci pommai*) and a few others. Over the years, when she can afford to, the householder adds new dolls to this collection. Once married, a Brahmin woman is responsible for making and assembling her own *kolu* every year and inviting at least five married women (Tamil: *cumaṅkali*; Sanskrit: *sumaṅgalī*) and their daughters to her home. These guests are often other Brahmin neighbors. Just by looking at pictures of a *kolu*, one can have a pretty good sense of the time period in which the householder got married, along with some key elements in her personal life: her native city; her sectarian affiliation or family deity; and, with some certainty, her caste. A *kolu* becomes a different visual display with each passing decade, depending on the changing societal and institutional influences upon one's identity and the materials available to make the dolls. *Pommai*, after all, represent identities of people and landscapes. These influences exert themselves materially and meaningfully into domestic spaces, transforming them from what was thought to be traditional.

Most of the unique dolls not made locally were in homes that had foreign travelers (i.e., upper-class and caste families) like Sarasvati, Mrs. Seshadri, and the Trio's parents. In the early eighties and nineties, there was a flourishing of global figurines among all economic classes, ones that tell a story of the ubiquity of travel in these Brahmin communities. Most members of the household between the ages of twenty-eight and thirty-five were starting to travel and brought back souvenirs. In addition, the local doll-market trends changed. Instead of having sets of nationalist figures like Gandhi and colonial officers made of clay, more plastic and plaster toys became available. With all these changes in styles and trends certain questions arise about *kolus*, materiality, and memory. How does one individual fit into their culture, environment? What is the relationship of individual identity/life history to social history? By evoking the question of identity in relationship to visual culture, Pommai Kolu functions as a vast repository of social and religious life histories.

For the *kolu* display, many householders erect a triangular and/or tiered arrangement of steps in odd numbers (3, 5, 7, 9), upon which they neatly arrange dolls depicting gods, saints, characters, and dioramas from mythology. Often, the upper tiers are reserved for gods and kings, the middle tier for saints, and the lowest level for human caste groups. Sand, trees, and various animals are placed on the ground surrounding the tiered tower. *Kolu* dolls are ordered and arranged neatly, but the tiered *kolu* also displays social order. While gods and goddess can be placed on any step, the social world—humans, plants, animals—is not allowed to move up so freely. The natural world we live in forms the base of the triangular tier flanking and surrounding the *kolu* display. What characterizes the display is that gods and goddesses are placed above the Tamil saints, sages above Brahmins, merchants above common folk, fishermen above animals and plants. These choices make neat the murkiness of the social world, reestablishing the structural hierarchies that distinguish deities from people, one community from another, humans from animals, and animate from inanimate. Once the dolls are ordered within a visual space, the entire *kolu* takes on material significance and hence needs to be read as materially different from the dolls themselves. They signal the relationships between and among the dolls and the divine and social worlds. The neatness and the demarcation of the social world through spatial arrangement marks the orderliness of a *kolu*, displaying the boundaries that distinguish and establish identity.

The tendency to categorize and hierarchize within *kolu* displays was evident in the *kolus* described above. After moving back from a multiyear posting in Zambia, Mrs. Seshadri always puts up her African nativity scene alongside the other religious objects in the main triangular *kolu* display. This shows that the display of religious objects extends to include other religious traditions. The Trio also group religious dolls in this way. Their Viṣṇu dolls are placed in Vaikuṇṭha alongside the Hare Krishnas and many girls in Vṛdāvana, the deity Kṛṣṇa's childhood abode. Their village scene included all kinds of villagers from Gujarati weavers to Tamil fishermen. Apart from religion, the *kolu* makers also tend to order dolls of similar type together. Sarasvati's father-in-law spent a few years in Japan, so she added a Japanese queen doll to her own royal *kolu* step. She also displays nesting dolls from different countries. Grouping dolls within the displays shows that the *kolu* makers are actively categorizing their dolls within the display for their viewers. Ordering tradition for the *kolu* participants, *kolu* displays showcase how materials and people can be structured in society.

Organizing our memories or life histories and society, *kolus* also show the major demarcation between god and human. Deities, free from societal and human categorizations, still play many roles in Pommai Kolu. In one, we may see the multiple versions of Kṛṣṇa and none of Śiva. In another, we may see only Rāma and Sītā in the forest while Hayagrīva also features prominently. In yet another, we may not see male deities at all but see a *kolu* filled with goddesses. It is this kind of prioritization that shows how religious memories may also be structured according to material alliances. The *kolu* maker is always sure to keep his or her its theme in mind. The Trio's display of their deceased adopted parents is quite similar. Although dead relatives' photographs rarely may be displayed for *kolu*, photographs of deities, landscapes, and other inanimate objects are not uncommon. Moreover, photographs of dead relatives maybe found on household *pūjā* shelves. The similarities between the *kolu* and *pūjā* shelf are evident in how they are treated, but not necessarily how they come to be displayed. The commonality between the Trio's *kolu* display and a typical Brahmin *pūjā* shelf is worth noting. Their reverence to their ancestors and their treatment within the *kolu* displays signifies the Trio's association to their adopted parents. Their parents are not deities, but they are *like* deities. Furthermore, *kolu* dolls are not considered "deities" until they are placed upon the display. Only once it is within the *kolu* does the eagle doll pulling Viṣṇu's palanquin while people cheer on in the streets become Garuḍa. Various materials and representations also enter the *kolu* space in the form of dolls and transform into deities upon their special treatment over the ten-day festival. Typically, before going to bed at night, the *kolu* maker disperses the day's *ārti* (a copper plate, usually filled with water, vermillion, and a few *tulasī* [holy basil] leaves) water to wash off the *kōlam* (geometric pattern made with rice flour) in front of the *kolu* and her front door. Every night, the *ārti* is thrown away in secret and freshly prepared the next evening. This process renews the potency of the *ārti*, protecting the *kolu* from the numerous eyes that will pass through the home during the ten consecutive days. On the preceding night of the last day of Pommai Kolu, Vijayadaśmi, the red sandalwood couple dolls are made to lie down, marking the end of the year's *kolu*. The final *ārti* on the tenth night is used to wash away and cleanse the entire space upon which the *kolu* was constructed. All these rituals attest to the religious nature of the *kolu*. Also, like a *prasāda*, every guest is sent home with a little offering from the householder's *kolu* viewing. Each guest may receive a packet of *sundal* and a *tambōlam*/offering plate containing some betel leaves, areca nuts, vermilion and turmeric, a piece of fabric to sew a blouse, and some cosmetic gift, like face creams, sandal paste, or a comb and mirror.

Kolu displays also venerate the goddess and bring her alive in her multiple forms. As Sarasvati once told me, "Durgā is the mother of everything and everyone." Utilizing the variety of materials associated with the goddess in household religious rituals, *kolus* showcase the potentiality of the goddess. For example, the *varalakṣmī nonpu mukham* (face of the Goddess Lakṣmī used for an annual vowing ritual) will be seen on some families' shelves. In other homes, where a lamp decorated as the goddess is used for the same vowing ritual, you will find lamps dressed in saris also upon their steps for Pommai Kolu. The various sprouts and *nāvadhānyams* offered in the *sundal* preparations are also symbols of the fecundity of the earth and the goddess. The goddess also comes to life in the numerous songs sung, hymns of praise recited, and various narratives shared through dioramas and dolls assembled during Pommai Kolu. *Lalithasahasranāmam* and *Devī Māhātmya stotras* (hymns) are popular ways to recall the goddess. The former text recites her thousand names and forms and is often also used to pick baby girl names. The latter text narrates the famous story retold every Pommai Kolu of the goddess destroying the buffalo demon Mahiṣāsura. The dolls themselves are sometimes arranged to venerate different actions of female figures from epic texts as well as local myths about the goddess. Finally, the guests themselves, the married women and pre-pubescent girls are also invited to this festival to embody the goddess in real life.

Kolus can be traditional while pushing the boundaries of what tradition may mean. In one home I saw a family add to their temple procession a couple of blonde-haired dolls holding cameras depicting foreign tourists who visit India to take pictures of religious festivals. In another I saw dolls of couples of different ethnicities and from different cultures in wedding costumes to symbolize interracial marriages and travel souvenirs. I have seen Barbie dressed in a sari wearing a *poṭṭu* (forehead vermillion dot) shopping for vegetables in a Mylapore marketplace. These displays are always done in conscious ways depicting scenarios that populate the memories of our *kolu* makers. They are actively transformed, and each year the *kolu* takes on a new flavor depending upon the *kolu* maker's life events. We could also look at the materials from which the dolls are made as part of the negotiation of tradition since *kolu* dolls are made and collected specifically for *kolus*. More recently, dolls are also borrowed from the children's playroom. They are gaily colored and fashioned from many materials, including paper, clay, plastic, fur, or wood. The possessions displayed may include plastic toys and mass-produced plaster images which cost less and are easily replaceable, alongside valuable old brass dolls, ritual implements like pots and lamps, and expensive large clay images. *Kolu* dolls nowadays are also commercially available as sets, so dioramas need not be assembled. For example, since India's major World Cup victory in 1983, cricket team sets are available to include in *kolus*, some even with Kapil Dev prominently visible as a batsman.

Apart from displaying tradition and order, *kolus* as we saw here, also display prosperity. Each of the three displays we discussed are very high in monetary value but for different reasons. Mrs. Seshadri has an extremely large collection of dolls from all her family's travels. The Trio and Sarasvati have dolls and objects valuable for their traditional history, comparable to those found in a museum as well as those made of high-priced metals such as silver and brass. Traditional *kolu* often means a valuable *kolu*. Today the materials used to make the dolls and the availability of bronze, brass, and silver dolls in traditional designs are fewer and more expensive. It is almost as if the three *kolu* makers today find themselves sitting upon an antique treasure chest whose value is only evident to the most avid *kolu* fanatic. "Displaying of prosperity" continues to be a theme in *kolu*. Though the materials may have changed, *kolu* displays continue to grow, and their dioramas spill over to the floors beside them to show off the variety and abundance experienced by the household. Women look into their homes, into their lives, and design and build something worthy of display to commemorate the year's prosperity. A *kolu* becomes an avenue for her creativity as designs once displayed require a special kind of attention, one that is shared, respected, and celebrated among the viewers. Apart from displaying her own *kolu* the householder also goes to view other married women's *kolus* and shares in the fun and excitement of seeing a truly unique *kolu*. Part of this ritual of viewing is showing and showing off prosperity through one's collection of dolls. The prosperity of the family corresponds to the quality and number of dolls displayed and the extent of their ability to host several female guests.

The number of steps, the elaborateness of the dioramas, and the ability to host several guests and present them with gifts and *sundal* display the prosperity and wealth of the household. Instead of being at odds with society and social order, displaying prosperity is viewed as necessary and good. As one informant told me, "Whatever Lakṣmī gives us, we have to show." The rarity of the collections of dolls, the uniqueness of the dioramas, and the ultimate size of the *kolu materially* reflect the boons acquired from Lakṣmī. Pommai Kolu provides a grammar through which displayed materiality can be understood as auspiciousness and wealth. Showing one's possessions may seem pompous, but it is also necessary, as my informant emphasized, showing visitors that Lakṣmī has blessed you. Displaying prosperity functions as both an aspiration and an assertion. What you have must be shown and if you show, you will get more. Prosperity is both celebrated and created through display.

What is the relationship between order, life histories, and prosperity? Moreover, how do these relationships come to be displayed aesthetically? From the perspective of the householder, boons and prosperity are what allow life histories to grow and change. On the one hand, the travels and souvenirs, the various rituals a family gets to partake in, the sheer magnitude (height and width) of the *kolu* are only made possible through prosperity or wealth. The *kolu,* on the other hand, requires structure, ordering through memory on a trajectory or life history. Just like marriage or the birth of a child, each *kolu* brings with it new changes in the household where it is presented. The visitors come to partake in that prosperity in the form of a *kolu,* which is displayed as tableaus within a larger social and religious world.

Since visitors are very important to the householders, they tend to shape the aesthetic choices made while arranging their display. Mrs. Seshadri always placed gifts from her friends and family upon the top three tiers of her *kolu,* making them visible to her guests. She said it was important to remember her guests, showing that she was utilizing their presents. In planning their five-room *kolu,* the Trio paid careful attention to plot various memories of rituals and narratives from their childhood experiences and used some rooms to organize based on characters or deities, and other rooms to organize based on moral teachings. Sarasvati too made sure to include embellishments to her adornment of the *kolu* space, feeling that the purchased or collected dolls didn't convey the whole picture or narrative. She believed that these dolls had to be altered to come into their identity on the steps of a *kolu;* otherwise they wouldn't be recognizable to the viewers.

I spent time lingering in each of these contexts for several hours, pausing to ask many visitors about their reactions. Almost all the intended messages were conveyed just as the householders had wished. Additionally, some new questions arose. One visitor in Sunnyvale, a newer participant to Pommai Kolu from North India, inquired of me about the pot dressed as the goddess (*kalacam*), asking its significance to the festival. After my explanation, she said that she understood that the goddess can be depicted in many novel ways. After a particularly informative workshop at the Trio's house, a group of women were chatting with me about the uniqueness of the five-room *kolu.* They were enraptured by the Trio's chosen variety of narratives and how each story had "hit home," showcasing allegories to modern themes and social problems. The Trio's workshops worked as artistic inspirations for these householders, who went on to replicate these themes and popularize them with their neighbors and friends. Sarasvati never depicted scenes or dolls from popular culture, but her Pommai Kolu always venerated gods, goddesses, and rituals important to her Brahmin community, the early Tamil freedom fighters, Subash Chandra Bose and Gandhi. In many ways, the viewers of these *kolu* are reminding the viewers, not only of what memories are important to the householder, but what makes up the variety of identities of those who maintain this festival.

Recalling the Ordinary Creates the Extraordinary

Memories, like oral narratives, seem unreliable unless recorded, unless accompanied by tangible materials that validate their being. Since *kolu* displays are transient, in some senses they record the ephemerality of memory. Next year, a new display can outshine the one made this year, and faults will be forgotten. Susan Pearce has observed that the motivations to collect could include keeping objects having religious significance, objects that are specific to a time period, objects that replicate reality ("as-if" miniatures), objects that are similar but different, and objects that have material effects (Pearce 2003, 157). Images collected for Pommai Kolu fall into similar categories, and almost all of them have "material effects" in the world. While Pearce has utilized this former definition only to depict objects that are effective, like charms or amulets, I would like to include that all materials displayed for Pommai Kolu have material effects in the sense that they bring the goddess and thus prosperity and order into the householder's family. The deities' images in *kolu* also function as storehouses of cultural and religious knowledge of a prosperous community, and talking about and remembering this prosperity and order tend to create auspiciousness for the coming year. The sort of belief conveyed by the statement "Whatever Lakśmī gives us, we have to show" emphasizes that Pommai Kolu has a "material effect" where it is created, exhibited, and viewed. It also emblematizes the significance of aesthetic display itself, giving prominence to the visual appeal and reception of our personal and communal life histories.

When reflecting upon the aesthetic principles at play during Pommai Kolu, we see the displayer and the viewer uniquely bound in a relationship around that which is displayed. Pearce has also observed that the relationship between the displayer and the objects collected can be multifold, encompassing the memories, experiences, and aesthetic taste of the collector. She likens collectors to curators of museums, who function as custodians of vast collections, lavishing great care upon the objects (Pearce, 1999, 7). Collecting objects for Pommai Kolu is a means to an end, and this means that *kolu* dolls are treasured for their aesthetic qualities and relevance to the festival. The aesthetic depictions, as seen in the three contexts presented in this chapter, must be read as a way in which narratives about one's family and community are visually and materially shared and archived.

The creators of *kolu* must think about representation, how they want to talk about their memories during this Navarātri, and the viewers must ask themselves about the associations that provoked the householder to arrange a display in a certain way in relation to their own memories. The dioramas are not taken to be arbitrary; the visitors are expecting to be entertained. The *kolu* displays and their dolls are always in conversation with the people they are built around. Not only do they ossify hierarchies and distinguish the social and religious worlds, but they also create a vocabulary, providing value to the materiality of the world. Since *kolus* create memories and trigger them, then not only can the dolls speak, but the goddess can come alive for ten days, celebrating among her children and devotees.

Notes

1. "Mylaipūr," as it was noted in early travelers' accounts, was a bustling trading post even since the fifth century. It is also home to St. Thomas Cathedral. St. Thomas is also buried in southern India. Mylapore holds witness to historical events for both Christians and Tamil Brahmins. Mylapore is well known as a trading post due to its proximity to the sea, making it a vibrant marketplace.

2. "Bay Area" refers to the collection of suburbs surrounding the city of San Francisco, including Oakland, Lafayette, Livermore, Sunnyvale, Cupertino, Fremont, San Jose, Santa Clara, Belmont, San Mateo, and Redwood City. Sunnyvale, Cupertino, Fremont, San Jose, Santa Clara, Belmont, and San Mateo are popularly called "South Bay" and are home to many Indians and specifically Tamil Brahmins.

3. Rukmani Arundale is well known for emblematizing the classical dance Bharatanaṭyam and leading a movement to learn and teach a "dying *devadāsī* art form." In the process, classical dances (in several Indian states) were intertwined with nationalist interests and promoting Hindu culture. Davesh Soneji is currently preparing a manuscript criticizing this usurpation with fieldwork notes with the last few dancing girl communities in Andhra Pradesh.

Bibliography

Appadurai, Arjun. 1986. *The Social Life of Things*. Cambridge: Cambridge University Press.

Bynum, Caroline W. 20111. *Christian Materiality: An Essay on Religion in Medieval Europe*. Cambridge, MA: MIT Press.

Coburn, Thomas. B. 1991. *Encountering the Goddess: A Translation of the Devī Māhātmya and a Study of Its Interpretation*. Albany: State University of New York Press.

David, Richard. 1997. *Lives of Indian Images*. Princeton: Princeton University Press.

Fuller, Christopher, and Haripriya Narasimhan. 2010. "The Agrahāram: The Transformation of Social Space and Brahman Status in Tamilnadu during the Colonial and Postcolonial Periods." In *Ritual, Caste, and Religion in Colonial South India (Neue Hallesche Berichte 9)*, edited by Michael Bergunder et al., 219–37. Halle: Verlag der Franckeschen Stiftungen.

Fuller, C. J., and Penny Logan. "The Navarātiri Festival of Madurai." *Bulletin of School of Oriental and African Studies* 48 (1985): 79–105.

Hancock, Mary. E. 1999. *Womanhood in the Making: Domestic Ritual and Public Culture in Urban South India*. Boulder, CO: Westview.

King, Frances. E. 2010. *Material Religion and Popular Culture*. New York: Routledge.

Kratz, Corrine. 2011. "Rhetorics of Value." *Visual Anthropology Review* 27 (Spring): 21–48.

———. 2002. "Photographs on Display." In *The Ones That Are Wanted: Communication and the Politics of Representation in a Photographic Exhibition by Corrine A. Kratz*. Berkeley: University of California Press.

Kurien, Prema. A. 2007. *A Place at the Multicultural Table: The Development of an American Hinduism*. Newark: Rutgers University Press.

Nagarajan, A. P. *Tiruvilayādal*. 1965. Written and Directed by A. P. Nagarajan. Madras, Tamil Nadu: Vijaya Pictures, Youtube. http://www.youtube.com/watch?v=zztzKqHb66c&list=PLC4D63EC5B1B95A7F&index=5

Pearce, Susan. M. ed. 2003. *Interpreting Objects and Collecting*. New York: Routledge.

———. 1999. *On Collecting*. New York: Routledge.

Pintchman, Tracy, ed. 2007. *Women's Lives, Women's Rituals in the Hindu Tradition*. New York: Oxford University Press.

Selby, Martha, and Viswanathan Peterson, eds. 2008. *Tamil Geographies: Constructions of Space and Place in South India*. Albany: State University of New York Press.

Tanaka, Masukazu. 1992. "The Navarātri in Chidambaram, South India." In *Living with Śakti*, edited by Masukazu Tanaka and Musashi Tachikawa. Osaka: National Museum of Ethnology.

14

Royal *Darbār* and Domestic *Kolus*

Social Order, Creation, Procreation, and Re-Creation

VASUDHA NARAYANAN

By the middle of September, many people—especially women—from and in Karnataka, Tamil Nadu, and some areas of Andhra Pradesh and Kerala are gearing up for Navarātri. In these states and for people from them who reside in other parts of the world, this festival will be celebrated by setting up a *kolu* (pronounced and sometimes spelled as *golu*), a temporary, tiered display stand, covered with cloths and populated with dolls. The dolls may be made of clay, marble, papier-mâché, porcelain, or any other material, and the *kolu* may include cheap to high-end railroad sets, Barbies, or elaborate doll sets showing scenes from Hindu epics. Weeks before the decorating begins, stores in these states, as well as those that cater to diaspora populations in New Jersey and California have stocked up on clay dolls depicting deities, holy men and women, popular stories from both India and other parts of the world (e.g., Aesop's fables), and scenes from everyday life. Stores such as Poompuhar, the official state handicrafts outlet in Tamil Nadu, are transformed and showcase huge *kolus* filled with hundreds of dolls. Street vendors have a brisk business selling clay and papier-mâché dolls at lower prices than the retail stores, and TV reporters scour the streets for the latest trends. School children, as well as men and women of all ages, rehearse classical music they will perform at various homes and in public celebrations of Navarātri. Many public venues have Navarātri festivities with vocal and instrumental music, dance, and the *kolu*. The schedule for the prestigious Navarathri Mandapam

Concert at the Padmanabhaswamy Temple, in Thiruvanantapuram, Kerala, featuring classical Carnatic music, has been drawn up accompanied by strict rules for the devotees' behavior (Navarathri Mandapam Concerts, Schedule 2016). In the different parts of Chennai, Tamil Nadu, newspapers advertise *kolu* contests. Television and YouTube channels are populated with segments of how to set up *kolus*, where to buy the dolls, what food to prepare on what day, and interviews with random shoppers to get their views on what Navarātri *kolu* means to them. From just this small cross-section of activities, we can see that Navarātri is celebrated across domestic and public spaces.

In domestic celebration, from little apartments to large bungalows, women and children set up the tiered *kolu* in the central room of the home. Here, family and friends will drop in briefly to look at the *kolu* during the nine days of Navarātri, perhaps sing a song, and receive the *prasād*, which is usually *sundal*. *Sundal* is a slightly salty saladlike dish, which is made with different kinds of beans, such as garbanzo, every day during the festival; the goddess, to whom the *kolu* is dedicated, is said to favor beans. This domestic form of Navarātri celebration that involves the setting up and arrangement of a large display of images and dolls in the homes has developed among Tamil-, Telugu-, and Kannada-speaking women in the last two hundred or so years. This tiered tableau is called *koluvu* (Telugu) and *kolu* (Tamil and Malayalam).

The Tamil lexicon gives the following meanings for the word *kolu*: "1. royal presence, durbar, sitting-in-state, presence of the deity in the temple; 2. Decorations in a Hindu house at the time of the Navaratri festival" (*Tamil Lexicon*, vol. 2, 1158). The *kolu*, therefore, is etymologically linked to the act and spectacle of a king sitting in state, as in a royal *darbār*. More descriptively, the festival is known in Telugu as Bommala Koluvu, or (dolls holding a *darbār*), a sentiment captured in the Kannada name Boṃbe Habba or Goṃbe Habba (festival of dolls). A popular blog gives a description of the festival. Although this is for the state of Karnataka, the description would apply to the way in which hundreds of thousands of Hindus in south India and in the diaspora celebrate it:

> The Dasara doll festival is celebrated in Karnataka through an exhibition of various dolls and figurines arranged as per custom. The dolls are arranged and exhibited on a stepped platform having an odd number of steps or tiers (usually 7, 9 or 11) and usually covered with a white or light color cloth. Many households use nine steps for the exhibition of dolls to signify the nine nights of Navaratri. The dolls are ritually worshipped during the celebrations. (Rotti 2016)

The *kolus* of today are embedded in narratives and nostalgia about kings and commoners, deities, demons, and devotees, and increasingly concerned with intergenerational relations, food, and social displays of cultural capital. Where did this tradition of tiered arrangement of dolls on bleacher-like steps and the emphasis on performing arts in Navarātri come from? Does the time period when Navarātri is celebrated tell us anything about its meaning?

My chapter explores the historical and temporal contexts of these life-affirming performances where the visual and performing arts are valorized and how these observances have been shaped by both pan-Hindu considerations in terms of temporal location and local history. I examine the evidence to see if this is a "domestication" of a festival that was once a royal, public affair during the time of the Vijayanagara kings, and I discuss its temporal connection with the dark fortnight dedicated to the ancestors. In the possible movement from the Vijayanagara festivities to the current *kolu* scene, the festival has shifted from the public sphere to the domestic, and now back to the public; and from male-royal military exercises to the renewal of learning and honoring of tools of one's trade.

This chapter, therefore, is about connections. I begin by first looking at the Karnataka tradition of giving primacy to dolls of the king and queen and the Tamil customs, which privilege images of deities and dolls depicting everyday life in the *kolu*. I connect these to the traditions of arts and music during the celebration of this festival in the Vijayanagara kingdom (fifteenth–sixteenth centuries CE) as described by foreign emissaries to the court. More specifically, pictures of the king sitting in state on his throne with his courtiers (known in later centuries as the *darbār* or "durbar") and the *kolu* in homes seem to belong to the same family of visual imagery. The social and divine orders in the display, as well as the life-affirming rituals and performances seen in many Hindu communities, I argue, are specially valorized in this period because it follows the most inauspicious fortnight connected with ancestors (*pitṛ pakṣa*) in the Hindu calendar. I describe the enduring importance of the rituals connected with this inauspicious time among Hindus in the diaspora and finally connect some of the themes and rituals of *pitṛ pakṣa* with the life-giving and creative forces of the goddess.

There are many filters through which I interpret this autumnal festival in this chapter. One such filter, which is explicit in the next few pages, comes through my lifelong connections with this festival that I integrate with academic sources. Traditional academic sources for this chapter include Sanskrit and Tamil works, historical texts, secondary literature (primarily on kingship and the Vijayanagara kingdom), and ethnography. Many of these texts are snapshots (or, more correctly, short, fluid motion pictures) in a specific time, revealing the viewpoint, the perspective of one patron, one author, or a set of authors in a distinct sociocultural milieu. Frequently, the texts that have survived showcase the perspectives of those who could afford to fund such enterprises.

More often than not, they only describe the world of the upper-class people, especially men, and do not necessarily represent society as a whole. But what if, to understand contemporary ideas today, we include expressions of popular culture through cartoons, ephemera, and YouTube videos, thinking of blogs as inscriptions and YouTube as part of the visual culture? These too are commentaries of social practices and trends, also limited in their viewpoint, but definitely expressing the sentiments of vast segments of the population today. Thus, in my quest to investigate the possible royal roots that led to the proliferation of the contemporary celebration of Navarātri, I not only draw from historical narratives and primary texts but also upon blogs and television news reports and social media, including popular video presentations.

In addition to these, I bring the knowledge from my own connections with the festival to this research. My grandmother and aunts celebrated Navarātri with considerable enthusiasm when I was growing up in Madras (now Chennai), and the traditions were continued by my mother in Bombay (now Mumbai). As a child, I accompanied family on trips to Mysore to see the public processions of the Mahārāja and see the Dasara (the name for Vijayadaśami that is popular in Karnataka) festivities. Many of our neighbors and friends also celebrated the festival, and the women in all these homes went "*kolu*-hopping," that is, visiting many homes during the nine evenings of Navarātri to see the *kolu*, hear the music, and consume the *sundal* given to them as a symbol of divine favor. I have continued to celebrate the *kolu* in Florida since 1986. My interest in the festival led me to visit small communities that make clay dolls in Panrutti, Tamil Nadu, in 1996, take extensive pictures, and write notes, long before I thought of doing anything formal with the material. Watching and keeping the *kolus* over decades and noting trends in friends' homes in India and in the United States has given me a special relationship to the festival, and some of these connections inform the narrative of this chapter.

While at times in the twentieth century it was connected with Brahmanical homes in Tamil Nadu, the *goṃbe habba* has been practiced by many castes in Karnataka. In the late twentieth and early twenty-first centuries, *kolu* has become part of state identity and revived as a heritage festival in Tamil Nadu, Karnataka, and Andhra. People from many walks of life and many castes—showcased on television—have started to practice this ritual as emblematic of a shared history and culture. Certainly, it is a significant feature of statehood and Karnataka identity, where we see a coming together of royal, religious, and public secular rituals. In homes, the domestic *kolus* still remain women's ritual in India, but everyone participates in them in the United States. Public celebrations of Navarātri in South Indian states have become more secular and involve performing arts with men and women singing on stages and large *kolus* sponsored by businesses (figure 14.1). What gave rise to this popular tradition?

The question of origins is always vexing, and the origins of the *kolu* as a celebration of Navarātri are not clear. We do not hear about this tradition even in early modern texts. Given that until recently this was largely a domestic ritual only done by women, who handed the lore through oral tradition, and given the largely androcentric nature of many surviving texts, it is not surprising that there is no mention of domestic *kolus* in literature even in the nineteenth century. Information given by family and friends over the years, as well as learning the history about the dolls that I used to place on *kolus* as a child, has made me realize that as a domestic festival it was certainly prevalent by at least the mid-nineteenth century in Tamil Nadu. Television shows, which feature *kolus*, however, speak about this as an ancient custom.

Placement of the Dolls and the Depiction of Social and Evolutionary Hierarchies

Do the tiered *kolu* steps at homes possibly simulate the royal *darbār* (sitting in state), which became increasingly important during and after the Mahānavamī (lit. the "great ninth" day, the preferred name of the

Figure 14.1. Singing and dancing before the *kolu* is a significant part of the *kolu* activities.

Navarātri festival in the Vijayanagara period) celebrations of the kings, especially King Kṛṣṇadevarāya (reigned 1509–1529), or do they show the hierarchy of creation? We turn to this issue now.

The placement of dolls in the Navarātri *kolu* is important in many families. In general, one notes three ways in which dolls are placed. The first—and probably the most common—is to keep dolls wherever they fit, wherever there is place, and wherever it is convenient, in other words, in random order. But there are also two other ways of arranging the *kolu*, which are important in terms of hierarchy. Many in Tamil Nadu place the deities up on the top, in the highest row; immediately below them come the kings, queens, and dolls depicting royal figures; followed by dolls of human beings, animals, and so on. Many people from Tamil Nadu say that the steps of *kolus* denote the various parts of the universe, with animals, human beings, and celestial beings on the lower tiers, and representations of the Supreme Being on the highest step, creating a hierarchy of creation in a universe of devotion.

There is yet a third way, one that is popular in Karnataka, with importance given to the dolls of a king and a queen. These rationales seem to parallel, in my opinion, what Ikegame observes about Navarātri or Dasara in general:

> It seems that there are two forms of the celebration of Dasara. One form focuses mainly on rituals of the goddess. The Navaratri festival celebrated in the Minakshi temple in Madurai clearly belongs to this type. . . . Dasara in Mysore constitutes another form in which the emphasis is placed, not only on the worship of the goddess, but also on kingship. These two forms of Dasara are, however, never in opposition to one another and nor are they self-sufficient, but rather are strongly interrelated and interdependent. (Ikegame 2012, 143)

In many *kolus* in Karnataka, the dolls of the king and queen are placed in such a way to show their primacy. They are, however, not kept on top, symbolically showing that they are the highest but, interestingly enough, in the lowest row, so they can be venerated easily.

The Primacy of the Supreme Beings and Spiritual Evolution in the Placement of Dolls

One popular arrangement that seems to have gathered momentum in recent years as a "correct" way of doing things in Tamil Nadu is said to depict the hierarchy of creation: the supreme beings on top, followed by lesser deities, mortals, and finally other forms of creation. It is a carefully organized, ordered hierarchy with the gods on top and with the deity considered by that family to be supreme on its top tier. The *kolu* becomes a microcosm of the universe. There is no textual basis for this, or even for this specific celebration of Navarātri. Like many ideas, this rationale takes a life of its own. This sentiment is confirmed in internet blogs, in interviews conducted by popular television stations in Chennai during the Navarātri, and in popular discourse, as people who celebrate this festival say that the steps denote the various parts of the universe, creating a pyramid of devotion. Others say that this is the time that is sacred for the Goddess and that by arranging the dolls, the whole area becomes the play, the *līlā*, of the deities. One of the most elaborate expositions of this sentiment in popular culture is seen in a YouTube video uploaded on October 1, 2016, on the Tamil Channel titled *Navarattiri kolu vaikkum muraiyum viyakka vaikkum vijnjnanamum* (The way to keep a Navaratri *kolu* and its science which will astonish you): Navaratri Celebrations and Golu." This video gives a very detailed exposition of the hierarchy of the cosmos. It also dictates that one should keep the dolls in a particular hierarchical order, starting with the inanimate objects and those with "one level of awareness, like conchs" on the bottom and slowly upgrading levels in relation to higher levels of existence, including animals, human beings, spiritual beings, lesser divinities, and finally the supreme being on the very top, highest row (figure 14.2). It also connects the tiers of the *kolu*

Figure 14.2. A *kolu* display with the deities—Viṣṇu with Lakṣmī and Bhū Devī (the Earth Goddess) on the top tier.

steps to a kind of spiritual evolution, that is, the slow growth of wisdom and self-realization of a created being. Thus, according to this video, one evolves from being a lesser being to a human being, to a spiritually luminous being, to a divinity, and finally realizing that we are in close communion with the supreme deity, conceptualized as Devī, Viṣṇu, or Śiva. This pilgrim's progress is said to be depicted in the dolls arranged in the tiered steps of the *kolu* ("Navaratri Celebrations and Golu" 2016).

The Primacy of the Royal Court in Mysore and the Significance of the Darbār

While the explanation in popular culture and social media in early twenty-first-century Tamil Nadu has focused deliberately on the depictions of human-divine hierarchy in *kolu* formats, Karnataka-based blogs, as well as colonial literature, have focused on royal connections. Works, which are deferential to royalty in the colonial times (Hayavadana Rao, 1936), as well as modern state literature and web lore connect the pageantry of royal Dasara in Mysore to the Vijayanagara empire as part of the founding myth of the festival and to the *Devī Māhātmyam* as a source for religious authority. These connections are certainly plausible, and one can show the evolution of the *darbār* through the centuries. What is less clear is its connection with the domestic festival of *kolu* done at the same time. It is this area that we will now explore.

One clue comes from the practice seen in Karnataka where the king and queen (*rāja-rāṇī*) dolls, sometimes known as the *paṭṭada goṃbe* (from *paṭṭa* or the silk turban or crown worn by a ruler; connected with *paṭṭābhiṣeka* or consecration of a tiara, implying a coronation) dolls, are considered to be the central pieces of the *kolu* (figure 14.3). The practice of giving a pair of these wooden *rāja-rāṇī* dolls dressed in a grand manner to young women when they get married is attested to in many blogs that reflect popular practice. One author notes that during the Navarātri season, "enthusiastic kids help their mothers in bedecking "Pattada Gombe" (Raja Rani dolls) and other dolls, and help their fathers in building the platform to arrange the dolls" (Bennur 2011). Another blogger, writing about the Karnataka customs, gives directions on how to decorate these dolls, and writes:

> Pattada gombe in Kannada means, the royal dolls . . . Many households have a custom of arranging dolls during Dasara festival in Mysore and distribute sweet and savories to children. This is also known as *Kolu* in Iyengar households. Various idols are arranged and the main dolls are the King and the Queen. The King and Queen dolls are made of Chandana / Rosewood. These dolls are gifted to the girl on her wedding day by her

Figure 14.3. *Paṭṭada* (king and queen) dolls are set on the lowest tier of the *kolu.*

> parents. . . . Every year, few days before Dasara, the Pattada Gombe/ King and Queen dolls are decorated using different materials. (Shantha 2015)

While wooden dolls, similar to the *rāja-rāṇī* dolls, known as *marappaci* in Tamil, are important in Tamil Nadu, they are not understood to be a royal couple, a meaning that is so prominent in Karnataka.

Aya Ikegame has shown the connection between the royal exercises of kingship and the *rāja-rāṇī* dolls of the household *goṃbe habba* in Mysore, Karnataka:

> Their arrangement of the dolls was very similar to the manner Nanjammanni has described: the raja and rani dolls on the lowest step and the dolls of the gods on the higher steps. They perform *pūjā* for raja and rani dolls on the podium itself, not in the worshipping room. They told me that they used to perform *pūjā* on the raja and rani dolls at precisely the same moment as the maharaja ascended to the throne during the durbar in the palace. . . . They knew exactly when they had to do so because a salute of twenty-one guns, which the people in the city could hear, was fired at the moment when the maharaja climbed onto the throne. The salute of guns,

> which was introduced by the British in order to create and fix the imperial hierarchy, became an important device for people by which they could know what was going on in the palace. . . . The domestic worship of the raja and rani dolls, and the royal ritual in the palace, were thus linked by this Anglo-Indian ritual device. (Ikegame 2012, 161)

Placement of the king and queen on the lowest tier here does not mean that they are the lowest beings; they are kept in a low shelf because they are closest to the people who are installing the *kolu* and therefore can be easily worshiped.

The Testimony of Travelers to the Vijayanagara Court

How can we link these customs of the *kolu* or *goṃbe habba* to the history of Mysore from Vijayanagara to the Woḍeyar times? To explore possible connections, we can turn to the accounts of travelers to the Vijayanagara court over a period of about a hundred years. In this process, I will show how classical studies by Sewell and others on the Vijayanagara kingdom as well as current textual and ethnographic scholarship also effectively help our arguments.

Nicolo dei Conti came in 1420 CE. He was possibly one of the earliest-known European travelers, and "if he was not the earliest European visitor, he was at least the earliest that we know of whose description of the place has survived to this day" (Sewell 1900, 81). Sewell, however, notes: "Nicolo never apparently wrote anything himself. His stories were recorded in Latin by Poggio Bracciolini, the Pope's secretary, for his master's information. Translated into Portuguese, they were re-translated from the Portuguese into Italian by Ramusio, who searched for but failed to obtain a copy of the original in Latin" (Sewell 1900, 81). A few years later, Abdur Razzak, who left Persia in January 1442, arrived in Vijayanagara (via Calicut) in April of the same year and stayed there until December. He wrote about what he calls the magnificent *mahandi* (Mahānavamī). The most elaborate accounts, however, come from the sixteenth century and are found in the works of Domingos Paes (c. 1520) and Fernao Nuniz (c. 1536–37; see Ikegame 2012, 144; Sewell 1900, v–vii, 81–95). These accounts collectively focus on several aspects of the Mahānavamī festival: the king's splendor; the activities of the citizens and the tributes they paid to the king; the entertainment involving wrestlers, musicians, dancers, the elaborate decorations; and the king's magnificent court. Of these, I will note a few passages relating to the last two subjects to show that these may be connected with later "spin-off" celebrations like that of the *kolu*.

The decorations noted by Razzak include "raised pavilions (*chahartaq*) of three, four and five stories, completely covered from top to bottom with pictures, every picture that could be imagined, of humans, beasts, birds and all other animals, even flies and mosquitoes–all executed with precision and mastery" (Thakston 1989, 299–321). There was, apparently, a lot of music and dance, circus acts, magic tricks, acrobatics, fireworks. Razzak writes that for three days, "from the time the peacock of the sun stands in the midst of heaven until the raven of evening spreads its wings, the regal celebration is conducted" (Thakston 1989, 314). Given the dates Razzak mentions (the month Rajab and a full moon) and his assertion that it lasted three days, Sewell speculates it may have been a different festival. While the first two factors make us pause, the third can easily be explained in that it is the last three days that are considered by many to be the most important and when most of the celebrations take place. The *dharmaśāstras* also give considerable latitude to the number of days in which we can celebrate this festival (Kane 1958, 154–55; 159–60).

Domingo Paes, who came around 1520, is more specific in his description of the structures. In his account, we read of the "narrow scaffoldings made of wood . . . covered at the top with crimson and green velvet and other handsome cloths, and adorned from top to bottom . . . [T]he walls were adorned with figures" (Sewell 1900, 263–64). These temporary scaffoldings were covered with elaborate decorations. It is interesting that there were eleven of the temporary structures, a number that becomes popular in very large *kolus*. Paes also speaks about tiered platforms upon which people sit; he notes that "[o]n the upper platform, close to the king, was Christovao de Figueiredo, with all of us who came with him, for the king commanded that he should be put in such a place as best to see the feasts and magnificence" (Sewell 1900, 264). Their reports show that during these Mahānavamī celebrations, the king in his capital city of Vijayanagara (Hampi) watched royal processions from the pavilion dedicated for this royal seating and viewing. We certainly know from Domingo Paes that during the festival, the king ascended a structure, at the top of which was a "throne of state" (Sewell 1900, 265). This massive stone platform, known as the Mahānavamī *dibba* (throne platform), was built in the fourteenth century (Rao 1991, 166). Nalini Rao highlights the imperial program of the Mahānavamī *dibba* and makes a close connection between kingship, holding the royal court, the arts showcased at Navarātri, and the festival itself (Rao 1991, 165–228). Rao says there were also wooden platforms that formed elevated tiers erected on the Mahānavamī dais upon which the king and his subordinates would sit (Rao, 1991, 165). If its purpose was, indeed, to serve as a dais for the king and the courtiers, the idea of a tiered seating arrangement evidently goes back several centuries to the Vijayanagara Mahānavamī and the king's tiered *dibba*. The festival culminated in a grand celebration with the king holding court. Ikegame notes that "the description by Paes and Nuniz clearly shows that the durbar was a powerful tool of control in the Vijayanagara kingdom" (2012, 145).

Further, during this Navarātri festival, we have a display of female auspiciousness in the king's court. Price notes that Kṛṣṇadevarāya had three principal queens and that "[e]ach of the nine days of the festival was designated as special to one of the three queens. Each queen, on one of her special days, sent her retinue of women, such that there was a representation of the principal wives each day of the festival" (Price 1990, 595). In passing, we should note that in contemporary understanding of the Navarātri festival in Tamil Nadu, many women think of the nine nights as devoted to the three goddesses Durgā, Lakṣmī, and Sarasvati. Price also notes the prevalence of this idea of the nine nights being divided between the three goddesses in later courts and seats of power in Tamil Nadu (Price 1996, 137). The presence of women seems to mark more than just a representation of the queen; Price notes that

> Domingo Paes's description of state ritual in the famous late medieval Navaratri festival shows women representing auspiciousness and material well-being. These women were not presented to the king in order of rank but appeared more as undifferentiated, abstract qualities necessary to the successful maintenance of the kingdom. (1990, 597)

The women who were present were involved in multiple activities, including performing arts and processions, but the queens themselves were not present in public. Kings sitting in state and giving audience to visitors continued to be important features of the post-Vijayanagara period. One may note two aspects that dominated these courtly sessions. The first was the giving and receiving of gifts between the ruler and the subject, which created a political and hierarchical bond between them; the second was the seating of the members such that it was "an occasion for the public display of the hierarchical structure of the kingdom. Subordinate chiefs, noblemen, officials, and prominent citizens had a seat at the durbar according to their status" (Fuller 1992, 126). However, Fuller says that in later times, the giving of a presentation was less important than the public display of social hierarchy, which was firmly maintained (quoted in Ikegame 2012, 148).

Thus, the Dasara festivities in the Vijayanagara period included components that suggest they were the model for the *kolu* decorations in many parts of south India in later centuries. There was an efflorescence of performing arts and opulent decorations. Also, from the reports of the foreign visitors, we know that the king held court in many different ways: in private chambers and publicly seated on a royal dais, the Mahānavamī *dibba*, with wooden platforms, in raised tiers, again, decorated in sumptuous manner. The king and courtiers seemed to have been seated on various levels watching the festivities.

Many of these protocols seemed to have continued into the nineteenth century in colonial times and into the "European" *darbārs* that were staged for the British Resident–the royal representative—and royal guests in Mysore. They also became part, to some extent, of this ritual when it was coopted by British Viceroys who staged "durbars" in honor of the British crown. A picture from the British Library entitled *The Dusserah Durbar of His Highness the Maharaja of Mysore*, engraved by C. F. C. Lewis senior in 1848–49 shows the seating in a Navarātri *darbār* . The engraving (reproduced in Ikegame 2012, 149) depicts the king and the royal courtiers, guests, and other luminaries sitting in what looks like a cross-section of a football stadium, on bleachers, watching the entertainment below. They seem to be seated on a platform with the king on the lowest row, center, on his throne, under a large pavilion. There are several tiers, with people standing on them.

In the *Kaṇṭhīrava Narasarāja Vijayam* (c. 1648) we find in considerable detail "the programme of the King's daily Durbar during the nine days and his State Procession on the tenth day (Vijayadasami)" (Hayavadana Rao 1936, 25). Apparently, this festival was continued even during the period of Haidar Ali and Tipu Sultan (1761–99). The *darbār* seems to have gained further prominence around 1805, during the time of Kṛṣṇa Rāja Woḍeyar III, and by 1814 a special foreign (i.e., European) *darbār* day was fixed and ritually performed with much pomp and pageantry (Hayavadana Rao 1936, 25).

Darbārs and *Kolus*

It appears from these descriptions that the royal court (*koluvu* or *darbār*) is what is recreated today in the domestic celebration of *kolu* or *koluvu* in south India. The visual of the mahārāja's *darbār* and the *goṃbe habba* (festival of dolls) clearly fall in the same family of visual imagery. As we noted earlier, in the Karnataka festival, the *rāja-rāṇī* dolls are kept on the tiered platforms, but at the lowest row in the *kolu*, almost exactly as we saw in the engraving by Lewis. What we find in the public Dasara *durbar* is a clear hierarchy of royalty and subjects, sloping down from the raised platforms into the "real" world of ordinary people and animals.

Although the visual imagery confirms it, the very term *koluvu* (sitting in state), or *darbār*, points directly to the connection. The Nāyakas and Poligārs who had been prominent vassals in the Vijayanagara empire eventually inherited the Vijayanagara mantle and spread the local culture to large parts of Andhra Pradesh and Tamil Nadu. It is probable that between the late seventeenth and early nineteenth centuries this practice was adopted in royal and then other households and spread to those parts with the Nāyaka ethos. During this time, we should remember that Navarātri was "[t]he main annual festival of kingdoms from Vijayanagar times to the nineteenth century" (Price 1996, 27) and that "durbars were an essential feature of Navaratri" (Price 1996, 147). The common conceptual ideas of both the deity and a king sitting in state as well as generic ideas of god-as-king and king-as-god would certainly have allowed other interpretations by the time it became popular in Tamil Nadu. Hence the primacy to the *rāja-rāṇi* (*paṭṭada*) dolls in Mysore and to the deities in Tamil Nadu in the *kolu*.

The idea of the deity sitting in a *kolu* or *darbār* is seen in classical music of that period in the Tanjore (Tañjāvūr) area of Tamil Nadu. In *Koluvamare Gada* a well-known, Carnatic music song composed by Tyāgarāja (1767–1847) in the Todi Rāgam (metrical composition), he describes the royal splendor of Rāma with his valorous bow sitting in state, as in a royal court. The reference to the deity holding court (*kolu*) is also seen in the lyrics of another Tyāgarāja *kṛti* (song) *Koluvai yunnāḍe* in Bhairavi Rāgam. In both these songs, Tyāgarāja visualizes Rāma as a divine king in a *darbār* with his family and courtiers. Another notable instance from this period that connects divinity and *darbārs*—and certainly one that has been extensively studied—seems to be the ritual state of Ramnad (Rāmanāthapuram), where the "spacious hall in which the Amman, in her processional form (*utsavar*), sat in state, was divided into elevated and terraced verandas" (Breckenridge 1977, 81; see also Waghorne 1994).

The last day, the "victorious tenth" day of Navaratri ("Vijayadaśamī" or "Dasara" in south India; "Bijoya Daśamī" in Bengal), when kings formerly did their symbolic conquests of other land, is dedicated to Lakṣmī, the goddess of good fortune. This is a time for renewal; people start new ventures and new account books and learn new things on that auspicious day. Students in performing arts frequently meet and honor their traditional teachers—a practice very much encouraged among Hindus in the diaspora—and learn new pieces of music or the first steps of a new dance, and acquire new knowledge. While spiritual gurus who lead one on a spiritual path are venerated on Guru Pūrṇimā, teachers of the arts and other forms of learning have been honored, at least in the last century, on Vijayadaśamī when they should learn something new from them. It may be a coincidence, but it was on this Vijayadaśamī day that Tipu Sultan wrote his longest letter to the Śṛngeri *jagadguru*; Simmons notes, "In fact on the day of Dasara, perhaps inspired by the other rituals that he had observed, Ṭīpū Sultān penned the longest letter that he ever wrote to the *jagadguru*" (Simmons 2014, 238). In the diaspora we see many variations of this sentiment; a few years ago, in Gainesville, a friend invited her daughter's schoolteachers for lunch that day. On the last days of the Navarātri festival, the fortune of learning, the wealth of wisdom, and the joy of music are said to be given by the grace of the goddesses and of the gurus.

While the ritual of *kolu*/*darbār* is important for both deity and royalty at special times of the year, the act of women keeping the *kolu* in their homes is restricted to two times a year. The best-known and the most popular time is during the *śarad* or autumnal Navarātri, the Navarātri that comes soon after the new moon in the month of Puraṭṭāci in Tamil Nadu and Āśvina in other parts of South India. But there is a second time, much less known than the Fall Navarātri.[1] This is during the time of Makara Saṅkrānti, the transition between *dakṣiṇāyana* (when the sun appears to be going south to the Tropic of Capricorn) and *uttarāyana* (when sun starts to travel north, in mid-January). The *uttarāyana* marks the winter solstice in the Hindu calendar, but because the local calendar did not make necessary corrections to specific astronomical movements, it now comes in mid-January in India, about twenty-three or twenty-four days after its astronomical occurrence. The *bommala koluvu* kept during the Makara Saṅkarānti time is now seen only in parts of Andhra Pradesh and is practiced by some of the Telugu people in the diaspora as *Poṅgal Bommala Koluvu*. The word "*poṅgal*," which is the name of a famous south Indian festival that comes at this time, is used with "*bommala koluvu*" to distinguish this *kolu* from that which is celebrated in autumn. Purnima Sonti, who lives in Arizona and keeps the *kolu* during Makara Saṅkrānti, says she follows the tradition of her mother-in-law, and she blogs about how to be creative in these displays, and through them the information about celebrating the display at this time of the year is disseminated to a wider public.

In the following section, I will argue that the celebration of the Navarātri *kolu*, with its focus on fecundity, creation, and order comes after two periods that focus on death and the ancestors. The times when the *kolu* with all its abundance and fanfare are celebrated are (1) mid-autumn, soon after the *pitṛ pakṣa*, the inauspicious time when the ancestors are venerated and (2) Makara Saṅkrānti, the Hindu winter solstice, which comes soon after the six-month period of the ancestors. As early as the *Bhagavad Gītā* (8:25) the association is made between *dakṣiṇāyana* and the death-rebirth; this is the path of the *pitṛ* (ancestors).

Creation and the Potential for Life

What we see in the *kolu* scenes in royal arenas and in the doll displays is a cosmos of creative possibilities and complex hierarchies: royal, divine, social, and even biological and spiritual. That this is true of the *kolu* presentation at homes is fairly clear. What the *kolu* shares with celebrations of Navarātri across the country is a very explicit across-the-board potential for creation, order, life, and prosperity. The bursting forth and celebration of life seen in *kolus* and so palpable in the travelers' accounts of the Mahānavamī celebrations is congruent with ideas of creative energies embedded in the Navarātri festival in other parts of India. The display of new life and new creation is made obvious in many ways in pan-Hindu ethnic and sectarian traditions. This emphasis on life-affirming symbols, objects, and rituals is seen in a number of ways including (but not limited to) the following: the abundant use of ritually grown grain, lentils, beans, and seeds; the use of material objects invested with spiritual meaning, like a metal *kalaśa* (jar) filled with the waters of life or an earthenware pot with holes within which the fire of creation burns through the nine nights; a ritual veneration of young, prepubescent girls who are considered to be manifestations of the Devī and filled with the potential to give birth to children; and music and dance that celebrate creation, procreation, and recreation.

It is perhaps the emphasis on grain and sprouting beans that is most tangible and most visible among many Hindu communities. In an eyewitness account in 1892 of the state celebrations in Ramnad, quoted by Breckenridge, we read that "to invite prosperity, five married women (*cumaṅkalis*) planted two seeds of different lentils in each of the vessels with the hope that they might sprout before the nine-day festivities were concluded" (Breckenridge 1977, 83). During this time, in most south Indian households where Navarātri is celebrated, *sundal,* a dish made of various kinds of dried beans or lentils is offered to the goddess everyday. These lentils and beans are seeds of life, ready to sprout. In Gujarat, women ritually plant *jowar* (sorghum; occasionally barley or wheat) seeds in little containers in front of the goddess at the beginning of the Navarātri festival, which sprout within a couple of days (figure 14.4). Neelima Shukla-Bhatt also describes the creation of a goddess-image by installing

Figure 14.4. Women from Gujarat venerate the creative energies of the goddess. A clay jar (*garbo*) and freshly sprouted *jowar* plants are arranged at the altar.

> a clay pot filled with water and decorated with a colorful sari as well as jewelry. On its top is placed a clay platter or a basket filled with soil. A coconut is placed in its center, and five types of grain are scattered around it. The image is put on an altar made of soil where grains are scattered as well. With the water seeping through the pot, the grains sprout during the festival. The sprouts are considered a part of the image. (2015, 93)

Hillary Rodrigues, in his discussion of this form of the goddess, has noted that this shape of the jar, the sprouted grains, and the earth powerfully speak about ideas of pregnancy and birth (Rodrigues 2003, 262).

Jars of water, noted by Rodrigues, seem to be one of the most ubiquitous examples of material culture in this festival, cutting across state and ethnic lines. Tender green mango leaves are kept in the neck of the jar in some areas, and a coconut sits on top of its lip. Most Hindus, if questioned, would say that the rounded *kalaśa* with water is the womb of the goddess. This jar with life-giving waters is the Devī, the creative energies of the universe. In many areas of south India and in Maharashtra, this jar or *kalaśa* is an important part of the nine-night celebration. A blog on *kolu* in the website of the transnational Art of Living movement says what is known to most families setting up this display: "Setting up of the Bommai Golu starts with a *kalash* (ceremonial jar) with fresh water covered with a coconut and mango leaves ("7 aspects of Golu"). The *kalash* is placed on the top step in the center and is considered to represent the Goddess Durga. Idols of Deities are placed to the left and right of the *kalash*" ("7 aspects of Golu").

Shukla-Bhatt compares these jars filled with water with clay jars called *garbo/garba* (Sanskrit: *garbha*; lit. "womb") which are popular in Gujarat (2015, 93–94). A lamp is lit inside them by women at the beginning of Navarātri, and the light inside the jar shines through the perforations. This jar is the goddess with the whole cosmos inside her. Throughout the nights of the festival, women sing and dance with this aniconic form of the goddess. These performances are called *garbo* and have become popular in many diaspora Navarātri celebrations.

Perhaps the joy and celebratory nature of life are best seen in the performing arts, which are showcased during Navarātri. We noted that the travelers to the Vijayanagara empire wrote about them in considerable detail. In the celebration of *kolu*, too, the evenings are filled with classical music, recitations, and dance. Women go to various houses and perform even if they are the only visitors. The audience is the *kolu*, those seated in the *darbār*: the deity, the royalty, and all the denizens of this cosmos. In Gujarat, too, women dance the nights away with the goddess, singing songs (*garbo*); music and dance are central to our understanding of the creation and recreation in the Hindu traditions.

The Time of the Ancestors

One may ask why this extended period of celebration of life and creative energies is seen at this time of the year in Navarātri and why the *śarad* Navarātri is celebrated at a particular time of the year. In the charter myth for this festival, Durgā kills Mahiṣa, the water buffalo, but there is nothing in that story that fixes it to this season. The explanation for this burst of creative energies and celebration of life may lie in the calendrical position of this festival in the Indian almanac, one that was common in multiple traditions, including Buddhism. Navarātri begins, as we noted earlier, on the new moon day in the Tamil month of Puraṭṭāci, or the month known in many parts of India as Āśvina (c. mid-September to mid-October). It is on that first day that the life-giving waters are placed in the *kalaśa*, the lamp is lit in the clay *garbo*, the *jowar* seeds are planted, the *rāja-rāṇī* dolls are placed, the sprouting *sundal* is made, and the cosmos of possibilities is set up in the *kolu*.

This first day of Navarātri comes at the end of two weeks of one of the most inauspicious times of the year in the Indian calendar: the *pitṛ pakṣa*, or the dark, waning phase of the moon dedicated to the ancestors. Kane notes that in the month of Bhādrapad (the one that precedes Āśvina), "the Sun is in the middle of its apparent motion in daksināyana [the six months when the sun seems to be going south]. Therefore, the dark half of Bhādrapada is specially chosen as the best period for śraddha [*śrāddha*; funerary rites] to the *pitr*s i.e. for the Mahālaya." (Kane 1953, 531). Kane adds that while the *dharmaśāstras* say there are "numerous śrāddhas described by the Purānas, all of them yield rewards but the Mahālaya (śrāddha is the most eminent among them" (1953, 532).

Thus, this fortnight just before Navarātri is not just one of the many times dedicated to the ancestors; it is the most important of them all. Nothing new is started during this period; it is a time to do *tarpaṇa* for the ancestors and feed them *piṇḍa* (balls of rice) (figure 14.5). This is not just in the many Hindu traditions; it is also in the Buddhist traditions. In Cambodia and those parts of Southeast Asia where the common Hindu/Buddhist calendars were adopted, the same *mahālaya* or *pitṛ pakṣa* is the time of the Pchum Ben festival when ancestors are fed and venerated. This is the time when the Cambodian Buddhists also give *piṇḍa*s (pronounced as "ben" in Khmer) or rice balls for the ancestors (Chouléan 2006, 238–42).

The conscientious observation of *pitṛ pakṣa* by Hindus, who migrated to other parts of the world in the nineteenth century, and its survival among Hindus well into the twenty-first century attests to its importance among many castes. I will cite two examples from social media, one referring to the observances in Trinidad and another from Bangkok, to show the enduring importance of this ritual to observing Hindus. Hindus in Trinidad in the twenty-first century observe this period of the ancestors in the following manner:

Figure 14.5. Rice balls (*piṇḍa*) are kept in an outside area in Bangkok to venerate the ancestors in *pitṛ pakṣa,* the fortnight before Navarātri begins. Picture by Aditya Bhattacharjee.

> [W]hen *pitr* paksh is observed, Hindus make daily offerings in morning . . . as it is believed that this is the only time the souls are wandering and able to partake. Both water (tarpan) and food offerings are prepared and offered . . . The general understanding is that spirits come in their astral bodies (sukhshma sharira) and are able to "eat" through their sense of smell. The tarpan is offered from a vessel called a *lota* . . . [which] holds (tilanjali) a mixture of water, rice and black sesame seeds. The water is offered on a specific type of grass called kusha. Most Hindus grow kusha grass in their gardens for the sole purpose of using for *pitr* offerings once a year. . . . There are also cultural implications as to how Hindus behave during *pitr* paksh. Generally, life is restricted to normal activities and nothing new is started . . . Signing contracts of any type, job interviews, engagement or marriage ceremonies are prohibited. (Ramlakhan)

We find references to these rituals in social media also; Aditya Bhattacharjee, a graduate student at McGill University, posted pictures of rice-ball offerings made during this fortnight with the caption: "My father places 'pind daan' (offerings of cooked rice etc.) on his balcony to appease the spirits of 4 generations of our ancestors during *Pitr* Paksha. . . . If the crows eat these, it is said the ancestors have accepted our offerings" (Bhattacharjee 2016). His father, he says, is from Bengal but has lived in Bangkok for over twenty-five years; a testimony to the enduring belief in this ritual and the importance of this time. Examples such as these inform us that the offerings of *piṇḍa*s during *pitṛ pakṣa* are not simply rituals described in the *dharmaśāstras;* they are a palpable part of living religion today.

This dark half of the month is followed immediately with Navarātri and its charter myth of Durgā slaying Mahiṣa, the water-buffalo demon. While there is no obvious connection that one can immediately see, we can discern both direct and indirect lines between the ideas of *pitṛ* / death and Durgā / creation. The indirect connections can be seen through the importance of Mahiṣa, the buffalo. The buffalo is at once a symbol of death on the one hand and of chaos, on the other. The death symbolism comes from its connection with Yama, the god of death. His vehicle, the animal he is connected with, is the water buffalo. Thus, it is possible to interpret the slaying of the buffalo as a conquest over death and the efflorescence of life in the Durgā story.

There is yet another side to the buffalo symbolism. Halperin, quoting several authors, including Biardieu, points out that the primeval buffalo is a potent symbol of chaos and disorder. The demon slain by the goddess in the myth serves as a "substitution for the Self in a sacrificial process that is necessary for the restoration of dharma and order . . . Sax, who also sees this ritual as a mechanism for establishing order, notes in passim the low economic value of buffalos in Uttarakhand, thus adding a materialist perspective to the issue" (Halperin 2012, 122). The death of the buffalo, therefore, leads us from the period of death, chaos, and disorder into one of creation, life, dharma, and order. The realms of life, order, and dharma are all brought together in the *kolu* / *darbār* and the accompanying food, music, and celebration, at home and in the kingdom.

There is also a textual connection linking Durgā and the ritual of giving *piṇḍa*s. It is seen in the *Ānanda Rāmāyaṇa,* a text of unknown date, but possibly contemporary with the early years of the Vijayanagara kingdom or a bit earlier. It speaks about an unusual incident, which provides a temporal frame for this festival, which is connected to the *pitṛ* on the one side and to Durgā on the other. In this story, Rāma, Sītā, and Lakṣmaṇa are visiting the holy place of Gaya to offer *piṇḍa*s for Rāma's father, Daśaratha who had died several years ago. Rāma makes the offerings and apparently waits for the hand of the dead Daśaratha to come and receive the *piṇḍa*s (something that seems to have been expected in those days). However, at the same time, unbeknownst to Rāma, Sītā is doing a *pūjā* for Durgā. She makes five *piṇḍa*-like balls with mud to make an image of Durgā on the riverbank. As she is making these sand/mud balls for an entirely different purpose than the rice balls her husband is making elsewhere, she notices that Daśaratha's hand is stretching out and accepting them as though they are real *piṇḍas*. Sītā ends up offering him 108 mud *piṇḍas*, and the after-death form of Daśaratha is satisfied, and does not accept any that Rāma offers. After much agitation on Rāma's part, and Sītā's confession, Daśaratha tells Rāma that he is satisfied and will not suffer in hell (*Ānanda Rāmāyaṇa, sarga* 6, *yātrakāṇḍam;* Dvivedi, 191).

The story is unusual in many respects but does reiterate the traditional notion of ancestors being saved from hell with the offering of *piṇḍas*—in this case, mud-balls that were made by a woman and intended for the image of Durgā. It is almost like Durgā, who is in all things and contains all things, *is* also the mud that is supposed to create her image, just as it creates the clay pot (*garbo*) that becomes the goddess. As such, Daśaratha is satisfied with what is offered, and all is well.

These connections between the *pitṛ*, disorder, and Durgā who is the seed of creation and the food in creation are brought together in multiple registers in the enactment of the Navarātri *kolu*. The *kolu* with all its ebullience and hierarchies of creation follows the dark fortnight and, in some parts of Andhra, the dark half of the year. The placement of the second *kolu* in Andhra is, as mentioned earlier, during Makara Saṅkrānti, the end of *dakṣiṇayana*. *Dakṣiṇayana* is the period of the *pitṛ*, the period of smoke, lasting for the six months when the sun begins to go south to the Tropic of Capricorn after the summer solstice. During Makara Saṅkrānti, the *pitṛ* are remembered in the celebration; Kane notes that on Saṅkrānti day a person should have a bath with water and *til* (sesame) (1958, 212). *Til* is the most important material substance, along with water, in ancestral offerings, and the predominance of this substance soon after *dakṣiṇayana* affirms that the dead have been honored is a way of marking the triumph of life over death. Thus, the Andhra *kolu* in *Poṅgal* or Makara Saṅkrānti also affirms life after a period of comparative darkness.

Out of this time of death, life emerges, goddesses spring to life, and creation begins again. And out of this comes the *darbār* or *kolu* of created order. The intersection of the *pitṛ pakṣa* and the waking of Durgā becomes a liminal time of great potential, growth, prosperity, and creativity. The creative aspect is particularly explicit in the emphasis on sprouting grains and beans, which form the main food that is given out as *prasād* during the festival—quite unlike the rich and satiating foods of Dīpāvaḷi—and in the *garbo* dances. The *kolu*—and time of Navarātri—is a site for creation and procreation, as well as re-creation of the social order and recreation through music and dance.

Notes

I am grateful to several people who helped me think through this chapter over the years. My thanks to Ute Hüsken, Vidyut Aklujkar, Anna Dallapiccola, Anila Verghese, Anna Seastrand, and Caleb Simmons for hearing me out patiently, to Kausalya Hart for her insightful comments when I first presented this work at the University of California, Berkeley, in 2010, and to the University of Oslo, who hosted the first conference on Navarātri.

1. In very few parts of Andhra, the *kolu* may also be shown a third time, during the festival of Dīpāvaḷi.

Bibliography

Ananda Ramayana. N.d. Accessed on October 31, 2016. http://www.ramanuja.org/sv/bhakti/archives/jun97/0097.html.

Bennur, Shankar. 2011. "Tradition and the 'Gombe Habba." *The Hindu*, September 4. http://www.thehindu.com/todays-paper/tp-features/tp-districtplus/tradition-and-the-gombe-habba/article2480503.ece.

Bhattacharjee, Aditya. "Facebook posting September 25, 2016." Quoted with permission.

Breckenridge, C. A. 1977. "From Protector to Litigant: Changing Relations between Hindu Temples and the Raja of Ramnad." *Indian Economic and Social History Review* 14 (1): 88–94.

Choulean, Ang. 2006. "Vom Brahmanismus zum Buddhismus Betrachtungen zum Totenfest in Kambodscha." In *Angkor: Göttliches Erbe Kambodschas*, edited by W. Lobo and Helen Ibbitson Jessup, 238–242. Bonn: Prestel Verlag.

Dvivedi, Pandit Yugalkishor, ed. 1997. *Ānanda Rāmāyaṇam*. Varanasi: Pandita Pustakalaya.

Fuller, C. J. 1992. *The Camphor Flame: Popular Hinduism and Society in India*. Princeton, NJ: Princeton University Press.

Halperin, Udi. 2012. "Haḍimbā Becoming Herself." PhD dissertation, Columbia University, New York.

Hayavadana Rao, C. R. 1936. *The Dasara in Mysore: Its Origin and Significance*. Bangalore: Bangalore Press.

Ikegame, Aya. 2012. *Princely India Re-imagined: A Historical Anthropology of Mysore from 1799 to the Present*. New York: Routledge.

Kane, P. V. 1958. *The History of Dharmashastra Volume* 5.1. Pune: Bhandarkar Oriental Research Institute.

"Navaratri Celebrations and Golu." N.d. Accessed on October 31, 2016. https://www.youtube.com/watch?v=-2HIP0Sml8Q

"Navaratri Mandapam Schedule." N.d. Accessed October 2, 2016. http://www.webindia123.com/festival/events/navarathrimandapamconcertschedule.htm.

"Pongal Bommala Koluvu/Golu." N.d. Accessed October 15, 2016. https://nimasonti.wordpress.com/2016/01/19/pongal-bommala-koluvugolu/.

Price, Pamela G. 1996. *Kingship and Political Practice in Colonial India*. Cambridge: Cambridge University Press.

———. 1990. "The State and Representation of Femaleness in Late Medieval South India." *Historisk tidsskrift udgivet af den Norske historiske forening* 4: 589–97.

Ramlakhan, Priyanka. Personal email. Quoted with permission.

Rao, Nalini. 1991. "Royal Artistic Imagery at Vijayanagara." PhD Dissertation, University of California, Los Angeles.

Rodrigues, Hillary. 2003. *Ritual Worship of the Great Goddess.* Albany: State University of New York Press.

Rotti, Jolad. 2016. "Dasara Doll Festival–Significance and History." N.d. Accessed October 9, 2016. http://www.karnataka.com/festivals/dasara-doll-festival/.

7 Aspects of Bommai Golu. N.D. Accessed October 15, 2016. http://www.artofliving.org/navratri/bommai-golu.

Sewell, Robert. 1900. *A Forgotten Empire: (Vijayanagara) A Contribution to the History of India.* London: S. Sonnenschein.

Shantha. "Pattada Bombe Alankara." N.d. Accessed August 15, 2015. http://www.itslife.in/do-it-yourself/pattada-gombe-alankara.

Shukla-Bhatt, Neelima. 2015. "Celebrating Materiality: *Garbo*, a Festival Image of the Goddess in Gujarat." In *Sacred Matters: Material Religion in South Asian Traditions,* edited by Tracy Pintchman and Corrine G. Dempsey, 88–113. Albany: State University of New York Press.

Simmons, Caleb. 2014. "The King and the Goddess." PhD dissertation, University of Florida, Gainesville.

Tamil Lexicon Volume 2.1. 1982. Madras: University of Madras.

Thakston W. M., trans. 1989. "Mission to Calicut and Vijayanagar." In *A Century of Princes: Sources on Timurid History and Art, Cambridge,* edited by W. M. Thakston, 299–321. Cambridge, Massachusetts: The Aga Khan Program for Islamic Architecture at Harvard University and the Massachusetts Institute of Technology.

Waghorne, Joanne Punzo. 1994. *The Raja's Magic Clothes.* University Park: Pennsylvania State University Press.

15

Navarātra and Kanyā Pūjā

The Worship of Girls as Representatives of the Goddess in Northwest India

BRIGITTE LUCHESI

This chapter deals with Navarātra celebrations in the north Indian state of Himachal Pradesh, focusing on one of its prominent aspects: the worship of young girls (*kanyā pūjā*) as representatives of Hindu goddesses (*devīs*). The first part will give a short depiction of the ways Navarātra is celebrated in this part of India, after which the two prevalent forms of *kanyā pūjā* in the Kangra region are described. In the last part, several aspects of this worship will be discussed that may explain its popularity during the two grand festivals in question.

Navarātra Celebrations in the Southern Part of Himachal Pradesh

The great festivals in honor of the Goddess in spring and autumn, known under various names throughout South Asia, are celebrated with great dedication in parts of Himachal Pradesh.[1] Both of these festivals are known as Navarātra (lit. "nine nights"), start on the first day of the light half of the lunar months Caitra (March–April) and Āśvina (September–October) and usually last nine days.[2] The form and intensity of the celebrations during these days vary, normally depending on the regional customs and the caste and family traditions of the devotees. Differences may also occur between rural and urban settings. I will concentrate on the Kangra Valley in the southern part of Himachal Pradesh, which I have visited repeatedly during the last thirty years. It is a predominantly rural area with many small towns.[3] Only a few sites in this region, such as Dharamsala and Kangra Town, are classified as cities.

A large part of the Hindu population in the valley seems to celebrate the Navarātra days with religious practices of some kind. They often take place in the privacy of the individual homes, but they may also be performed in public places, above all, in temples dedicated to a goddess. Many people make it a point to visit a goddess temple at least once during Navarātra. The well-known great Goddess temples of the region—among them the Brajeśvarī Mandir in Kangra Town, the Jvālā Mukhī temple in Tehsil Dera Gopipur, and the Cāmuṇḍā temple near Dadh—are particularly popular with numbers of devotees seeking the divine sight (*darśan*) of the residing goddess during these auspicious days. Pilgrims from other north Indian regions also prefer these days for having *darśan*, so the temples and surrounding areas are usually densely packed with devoted men and women throughout Navarātra. The buses are filled with people wearing special outfits or carrying sticks, flags, or other objects that clearly identify them as visitors to one of the important temples. Women often gather in the smaller village and neighbourhood temples in the evening to celebrate the Goddess with religious songs accompanied by the beating of drums and playing of other instruments. The organizers of these temples frequently arrange a communal meal at the end of the festival on the ninth day (*navamī*).

Apart from the omnipresent temple visitors, the most conspicuous signs underlining the religious importance of these days are drawings made by many women in front of their houses. On each of the nine mornings a design, locally known as *apan,* is drawn on the courtyard floor, usually near the one of the previous day so that in the end a long strip or "carpet" has emerged. The designs serve as the basis for the special ritual offerings—water, flowers, food grains, and red powder—presented to the goddess every morning. *Apan* in the courtyard may be connected to an even more elaborate domestic form of worship, which takes place inside the house in front of the house shrine. Here special temporal arrangements to venerate the deity may be made. Quite widespread is the practice of placing an image of the venerated goddess near or amidst a flat vessel filled with earth in which grain seeds are sown. The sprouting seeds are equated with the goddess, and by the ninth day, they will have grown into finger-long green shoots that will then be immersed in a river, preferably near a temple. Less widespread—as the services of a priest are required—is the representation of the goddess in the form of a clay pot (*ghaṭa*) filled with sanctified water and closed with a coconut and mango leaves. Devotees who choose this type of worship will usually keep a fast (*vrata*) for the entire period of the festival and will end the devotional acts with oblations to a sacrificial fire (*havan*), followed by a meal for the extended family and the neighbourhood (for more on *vratas*, see Pearson 1996 and Bose 2010, 138–48). It seems more usual, however, to follow dietary restrictions only for one day, preferably the eighth day (*āṣṭamī*). I was told that it is also common to read or recite appropriate religious texts, which glorify the deeds of the Goddess, as for example the *Devī Māhātmya*.

Another widespread practice is to worship young girls as living embodiments of goddesses, the main topic of this chapter. Before turning to this practice, it should be pointed out that the preparation of clay images of the goddess Durgā, which are popular in Bengal and used by Bengali communities in other Indian regions, is practically unknown in Himachal Pradesh. The tenth day, Daśahrā, which in other parts of India is the day to remember the victory of this goddess over the demon Mahiṣa is also not a prominent festive occasion. An exception is the grand Daśahrā festival in the capital of Kullu District which starts on Daśahrā and ends after seven days with the sacrifice of a buffalo in honor of Durgā, who, according to the great epos *Rāmāyaṇa*, helped Rāma in his battle against Rāvaṇa (e.g., Goswamy 2014 and Luchesi 2006).

Kanyā Pūjā in the Kangra Valley

The worship of young girls is known in many parts of India (e.g. for Punjab, see Hershman 1977; for Benares, see Rodrigues 2005 and 2009; for Bengal, see Foulston and Abbott 2009, 166). It is especially widespread in Kangra and the neighbouring districts of Himachal Pradesh as well. This practice is usually known as *kanyā pūjā*. *Kanyā* is the usual term for a young girl (cf. Khare 1982, 149–53); however, the Punjabi term *kanjak* or the synonymous word *kumārī* may be used. In most cases it is not a single *kanyā* but several girls who are made to represent the goddess Durgā or other manifestations of the Great Goddess and to receive the services and gifts intended to please the goddess to whom the worship is directed. *Kanyā pūjā* may take place at many occasions on which the blessing of a goddess is desired: at the end of life-cycle rituals, at the conclusion of a house-opening ceremony, or after having completed a series of fasts. The occasion for a great number of simultaneous *kanyā pūjās*, however, are the two Navarātra festivals in spring and autumn, with the spring celebration being perhaps the slightly more preferred occasion for the worship of girls.

One can distinguish between two versions of *kanyā pūjā*; one is a private affair and not easily observable, and the other takes place in public, most often in a temple courtyard. It is not only the setting that distinguishes the two versions but also the type of girls selected for worship. In private *pūjās,* the daughters of close relatives and neighbours are chosen, that is, known children. In temples, unknown girls or even entire groups of *kanyās* make themselves available to be chosen by visiting devotees then and there.

Privately Performed *Kanyā Pūjās*

Private *pūjās* usually take place at home. Very often they are done on Naumi, the ninth and last of the days in honor of the Devī during Navarātra. In cases where people have kept a fast and performed a full Navarātra *pūjā* with the help of a priest, this worship marks the conclusion of the entire sequence of religious practices. In general, however, *kanyā pūjā* is an independent devotional act. Several girls are called for, usually at least three, but, ideally, nine (though there can be more). In addition, one small boy may be asked to participate. In the local dialect, the boy is called "*loṇkṛu*" or "*lāṇkṛa,*" which may be translated as "very small boy" (cf. Hershman 1977, 279, n. 17). People understand him as a sort of protector (*rakṣak*) or "bodyguard" and compare his role with that of Bhairava or Hanuman, both of whom are repeatedly described as protectors of a goddess in Hindu mythology and are depicted on popular posters of the famous regional goddess Vaiṣṇo Devī as her guardian gods. In many cases, the children come from families who are related by descent or marriage to those who perform the *pūjā* or that live nearby, as paternally related households often live together in the rural areas, and neighbors are frequently close kinsmen as well. If the households are not related, they are most often considered to be of roughly the same standing in the local caste hierarchy and therefore eligible for the ritual. In all these cases, the children invited for the *pūjā* are more or less known to those who perform it. The families' own daughters may be included, but it seems that not all families with daughters do so.

The *pūjā* can be simple or elaborate, but the main features are nearly always the same. The children are made to sit down on the floor, often on cushions spread out for them. Then one of the main devotees, frequently the male householder, washes their feet. This is generally a genuine footbath in a basin with warm water put before them. This sort of service, mostly offered to guests and elders, is still widespread in many households in Kangra. Then a mark (*ṭikā*) with red powder is put on the forehead of the children, followed by the tying of a red thread around their wrists. The next sequence consists in spreading red veils (*cunnī*) over their heads, on which a few flower petals may be sprinkled. The feeding of the girls follows, starting with the placing of plates before them. These may be the usual steel plates or even the traditional leaf plates that are still in use at family functions and community feasts for feeding large groups, but lately fancy paper plates from the bazaar have come into fashion. The food served may be freshly fried bread, *halva* (a sweet mash) and seasoned chickpeas (*canā*), or a full meal consisting of boiled rice, lentils, and vegetables with an extra sweet dish. Either shortly before the food or together with it, the children receive a small gift, such as red bangles, red ribbons, hairclips, or a handkerchief. Frequently, these things are not given separately but packed in *suhāgī* (transparent bags), which can be bought from special shops. These bags typically also contain a small comb and mirror, *bindīs* (small ornaments for the forehead), a small quantity of henna, face cream, and the like. These bags are also presented to goddesses when visiting *devī* temples and are popular gifts exchanged between married women. When the children have finished their meals, the main devotee bends down and touches the feet of all the girls. They respond by touching the devotee's head. All other members of the household follow suit.[4]

As already mentioned, inviting children from related or neighbouring families is the usual practice for private *kanyā pūjās*. If devotees want to involve many girls but cannot find enough in the immediate vicinity, they may call for children from a nearby school or similar institution. The shortage of eligible girls in the neighborhood is often given as the reason for performing the *pūjā* at a temple with unknown girls.

Public *Kanyā Pūjās*

This type of the worship primarily takes place at goddess temples. The Kangra Valley is home to several famous *devī* temples, including the most popular ones mentioned above: the Brajeśvarī Mandir in Kangra Town, the Cāmuṇḍā temple in Dadh, and the Jvālā Mukhī temple in Tehsil Dera Gopipur. Apart from these, nearly all towns and villages have a religious place dedicated to a *devī*. The neighboring districts equally abound in goddess temples, most prominently the temples of Nainā Devī in Bilaspur District, Cintpūrṇī Devī in Una, and Vaiṣṇo Devī in Jammu and Kashmir. Pilgrims from the plains, especially from Punjab and Uttar Pradesh who are on a pilgrimage tour to holy places in the mountains usually visit two or more of the renowned temples in Kangra. The temple of Brajeśvarī Devī in particular is the pilgrimage goal of devotees from western Uttar Pradesh who consider this goddess as their *kul devī* (lineage goddess). They often come during the spring Navarātra to honor her and have their small sons' first haircut (*muṇḍan*) performed behind her main shrine (cf. Erndl 1993, 50; Bhardwaj 1973, 132).

Both local devotees and visitors from distant places may choose to include *kanyā pūjā* in the sequence of religious practices performed at the goddess temples. There is no official organizer whom one can approach for the arrangement of this event. People who wish to do this *pūjā* must look for girls who are willing to participate. There are usually several girls in the temple courtyards during the Navarātra days who are eager to participate and are on the lookout for visitors in search of *kanyās*. They may be daughters of the temple personnel, but frequently they come from nearby places. They often form groups of up to ten girls between four and twelve years old, and several boys and are led by the eldest girls. Some children come with their mothers or elder brothers.

As soon as the devotees have chosen the number of girls they have decided on—which may take a while, as often more girls than desired appear—they make them sit down in a circle or a row. The sequence of a public *kanyā pūjā* is basically the same as the one performed at home. It, too, can be elaborate, and the gifts may vary. As a rule, the number of girls on the last two days is high, that is, rarely less than eight or nine girls. This may be explained by the ready availability of children on these days, but also by the tendency of the devotees to choose the number of *devīs* according to the number of the day in question (e.g., eight *devīs* on the eighth day). A certain difference from the domestic *pūjā* can be observed regarding the footbath. A proper wash is only done where there is a tap nearby. Usually, the feet of the children are sprinkled with water, which

Figure 15.1. *Kanyās* being fed by a young man at the Cāmuṇḍā Temple in Kangra during the Navarātra 2017.

may be ritually purified by dropping flowers into it and waving incense over it. The devotee—in the case of a group, typically it is the eldest male member, otherwise the eldest woman—starts the *pūjā* by placing a piece of red cloth or a gold-bordered red veil over the heads of the *kanyās*.

Thereafter, a red mark is applied to the foreheads of the children and/or a red string is knotted around their wrists. Then food and gifts are distributed. The food items vary. The simplest seems to be the offering of a banana and a small sweet, which is typically given by pilgrims from far away who must buy food items in the bazaar. Local devotees frequently carry food prepared at home, like *halva*, *capātīs* (flat bread), *canā* (chickpeas), and a piece of fresh fruit. It may be served in different ways. The simplest is to put it directly into the outstretched hands of the children. As in many of the privately performed *kanyā pūjās*, traditional plates and bowls made out of leaves may be used. Also very common is the use of paper plates, especially the very fancy coated ones, and the latest custom is colorful plastic plates, which the girls are expected to take home. A gift is given along with the food. Here, too, it may be a set of red bangles, a necklace, red hair ribbons, a handkerchief, or a ready-packed assortment of items in transparent bags from the bazaar. Sometimes the items in the *suhāgī* include money, but it is more common to distribute money separately. Although a one-rupee coin for each of the children is still considered adequate by many, ten-rupee notes seem to have replaced coins recently. Finally, the devotee bends down to touch the feet of the girls. A man will make sure that his head is covered by a handkerchief or something else, whereas a woman is not in need of this additional reverential gesture as she will have followed the common north Indian custom of wearing a headcovering when entering the temple. After the main devotee, his wife or other family members will follow suit. Should a son be present, he is nearly always made to participate, too. The girls respond to the feet-touching by slapping the backs of the devotees with their right hand.

As soon as the *pūjā* is over, the children quickly get up. When there is a high demand of girls, they often just switch over to the next devotees and sit down again. The children usually sit patiently and submit passively to the actions of the devotees, but not all are always so compliant. Girls who are part of groups and have gained a certain experience as *kanyās*—sometimes over several years—show signs of restlessness if the *pūjā* takes too long for their taste and often do not conceal their displeasure when the gifts are not to their liking. This behaviour differs considerably from that of the *kanyās* who are invited by relatives or neighbors to take part in private *pūjās*, who even in the case of discontent would never behave in this way. The conduct seems to be an outcome of the experience level of the temple *kanyās*, which in turn points to a certain professionalization. The professional attitude of the girls is not limited to the time before or after the *pūjā;* it is also discernable in the very act of offering their services as *kanyās* to unknown clients in public places.

Different from the intimate and protected character of private houses, the public domain is often seen as potentially endangered by negative forces, especially ritually polluting influences. Ute Hüsken has shown that in the case of certain south Indian temple priests, who hold a highly respected position as mediators of the presiding temple deities, the "practice of their office as profession" often diminishes their status outside the temple (2010, 75). "[T]he ritual activity *for others,* or as a profession" can be regarded negatively because being in contact with strangers and accepting gifts from them involves a risk of ritual pollution, which is why the priests are often "viewed with suspicion" (Hüsken 2010, 75). I lack fieldwork data which would allow me to arrive at the same conclusion with respect to the temple *kanyās,* but there can be no doubt that the seasoned "self-appointed" girls at temples are less appreciated than the ones worshipped at home. It is possible that the girls, being aware of this, react with contempt.

Girls as Goddesses: The Characteristic Features of *Kanyā Pūjā*

The descriptions of the two types of *kanyā pūjā* have shown that this kind of worship plays an important part in the Navarātra celebrations in the Kangra area. It is a well-known and widespread devotional practice in honor of the Goddess, either combined with other forms of worship or even as an independent practice. Its way of approaching the Goddess is quite unusual: it is not done by means of her cult image in a temple or one installed in a private shrine, be it anthropomorphic in shape or otherwise designed. Nor is a device for the mental realization of the *devī* employed, as for instance a ritual design (*yantra*) (e.g., Zeiler 2015). Instead, young girls are made to represent the Goddess and to receive the immaterial and material offerings in lieu of her. As representatives of the Goddess, the girls turn into objects of worship as well. As is the case with other cult images and objects of worship, they are believed to be charged with the presence of the deity whom the worshippers wish to approach.

This understanding is given expression in the various acts performed by the worshippers. Most of them are in accordance with those found in other types of *pūjā*. The footbath, the provision of a veil and decorative items, and the offerings of flowers and food correspond to the ritual services (*upacāras*) of *pādya* (footbath) or *snāna* (bath), *vastra* (investiture), *puṣpa* (flowers), and *naivedya* (food) that form the core of *pūjās* in general (see Bühnemann 1988; Falk 2004). The same goes for the final act of bowing down and touching the feet of the girls, which is clearly the same as the bowing or prostration before an image (*namaskāra/pranāma*) of a deity.

All these acts are usually done with great care. The girls are properly seated. The headcovering and all the other items given as offerings are always new. The food as a rule is well prepared at home or carefully chosen, and it is served in a pleasing way. The act of feet-touching is never omitted. Bending the most exalted part of one's body (the head) toward the lowest parts of another person and touching his or her feet with one's hands is a demonstration of utmost respect and humility in Indian culture. It is widely practiced in everyday life, too, to honor elders and esteemed guests. The responses of the girls, namely slapping the devotees' backs or touching their heads, are locally understood as forms of blessing and a common gesture of dismissal used by women possessed by a goddess who are also often at goddess temples during the Navarātras. These gestures may also be understood as a way to replace *prasād* (boon or blessing), the food which is offered to a deity and at the end of a *pūjā* distributed among the worshippers as consecrated matter. Both the partaking of the food and being touched by the *kanyās* are believed to have beneficial effects on the recipients. By means of the honor offerings, what Diana Eck has called the *upacāras* (1985: 47), the *kanyās* are divinized. They are perceived to be *devīs* themselves.

Having pointed out the similarities in the ways the *kanyās* and cult images, especially those in temples, are treated, the differences too should be noted. Before being considered to be appropriate receptacles of divine powers, temple images have to undergo lengthy and intricate consecration ceremonies. In the case of the *kanyās,* however, there are no such preparatory acts. Once chosen, the girls are immediately eligible to represent goddesses. This state, however, is limited. It starts with the *pūjā* and ends with the *pūjā*. The moment the worship is over, the extraordinary temporary condition of the girls comes to an end. Because of this, I would group them with the various temporary cult images or impermanent objects of worship one can find in Hindu religious tradition (for more on temporary cult images, see Preston 1985, 10; Luchesi 1995). In this way, they can be likened to the elaborate Durgā images so prominent in Bengal that are exclusively made for the celebration of Durgā Pūjā and are immersed in a river after the festivities, the temporary Gaṇeśa statues in Maharashtra used exclusively on Vināyaka Caturthī (Courtright 1985, 49), and the tableaux vivants (*jhāṅkīs*) of gods displayed at certain religious festivals in Kangra (Luchesi 2015). *Kanyās,* too, are required only for a specific occasion and only for a limited length of time. What distinguishes them from the other impermanent objects of worship is that they can be used whenever they are needed. They are, as it were, ready on demand; the only precondition is their consent to participate.

The short time-span of the actual divinization distinguishes the girls in Kangra from the well-known Royal Kumārīs in central Nepal who are considered living goddesses as long as they are in a prepubescent state

(Allen 1975; Letizia, forthcoming). Besides these exceptional *kumārīs* the practice of *kanyā pūjā* in the form described here is known in Nepal, too. It may be even performed on a very large scale, as once witnessed by Gutschow and Michaels in Banepa where hundreds of girls were lined up in the main street and given "offerings such as rice, sweets or small gifts" (2008, 152).

As already mentioned, the worship of girls is known and practiced in many parts of India. It seems a widely shared belief that young girls are especially suited to represent goddesses. It is first and foremost their unmarried, prepubescent condition that qualifies them to receive the honor offerings, which characterize a *kanyā pūjā*. In Kangra, too, this belief is prevalent. The answers I got when asking why this kind of worship is chosen were unanimous: because young girls are *śuddh* (pure). This term comprises various meanings (Malinar 2010). It often refers to ritual purity, but may also point to sincerity in the sense of innocence and simplicity. To call girls *śuddh* implies that their virginal state before menarche is intrinsically pure. Being prepubescent and unmarried, they are understood as not yet affected by the impurity, which is commonly believed to accompany menstruation and the sexual activities connected with marriage. Both menstruation and sexual intercourse are considered polluting and leave women impure (*aśuddh*) for certain periods. While in this condition, they are barred from entering temples or approaching the deities in private worship. Young girls, however, are at no time subject to these restrictions. They also enjoy certain other prerogatives, as for instance not being obliged to touch the feet of their elders or cover their heads in front of them. Sometimes they are even referred to as "*devīs*" (e.g., "our *devīs* in the house"). Jonathan Parry therefore speaks of an "aura of sanctity which surrounds all prepubescent girls" in Kangra (1979, 147). Apart from being pure, *kanyās* are thought of as simple and honest, especially the very small ones. This seems to be the reason why people often prefer to call for very young girls who may not yet be aware of their role in the *pūjā*. Yet another reason may influence their choice: people obviously love to adorn and feed the little ones. Serving them seems to be emotionally satisfying.

While there is an element of choice in the selection of the girls who participate in *kanyā pūjā*, it is necessary to distinguish between the private and the public forms of worship. As mentioned above, the practice in private *pūjās* is to invite girls from related or neighboring families to participate in the ritual. This results in having girls of the same descent group and caste (*jātī*) as the worshippers or of castes that are considered to have roughly the same social standing. The caste background of the girls available at temples, however, does not seem to matter. As I normally did not want to ask the girls about their caste directly, I sought the opinion of other people, including the temple priests. At the Jvālā Mukhī temple, they informed me that children of all castes except the very lowest are eligible. At the Cāmuṇḍā temple, the bulk of children come from Brahmin families, settled in nearby Dadh, whose male members work as family priests and ritual cooks, but other girls were also present whose accompanying mothers were discernably Biharis and Rajasthanis and known to live in the work camps near Dharamsala. Other visitors whom I asked about them suspected that they belonged to a low *jātī* but emphasised that they would not mind. I do not know whether Dalits (Untouchables) take part.[5] But I never witnessed any girls available at temples being asked about their caste.

Kanyā Pūjā as a Favorite Devotional Practice in Himachali Navarātras

I have mentioned above that *kanyā pūjā* in Kangra is not limited to the time of the Navarātras but may be performed whenever there is the wish to honor a goddess and to receive her blessing. But there can be no doubt that the worship of girls is most prevalent during both of the nine-day festivals in honor of the Devī in spring and autumn. In the following section I will try to explain why this is the case.

Adhering to Old Ways: *Kanyā Pūjā* as a Local Tradition during Navarātra

I repeatedly tried to find out from various people why the worship of girls is so popular during the two Navarātras. They explained that it is a very old custom. They were doing it because their forefathers had done it before. The practice indeed seems to be quite an old phenomenon. The British administration officer A. H. Rose mentions it in his *Glossary of the Tribes and Castes of the Punjab* from 1919 (Vol. 1, 327): "Devī is personified in a girl under ten years twice a year and offerings are made to her as if to the goddess on these occasions." He then quotes an even older report: "Special feasts are given to little girls twice a year and they are given fees, as if they were Brahmans (*Panjab Notes & Queries* III, § 416)" (Rose 1919, Vol. 1, 327, n. 3).

Interested in the more recent past, I asked several middle-aged and elderly women if they had been *kanyās* in their childhood. It turned out that many, especially Brahman and Rajput women, participated in or witnessed *kanyā pūjās* when they were small. Remembering the occasions often brought smiles to their faces. Younger women reacted similarly. For instance, twenty-two-year-old Priyanka told me, "I felt wonderful. It was so great having my father touch my feet and giving me nice presents."

Approaching the Goddess: The Auspiciousness of the Navarātras and *Kanyā Pūjā*

According to general belief both Navarātras mark a period when the goddess Durgā, as well as all other forms of the Devī, are more accessible than usual. The days in question are therefore regarded as most suitable to approach her, and devotees of the Goddess will make use of these occasions, in one way or other, to visit one of the many goddess temples in the region, which are often given first priority. To have *darśan* of the Goddess in one of her earthly abodes is considered *śubh*.

As alluded to above, there are several possibilities to render "*śubh*" into English, all of which have a clearly positive connotation. As a noun it may translate as "auspiciousness," "good fortune," "welfare," "happiness," "bliss," "beauty," "charm," or "prosperity," and as an adjective as "auspicious," "lucky," "favourable," or "good." Its counterpart, "*aśubh*," connotes "misfortune," "calamity," "evil" or something being "inauspicious," "unlucky," or "sinister" (cf. McGregor 1995, 953, 66; Narayanan 2010, 694). When people call *darśan*, the divine sight of the deity in the temple "*subh*," they want to emphasize that it is a particularly auspicious act, which is bound to bring about positive outcomes.

The same term, *śubh*, was used in answers to my questions about why *kanyā pūjā* is performed as part of the Goddess worship during the Navarātras. In most cases, I was told that the worship of girls is *śubh*. It would be a good thing to perform this *pūjā*. It would please the Goddess, make her happy. Kathleen Erndl reported the same, "The worship of *kanyās* is considered to be extremely pleasing to the Goddess, and almost every pilgrim will perform it with a greater or lesser degree of formality" (1993, 73). The implication is that a pleased, happy goddess would be inclined toward the devotee and willing to give her blessings. Positively disposed in this way, she is said to grant whichever wish is brought before her, be it the wish for well-being, prosperity, happiness, or other things. Doing an auspicious act like *kanyā pūjā* during a time that is considered *śubh* is seen as possibly increasing auspiciousness even more and thereby increasing the chances of the devotees to come close to the deity.

Another aspect that Vasudha Narayanan suggested may be of importance in this context. Auspiciousness is permanently threatened by inauspiciousness and must be safeguarded from this opponent (2010, 695). It therefore needs to be strengthened or "cultivated," as Narayanan calls it, by seizing "the opportunity, when the potential for success and happiness is present, to make it work for the individual or community" (Narayanan 2010, 695). This potential is clearly present. It is embedded within the Navarātras. Their auspicious character derives from being outstanding days of the Goddess, but also from their special ritual timing. Both Navarātras are invariably celebrated during the 'bright' part of the lunar months in question (i.e. in the period of the waxing moon), which is considered the positive, favorable half of the month.

The ritual performance of *kanyā pūjā* itself also cultivates auspiciousness, or *śubh*. The most important is naturally the employment of pure virgins, but there is more. The small items used in worship and presented to the girls connote auspiciousness as well, especially the red veils and the various adornments. Red scarves—and they must be red—allude to the full outfit of a bride, a most auspicious human being. The other highly *śubh* human being is a *suhāgin*, the wife of a living husband and mother of children, preferably boys. At various occasions small decorative items like *bindīs* (forehead marks), bangles, red powder, and so on may be given to *suhāgins* or exchanged between them. The ready assortments called *suhāgī* take their name from this custom. These small gifts are signifiers of the auspicious marital state (*suhāg*) of the women in question, and in an extended sense also of auspiciousness. In the context of *kanyā pūjā*, they seem to serve the latter function. Auspiciousness is also derived from the food served to the children and sometimes to the bystanders, too. Soaked and spiced chickpeas, especially, is a dish that is quite regularly distributed among women at the end of all occasions that are considered "*śubh*," like singing sessions of devotional songs or other religious events jointly undertaken.

Acquiring Merit: *Kanyā Pūjā* as an Occasion for Gift-Giving

It cannot be overlooked that gifts play a very important role in the *kanyā pujas*, which I have described. Food, a variety of small things, and money are given from donor to the recipients. The addition of money to the other gifts seems to be mandatory. Even in the shortest version of this *pūjā*, which may consist of just distributing some sweets and touching the feet of the girls, at least one coin is given. Noteworthy in this context is that the material gifts flow in only one direction; they are not reciprocated, at least not in kind. In this the gifts closely resemble the religiously motivated offering (*dāna*) given to Brahmins at the end of rituals that they have performed for a donor. The early twentieth-century colonial British administrator Rose noticed this similarity when he included the views of an earlier observer, who wrote that the girls, "are given fees, as if they were Brahmans" into his report (Rose 1919, Vol. 1, 327, n. 3). The scholarly discussion on the Brahminic legal theory of the gift is extensive, and it would be out of place to enter it here. I therefore restrict myself to two short quotations from Axel Michaels (2003): "Dāna should be given mainly in a generous spirit, without regarding or speculating on the advantage or utility" (198); and "The receiver of a Dāna may give nothing in return except religious merit (*puṇya*)" (197).

In my understanding, the gifts given in *kanyā pūjās*, especially the money gift at the very end of the worship, are forms of *dāna*. It should be given without expecting anything in return. At most, it will result in an increase of *puṇya*, religious merit. This merit is not something that can be reciprocated immediately; it is an immaterial good from which devotees may hope to benefit in a distant future. As the emphasis lies on selfless, disinterested generosity, it is also understandable why people do not expect any gestures or words of gratitude from the children, or why they are not annoyed by the sometimes business-minded girls in public *pūjās*. The behavior of the girls is not crucial in this context, but the important question is whether they are suitable recipients. Michaels has emphasized this point: "Dāna must be given to a worthy recipient, for example to a Vedic scholar or an ascetic. Then, religious merit (*puṇya*) comes to the giver" (2003, 298). The worthiness of the *kanyās* is beyond all doubt; it comes from their particular ritual purity—the same quality that makes them eligible to represent goddesses.

Taking Pleasure in Giving: *Kanyā Pūjā* and Emotional Satisfaction

When I asked people why money should be given to the *kanyās* in addition to the honor offerings, they often answered: "It is good to give," "It makes you feel happy to be able to give," and so on. These statements point to the emotional side of a *kanyā pūjā*. As mentioned above, people clearly like to perform this kind of goddess worship. Observers gain the impression that most devotees love to adorn and feed girls, especially the very small ones, and to have a close physical contact with the little "living goddesses." I was told that women as well as men look forward to it. Whether they take place at home or in a temple, *kanyā pūjās* appear to be accompanied by positive feelings, not only while they are performed but also before and afterward. It may be argued that these feelings run counter to the disinterested attitude the medieval authorities prescribe for the donors. Maria Heim, who has studied classical theories of the gift in South Asia in great detail, has shown that this is not the case: "Not only did most of the medieval authors not prohibit the donor's interest and pleasure in making a gift, but sometimes even prescribed them. The various moments of feeling and thought that comprise a gift are elaborated in great detail, and pleasure and good feeling are to be present throughout" (2004, 42). I would argue that people use *kanyā pūjā* to follow the prescribed traditional rules of gift giving and to experience pleasure as well, whereby the pleasure derives not only from the act of giving but also from the encounter with pleasant recipients.

Conclusion

Navarātra celebrations and the practice of *kanyā pūjā* seem to go hand in hand in the Kangra area. Although the worship of goddesses in the form of *kanyā pūjā* may take place at nearly all times of the year, it is most frequently performed during the two Navarātras. While sometimes the desire to perform *kanyā pūjā* outside of these two periods of time arises because of an extraordinary event in an individual household (i.e., opening a new house, successful completion of a family ritual), Goddess worship in the form of *kanyā pūjā* during the Navarātras is common among all who want to honor the Goddess because they are favorable periods for approaching her. The decision to choose young girls as her representatives and worship them is based on the religious belief that prepubescent, unmarried girls are exceptionally pure human beings and, therefore, highly auspicious. They are also seen as worthy recipients of the gifts, which otherwise are offered to a goddess in front of her temple image. These gifts consist of various beautifying items as well as money. The money gifts may be understood as *dāna,* which can, when offered without calculating the possible advantages of this act, result in *puṇya* (merit), an immaterial future reward for the donor. And finally, *kanyā pūjā* seems to provide considerable emotional satisfaction for those performing it. For all these reasons, *kanyā pūjā* and temple visits and *pūjās* at the home shrine are integral parts of ritual performance during the Navarātras in Kangra.

Notes

1. I use the words "Goddess" and "Devī" when referring to the supreme Divine Feminine. When talking about a particular goddess or several goddesses I use "goddess" and "*devī.*"

2. The Caitra Navarātra is also known as Vāsant (spring) Navarātra, the other one as Śarad (autumn) Navarātra. When referring to both festivals, I use "Navarātras." Occasionally a Navarātra lasts only for eight days, as was the case in spring 2015.

3. According to the 2011 census, 94.29 percent of the population of Kangra District lived in rural areas or villages. See http://www.census2011.co.in/census/district/230-kangra.html, accessed February 11, 2016.

4. The *bali dāna* (blood sacrifice) described by Rodrigues (2009, 268, 273–77) which in the Bengali type of Durgā Pūjā should be performed at the same time as the *kumārī* (girl) worship, i.e. during the night following the eighth day or early on the ninth day, is to my knowledge not part of the Navarātra celebrations in Kangra. I am therefore not able to confirm Rodrigues's most interesting contention "that the blood sacrifice is also intended to provoke the *kumārī's* menarche" (274). Neither did I witness the offering of a substitution, such as a pumpkin. However,

an indication that the eventual transformation of the premenarche girls into marriageable young women and finally married wives is wished for is the fact that the *suhāgī* bags are usually given as presents to married women.

5. *Kanyās* at the famous Haḍimbā temple near Manali belong to the Dalit community of Dhungri where the temple is situated. They receive food and money from visitors of all ranks.

Bibliography

Allen, Michael. 1975. *The Cult of Kumari: Virgin Worship in Nepal*. Kathmandu, Nepal: Institute of Nepal and Asian Studies, Tribhuvan University.

Bhardwaj, Surinder Mohan. 1973. *Hindu Places of Pilgrimage in India*. Berkeley: University of California Press.

Bose, Mandakranta. 2010. *Women in the Hindu Tradition. Rules, Roles and Exceptions*. London and New York: Routledge.

Bühnemann, Gudrun. 1988. *Pūjā: A Study in Smārta Ritual*. Vienna: Institute for Indology, University of Vienna.

Courtright, Paul B. 1985. "On This Holy Day in My Humble Way: Aspects of *Pūjā*." In *Gods of Flesh, Gods of Stone: The Embodiment of Divinity in India*, edited by Joanne Punzo Waghorne, Norman Cutler, and Vasudha Narayanan, 33–50. Chambersburg, PA: Anima.

Eck, Diana L. 1985. *Darśan. Seeing the Divine Image in India*. Second revised and enlarged edition. Chambersburg, PA: Anima.

Erndl, Kathleen M. 1993. *Victory to the Mother: The Hindu Goddess of Northwest India in Myth, Ritual, and Symbol*. New York and Oxford: Oxford University Press.

Falk, Nancy Auer. 2005. "Pūjā: Hindu Pūjā." In *Encyclopedia of Religion*, edited by Lindsay Jones. 2nd ed. Vol. 11, 7493–95. Detroit: Macmillan.

Foulston, Lynn, and Stuart Abbott. 2009. *Hindu Goddesses: Beliefs and Practices*. Eastborne: Sussex Academic.

Goswamy, Karuna. 2014. *The Dussehra of Kullu. History and Analysis of a Cultural Phenomenon*. Shimla: Indian Institute of Advanced Studies, and Delhi: Aryan Books International.

Gutschow, Niels, and Axel Michaels. 2008. *Growing Up: Hindu and Buddhist Initiation Rituals among Newar Children in Bhaktapur, Nepal*. Wiesbaden: Harrassowitz Verlag.

Heim, Maria. 2004. *Theories of the Gift in South Asia. Hindu, Buddhist, and Jain Reflections on* Dānā. NewYork and London: Routledge.

Hershman, Paul. 1977. "Virgin and Mother." In *Symbols and Sentiments. Cross-cultural Studies in Symbolism*, edited by Ioan Lewis, 269–92. London and New York: Academic.

Hüsken, Ute. 2013. "Contested Ritual Mediation: Tamil Tempel Priests in South India." In *Religion across Media: From Early Antiquity to Late Modernity*, edited by Knut Lundby, 71–86. New York: Peter Lang.

Khare, R. S. 1982. "From *Kanyā* to *Mātā*: Aspects of the Cultural Language of Kinship in Northern India." In *Concepts of Person: Kinship, Caste, and Marriage in India*, edited by Ákos Östör, Lina Fruzzetti, and Steve Barnett, 143–71. Cambridge, MA: Harvard University Press.

Letizia, Chiara. Forthcoming. "What Is Left of the Divine in Kumari? Responses to Modernisation, Secularisation and Human 'Rights' Challenges to the Tradition of the Living Goddesses in Nepal." Paper held at the 23rd European Conference on South Asian Studies, July 1914.

Luchesi, Brigitte. 2014. "Jhaṅkis. 'Living images' as objects of worship in Himachal Pradesh." In *Objects of Worship in South Asian Religions: Forms, Practices, and Meanings*, edited by Knut A. Jacobsen, Mikael Aktor, and Kristina Myrvold, 35–50. London and New York: Routledge.

———. 2006. "Fighting Enemies and Protecting Territories: Deities as Local Rulers in Kullu, Himachal Pradesh." *European Bulletin of Himalayan Research* 29–30: 62–81.

———. 1995. "Temporäre Kultbilder hinduistischer Gottheiten." In *Lokale Religionsgeschichte*, edited by Hans G. Kippenberg and Brigitte Luchesi, 223–233. Marburg: diagonal Verlag.

Malinar, Angelika. 2010. "Purity and Impurity." In *Brill's Encyclopedia of Hinduism*, edited by Knut A. Jacobsen. Vol. 2, 435–49. Leiden: Brill.

McGregor, R. S., ed. 1995. *Hindi-English Dictionary*. Oxford and Delhi: Oxford University Press.

Michaels, Axel. 2003. *Hinduism: Past and Present*. Translated by Barbara Harshav. Princeton: Princeton University Press.

Narayanan, Vasudha. 2010. "Auspiciousness and Inauspiciousness." In *Brill's Encyclopedia of Hinduism*, edited by Knut A. Jacobsen. Vol. 2, 693–701. Leiden: Brill.

Parry, Jonathan P. 1979. *Caste and Kinship in Kangra*. London, Henley and Boston: Routledge and Kegan Paul.

Pearson, Anne Mackenzie. 1996. *Because It Gives Me Peace of Mind: Ritual Fasts in the Religious Lives of Hindu Women*. Albany: State University of New York Press.

Preston, James. 1985. "Creation of the Sacred Image: Apotheosis and Destruction in Hinduism." In *Gods of Flesh, Gods of Stone: The Embodiment of Divinity in India*, edited by Joanne Punzo Waghorne, Norman Cutler, and Vasudha Narayanan, 9–32. Chambersburg, PA: Anima.

Rodrigues, Hillary Peter. 2009. "Fluid Control: Orchestrating Blood Flow in the Durgā Pūjā." *Studies in Religion/Sciences Religieuses* 38 (2): 263–92.

———. 2005. "Women in the Worship of the Great Goddess." In *Goddesses and Women in the Indic Religious Tradition*, edited by Arvind Sharma, 72–104. Leiden: Brill.

Rose, A. H. 1980. *Glossary of the Tribes and Castes of the Punjab and N.W.F. Province*. Vol. 1, (First published 1919). New Delhi: Amar Prakashan.

Zeiler, Xenia. 2015. "*Yantras* as Objects of Worship in Hindu and Tantric Traditions: Materiality, Aesthetics, and Practice." In *Objects of Worship in South Asian Religions: Forms, Practices, and Meanings*, edited by Knut A. Jacobsen, Mikael Aktor, and Kristina Myrvold, 67–84. London and New York: Routledge.

Conclusion

HILLARY RODRIGUES

This volume goes some distance in rectifying a lacuna in scholarly work on the Hindu tradition, namely, the absence of substantive studies on popular Hindu festival traditions. My students are fascinated when they hear about Hindu festivals such as Divālī or Holī, and they frequently ask if they can learn more about them. To my chagrin, I can often at best point them to a single influential paper, such as McKim Marriott's "Feast of Love," which speaks of his experience of Holī in the village of Kishan Garhi, or to some generalized descriptions in a book about Indian or Hindu festivals written for popular consumption.[1] In his study of festival religion in the south Indian tradition, Paul Younger (2002, 3–4) identifies two main reasons for this academic neglect. The first is that both Brahmin scholars and temple priests themselves had undervalued festival religion, which often originated in the rites of communities that were marginalized from full participation in the temple traditions. Even after temples developed their own festival styles, typically with temple and priest-affirming ritual features, these stood in contrast to popular manifestations and their malleable forms. The second reason is that the early history of Western scholarship shows a distinct bias toward the textual traditions of Hinduism. These too tend to privilege male, upper-class perspectives at the expense of marginalized voices, such as those of women, the lower castes, and casteless segments of Indian society. It is only with the realization—particularly through the contributions from anthropological studies—that the vibrant, lived practices of religion had been ignored that we have seen a shift in academic interest and research. If I might add a third reason, it would simply be that studying festivals is logistically challenging. This is why, even in practice-oriented studies, the tendency has been to focus on a particular pilgrimage, ritual celebrations in a particular temple, or festivities in a particular village. It is not easy, or prudent, for a scholar to attempt to generalize about a festival tradition that is widespread throughout the Hindu world, when one has only managed to observe one or at best a few regional manifestations. Although the throwing of color may be widespread in the celebrations of Holī (and Marriott's discerning analysis holds broadly true despite regional variations), surely the festival's duration, religious connotations, mythic attributions, defining activities, and a host of other features vary widely in other regions from what he described and experienced in Kishan Garhi. A collection of scholarly studies on Holī is what is actually needed.

Unlike scholarly studies on various types of Hindu practices, or even on various Hindu festivals, a distinctive feature of this collection is that its focus has been entirely upon a single festival, Navarātri (a.k.a. Navarātra, Dasain, etc.), whose widespread popularity rivals both Holī and Divālī. While Holī and Divālī may regionally vary considerably in their durations, and rarely span more than a few days, Navarātri clearly asserts for itself in name "nine nights" of the calendar year. Even though it may actually span more or less than its designated nine nights, it is a long and hugely important festival. And although Rāma's victory over Rāvaṇa is a mythic rival to Durgā's defeat of the buffalo demon Mahiṣa as the rationale for Vijayadaśamī (Tenth for Victory), the day following Navarātri, there is no dispute among virtually all celebrants that Navarātri is intimately connected to the worship of Devī, the Goddess. True, there are dissenting voices, such as those that commemorate Mahiṣa during this period, but they are currently marginal, minor, and have only recently been garnering media attention (see the introduction). Even though the persona and names of the Goddess may vary, leading one to wonder if Śakti, Umā, Durgā, Taleju, Kālikā, Cāmuṇḍēśvarī, Caṇḍī, Ambā, Kāmākṣī, and so on are indeed all the same Goddess, the mythic persona of the Goddess, alluded to by Balkaran (chapter 1) in his examination of the *Mārkaṇḍeya Purāṇa*, is that all goddesses are indeed Devī, the recipient of glorification in the *Devī Māhātmya*. This almost unequivocal identification of Navarātri with Devī is akin to festivals such as Mahāśivaratrī, which is clearly dedicated to Śiva and differs from Divālī and Holī, where the exuberant celebratory features of lights and color overwhelm their precise religious underpinnings. Devotees differ in whether they consider Divālī a celebration of Rāma's victorious return to Ayodhyā, the beneficence of Lakṣmī, or Kṛṣṇa's defeat of the demon Narakāsura. Is Holī a celebration of Prahlāda's victory over the demoness Holikā or a spring fertility rite with connections to the Kṛṣṇa-Rādhā myth cycle? Even if seasonal or astronomical cycles marked the ancient origins of Navarātri, it has long been firmly associated with the worship of Devī and speaks to her enormous popularity within Hinduism. Navarātri (Dasain) in Nepal is that country's most important religious celebration. A study of this grand festival, widely celebrated throughout India and among Hindu communities transnationally, spanning many days in the annual cycle and clearly dedicated to the Divine Feminine, is long overdue. This volume is a notable, albeit modest, initial contribution to the study of this festival tradition with a rich and ancient pedigree that is and has been celebrated by millions of people.

In this concluding chapter, I shall not summarize the content of the contributed articles. Not only would that be redundant, but it might insinuate a distorting fixity to Navarātri. It would be akin to saying that despite the many variations in how Navarātri is celebrated, let us now delineate its contours armed with this array of incisive snapshots. In truth, every chapter in this volume dealing with the ways in which the festival is practiced reveals that it is a phenomenon in flux. Not only are the contours of Navarātri rapidly changing, so are its internal forms.[2] And the historically oriented chapters indicate that this was also true in the past. I wish instead to draw attention to four salient dynamics in the Navarātri festival tradition. These are progressive democratization and secularization, the fluidity of symbolic power, embodied display and play, and theologies of transformation.

Progressive Democratization and Secularization

The process of democratization follows a trajectory from Navarātri's ancient origins to its present configurations. The *Devī Māhātmya* (13.6–16) tells how king Suratha and the merchant Samādhi went off to a river bank to worship the Devī. Through their own ascetic and devotional efforts, these members of the warrior (*kṣatriya*) and merchant (*vaiśya*) classes managed to obtain a vision of the Devī and secure her blessings.[3] Evidently, even prior to but certainly at the time of that text's composition (certainly before the ninth century CE), there was a shift in the style of ritual practice and access to the Devī's beneficence away from the ministrations and mediation of the priestly class. Even so, it was mainly members of the royalty that staged grand public celebrations during Navarātri with the aid of an elite priesthood (e.g. *rāj-purohita*) in subsequent centuries. The exact contours that worship took among the masses—probably within the confines of their homes or in village settings—is difficult to trace. However, with the decline of Mughal power and the revival of Hinduism, even during the period of British colonial rule, we note a flourishing in Navarātri celebrations. One certainly should not discount the effects of sociopolitical values on the democratization of the festival, for as wealth and power shifted from Hindu monarchs to the people, the locus of celebrations also moved away from kings and landlords to wealthy merchants, and eventually to Hindu communities of all stripes.

The recent history of Navarātri celebrations in Bengal illustrates this shift in locus. Once staged in the homes of wealthy landlords (*zamīndār*), the Navarātri celebrations—centered on the Durgā Pūjā—shifted in 1790 to what are called the Barowari (Bengali: *bāroiyāri*) Pūjās, initially instituted by twelve friends. This change was simply driven by economic factors; escalating costs combined with the declining fortunes of the *zamīndārs* made the Durgā Pūjā progressively difficult to stage with the grandeur that it demanded. As a result, it became a collective event. In time, this process led to the development of the so-called *sārvajanīna* (public) *pūjās*, common today in which companies, civic organizations, and neighborhoods contribute to the costs and labor to stage elaborate celebrations. My contribution (chapter 10) in this collection refers to celebrations of the Durgā Pūjā within the Benares home of a once wealthy Bengali landlord family. The Lahiris were among the handful of families in Benares still financially capable of staging such a grand celebration domestically. Einarsen (chapter 7) tellingly reveals the growth in popularity of the phenomenon of public Durgā Pūjās in Benares, which have grown from a few dozen to several hundred within the last century. It is important to recognize that the phenomenon of Durgā Pūjā–styled public celebrations, with large temporary shrines (*pandal*) and polychrome deity image clusters, has moved well beyond the Bengali communities and are embraced by Hindu groups across India as components of Navarātri celebrations. The grandest of the Bengali Durgā Pūjā celebrations are, of course, staged in Kolkata. Sen's (chapter 5) description of the Kolkata context points to broader factors of "democratization" at work.[4] Not only are larger swaths of populations being involved in paying for and contributing energies toward the staging of the Durgā Pūjās, but the *pandals* have also become significant nexuses of both secular and religious participation. The artistry of the *pandals*, as well as the creative ways in which the deities are fabricated and staged, transform entire cities such as Kolkata into museumlike spaces. Simply bigger is not always better when appraising *pandals* and tableaux; aesthetic merit and authenticity vie with scale and grandeur for public appeal and acclaim.

Secularization has accompanied democratization in recent centuries. We know that the royal Navarātri celebrations in nineteenth-century Bengal, for instance, were replete with entertainment, often including music and dance performances to which non-Hindus such as members of the ruling British elite were invited (McDermott 2011, 27). Such secular dimensions are integral to the modern community celebrations and will almost certainly continue to grow. Social media has accelerated rapid sharing of information about noteworthy sites and events occurring during Navarātri, encouraging more secularized, widening modes of festival participation (see Zeiler, chapter 6). People quickly learn where to go, sometimes simply to view particular displays, and they need not be Śāktas or Hindus or even have any religious affiliation or inclination whatsoever. It might be erroneous, however, to assume that this progression toward enhanced democratization and secularization is cannibalizing religious sentiment. It is beyond the scope of this conclusion to elaborate upon current theories concerning secularization and its countervailing movements of desecularization, religious reenchantment, and so on. Suffice to say, the overly simplistic notion of progressive secularization has been rejected, even by some of its early proponents such as Peter Berger (see Berger 1999).[5] The growing numbers of people (Hindu and non-Hindu) exposed to Durgā Pūjā displays in cities, on websites, and particularly through social media, will almost certainly have effects (secular and nonsecular) that are too incipient to appraise adequately at this time.

The Fluidity of Symbolic Power

The dynamics of democratization and secularization discussed above are related to ongoing shifts in the loci of symbolic power. When kings staged or patronized grand celebrations during Navarātri, their actions functioned at various levels. There was an overt display of the wealth and majesty of the ruler. The lavish scale of the celebrations worked to visually assert one's position in a hierarchy of sovereign power. The symbolic dimensions are evident because power was not actually exercised, but merely evoked. Grand military parades, or extravagant sacrificial offerings stood as emblems of martial and economic power. There was also an implicit sense that the Devī herself favored such worship and conferred her favor upon the kingly patron as she did to king Suratha in the *Devī Māhātmya*'s account. The ruler patron's special relationship to the Goddess was a crucial theme underlying the external activities.

Political democratization then mirrors the shifts in where the Devī's favor now resides, for we note an ongoing ascension in the scale of celebrations staged by business and social organizations and neighborhood communities. Skoda's (chapter 4) observations in the former princely state of Bonai, Odisha, are suitably representative. They reveal the relatively rapid ascendency of the "market-centered" and well-funded Durgā Pūjā and the decline of the "fort-centred" Dasara of the king, which is now an impoverished enactment when compared to its past. The case of the Woḍeyar rulers of Mysore discussed by Simmons (chapter 3) illustrates similar changes. His study also notes that where the ritual performances of Dasara once symbolically represented sovereign power and largesse, they have progressively become venues for celebrations of arts and culture, not for an elite audience, but for the masses. Sen, Skoda, and Simmons offer valuable observations of how modern-day politicians seek to bathe in the waters of symbolic power, by aligning themselves with ritual activities of Navarātri (e.g., by serving as honorific presidents of organizing committees, or through overt political advertising at *pandals*).[6] However, the floodgates of this fluid movement have not been fully opened. Sovereigns have not wholly capitulated and continue to utilize various strategies to restrict or even reverse back to themselves the flow of empowerment that comes from association with ritual worship of the Goddess.

Zotter's (chapter 2) observations of the transformations of the style of Navarātri royal rituals with the transition of rule from the Malla dynasty (c. 1200–1768/9) to the Shahs is especially instructive. To facilitate the legitimacy of their sovereignty, the Shahs skillfully melded the Tantric rites of the Mallas—centered on the worship of Taleju Bhavānī—with their own Navarātri rituals dedicated to Kālikā. A crucial point, of course, is that both dynasties recognized the vital symbolic role of Navarātri in their claim to power. The abolition of the monarchy in Nepal in 2008, which put an end to the world's last Hindu kingdom, offers us an ongoing opportunity to examine the shifting dynamics of symbolic power. With the Kathmandu palace of the last Shah king, Gyanendra, transformed into a museum, diminution in the scale and significance of royal Navarātri rites with each passing year is inevitable. Since the autumnal Navarātri is undoubtedly the nation's most important religious festival, it will be vital to observe where and how symbolic power flows from a sovereign center that has dissolved.

Simmons and Sen (introduction) point to the emergence of Dalit groups seeking empowerment in a highly creative reinterpretation of normative symbols in their celebrations of Mahiṣāsura Pūjā. The Devī is portrayed negatively, and Mahiṣa, whom they identify as a divine ancestor, is elevated. Even so, the dynamics of symbolic power and its endurance are evident. Although meanings ascribed to the polar symbols (divine/demonic, oppressor/oppressed) are reassigned and even inverted, power flows through new causeways through ritual enactments utilizing the same symbol set.

Embodied Display and Play

Although sovereign and communal empowerment are crucial features of Navarātri, and sober religious rites are conducted everywhere, one ought not to forget that it is also a great festival (*utsava*) and has been thus since antiquity. Even today, businesses close; national holidays are declared; families reunite; and there are festive celebrations in homes and public venues. Celebrants often dress in their finest, prepare special meals and delicacies, spend lavishly and incur debt, and enjoy themselves by attending music and dance performances. Just as Christians may put up Christmas trees in their homes and offices, with particularly notable ones for public viewing (e.g., at Rockefeller Center or on the South Lawn of the White House), the installation of the Goddess in various forms is a ubiquitous feature of Navarātri. These manifest forms may vary from a simple jar (*ghaṭa, kalaśa*), to a cluster of nine plants (*navapatrikā, phūlpātī*), a virgin girl (*kumārī, kanyā*), a cosmograph (*maṇḍala*), or an anthropomorphic earthen image. Luchesi (chapter 15) closely unpacks some variations in the dynamics of embodiment of the Devī in her study of maiden (*kanyā*) worship in private and temple settings in Himachal Pradesh. Such divine embodiment of the Goddess in the form of a living female is a theme found in other chapters, including those by Zotter, Rodrigues, and Ilkama. In elaborate Navarātri rites, the Devī may be invoked into several types of manifest forms. A crucial contrast with the Christmas tree analogy is that the Goddess is believed to take up her abode—is embodied—in these various forms.

Therefore, there is a significantly different stratum of meaning attached to a devotee's viewing of any installation of the Goddess than when gazing at a dazzlingly beautiful Christmas tree. In the former case, it is *darśana*, sensory communion with the Devī, while the latter scenario possesses no meaningful allusions to embodied divine presence. During the autumn Navarātri, the Goddess is believed to arrive and take up her abode in locales where she has been invited. The grandeur of her abode reflects the sentiments of her host, and it is incumbent on those who have invited her to provide their divine guest with the very best that they can muster. The mechanics of *pūjā* are likened to the traditional procedures of welcoming and honoring a guest who has traveled from afar, and the establishment of elaborate pandals and imagery are like preparing the guest room or guest palace for an important visitor (Östör 2004, 70–72). Once the guest has arrived and taken up residence, others may be invited to visit with her. Such divine hospitality arrangements exist in a type of tension with temple traditions in which temples assert the ongoing and constantly accessible presence of the Goddess in her own abode. She is not a guest who has arrived but more like a queen in her palace. Temples also clean up and decorate the premises, clothe the Devī specially, and offer distinctive rituals of worship, but their rites typically affirm indispensable priestly roles in orchestrating those rites.

Hüsken, Ilkama, and Luchesi in various ways offer insights into features of embodiment and the dynamics at play within temple traditions. Ilkama's (chapter 8) observations of Navarātri rites at the Kāmākṣī and Patavēttamman temples reveal that in both cases the Devī's act of destroying the demon (embodied in the form of a tree) require priestly ministrations. At Kāmākṣī temple the rationale is expiation or atonement for the act of killing, and at Patavēttamman, it is to cool down a hot goddess. Hüsken's (chapter 9) study reveals a contrast between modes of worship at the Kāmākṣī and the Varadarāja temples. While the Kāmākṣī temple is dedicated to the Devī, in the Varadarāja—a Viṣṇu as Perumāl temple—the role of the Devī is somewhat understated. Here we see an illustration of Younger's (2002) observation that temples construct normative traditions to serve their own interests, often crafted in response to popular needs. Hüsken notes how the realities of the Varadarāja temple celebrations deviate from their own textual prescriptions in the Pāñcarātra Saṃhitās and are shaped more tellingly by the styles demanded by the local populace.

Ilkama, Sivakumar, and Wilson's chapters also draw attention to the south Indian domestic worship tradition during Navarātri of setting up *kolus* in one's homes. *Kolus* are tiered altars upon which celebrants display doll collections, as well as other objects. Ilkama reiterates the significance of "embodiment," for these are manifestations of the Devī, with agency, and not mere representations of the divine. Sivakumar (chapter 13) and Wilson (chapter 12) describe and analyze how *kolus* reveal dynamics at play among high and low castes, as well as within socioeconomic classes, particularly in urban environments. Everything is significant, including what is displayed and who is invited to view the tableaux. Narayanan (chapter 14) offers us a valuable glimpse into how the *kolu* custom is expressed in parts of the United States. She notes how within such transnational communities Navarātri serves to sustain and impart tradition, in contrast to Indian contexts where normative conventions may be challenged and innovation is commonplace. Moreover, the symbolic structure of the *kolu* may derive from sovereign display, while Navarātri's timing resonates with a hopeful cosmic reinvigoration after a dark period in the annual cycle.

Alongside the clear evidence of dynamism in all these aforementioned Navarātri rites, which may reinforce or disrupt tradition, we see the crucial significance of embodied display. Moreover, one must not forget the element of play—alluded to earlier—within many of these very same festive activities. Display and play are juxtaposed in Navarātri. Divine play (*līlā*), or purposeless play, is a recurring motif and metaphysical rationale for why deities may choose to act as they do. From this perspective, the entire creation is the divine *līlā* of the Goddess, and the Navarātri is a period to honor and celebrate that affirmation of her cosmic role.[7] However, here we have yet another type of divine *līlā* at work because the festive nature of Navarātri also highlights human play. Kings, businesses, communities, and individuals display their wealth and playfully share their bounty with others. This is display as play. Devotees playfully enact dramas, play or listen to music, and enjoy the festival atmosphere of social gatherings by eating together, visiting *pandals*, and so on. The context of this human playfulness is the embodied arrival of the Devī. She not only appears in earthen, vegetative, and other symbolic embodiments but is also vibrantly displayed in the form of young maidens (*kanyā*) and married women. Navarātri is a time when married women often return to their paternal homes and are treated like living embodiments of the Goddess (see Rodrigues, chapter 10). Maidens and married women are dressed in finery, adorned, fed, and given gifts. In south India, the *kolu* enacts a paradigmatic act of girl's play, namely, playing with dolls, which are displayed and collectively shared with friends. The Devī is embodied within these dolls, and thus here one actually plays with the Goddess.

These playful dimensions of Navarātri have a conceptual framework that differs from other types of festival celebrations. The Goddess comes in various forms, including as maiden girl and married daughter, but these human embodiments evoke something larger. When she arrives during Navarātri, everyone, both male and female, is made unmistakeably aware—through her ubiquitous embodiments on display—of the presence of the Divine Feminine. This gives the spirit of playfulness within Navarātri celebrations a distinctive character, for all celebrants are akin to her children, able to play freely and securely under the watchful and protective presence of the Cosmic Mother.

Theologies of Transformation

It would be a reductive oversight to ignore the personal religious dimensions of Navarātri, even though these are difficult to appraise when compared to the overt activities of temple rituals and public festivities. Despite the progressive secularization of the festival, its commercialization, and its social, political, and economic dynamics, Navarātri provides individuals with an opportunity to reflect upon deeper spiritual realities. In fact, Navarātri is regarded by most devotees as the most efficacious period to encounter the Goddess. Devotees' devotional acts during Navarātri are evident in temple visits, simple *bhakti*-oriented *pūjās*, and even hearing recitations of the *Devī Māhātmya*. But there is more afoot, because the Devī offers the promise of more than the sort of temporal power and cosmic sovereignty bequeathed to king Suratha. In the *Devī Māhātmya's* account (13.16), the Goddess granted the merchant Samādhi the knowledge that leads to perfection.

Shankar (chapter 11) ably reveals how Aghor ascetics and devotees utilize the festival period in pursuit of the merchant Samādhi's goal of spiritual self-transformation. Essentially, the external form of the jar (*kalaśa*) into which the Goddess is installed is but a starting point for this process. Through austerities, devotional acts, and creative visualizations, those seekers strive to become one with the Goddess who has taken up her abode within their midst. The Tantric dimensions of this spiritual practice are evident and are mirrored in other contexts, such as within the activities of the *purohita* who presides over the Bengali style of the

Durgā Pūjā ritual (see Rodrigues). Through purification rites (e.g., *bhūta śuddhi, prāṇāyama*), bodily imprintments (e.g., *nyāsa*), and creative visualizations, the *purohita* repeatedly transforms himself into the Goddess before establishing her into various material forms. The capacity of the Goddess to become present in such a plethora of images, which abound during Navarātri, speaks to metaphysical notions that virtually any fragment of the creation can serve as a habitat for or seat of her divine presence. This includes the individual human being, female or male. Once such a transformation has transpired, an abiding sacralization of the material abode, namely, one's own being, is believed to have occurred.

Some Final Thoughts

Although I have only touched in broad strokes upon a few themes found within the rich material of the foregoing chapters, readers are invited to delve deeper into these themes and to extract different, unmentioned ones. Each theme reveals the fluid nature of Navarātri, and I have alluded to seeming flows in direction of these changes. One can certainly imagine yet greater democratization and secularization processes at work as the festival garners larger public participation. These forces are likely to be catalyzed as Hindu communities grow more connected through mediatization and through the burgeoning middle-class's enhanced affluence. As the numbers of participants grow, and the scale of the celebrations increases, so will the celebratory dimensions of the autumn festival. Both display and play will evolve in new and creative ways.

The loci of symbolic power will continue to shift away from monarchs, but it is yet premature to predict to what extent it will flow primarily to the people instead of being absorbed by demagogic leaders for less than democratic ends. Just as Rām Rāj (the [righteous] rule of the mythic king Rāma) has been an effective clarion call for political action, sweeping particular groups into governing roles, the Devī's persona through the rites of Navarātri may work similarly. There are ample examples of political leaders being compared to the Devī, or eliciting such comparisons themselves (see Sen), and political opponents, rival religions, and so on have often been equated with Mahiṣa, the demon in the Goddess's best-known mythic conquest. The rich polysemy of the symbols of the Devī's defeat of Mahiṣa will continue to accrue layers of meanings, or even upturn them over time and within diverse cultural contexts.

The Goddess and Navarātri offer powerful symbols and opportunities to celebrate womanhood in manners aligned with burgeoning women's movements, particularly as these continue to blossom more fully. Of course, the vision of the Goddess functioning as an emblematic force for empowerment must be situated alongside the very real ways in which such idealized feminine models of perfection may serve to undermine the realization of social, economic, and political equality for actual women.[8] After all, the Goddess and Navarātri have been around for centuries in the Hindu world, and, as some might argue, they have functioned to maintain a disempowering hierarchical status quo. What is different, however, is that despite their faltering forward march, feminist movements now routinely do challenge and reframe hegemonic, patriarchal interpretations of normative symbol sets within all the major religious traditions.[9] Mediatized interconnectivity could assist in the rapid and widespread dissemination of Navarātri beyond its Hindu, Indian, and even transnational religious contexts. One already notes that religiously inclined, non-Hindu women discover in the Goddess a symbol of feminine divinity deprived to them within their own religious cultures, which have been dominated by male deities. Secularization of the rite might enhance and broaden Navarātri's appeal among all women worldwide, who see in the Devī a model of feminine strength and empowerment, not unlike a fantasy super-heroine.

The trajectories of the aforementioned developments are uncertain. However, the burgeoning academic interest in Navarātri is not, and is not restricted to the production of this volume. There are many doctoral dissertations with substantial emphases on Navarātri currently underway, a few by contributors to this volume. This volume was itself the outgrowth of a series of conferences (in Paris and Austin), panel presentations (at the IAHR in Erfurt, and the annual AAR gatherings in San Diego and San Antonio), and conversations among a group of scholars assembled primarily through the efforts of Dr. Ute Hüsken. This working group continues to grow, and a new volume edited by Drs. Hüsken and Vasudha Narayanan, on Navarātri's agency, namely, its capacity to accomplish things, is already underway. Primarily through the efforts of Dr. Caleb Simmons, the American Academy of Religions (AAR) has recently accepted a five-year Navarātri seminar, which will run from 2017 to 2021. Not only is this a recognition of the significance of the festival, but it ensures a venue for scholars to disseminate their research over the next several years. Such activities will undoubtedly lead to the production of journal articles, edited volumes, and monographs further enriching our understanding of Navarātri and spearhead similar broad-ranging studies of other Hindu festival traditions in the near future.

Notes

1. An example of this might be Om Bahadur's "Divali: The Festival of Lights," in Hawley and Narayanan, eds. (2006).

2. Even the Devī's supreme position as the central focus of the festival period is being challenged by certain Dalit groups that recast Navarātri as Mahiṣāsura

Pūjā or Mahiṣāsura Commemoration Day. We do not have adequate evidence-based knowledge whether such contestations of Navarātri rites occurred in the past, or what forms they might have taken. We do know that blood sacrifice was problematic to Buddhists and Jains, who likely provided alternative opportunities for celebrants during the autumn Navarātri.

3. Verse numbers of the *Devī Māhātmya* follow the scheme utilized in Coburn (1991).

4. McDermott (2011, 147–57) identifies and articulates features of this democratizing process, but discusses it primarily as the vector from royal, private, and regal to public and even low-brow.

5. A pertinent collection on the topic is found in Calhoun, Juergensmeyer, and VanAntwerpen (2011).

6. Theoretical underpinnings of symbolic power and its dynamics are found in Max Weber's analysis of status, class, and power, and most thoroughly developed in Pierre Bourdieu's (1984) notions of symbolic capital.

7. Kinsley (1979, 19–27) provides an extensive treatment of the Goddess as Divine Player, but does not touch upon the features of human play under the protective presence of the Divine.

8. Along these lines, Kishwar (1999) argues that, although powerful, Durgālike women, such as Mayawati and Mamta Banerjee, may acquire and utilize political power, these leaders often do not further the cause of ordinary women.

9. The complexities embedded within the diverse objectives and approaches of feminist movements, issues of cultural appropriation without full appreciation of cultural contexts, and the polyvalent character of the Goddess (e.g. virgin, mother, nurturer, and warrior) are explored in Hiltebeitel and Erndl (2002).

Bibliography

Bahadur, O. 2006. "Divali: The Festival of Lights." In *The Life of Hinduism*, edited by J. Hawley and V. Narayanan, 91–98. Berkeley: University of California Press.

Berger, Peter. 1999. *The Desecularization of the World: Resurgent Religion and World Politics*. Grand Rapids, MI: Eerdmans.

Bourdieu, Pierre. 1984. *Distinction: A Social Critique of the Judgment of Taste*. Translated by Richard Nice. Cambridge, MA: Harvard University Press.

Calhoun, C., M. Juergensmeyer, and J. VanAntwerpen, eds. 2011. *Rethinking Secularism*. New York: Oxford University Press.

Coburn, Thomas. 1991. *Encountering the Goddess: A Translation of the Devī-Māhātmya and a Study of Its Interpretation*. Albany: State University of New York Press.

Hiltebeitel, A., and K. Erndl, eds. 2002. *Is the Goddess a Feminist? The Politics of South Asian Goddesses*. New Delhi: Oxford University Press.

Kinsley, David. 1979. *The Divine Player: A Study of Kṛṣṇa Līlā*. Delhi: Motilal Banarsidass.

Kishwar, Madhu. "Indian Politics Encourages Durgas, Snubs Women." *Manushi* 111: 5–9.

Marriott, McKim. 2006. "Holi: The Feast of Love." In *The Life of Hinduism*, edited by J. Hawley and V. Narayanan, 99–112. Berkeley: University of California Press.

McDermott, Rachel Fell. 2011. *Revelry, Rivalry, and Longing for the Goddesses of Bengal: The Fortunes of Hindu Festivals*. New York: Columbia University Press.

Östör, Àkos. 2004. *The Play of the Gods: Locality, Ideology, Structure, and Time in the Festivals of a Bengali Town*. Reprint. New Delhi: Chronicle Books. First Edition: University of Chicago, 1980.

Younger, Paul. 2002. *Playing Host to Deity: Festival Religion in the South Indian Tradition*. New York: Oxford University Press.

Contributors

Raj Balkaran is a mythologist and scholar of Sanskrit narrative texts, most notably the Vālmīki Rāmāyaṇa and Devī Māhātmya. His article "Violence in the Vālmīki Rāmāyaṇa" was published in the *Journal of the American Academy of Religion* (2012), and he is currently working on his book manuscript, *Mother of Power,* and numerous other articles. Balkaran has served as instructor at the University of Toronto School of Continuing Studies since 2010 and is currently appointed as World Religions Instructor at Ryerson University. In addition to his work at the academy, Balkaran founded the School of Modern Mythology, which focuses on harnessing mythological wisdom to ameliorate modern life.

Silje Lyngar Einarsen is assistant professor at Oslo Metropolitan University and PhD scholar at the Department for the Study of Religion at Aarhus University. Her research interests include Śākta traditions, medieval yoga traditions and the relationship between Hindu scriptures and religious practice. She has conducted research on the role of Sanskrit texts and ritual performances during Navarātri in Benares, combining textual and ethnographic research methods. She is currently co-manager of the Śākta Traditions research project at the Oxford Center for Hindu Studies and works on a Danish translation of the *Haṭhapradīpikā.*

Ute Hüsken is a professor and head of the Department of Cultural and Religious History of South Asia (Classical Indology, South Asia Institute), Heidelberg University. She studied at Göttingen University (Germany), was a member of the collaborative research project Dynamics of Rituals at Heidelberg University, and until 2017 was a professor in the field of South Asia studies (Sanskrit) at Oslo University (Norway). Hüsken's main fields of interest are Buddhist studies, Hindu studies, ritual and festival studies and gender studies. Her major publications include *Die Vorschriften für die buddhistische Nonnengemeinde im Vinaya-Piṭaka der Theravādin* (Reimer, 1997), *When Rituals Go Wrong: Mistakes, Failure, and the Dynamics of Ritual* (Brill, 2007), and *Viṣṇu's Children: Prenatal Life-Cycle Rituals in South India*

(Harrassowitz, 2009). Together with Ronald Grimes and Barry Stephenson, she edits *The Oxford Ritual Studies Series* (OUP).

Ina Marie Lunde Ilkama is currently a doctoral research fellow at the Department of Cultural Studies and Oriental Languages, University of Oslo. Her PhD project explores the Navarātri festival in Kāñchipuram by investigating roles and images of the feminine (goddesses and women) and the play (*līlā*) of the goddess as expressed in mythological narratives and in the festival performances. She holds a Master's in Sanskrit from the University of Oslo (2012) and has a background in religious studies. Her academic interests include goddess traditions, women in Hinduism, religious festivals, vernacular religion, Sanskrit textual traditions, ritual, and mythology.

Brigitte Luchesi is a trained sociologist, historian of religion, and social anthropologist. She has taught at the Free University of Berlin and from 1989 to 2008 at the Department of Comparative Religion at the University of Bremen, Germany. After her retirement, she moved back to Berlin where she continues to work in the fields she always has been most interested in: forms of local religion in North India and the religious practices of Hindu and Christian immigrants from South Asia in Germany. Another ongoing field of interest is visual perception.

Vasudha Narayanan is a distinguished professor in the Department of Religion and director of the Center for the Study of Hindu Traditions (CHiTra) at the University of Florida. She was educated at the Universities of Madras and Bombay in India and at Harvard University. She is a past president of the American Academy of Religion and the Society for Hindu-Christian Studies. She is the author or editor of seven books and the associate editor of the six-volume *Brill's Encyclopedia of Hinduism*. She has also written numerous articles, book chapters, and encyclopedia entries. Her research has been supported by grants and fellowships from several organizations including the Centre for Khmer Studies; the American Council of Learned Societies; National Endowment for the Humanities; the John Simon Guggenheim Foundation, the American Institute of Indian Studies/ Smithsonian, and the Social Science Research Council. She is currently working on Hindu temples and traditions in Cambodia.

Hillary Rodrigues is a professor of religious studies at the University of Lethbridge (Canada) and author of several books, including *Ritual Worship of the Great Goddess* and *Introducing Hinduism*. His edited volume, *Studying Hinduism in Practice*, in the Studying Religions in Practice series, is a collection of essays by experts written for novice undergraduates.

Moumita Sen is a visual studies scholar and is currently a postdoctoral fellow at the Department of Cultural Studies and Oriental Languages (University of Oslo). She is studying Mahishasur *puja* as part of a larger project that looks at the rise of blasphemy accusations in South Asia. Her doctoral dissertation focused on the intersection between art, popular religiosity, and democratic politics in the clay-modeling industry of West Bengal and was awarded the Norwegian king's gold medal (2017) for outstanding scientific research. She is currently studying the contentious practice of Mahishasur *puja,* the celebration of a mythical figure by minority communities that is considered "demon worship" by dominant Hindu culture.

Jishnu Shankar is a senior lecturer at the University of Texas at Austin with the Department of Asian Studies and the Hindi-Urdu Flagship. Before coming to Austin in 2007, he was a Hindi lecturer and associate director for the South Asia Center at Syracuse University. He is a graduate of the Delhi School of Economics and the Indian Institute of Mass Communication and a certified trainer for Oral Proficiency Interview with the American Council on the Teaching of Foreign Languages (ACTFL). He also worked as a journalist in Delhi. Under the auspices of the Hindi-Urdu Flagship at the University of Texas at Austin, in collaboration with the New York University and Columbia University, he has participated in the joint creation of the Language for Health in Hindi and Urdu website. Besides teaching Hindi, Jishnu conducts research and translates literature from the Aghor tradition of India. Besides the United States and India, he has made presentations and participated in workshops in universities in Japan, Norway, Germany, France, and Italy on Hindi pedagogy and the Aghor tradition. His main publications in Hindi are *Aghor Vachan Shastra,* and *Bhagawanramleelamrit,* and in English *The Book of Aghor Wisdom* and *Mysteries of the Aghor Master*. He also serves as the scientific advisor on the board of the Venetian Academy of Indian Studies.

Caleb Simmons has a PhD in religion from the University of Florida. He is an assistant professor of religious studies at the University of Arizona. He specializes in religion in South Asia, especially Hinduism. His research specialties span religion and state formation in medieval and colonial India to contemporary transnational aspects of Hinduism. His current book project, *Devotional Sovereignty,* examines how the early modern court of Mysore reenvisioned notions of kingship, territory, and religion, especially through articulations of devotion within their genealogical material. He has publications and continuing research interests related to a broad range of contemporary topics, including ecological issues and sacred geography in India; South Asian diaspora communities; and material and popular cultures that arise because of globalization—especially South Asian religions as portrayed in comic books and graphic novels.

Deeksha Sivakumar is a PhD candidate in religion at Emory University in Atlanta. Sivakumar is an ethnographer focusing on the southern Indian celebration of Navarātri called *pommai kolu,* a festival arrangement of dolls. She has completed her master's in Asian religions from the University of Hawaii (2010) and her bachelor's (Hons) in philosophy and psychology from Linfield College, Oregon (2007). Her primary interests include ritual performance, healing, materiality, and femininity.

Uwe Skoda is an associate professor in South Asian studies at the Department of Global Studies, Aarhus University. His current work focuses primarily on political anthropology and visual culture in relation to India. He has recently co-edited "Contemporary Indigeneity and Religion in India" (special issue of *International Quarterly for Asian Studies* 46 [1-2]) and the volume *India and Its Visual Cultures* (Delhi: Sage, 2017).

Nicole A. Wilson received her doctorate in anthropology from Syracuse University. Her primary research interests include performances of middle-class Tamil identity through urban Hindu religious practice and marriage and matchmaking. Her dissertation research investigates how modern middle-class identities are related to religious affiliations and motivations, as well as how the building of new urban social networks in south India relates to narratives of caste, class, and morality. Nicole's work was funded by a Fulbright-Hays DDRA, as well as a Bharati Memorial Grant from the South Asia Center at Syracuse University.

Xenia Zeiler is tenure-track professor of South Asian Studies at the University of Helsinki, Finland. Her research is situated at the intersection of digital media, religion, culture, and India and the worldwide Indian community. Her research foci are digital Hinduism, global Hinduism, Ethno-Indology and Tantric traditions. She is the author of a monograph on current transformations of Tantric traditions and numerous articles and book chapters on mediatized and digital Hinduism, popular religion in contemporary India, and global Hinduism. Her current projects include an edited volume on digital Hinduism and co-edited volumes on mediatized religion in Asia and methods for researching video games and religion.

Astrid Zotter studied Indology and religious studies at Leipzig. Over the past ten years she has been doing research on Hindu traditions in the Kathmandu Valley (Nepal), combining textual studies with fieldwork. Her research and publications cover various topics, such as the use of flowers in worship, life-cycle rituals among Brahmins, and festivals. Currently she is employed as project coordinator and postdoctoral researcher in the research unit "Documents on the History of Religion and Law of Premodern Nepal" at the Heidelberg Academy of Sciences and Humanities.

Index

Ādivāsis
and Dasara, 84, 88, 95
and Kant Debī, 84, 88
Mahiṣāsura as hero of, 109
and the Paudi Bhuiyan, 85, 87
and sacrificial polity, 97
as "Scheduled Tribes," 7
and ties with king, 93, 97
and worship of Mahiṣāsura, 17n4
Ali, Haidar, 65, 287
Ambedkar, B. R., 108
Amma, Meenakshi, 248–50
Aryans, 7, 8
astrological mythology, 30–35. *See also* Jyotiṣa (classical Indian astrology)
Āśvina
and ancestors, 141
bright half of, 58n4
and Dasara, 87
and festivals in Benares, 141, 151
and Hindu month of Āśvin, 4
lunar month of, 33, 34, 299
military background of, 141
and Navarātra procedures, 44, 46–47
and Navarātri times, 33, 153n1, 197, 199–200, 289, 292
as September–October, 1, 292, 299
See also Jyotiṣa (classical Indian astrology)

Baba, Sarkar
and Aghor tradition, 216, 220
and austerity, 15, 217–18, 219, 222, 230
and becoming like the Goddess, 229, 230
name of, 215
and Navarātri, 217–19, 220, 221–23, 224, 225, 226, 228, 230–31
and offerings, 232n4
and presence of the Goddess, 226, 227
and ritual practice, 216–17, 223–24, 227
and sacrifice, 222
and Shri Sarveshwari Samooh, 216
stories of devotees of, 228–29
and visions of *Devī*, 219–20
and *yoga*, 218
Balkaran, Raj, 13
Banerjee, Mamata, 108, 109, 110–13, 114 fig. 5.2, 115, 116, 117
Basu, Jyoti, 112
Benares, India
Baba Kinaram Sthal in, 216
and Banarasi indentity, 14
and Durgā Pūjā, 34, 204, 320
and local youth clubs, 14
Navarātri celebrations in, 14
and Sarkar Baba, 15, 216
Shri Sarveshwari Samooh Kusht Sewa ashram in, 215, 216, 217–18
Bengal
and advertising of politicians, 116, 117
art and culture in, 111–14
Bengal Institute of Art & Culture in, 128
and chief minister Mamata Banerjee, 105, 107, 108, 109, 110–13, 114, 115, 116, 117

Bengal *(continued)*
and clay images of Durgā, 301
and Durgā Pūjā, 96, 105–7, 110, 112, 113–17, 122–23, 124, 125, 133–34, 140, 198, 199, 307, 320
greatness of, 105, 116
Navarātri in, 320
and Śākta *Mahābhāgavata Purāṇa,* 16n2
and *sarbajanīn* (public) *pūjās*, 124, 125
and secularism, 14, 107, 118n3
social and political life in, 106, 110–17
West Bengal, 14, 96, 105, 106, 107, 110, 111–12, 113, 114, 115, 116, 117, 118n3, 132
and worship of young girls, 313n4
and worship of young girls *(kanyā pūjā),* 301
zamīndār of, 123, 153n5, 198, 320
Bhagavad Gītā, 6, 289
Bharatiya Janata Party (BJP)
and Atal Vajpayee, 17n4, 109
and National Democratic Alliance, 17n6
and prohibition of cow slaughter, 17n5
as a right-wing party, 7–8
Smriti Irani of, 7–8
Bonai, Odisha
and Ādivāsis, 97
capital Bonaigarh of, 83, 86, 87, 89, 90, 95, 96, 97, 99n5
Dasara in, 84–94, 95, 97–98, 321
and Durgā Pūjā, 96–98, 321
former kingdom of, 84, 97
industrialization in, 83, 96, 97
palace of, 83
and sacrificial polity, 84, 94, 97
social and political life in, 84, 94, 97
sponge-iron factories in, 83, 96, 99n6
Brahmins
and Americans in San Francisco Bay, California, 258
Aryan Brahmins, 7
and *bhadraloks*, 111
and Brahminization, 240
and Brahmin Rajpurohit, 91, 99n3
Brahmin women, 181, 184, 244, 248, 249, 251, 265, 309
and censuses, 253n1
and class, 240–41
and Dasara, 91, 92
fees or offerings to, 309, 311
and festival religion, 317
and hierarchy, 40, 142
high tradition of, 192n20
interpretations of, 168
and *kolus*, 246, 250, 261, 262, 264, 265, 266, 267, 271, 278
and legal theory of gifts, 311
and Mylapore, Chennai, 258, 261, 262–63, 264, 272n1
and Navarātri, 17n3, 152, 237
of Nepal, 40, 49
Parbatiya Brahmins, 49
and planets, 37n11
and politics, 240
and Pommai Kolu, 16, 261
and priests, 88, 216
and religious knowledge, 244, 249
Tamil Brahmins, 258, 272n2
and Tamil dialect, 249
in Tamil Nadu, 240–41
temples of, 14, 157, 168, 169, 170, 190, 192n18
texts of, 2, 168, 264
traditions of, 191n4, 261, 262–63, 264
Upādhyāya Brahmins, 40
as upper-caste, 239
worship of girls from, 48, 309
Bṛhat Jātaka (Varāhamahira), 31, 33, 35, 37n8
Bṛhat Parāśara Hora (Parāśara), 31–32, 34–35
Britain
and Anglo-Mysore Wars, 65
and British East India Company, 66
and British India, 125
and British officers, 106
and colonial rule, 239, 287
and *darbārs*, 287
and defeat of Ṭippu Sultān, 64, 65

and development of kingship in India, 64, 66, 67–68
dynastic succession laws of, 64, 81n4
and governing in Mysore region, 64, 65, 66, 284
and Indian diaspora, 132
and Kṛṣṇarāja III's reign, 78, 80
police of, 92
and victory at Plassey, 122
Buddhism
and Buddhist *khaḍgapūjā*, 58n4
and Buddhist stupa, 96
and caste system, 47
and feeding of ancestors, 292
and Navarātri, 292
and participation in Hindu rites, 40
and Patan, 57n2
and sacrifices, 328n2
and state religion, 57n2
and worship of Buddhist girls for Navarātra, 47–48

caste
and *bhadraloks*, 111
in the *Bṛhat Parāśara Hora*, 35
Buddhist castes, 47
and caste-based customs and practices, 16, 174n1, 240, 246, 247, 248, 250, 278, 299
and casteless Indians, 317
and class identifications, 237–38, 240
communities of, 258, 264
and Dalit groups, 2, 7, 109, 149, 322, 327–28n2
and Durgā Pūjā, 149, 152
gardener subcaste, 53
Hindu castes, 111, 174n1, 237, 239, 240–41, 246, 247, 248, 250, 251, 302, 309, 324
and identity, 239–40, 243
and Indian community, 261, 262
and *kolus*, 244, 246, 247–48, 250, 251, 253, 265, 266, 278, 324
Kṣatriyas caste, 40
lower castes, 237, 239, 240, 248, 250, 251, 309, 317
and Mahiṣāsura as hero, 109
and Navarātri, 237, 238, 250–51, 253
in Nepal, 40, 41
and Pano community, 86
and *pitṛ pakṣa* observance, 292
of the Punjab, 309
and Rāma, 142
and the *Rām Līlā*, 142, 143, 151
and ritual displays, 244
and Sarasvatī Pūjā, 241
and social mobility, 239–40
and spacial categories, 238
and Śrī Maṅkala Vināyakar temple, 244
and stereotypes, 239
and the Sun, 35, 37n11
and urban areas, 240
and worship of young girls *(kanyā pūjā)*, 308–9
and youth clubs, 152
and zodiac, 37n11
See also Brahmins, Dasara
Chakravarty, Pandit Hemendranath, 198–99
Chatterjee, Sovandev, 105
class
and *bhadraloks* (aristocracy), 111–12
and blessing tickets, 244
and caste, 238–41
and cultural values, 240–41
and Durgā Pūjā, 115, 123, 128, 152
and employment opportunities, 239
and identity, 16, 238, 239, 243, 251, 252
Indian lower class, 252
Indian middle class, 95–96, 98, 112, 115, 128, 135, 146, 152, 238–39, 240, 243, 247, 248, 249–50, 251, 252, 253, 326
Indian upper class, 98, 111–12, 146, 239, 240, 247, 252, 266, 278
and *kolus*, 244, 245 fig. 12.1, 246, 247–48, 250–52, 253, 257, 263
and Mamata Banerjee, 112, 113
merchant class, 319
and Navarātri, 239, 253
and "Other Backward Classes," 109
and Sarasvatī Pūjā, 241

class *(continued)*
and stereotypes, 16
and textual traditions, 317
warrior class, 319
Communist Party of India, Marxist (CPIM), 108, 109, 111, 114

Dalit groups
and blasphemy charges, 109
and consuming beef, 17n5
hegemony over, 2
and king Rāma's power, 152
and Mahiṣāsura Commemoration Day, 2, 7, 8, 327–28n2
as a religious minority, 7
and worship of Mahiṣāsura, 17n4, 109, 322
and worship of young girls *(kanyā pūjā)*, 309, 314n5
Dasara
in the 1930s, 93, 94
in Bonai state (of Odisha), 13–14, 83, 84–92, 93, 94–95, 97–98, 321
in capital of Kullu District, 301
and contests, 92, 93
and *darbār*, 16, 63, 72, 93, 95, 285–87
and Dasara day hunt, 79
death during, 71
and divine kingship, 13, 65, 68–69, 79, 80
eighth day of, 88, 89, 90, 91
and first Woḍeyar Dasara, 70–71
fort-centered rituals of, 13, 14, 83, 84–87, 89–90, 93, 96, 97, 98, 99n2, 321
honoring of teachers during, 288
and identity formation, 14, 77
and Indian politics, 63–64, 80–81
and Kant Debī, 88–91, 92, 95
and king-making, 13, 63–64
and king's donative practices, 80
and kingship, 280
and *kolus*, 276, 280, 282–83
and Kumāri Pūjā, 91
and Mā Kumārī, 92
in Mysore, 63–64, 66, 74, 77–81, 278, 280, 282
ninth day of, 90, 91
and Pano community, 90
and the Paudi Bhuiyan, 88–89, 90, 93
and performing the continuity of lineage, 64–65, 68–69, 74, 77–81
and *pratipada* (commencement of Dasara), 87
and privy purses, 92
procession of, 13, 14, 63–64, 65, 68, 71, 72, 73, 74, 77–81, 85, 92, 95, 143
and public celebration of arts, 63, 321
reduction of rituals for, 93–94, 95
rituals of, 63–64, 68, 70–72, 77, 79, 80, 83, 84, 85–95, 96, 97, 98, 99n2, 321
and roots of the festival, 63
royal celebration of, 94, 97–98, 285–87
and royal power, 79, 80–81, 84, 97, 286, 321
and royal ritual on Dussehra, 153n3
and sacrifices, 84, 88, 89, 90, 91, 93, 94, 95, 97, 98
and sacrificial polity, 84, 87–88, 89, 91–92, 94, 97
in Sanskrit and Kannada, 81n1
seventh day of, 90, 91
sixth day of, 87
and sovereignty, 64, 80–81, 321
and the *Śrīman Mahārājavara Vaṃśāvaḷi*, 68, 80
and state of Karnataka, 276
and swords, 85–86, 90, 91, 92, 94
as a ten-day festival, 63, 72
tenth day of, 79, 91
as tenth day of victory, 301
and victory of good over evil, 139
See also Navaratri; Vijayadasamī
Devī Māhātmya (*Glorification of the Goddess*)
and Caṇḍī, 105, 191n13
and classical Jyotiṣa, 31, 33
and Dasara, 282
date of composition of, 212n3, 319
and deeds of the Goddess, 24, 25, 33, 34, 35, 158, 164, 185, 241, 301

and Devī, 318, 321
and equinoxes, 13, 23, 33
and Hindu Great Goddess, 23, 33, 34, 158, 164, 209, 210, 212n3, 219, 220, 232n3
invocations of Sun in, 33–34
and king Suratha, 24, 27, 29, 33, 211, 319, 321
manus in, 24, 28–29 table 1.1, 35
as a Navarātri ritual text, 13, 23, 33, 34, 47, 325
and parallels with *Sūrya (Sun) Māhātmya*, 28–29 table 1.1
and praise of the goddess, 24–25, 28, 33, 35, 203, 211, 212n4, 268
and preservation, 35
recitations from, 45–46, 47, 203, 325
and solar mythologies, 25, 28, 29–30, 33, 34, 35, 36n3
and worship of Durgā, 121
dharma (law)
and *dharmaśāstras*, 71, 72
Durgā as guardian of, 84, 142
and festivals, 105
and order, 142, 294
and Rāma, 143, 144
and Rāma's subjects, 143
Durgā
Abhinav Caṇḍī Durgā, 17n4
alaṃkāras (ornamentation) of, 158, 169
as Bana Durgā (forest Durgā), 84, 85
as Cāmuṇḍā, 204
and creation, 294, 295
and Dasara, 83, 84–87, 97, 98
and the *Devī Māhātmya*, 158, 164, 203, 210–11
and Durgā Vāhinī (Vehicles of Durgā), 109
and eighth day of Navarātri, 164
and establishment of a *kalaśa*, 291
female political leaders as, 108–9
as the feminine sacred, 84
and festival culture of Benares, 147
forms of, 84, 85–86, 91, 97, 98, 219–20
and giving of *piṇḍas*, 294–95
and Hinduization, 84
and hymns, 153n3, 203
image of, 107, 109, 110–11, 113–14, 117, 125, 139, 140, 147, 150, 164, 197, 198, 295, 301, 307
and killing of demons, 191n13, 198
and killing of Mahiṣāsura, 34, 50–51, 96, 108, 142, 148, 152, 164, 175n2, 198, 241, 245, 259, 292, 294, 301, 318
and *kolus*, 161, 245
in the *Mahābhārata*, 4, 141, 203
and Mahiṣa, 8, 12, 139, 142, 164, 198, 318
and Mā Kumārī, 85
and Mamata Banerjee, 108, 109, 110–11, 113–14
many names of, 197, 210
and military season, 141
as motherly protector, 242, 253, 268
Naba Durgā, 90, 93
and nation as Bhārat Mātā (Mother India), 8, 152
and nature, 84
and Navarātri, 3, 4, 8, 43, 158, 241
and Nine Durgās, 85, 91, 231n2
pandals (marquees) of, 110, 112, 140–41, 146, 147–148, 151
and ritual practice, 105, 111
as role model for women, 242
and *śakti*, 109, 117, 141, 146, 153n3
sexualization of, 8
and sex with Mahiṣāsura, 17n7, 17n8
and sword worship, 85
as Ugracaṇḍā, 51–55
unmarried status of, 242
and Vaishnavism, 242
veneration of, 2, 4, 7, 12, 83
and veneration of the state, 2, 8
warrior nature of, 84, 108, 153n3, 158
worship of, 34, 39, 46, 54, 55–56, 58n13, 85, 96, 97, 98, 109, 121, 122–23, 153n3, 153n5, 158, 175n2, 203, 204, 212n3, 242, 253n2
See also Durgā Pūjā; goddesses

Durgā Pūjā
and artist Sanatan Dinda, 113
and autumn, 200, 212n2, 258
in Benares, 14, 34, 139–41, 145–52, 153n2, 154n14, 197, 198–99, 204
Bengali Durgā Pūjā, 15, 34, 96, 105–7, 110, 112, 113–17, 122–23, 124, 125, 128–29, 133–34, 147, 153n2, 153n4, 198, 199, 200, 201, 204–11, 313n4, 320, 325–26
and Bengali *Kṛttivāsa Rāmāyaṇa*, 204
and Bengal Institute of Art & Culture, 128
budget of, 96, 106, 128–29, 133, 146
in Calcutta, 14, 105, 106, 107, 108, 110–11, 112, 114, 115, 123, 124, 125, 147, 148, 197, 320
and committee Mulund, 14, 122, 128–36
as community-centered, 123–25, 129, 133–34, 152
definition of, 197
diaspora community involvement in, 135
in domestic space, 117, 121, 123, 147, 153n2, 198, 204, 206, 320
and Durgā Pūjā Committees, 14, 98, 122, 124, 126, 128–36, 146–47, 148, 149, 150, 152
and *Durāapūjātattva* (Raghunandana), 6, 199
and employment opportunities, 106, 115
and empowerment, 211
and fire rituals (*homa*), 206
food of, 204
and globalization, 121, 145–46
and government control, 151
and "heterotopia," 17n9
and Hindu-Muslim riots, 149
history of, 122–25
and identity formation, 14, 124, 149
immersion (*visarjana*) parade of, 149–50, 151
increase in popularity of, 14, 95–97, 110, 121, 122, 124, 125, 140, 145, 146, 148, 151, 320
and installations as platforms for messages, 148
and killing of Mahiṣa, 198
and killing of native Mahishasur, 8
and *kumārā pūjās*, 205–6
and law enforcement, 149, 150
and local youth clubs, 14, 106, 107–8, 114–15, 148, 149, 197
locations of, 198, 199
and Mahāsaptamī, 202
and Mamata Banerjee, 105, 108, 113–14, 115, 116
as market-centered, 14, 84, 98, 99n2, 321
and media, 145
and mediatization, 14, 107, 113, 121–22, 125, 128–36
and *mudrās*, 209
and Navarātri rituals, 4, 12, 121
nine nights of, 130
in Odisha, 96, 321
organizations involved in planning for, 14, 96, 106, 107–8, 110–11, 113–14, 115, 123–24, 128–36, 148–49, 152
and other *pūjās*, 145–46, 206
pandal's role in, 124–25, 135, 140–41, 145, 146, 147–50, 152, 153n10, 153n12, 154n14, 198, 210, 247, 320
and participation since 17th century, 121
and personal austerity, 147
political patronage of, 14, 96, 106, 107, 108, 114, 115, 116, 123
politization of, 107, 108, 114–15, 117, 147, 148
private sector funding of, 106, 115, 125, 129, 146–47
public art installations about, 107, 110–11, 113–14, 147–49
in public places, 14, 97, 115, 121, 122–23, 124, 125, 133, 136n1, 139, 140, 141, 147–48, 151, 152, 153n2, 206
and *pūjā* designers, 107, 110, 116
as a racial festival, 8
of Rāma, 3–4
as reflection of modern society, 152
rituals of, 15, 96, 97, 98, 99n2, 107, 116, 117, 121, 125, 127, 136n1, 150, 152, 198, 198–99, 200–206, 207, 211

ritual texts of, 199
royal celebration of, 207
and royal power, 98
and sacrifices, 98, 204–205, 207, 210–11, 212n4, 313n4
and Śākta *Mahābhāgavata Purāṇa*, 16n2
and Sarvatobhadra Maṇḍala, 204, 208
and social media, 14, 135–36
social practices around, 127
in South Asia, 1
and sovereignty, 207
spectacle of, 97, 106, 107, 108, 110, 117, 123, 124–25
and status or authority claims, 123, 124, 133, 135–36
and symbolism, 113–14, 207, 208–10
and Tantric traditions, 204, 208, 210
and temple context, 204
and Vedic elements, 208
and Vedic *rājasūya* ceremony, 207
and *Vijayadaśamī*, 139, 206
in West Bengal, 105–107, 110, 117
and women, 208
and womens' life cycles, 176n12
and worship of girls, 204–205, 211
and worship of Goddess Durgā, 84, 86, 96, 98, 121, 197–98, 206–11
and *zamīndār* families, 123
See also Durgā Pūjā Committees; Navarātri; Vijayadaśamī
Durgā Pūjā Committees
and advertising, 130, 131, 132–35, 136
and Ajay Rai, 150
arrests of members of, 150
and Dalits, 149
Durgā Pūjā Committee Mulund, Mumbai, 14, 122, 126, 128–36
and funding for *pūjās*, 146–47
and Hindu-Muslim riots, 149
and immersion of *mūrtis* (images), 150
and installations as platforms for messages, 148–49
and kings, 98
languages used by, 129, 132
and mediatization, 14, 121–22, 126, 128–36
names of, 152
and public Durgā Pūjā, 139, 149–50
youth involvement in, 149
Durgāpūjātattva (Raghunandana), 6

Foucault, Michel, 17n9

Gandhi, Indira, 17n4, 92, 109
gender
and Brahmin wives, 181, 184
and class status, 253
and cross-dressing of children, 182
and Durgā, 253
and Durgā Pūjā, 152, 176n12
and female political leaders, 113
and feminine ritual roles, 253, 311
and festival at Varadarāja temple, 185
and identity formation, 249
and impurity of menstruation and sexual activity, 308
and *kolus*, 246, 247
and participation in piercing ceremony, 166
and power, 179
and roles for Tamil women, 175n4, 182
and roles in *Rām Līlā*, 142–43, 150
and Sarasvatī Pūjā, 241
and textual traditions, 317
and women's freedom of movement, 252
and women's movements, 326–27
goddesses
adornment of, 244
and Aghor tradition, 215
alaṃkāras (ornamentation) of, 157, 158, 159, 164, 165, 169–71, 174, 175–76n10
and alliance between Goddess and government, 14, 109, 112–14
Amaladēvate, 72
Ampāḷ, 248
and anointing procedures, 202–203
Aparājitā, 206
around Bonai's fort, 85, 86
and becoming like the Goddess, 229
and Bengali Goddess worship, 97

goddesses *(continued)*
and blasphemy connected to treason, 8
Blessed Trinity of, 220, 231–32n3
and the body, 15, 108, 224, 230
Brahmin goddesses, 170
Cāmuṇḍēśvari, 63, 64, 72, 74, 81n1, 318
Caṇḍā, 52, 53, 54, 55–56, 59n17
Caṇḍī, 72, 85, 105, 191n13, 318
Candika, 55, 231n3
consecration of, 113, 114
and court rituals, 97
and creation, 208, 209, 231n3, 290–91, 294, 295, 324
and *darbār*, 90
and *darsana* (viewing of a deity), 147, 170–71, 174, 175n3, 228–29, 300, 310, 323
and Dasara, 63, 83–92, 97–98
and Debī Pūjā, 90
and deeds of the Goddess, 3, 4, 5, 14, 23, 24, 25, 157, 170, 174, 301
and defeat of demons, 5, 6, 14, 28, 50–51, 74, 108, 109, 158, 164–65, 172, 174, 268, 326
Devī, 12, 28, 29, 164, 201, 205, 207, 210, 211, 212n2, 219, 282, 290, 291, 299, 302, 303, 304, 307, 308, 309, 313n1, 318, 319, 321, 322, 323, 324, 325, 327
and the *Devī Gītā*, 6
and the *Devī Māhātmya*, 13, 23, 24–25, 27, 28–29, 33, 34, 35, 164, 203, 209, 211, 232n3, 268, 301, 318, 319
and domestic space, 172, 191n4, 211, 300–301, 308
Durgā, 2, 3, 4, 5, 7, 8, 12, 33, 34, 39, 50–55, 58n13, 83, 85–86, 90, 96, 97–98, 108–11, 139, 141, 142, 147, 150, 152, 153n3, 153n5, 161, 164, 175n2, 197–98, 200, 203, 204, 210, 219, 231n1, 241, 242, 253n2, 286, 291, 294–95, 301, 307, 310, 318
and earth, 200, 208, 211, 291, 300, 323
Eight Mother Goddesses, 52–53, 54
embodiment of India in, 8, 108
and establishment of a *kalaśa*, 223, 230, 290–91, 323, 325
and feminine ideals, 179, 327
and fertility, 36n5, 87, 200–201, 290–91
and festival times, 33
and fire rituals (*homa*), 6, 163
forms of, 6, 12, 15, 34, 39, 45, 46, 52, 53, 54, 55, 85–86, 96, 98, 158, 159, 163, 164, 165, 169, 170, 170–74, 198, 200–203, 204, 205, 206, 208, 219, 220, 241, 243, 253n2, 268, 291, 300, 301, 323, 324–25, 326
and future manus, 33
and gift giving, 303
and globalization, 96
and Goddess as omnipresent, 224
goddess of Aryan Brahmins, 7
and Goddess Puranas, 4–6
and gods, 211, 302
healing power of, 95
human embodiment of, 172, 175n6, 208, 222, 230, 268, 301, 312, 323, 325, 326
images of, 89, 107, 108, 110–11, 113–14, 117, 125, 147, 164, 166, 169, 171 fig. 8.2, 172, 174, 182, 186, 206, 244, 290–91, 300, 301, 306, 307, 320, 326
increase in worship of, 122
and jars and sprouting plants, 201, 290–91, 300
Kālī, 109, 128, 136n4, 165, 169, 170, 185, 191n13
Kālikā, 318, 322
Kāmākṣī, 15, 158, 159, 160, 161, 163, 164, 165, 166, 167, 168, 169, 170, 172, 174, 175n2, 175n10, 176n10, 179, 180, 185–186, 188, 189, 190, 191n12, 191n13, 191n14, 192n18, 192n19, 192n22, 243, 318, 323–24
in Kāñcipuram, Tamil Nadu, 179–90
Kant Debī, 84, 86–87, 88, 90–91, 92, 95, 97–98, 99n5
Kant Kumārī, 86, 93
Kātyāyanī, 54, 55
Kaumārī, 59n22
and killing of demons, 157, 166, 167, 168, 169, 170, 171, 172, 173,

174, 185, 185–86, 188, 189, 191n13, 192n20, 205, 220, 323
and kingdom of Keonjhar, 86
and *kolus*, 159–61, 258, 266, 268, 271, 272, 275, 276, 277, 280, 281–82, 288, 324, 325
Kumārī Debī, 88, 90
and Kumārī Pūjā, 91, 208
Kumārīs, 47–48, 54, 307–308
Lakṣmī, 36n5, 54, 85, 105, 128, 136n4, 168, 175n2, 179, 180–81, 182, 183, 184–85, 186, 187, 190n2, 191n6, 191n10, 198, 201, 203, 237, 241, 243–44, 250, 253n2, 268, 269, 270, 271, 286, 288, 318
locality and tradition of, 11–12, 16, 86, 158, 168
Mahākālā, 220, 231n3
Mahālakṣmī, 220, 231–32n3
Mahāsarasvatī, 220, 231–32n3
Mā Kumārī, 85, 86, 87, 90, 92, 93, 97
and Mamata Banerjee, 110, 328n6
and *mantras*, 175n8, 224, 226, 229
many names of, 12, 45, 46, 54, 58n8, 58n13, 86, 268
Māriyammaṉ, 165
materiality of, 168–69, 173, 174
material representations of, 157, 167, 174
mohana khaṇḍa, 85–86
Mother Kālī, 216
Mother Vindhyavāsinī, 228, 229
and Navarātri, 1, 2, 3–6, 10, 11, 12, 14, 15, 16, 23–24, 33, 45–49, 140, 153n1, 163–74, 185, 190, 220, 230–31, 241, 326–27
and nine plants of the Navapattrikā, 203, 204, 206, 323
and palace of Gorkha, Nepal, 54
Pampā, 180, 187–88
pandals (marquees) of, 105, 107, 108, 110, 112, 115, 140–41, 147–48, 323, 324
and Pano community, 90
Patavēttamman, 14, 157, 158, 165, 166, 167, 168, 169, 170, 171 fig. 8.2, 172, 174, 323
and the Paudi Bhuiyan, 85, 86, 87, 97
and *pīṭhas* (seats of the goddess), 147, 208
power of, 152, 167, 172, 226, 277
and power of women and girls, 12, 172
and presence of the Goddess, 225–29
and preservation, 35
and *pūjās*, 11, 34, 90, 105, 136n4, 149, 163, 164, 172, 299–313
and relationship to blood, 211
representatives of, 160, 208, 299, 301, 306, 307–308, 312, 313
and ritual practice, 87–92, 163–67, 202–203, 319
ritual sacrifice to, 6, 49, 89, 90, 95, 192n19, 202, 208, 210, 211, 301
and royal power, 10–11, 23–24, 34, 35, 42, 54, 141
and Śākta narratives, 3, 4–6, 25
and *śakti*, 114, 141, 161, 209, 226, 231
and Śakti, 253n2, 318
and Sanskritic deities, 168
Sarasvatā, 175n2, 198, 203, 241, 243, 244, 247, 286
and Sarkar Baba, 216, 217
and Sarvatobhadra Maṇḍala, 204
Sarveśvarī, 225
Shah's Kālikā, 42, 47, 54
and Shaivite Tantric traditions, 41–42
Śiva, 54
and slaying of buffalo-demon, 74, 85, 96, 152, 175n2
and sovereignty, 34, 35
and speech, 208, 211
Śrī, 201
Śrī Maṅkala Vināyakar temple's worship of, 243–44
stotras dedicated to, 105, 113
and supreme Divine Feminine, 313n1
and sword form, 98, 202, 205
and symbolism regarding politicians, 109
Taleju, 42, 47, 48–49, 56, 58n7, 58n8, 318, 322
Tantric goddesses, 204

goddesses *(continued)*
and *tarpaṇa*, 222
and temple images, 167–71, 174, 306, 307, 313
and temples of the Kangra Valley, 300, 303–304
and term Mother, 230, 231n1, 325
and "tribal deities," 97–98
Ugracaṇḍā, 51–55, 56, 59n17
and universal power, 141
of Vaiṣṇava Varadarāja Perumāḷ temple, 179
Venus, 36n5
weapons of, 170, 204
and women, 175n4, 208, 211, 212n4
worship of, 3–4, 5, 6, 11–12, 15, 24–25, 26, 34, 35, 41–42, 45–46, 47, 48, 52–55, 56, 89, 90, 91, 93, 95, 97, 106, 147–48, 158, 159–60, 163, 167, 175n3, 180–81, 184, 186, 188, 190n2, 202, 204, 205–206, 208–209, 211, 218, 220–21, 230, 241, 245, 251, 280, 300–313, 318, 322
and worship of in home, 95, 147, 161–163
and worship of young girls, 10, 12, 47–48, 54, 58n13, 208, 230, 290, 299, 301–13, 323
See also *Devī Māhātmya* (*Glorification of the Goddess*); Durgā; Durgā Pūjā; *kolus* (dolls); Navarātra; Navarātri
gods
Aditi as mother of, 200
appeasement of, 141
and Āśvin twins, 31
and autumnal equinox, 23
Bhairavas, 46
Brahmā (creator deity), 27, 28, 69, 192n20, 216
and Brahmin goddesses, 170
Candra (Moon), 74
and cartoons, 224
and co-opting of deities, 39
and court astrologers, 30
and deeds of the Goddess, 5, 23, 28, 29
and deity of the Dasaĩghar, 58–59n14
and the *Devī Māhātmya*, 36n3
and dolls *(kolus)*, 159
and Durgā Pūjā, 200
female consorts of, 191n7
Ganeṣa, 198, 203, 252
genealogy of, 69, 70, 74
and globalization, 96, 146
and God, 158, 167
and gurus, 224
Hanuman, 78, 142, 143, 212n2, 302
of heaven, 27
images of, 244, 307
in Kāñcipuram, Tamil Nadu, 179, 188
in the Kangra Valley, 307
Kārttikeya, 198, 203
and killing of demons, 185
as kings, 288
and *kolus*, 259, 263, 266, 271, 275, 277, 280, 281–82, 288
Kṛṣṇa, 68, 69, 74, 77, 79, 80, 162, 267, 318
and local memorial practices in Nepal, 41
and Mahiṣa, 141–42
male gods, 170
and Navarātri, 140
and perception of God/Goddess, 227
and Pommai Kolu, 267
Pradyumna, 69
Rāma, 153n3
and the *Rām Līlā*, 143, 150
and ritual practice, 90
and sacrifices, 192n20
of the Sanskrit tradition, 186
and Sarvatobhadra Maṇḍala, 204
Śiva, 6, 74, 142, 150, 179, 186, 203, 204, 216, 261, 263, 282, 318
sovereignty of, 28, 29
and Sun, 26, 27, 28, 74
and temple images, 167
and temples, 11, 179, 180–81, 190n3, 323–24
and Vaiṣṇavism, 191n5
Varadarāja, 181, 182, 183, 184, 185, 187, 188–89, 190n2, 192n19, 192n20, 192n22, 323–24

Vasudeva, 74
Vināyakar, 248
Virūpākṣa, 180, 187, 188
Viṣṇu, 6, 17n4, 23, 68, 69, 74, 78, 142, 179, 188, 216, 261, 267, 282, 324
and women's performances, 191n15
worship of, 106, 183–84, 227
Yama, 26, 294
Yamunā, 26
See also *kolus* (dolls); Purāṇas; Surya (Sun); Woḍeyar dynasty

Hinduism
and BJP political agenda, 7–8
and Brahminical culture, 240–41, 261, 272n3
and Brahmotsava, 163
and Buddhism, 292
and community, 238
cult images in, 307
and Dasara, 80
and death, 168, 294, 295
and the *Devī Māhātmya*, 33–34, 241, 318
dharmaśāstras of, 71, 72
and diaspora, 125, 288, 289, 291, 319, 324
and domestic space, 192n22, 192n23, 319, 324
and Durgā Pūjā celebrations, 122, 320–21
and Durgā Vāhinī (Vehicles of Durgā), 109
and fasting, 301, 302
and "Gentoo" (Gentleman Hindoo), 106
and grains and sprouting beans, 290–91, 295
and Hindu Great Goddess, 23, 34
and Hindu identity, 124
and Hindu nationalism, 8, 109, 116, 144, 152, 153n6, 239
and Hindu society, 143, 162–63, 324–25
and Hindu symbolism, 149, 152, 324, 327
and Hindu women, 242, 248–50, 313–14n4, 324–27
and Indian Hindu majority, 7
in the Kangra Valley, 300–313
and king Rama, 142, 143, 294–95
and *kolus*, 276, 291, 295
and Mahānavamī festival, 72
as a majority religion, 146
and *mantras*, 223, 224, 226–27, 229, 230, 245
medieval ritual texts of, 192n23
and meditation, 217, 220–21, 222, 223, 226, 227, 230, 319
of modern middle classes, 152
and month of Āśvin, 4
and mythology, 159, 161, 163, 175n9, 182, 185, 186, 200, 208, 210, 211, 212n2, 294, 302, 318
and Navarātri, 4, 8, 176n11, 222, 238, 277, 291, 318–19, 326, 327
and Nepalese nation building, 40, 41
new media's shaping of, 128
and non-Bengali Hindus, 118n3
and non-dual Vedanta, 207
and number of wives, 82n6
and organizations' clash with law enforcement, 150
and participation in Durgā Pūjā, 123
and participation in Hindu rites, 40, 292–95
and period of ancestors, 289, 292–95
and *pitṛ pakṣa* observance, 292–95
and pluralistic traditions, 17n4
and pollution by death or women, 168
and popular festivals, 317
and popularity of Devī, 318, 326
and *pūjās*, 149, 174n1, 192n22, 207
and *rājas*, 153n5
and Rāmāyaṇa narrative, 4, 142
ritual calendars of, 4, 180, 188, 289
ritual cultures of, 43–50, 187
and ritual handbooks, 168
and role of women, 192n22, 192n23, 288–89
and royal legitimacy, 144
saints in, 179, 216
and Śākta Tantrism, 210

Hinduism *(continued)*
and Shaivite Hindus, 57n2
and South Indian temples, 168
Tantric traditions in, 41–42, 43, 187, 198, 199, 201, 210, 220, 224, 231n2, 325–26
and *tarpaṇa*, 222
and temple context, 192n21, 248–49
temple deities in, 167–68
textual traditions of, 317
and Vaishnavism, 242
and Vedantic philosophical tradition, 71
and Vedic elements, 189, 198, 199, 201
and weddings, 162
and women in domestic space, 191n4
and women's reproductive cycle, 189–90, 308, 313–314n4
and worship of Mahiṣāsura, 7–8, 17n4
and worship of planets, 253n4
and worship of women, 189
and worship of young girls, 189, 299, 301–13
See also Dasara; Durgā Pūjā; goddesses; gods; *kolus*; Navarātri; Purāṇas

Ilkama, Ina Marie, 14–15, 190, 192n18, 192n23, 323, 324
India
Andhra Pradesh, 275
anticolonial developments in, 124
astrological mythology of, 30–35
Ayodhyā, 3, 142, 318
and Bangladesh war, 109
Benares, 4, 14, 15, 35, 139–41, 150, 210, 212n4, 215, 301, 320
Bengal, 14, 16n2, 96, 105–7, 110–12, 125, 153n4, 288, 294, 301, 307
bhadraloks (aristocracy) of, 111–12
and British colonial rule, 239, 319
capital of, 125
and city planning, 148
and cultural values, 238–39
diaspora of, 122, 132, 136, 258, 259, 275, 276
and Dīpāvalī festival, 252, 258, 295, 296n1
and Dīvālī (Dīpāvalī) festival, 318
and Durgā Pūjā in Calcutta, 14, 105–8, 110–11, 115
Durgā Pūjā industry in, 117
eastern India, 7, 16n2, 85
economy of, 239
education in, 239, 240
18th and 19th century in, 106
environment of, 148, 150
Ganga river in, 150
government of, 98, 106, 107, 108, 111, 113, 115–17, 118n3, 148, 149–50, 240
Gupta Empire in, 30
hegemonic culture in, 7–8
and Hindu-Muslim riots, 149
and Hindu nationalism, 8, 109, 116, 144, 152, 153n6, 239
importance of Hinduism in, 146
independence of, 108, 145, 239
and Indian political theory, 66–67
and Indian Union, 84, 92, 97
Kashmir, 303
Kerala, 275
and kingship under British rule, 64, 67–68
as majority Hindu, 7
and Mandal Commission, 239
and mediatization, 127–28
medieval India, 106
middle class of, 95–96, 98, 238–39
monsoon season in, 258
Mylapore, Chennai, 258
and National Democratic Alliance, 17n6
national integration of, 13–14, 81n2
and nation as Bhārat Mātā (Mother India), 8, 108
North India, 144, 299–313
other festivals in, 116, 117
and partitioning into east Pakistan, 198
politics in, 7–8, 14, 16, 17n4, 17n6, 63, 64, 67, 68, 80–81, 84, 106, 107, 108–9, 111–13, 115–17, 118n3, 144, 146, 328n6

popular festivals in, 317
and prohibition of cow slaughter, 17n5
and public religion, 11, 63, 84, 123–25
Punjab, 301, 303, 309
purists in, 222
and royal celebration of festivals, 4, 63, 64, 80–81
and Sanskritization, 240
and *sarbajanīn* (public) *pūjās*, 123, 124, 125
and secularism, 107
social and political life in, 106–7
and social media, 135–36
socioeconomics in, 15–16, 238–39, 240
South India, 17n3, 63, 179, 192n17, 237–53, 276, 286, 288, 289, 291, 317, 324, 325
and sovereignty, 8, 63, 80–81
sponge-iron production in, 83, 96
and state of Himachal Pradesh, 299–313
and state of Karnataka, 63, 64, 81, 81n2, 275, 276
and state of Tamil Nadu, 109, 275, 276
territories of, 40
and terrorism, 148
and tribal people of Odisha, 14, 84
Uttar Pradesh, 303
during Vijayanagar period, 241
western India, 17n3
and worship of Mahiṣāsura, 7
and worship of young girls *(kanyā pūjā)*, 299, 301–13
See also Bengal; Bonai, Odisha; Britain; class; Durgā Pūjā Committees; Kannada; Mysore, India; Navarātra; Odisha; Sanskrit

Jainism, 5
Jawaharlal Nehru University (JNU), 7–8, 17n7, 154n14
Jayalalitha, 109
Jyotiṣa (classical Indian astrology)
asterisms in, 31, 32, 33, 36n4
and court astrologers, 30
and equine realm, 31
manus in, 36n4
and *Markandeya Purana*, 30–31, 32
mechanics of, 31–32
and Navaratri times, 33
royal majesty in, 34–35
and zodiac, 33, 36n5, 36n6

Kāmākṣī Ammaṉ temple
as a Brahmanical temple, 157, 163, 174n1
and Kāmākṣī, 179, 185–86
Navarātri in, 163–65, 173, 179, 184, 185–86
rituals of, 157, 163–65, 166, 169, 172, 173
and sage Durvāsa, 163
and worship of young girls and women, 172, 174
Kāñchipuram, Tamil Nadu
Brahmin temples of, 163, 169, 174n1, 192n18
Navarātri in, 14, 15, 157, 158, 161, 163–67, 169, 173–74, 179–90
principal goddess of, 163
as religious center, 179, 188, 191n9
and Śaivism, 179, 188
and Śāktism, 179
Vaiṣṇava Varadarāja temple in, 15, 179, 180–85, 189–90, 190n2, 191n4, 191n7, 191n8, 191n15, 192n22, 192n23
and Vaiṣṇavism, 179, 190n1, 191n4, 191n5
Kannada
and Dasara terms, 64, 81n1
doll festival in, 276
as language of Karnataka, 63
literature in, 65, 68, 69
royal dolls in, 282
and the *Śrīman Mahārājavara Vaṃśāvaḷi*, 68, 69
Kathmandu, Nepal
as capital, 42
dynasties of, 13, 39, 48, 55
and Kathmandu Valley, 39, 41, 42, 44, 47, 49, 52, 55

Kathmandu, Nepal *(continued)*
Malla dynasty of, 45, 54
and Malla's Taleju, 58n7
and Mother Goddesses, 54
palace of, 42, 45, 322
royal court of, 45
Shah dynasty in, 41, 42, 56
kings
and Adivasis, 97
and adoption of heirs, 66, 68, 70, 77, 81n6
astrologers in courts of, 30, 50
as authors, 58n10
and behavior of girl-goddesses, 47–48
and Benares, 143–44, 152
and celebration of the Maharāja, 139, 143
consecration of, 23
and continuity of lineage, 64–65, 67, 70, 77, 79
and co-opting of deities, 42, 56
and Dasara, 63, 64, 65, 68–69, 70, 71, 77–79, 80–81, 84, 87–88, 89, 91–92, 321
and Dasara's budget, 88, 91, 94–95, 96
and democratic state, 64
demon-king Mahiṣāsura, 7
and divine kingship, 13, 65, 66–67, 68, 69, 70, 72, 77, 79, 80, 152
Dravya Shah, 42
and Durgā Pūjā, 5–6, 98, 207, 211
as fathers of citizens, 67
and festivals, 192n17, 285–87
and gifts to subjects, 71, 72, 286
and goddesses, 84, 86–87, 88, 89, 90–91, 97–98, 141, 321
and gods, 9, 68, 72, 80, 84, 106, 187, 288
Gyanendra, 322
and hierarchy, 286
Hindu kings, 72, 319, 322
and hunting, 79
and immortality, 65, 67, 68–69, 80
from Indian epics, 74
and Indian religious thought, 35, 71, 72
Indra, 141
and Kant Debī, 87, 93, 97–98
King Daśaratha, 69
King Karandhama, 30
and king-making, 63–64, 65
King Pratapsimha, 46
and kingship, 277, 285, 321
King Suratha, 24, 27, 29, 33, 35, 211, 319, 321, 325
K.K.C. Deo, 87, 95
and *kolus*, 266, 276, 277, 279–80, 283–84
and Kṛṣṇarāja III's harem, 76–77
Kṛṣṇarāja Woḍeyar III, 13, 64, 65–77, 79, 80, 287
Mahālakṣmī worship of, 184
and Mahānavamī festival, 72, 284
and Maharāja's power, 143–44
Mahārāja Udit Narayan Singh, 143–44
and Mā Kumārī, 97
Malla dynasty, 39, 41–42, 48, 56, 57, 57n2, 58n10, 322
mortality of, 66, 67, 80
and mourning periods, 48
Mysore kings, 63, 64, 65, 66–80
and Navarātri, 1, 10–11, 23–24, 39, 40–42, 71, 190, 287, 319, 324
in Nepal, 39, 41–42, 49
palaces of, 11, 12, 39, 41, 42, 81n2, 90, 91, 97, 98
and Pano community, 86–87
of Patan, 48
and the Paudi Bhuiyan, 87, 88, 89, 93, 98
and public religion, 9, 11–12
and *pūjās*, 71–72, 90, 106, 144
pūjās and rituals for, 71–72
Rājyavardhana in *Sūrya (Sun) Māhātmya*, 27, 29
Rāma, 142, 143, 144, 152, 153n3, 326
religious roles of, 41–42, 49, 90, 91, 97, 98, 188
and royal *darbār*, 276, 277, 282, 285–286, 287, 288
royal display of, 16, 68, 77–79, 80, 92–93

and royal power, 10, 56, 64, 67, 79, 80–81, 84, 88–89, 98, 106, 123, 141, 143–44, 152, 187, 188
and sacrifices, 207
and sacrificial polity, 84, 87–88, 91, 97
Shah dynasty, 39, 40, 41–42, 46, 47, 48, 56, 58n10, 322
sovereignty of, 106, 141
and succession of kings discourse, 28–29 table 1.1
and swords, 91
Vibhuti Narayan Singh, 143
Vijayanagara kings, 187, 192n17, 277, 280
visible and invisible bodies of, 65–68
warrior nature of, 35
Woḍeyar dynasty, 63, 64, 65, 67–80
and women's performances, 191n15
worship of, 92
See also *King's Two Bodies, The* (Kantorowicz); Malla dynasty; *Mārkaṇḍeya Purāṇa*; Shah dynasty; *Śrīman Mahārājavara Vaṃśāvaḷi (The Annals of the Royal Family of Mysore)*; Woḍeyar dynasty

King's Two Bodies, The (Kantorowicz), 66–68

kolus
and Andhra Pradesh, 278, 289, 295, 296
celebration times of, 289
and cultural capital, 276
definition of, 159, 244–45, 275, 276, 324
different sets of, 162, 175n5, 260, 263–64, 266, 269, 275
and Dīpāvalī festival, 296n1
as display of prosperity, 269–70, 271, 289
and doll display for stories, 175n9, 257, 260, 262, 263, 265, 268, 271–72
domestic *kolu*, 16, 157, 159–61, 173, 174n1, 192n23, 247, 258, 259–60, 261–65, 266, 276, 277, 278, 279, 282, 287, 289
and establishment of a *kalaśa*, 291
and family relations, 162, 173, 259–60, 262, 263, 265, 267, 282–83
and gift giving, 162, 247–48, 250–51, 264, 268, 269
and goddess's fight with demon, 161, 245
and grains, 290–91, 295
and hierarchy, 266, 272, 279–80, 281, 282, 289, 295
and Hindu castes, 250, 253, 264, 278, 324
interpretations of, 245, 280–81
king and queen dolls of, 282–84, 288, 292
and *kolu* visiting, 158, 162–63, 244, 246, 247–48, 250, 251, 259, 260, 264–65, 269, 270, 271–72, 276, 278, 324
in Maduri, Tamil Nadu, 245 fig. 12.1
materiality of, 161–63, 263, 266, 269–70, 271, 290
and Mylapore, Chennai, 261–62, 264, 268
in Mysore, 282–84
and Navarātri, 237, 244–48, 250–51, 252, 257, 278, 279–80, 281, 282, 286, 287–88, 289, 295, 324
and participation in the United States, 258, 264, 270, 278
and political figures, 244, 266, 271
and Pommai Kolu, 16, 257–58, 259, 260, 262, 263, 266, 267–68, 270–72
and pots for godesses, 174, 174n1, 175n8, 270
and preservation of memories, 257–58, 259, 260, 264, 265, 266–67, 270, 271–72
public context for, 258
and *pūjās*, 162, 172, 267
religious significance of, 246, 259, 265, 266–68, 270, 271, 277, 280–82, 291
and ritual practice, 16, 162–63, 173, 175n8, 246, 264, 267–68, 271, 278
and royal *darbār*, 279, 286, 287–88, 291, 294

kolus (continued)
and Sarasvati's collection, 262–64, 265, 270, 271
and social mobility, 162–63, 246, 248, 250–51
social order in, 277, 295
and state of Karnataka, 278, 280, 282, 283, 287
in Tamil Nadu, 276, 278, 279, 280–82, 283, 288
and veneration of the goddess, 268, 281
and women, 247, 252, 260, 269, 276, 278, 279, 282, 288–89, 291
and worship of Kāmākṣī, 160 fig. 8.1
Krotz, Friedrich, 126–27

Mahābhārata
and Draupadi, 109
hymns in, 141, 153n3
Pāṇḍava brothers in, 4, 141
passages in, 185
and public lectures, 249
and *śamī* tree, 4, 153n3
and weapons, 4
Mahānavamī, 1, 5, 70–72, 279, 284–85, 286, 289
See also Navarātri
Mahiṣāsura
and blasphemy, 7, 8, 17n7
and commemoration of Mahiṣa, 318
and deity Śiva, 6
as a demon-king, 7, 141–42
as demon Mahiṣa, 210, 294, 301, 322, 326
as hero, 109
and Indian politics, 16n1, 109
and killing of by Goddess, 4, 5, 6, 8, 12, 34, 51–52, 96, 139, 142, 148, 185, 198, 241, 245, 246, 259, 268, 292, 294, 318
and Mahiṣa's demon forces, 28, 142
and Mahishasur's marriage to Durgā, 8
and name Makiṣāsuraṉ, 165, 166
and *pūjās*, 154n14, 203
and sex with Durgā, 17n7
worship of, 7–8, 17n4, 17n5, 109, 322, 327–28n2
See also Mahiṣāsura Commemoration Day
Mahiṣāsura Commemoration Day
contestations over, 7–8, 327–28n2
and Dalit groups, 2, 7, 327–28n2
on Jawaharlal Nehru University campus, 7–8
and worship of Mahiṣāsura, 7–8, 17n4
Malla dynasty
and Durgā as Ugracaṇḍā, 51–54, 55, 56
integration of previous rituals of, 56
of Kathmandu, Nepal, 13, 41–42, 43
and Kathmandu Valley, 55
libraries of, 58n10
and main goddess Taleju, 42, 47, 48–49, 56, 58n8, 322
and Newars, 43, 48–49, 53
palace of, 42, 43, 48, 53, 54, 55, 58n8
ritual procedures of, 13, 41–57, 322
royal priests of, 59n21
and state religion, 56
Tantric traditions of, 41–42, 322
and worship of Buddhist girls, 47–48
Mārkaṇḍeya Purāṇa
and Caṇḍikā, 231n3
and defeat of demons, 5, 28
Devī Māhātmya in, 5, 13, 24, 25, 27, 28–29 table 1.1, 30, 31, 35, 219, 241
and goddesses, 318
manus in, 24, 25, 26, 28–29 table 1.1, 35
Manu Vaivasvata in, 25, 26
and Navaratri, 5
principles of Indian astrology in, 30–31, 32, 35
and rituals, 30
and *śakti*, 231n3
solar myths of, 24, 25–30, 31, 32, 35, 36n3
and succession of kings discourse, 28–29 table 1.1

Sūrya (Sun) Māhātmya in, 27–29, 32, 36n3
See also *Devī Māhātmya*; Sūrya (Sun)
Marriott, McKim, 317, 318
media
and art installations, 107, 110, 113–14
and communication practices, 125–27, 129–30
and construction of reality, 125–27
digital media, 125, 129, 136
and Durgā Pūjā, 106, 107, 110, 113–14, 125, 129–36, 148, 149
and Durgā Pūjā Committee Mulund, Mumbai, 126, 128, 129–36
and Durgā's consecration, 113
entertainment media, 130
Facebook, 126, 128, 129, 130, 131–32, 134, 135, 136
films, 125, 127, 130
and globalization, 126
and goddess symbolism, 109
and Indira Gandhi, 109
and individual actors, 127, 128
and individualization, 126
information in, 225
and instruction for *kolus*, 276
internet forums, 125, 127, 129, 130, 131–32, 133, 134, 135, 136, 278
journalistic media, 130, 135
and Mamata Banerjee, 110, 113
and media research, 136n2
and mediatization, 14, 121–22, 125–36, 326
newspapers, 50, 106, 113, 130, 135, 146
rise of, 145
social media, 7, 14, 126, 128, 129–35, 136, 278, 282, 292, 293–94, 320–21
TV, 127, 130, 135, 278, 279, 281
visual media, 7, 130
Modi, Narendra, 108, 150
Mysore, India
and Anglo-Mysore Wars, 65
and British colonial rule, 13, 64, 65, 66, 287
and control of by war ministers, 65
court of, 6, 63, 65, 69, 71–72, 74, 76, 77
and custom of doll-arranging, 282–84
Dasara procession of, 13, 63–64, 72, 77–81, 278
history of, 70
hunting in, 79
Jaganmōhan Palace in, 73
and *Kālikā Purāṇa*, 6
king-making in, 13, 63–64
medieval rulers of, 65
and Mysore-French coalition, 65
Mysore Palace in, 73
as a princely state, 64
rāja-rāṇī dolls in, 282–84, 288
royal Dasara in, 282–84
Woḍeyar dynasty in, 65, 69, 70, 71–72, 321
See also Raṅgamahal (Hall of Color); *Śrīman Mahārājavara Vaṃśāvaḷi (The Annals of the Royal Family of Mysore)*

Narayanan, Vasudha, 16, 310, 324, 327
Navarātra
artistic celebration of, 300
and Āśvina, 44, 46–47, 197, 299
auspiciousness of, 310–11, 313
in domestic space, 300, 301–3, 304, 305, 306, 308, 312, 313
eighth day of, 45, 47, 50, 53, 198, 200, 301, 304
end of, 206
fifth day of, 200, 202
first day of, 45, 45–46, 47, 53, 55
food of, 300, 301, 302–3, 305, 306, 307, 308, 309, 311, 314n5
and gift giving, 303, 305, 306, 309, 311–12, 313, 314n4, 314n5
and goddess Taleju, 48–49, 56
at Gorkha, Nepal, 46
and jar *(pūrṇa kalaśa)*, 202
at Kathmandu, 46, 47, 48
and killing of Mahiṣāsura, 50–51
length of, 313n2
and lunar month Caitra, 299, 313n2
and mourning periods, 45, 48, 58n7

Navarātra *(continued)*
Nepalese autumnal Navarātra, 39–43, 47
and Nepalese Shah kings, 56
ninth day of, 45, 47, 49, 53, 54, 55, 198, 300, 302
northeastern Indian practices of, 46–47, 54
and Parbatiya priests, 49
and public space, 300, 301–6, 308–9
and pujas, 48, 299, 301–13
ritual cultures of, 55–57, 57n1
ritual handbooks for, 43–46, 50, 51–54, 56–57, 58n6, 59n22
rituals of, 39, 40–50, 52–55, 56, 300–301, 302, 303, 305–7, 308, 309, 311–13
and ritual timing, 49–50, 55, 56, 311
in royal Nepal, 39–58
in rural Kangra District, 313n3, 313n4
and sacrifices, 44, 45, 47, 49, 58n7, 301
seventh day of, 42, 50, 198, 202
sixth day of, 55, 58n7, 200, 202
in South Asia, 1, 299–313
and sovereignty in Nepal, 39
and state of Himachal Pradesh, 299–313
and temple context, 300, 301–6, 308–9, 310–13, 314n5
tenth day of, 42, 45–46, 47, 53, 57
and use of mandalas, 52–53, 55
and Vedic schools, 43
and worship of girls, 45, 47–48, 54, 58n13
and worship of young girls *(kanyā pūjā)*, 299, 301–13
See also Kathmandu, Nepal; Navarātri
Navarātri
Aghor tradition of, 215, 325
alaṃkāras (ornamentation) during, 169–71
and ancestors, 222, 277, 289, 292–94, 295
artistic celebration of, 275–76, 277, 278, 285, 286, 290, 291, 294, 295, 320, 324
in the ashram, 220–23, 224
and autumnal equinox, 1, 3, 13, 23
autumn festival of (in Asvina), 1, 5, 6, 14, 23, 33, 34, 139–41, 151–52, 153n1, 188, 215, 289, 322, 323, 326, 328n2
beginning of, 237, 238
in Benares, 14, 15, 139–41, 145, 147–49, 151–52
and birth *nakṣatra* of Vedānta Deśika, 191n9
birth or death during, 71
and the body, 15, 215, 217, 221
Brahminical texts about, 2, 190
and celebration of the Mahārāja, 139
in Chennai, 247, 278
as community-centered, 319, 321
and connection between earth, ancestors, and living, 9–11
and courtly life, 10–11, 13–14, 16
and creation, 289–91, 292, 295
and cultural values, 190, 277
and Dalit groups, 2, 7, 8
dancing during, 1, 215, 231, 275, 291, 295, 322
and *darśana* (viewing of a deity), 147, 158
and defeat of demons, 246
and democratization, 319–21, 326, 328n4
and the *Devī Māhātmya*, 13, 158, 318
and diaspora, 10, 291
in different periods, 2, 3, 319
differing aspects of, 1–2, 190, 216, 319
and diversity of belief, 2, 8, 13, 16, 16n1
and dolls *(kolus)*, 16, 158, 159, 160–63, 244–48, 250–51, 272, 275
and domestic space, 2, 8–13, 15–16, 147, 157, 158, 159–63, 171, 188, 220, 231, 241, 276, 277, 322, 323, 324
and Durgā as destroyer of evil, 242
early Sanskrit textual history of, 3–7
and earth's fecundity, 9, 10, 11, 290–91

eighth day of, 153n3, 164, 244
and embodied display and play, 319, 322–25, 326
and establishment of a *kalaśa*, 220, 223, 290–91, 292
and female divine power, 1, 6, 11, 170, 319, 325
and festival locations and times, 1, 3, 6, 9–10, 33, 141, 241, 275, 292
as a festival of kings and warriors, 1, 10–11, 141
and fire oblations (*havana*), 147, 221, 222
first conference on, 296
first day of, 237, 292
and fluidity of symbolic power, 319, 321–22
food of, 161, 163, 174, 181, 218, 219, 221, 231, 244, 248, 276, 278, 290, 292–94, 295, 322
forms of, 9, 13
gender dynamics of, 11
and gift giving, 160, 161, 237, 250, 251
and Goddess devotion, 4–6, 11–12, 197, 215, 217, 324
and grains and sprouting beans, 290–91
and harvest, 1, 9
and hegemonic culture, 7–8
and "heterotopia," 17n9
and Hindu nationalism, 8
and identity construction, 15–16
and ideological concerns, 12
increase in popularity of, 165, 319, 326
and Indian politics, 8, 14, 321–22
and *Īśvarasaṃhitā*, 180, 181, 182–83, 189, 190n1, 191n4
in Kāñchipuram, Tamil Nadu, 14, 15, 157, 158, 161, 163, 173–74, 179–90
killing of demons during, 1, 5, 6, 164–65, 172–73, 174, 188–89
and kingship, 241
and *kumārī pūjās*, 222, 230
length of, 1, 176n11, 190n1, 318
local, regional, and non-Brahminical versions of, 2, 14–15, 165–67
and local mythologies, 15, 165, 172, 175n9, 185, 186
and local pilgrimages, 147
in Maduri, Tamil Nadu, 238, 243–53, 253n2
and the *Mahābhārata*, 241
and Mahiṣāsura Commemoration Day, 2, 7, 8
and Mahotsava, 191n12
as a major festival, 163, 185, 318, 322
materiality of, 15, 157–59, 161–63, 291
and mediatization, 327, 185, 186
and nature, 23
Navamī (ninth day of), 4, 6, 147, 182, 191n15, 222
and nine forms of the Goddess, 219
nine nights of, 157, 184, 215, 218, 241, 245, 258, 278, 286, 290, 291, 318
number of, 153n1
organization of, 241, 244, 286
other names for, 1, 40, 241, 318
and *pandals* (marquees), 139, 140–41, 322
and Pommai Kolu, 16, 257–72
and presence of the Goddess, 229, 326
and public space, 2, 8–13, 14, 16, 139, 140, 145, 147, 231, 276, 277, 278, 320, 322
and *pujas*, 147, 160, 163, 164–65, 168–69, 237, 244, 320
in Puraṭṭāci, 191–92n16
and recitations *(japas)*, 220, 221, 230
as reserved for women, 248–49
rituals of, 2, 4, 5, 6, 9–12, 13, 14–16, 17n9, 23–24, 39–50, 71, 141, 147, 157–58, 162–67, 168, 172–73, 174, 179, 180–84, 187, 188–90, 219, 220–24, 238, 243, 244, 248, 250, 253, 277, 322, 323, 324, 325–26, 328n2
ritual texts of, 13, 15, 23, 33, 45–46, 47, 163, 179, 180, 181, 182–84, 185, 189, 224
and ritual timing, 33

Navarātri *(continued)*
royal celebration of, 4, 10–11, 13–14, 23–24, 39–50, 141, 180, 187, 277, 286, 287, 319, 320, 321, 322
and royal *darbār*, 288, 295
and royal power, 1, 10, 141, 186–88, 241, 321, 322
and sacrifices, 187, 222, 230, 321, 328n2
and Śākta *Mahābhāgavata Purāṇa*, 16n2
and Śākta Purāṇa (*Bṛhannandikeśvara Purāṇa*), 6
and *śakti*, 141, 167
and Śakti, 253n2
and *śamī* tree, 1, 183–84
Sanskrit texts about, 3–7, 15, 23
and Sarasvatī Pūjā, 241
and Sarkar Baba, 216, 217–23, 224, 225, 226, 228, 230–31
scholarly work on, 327
and season of warfare, 1
and secularization, 319, 320–21, 325, 326, 327
social aspects of, 222, 237, 325
and social media, 320–21
and social status, 252–53
and socioeconomic status, 238–39
in South Asia, 1, 2, 3, 7, 10, 12–13, 252
and spatial categories, 12–13, 15–16
spiritual element of, 15, 215, 217–27, 230, 231, 325
and spring equinox, 13, 23
spring Navarātris, 6, 153n1, 188, 215
and Śrī Maṅkala Vināyakar temple, 241, 243–44, 248–49, 253
and state of Karnataka, 277
and story of Rāma, 3–4, 5
in Tamil Nadu, 15–16, 157, 172, 179–92, 238, 243–53, 286
and temple context, 14–15, 16, 157, 158, 159, 163–67, 169–71, 172, 183–89, 237, 241, 323–24, 325
tenth day of, 183, 190n1, 241
and texts about festival, 1, 2, 3, 4, 5–7, 15, 121, 184
and theologies of transformation, 319, 325–26
in Vaiṣṇava Varadarāja Perumāḷ temple, 179, 184, 185, 186, 187
and Vedic and Tantric rites, 17n3
as veneration of the state, 2
and Vijayadaśamī, 1, 3, 4, 159, 161, 164, 165, 167, 169, 170, 171, 174, 176n11, 241, 259, 287, 288, 318
and Vijayanagara kings, 187, 280
and weapons, 1, 164, 183
Woḍeyar celebration of, 70
and women's freedom of movement, 252
and women's roles, 187, 286, 326–27
worship of women in, 1, 16, 160, 163, 171–72
worship of young girls in, 1, 10, 16, 147, 160, 163–64, 171–72, 290, 323
See also Dasara; *Devī Māhātmya*; Durgā Pūjā; goddesses; *kolus*; Nepal; *vrata*

Nepal
Bhaktapur in, 41, 43, 45, 50, 51, 53, 54, 57, 58n8
and Buddhist stupa, 96
and caste, 40, 41, 54
and Dasain, 318–319
Hindu agenda in, 40
and local memorial practices, 41
Malla period of, 39, 41–48, 49, 50, 51–54, 55, 56–57
Navarātra in, 39–55
and Nepalese National Archives, 57
and Newars, 43, 48–49, 50, 55
Parbatiyas of, 40, 43, 48–49, 55
and religion as promoted by state, 39–41, 50, 56
Royal Kumārīs in, 307–8
Shah period of, 39, 40, 41, 42–50, 54–55, 56, 322
state of Gorkha in, 40, 41, 42, 46, 48, 49, 54, 56, 58n11, 58n12
Tantric traditions in, 41–42
and Treaty of Sagauli, 40
and worship of young girls *(kanyā pūjā)*, 308

See also Kathmandu, Nepal; Malla dynasty; Shah dynasty

Odisha, 85, 86, 87, 92, 99n1. *See also* Bonai, Odisha

Patavēttammaṉ temple, 157, 165–67, 169, 170, 172, 175n6, 323
Purāṇas
and classical Jyotiṣa, 30–31, 32
and clay images of Durgā, 34
as deity narratives, 69
Devī Bhāgavata Purāṇa, 6, 121
Devī Purāṇa, 5, 121, 199
funerary rites in, 292
Goddess Purāṇas, 4–6
Great Purāṇas (*mahāpurāṇas*), 69
Kālikā Purāṇa, 5–6, 71, 72, 199, 206, 212n2
and killing of Mahiṣāsura, 34
and the *Mahābhārata*, 4
and Mahiṣa, 5, 6, 210
mantras and Tantras in, 5
Mārkaṇḍeya Purāṇa, 5, 24–30, 219, 231n3, 241, 318
and Purāṇic texts as authorities, 43
and *Rāmāyaṇa* narrative, 5
and relationship between Goddess and Sun, 25
as ritual texts, 6
Śākta *Mahābhāgavata Purāṇa*, 16n2
Śākta Purāṇa (*Bṛhannandikeśvara Purāṇa*), 6
and *Viṣṇudharmottara Puraāṇa*, 207
See also *Devī Māhātmya* (*Glorification of the Goddess*); *Mārkaṇḍeya Purāṇa*

Rāma
and Bengali *Kṛttivāsa Rāmāyaṇa*, 3–4, 200, 204
and *darbārs*, 288
and defeat of Rāvaṇa, 3, 4, 5, 6, 139, 142, 200, 212n2, 259, 301, 318
and Durgā Pūjā, 3–4, 5, 6, 204, 212n2
exile of, 142
and giving of *piṇḍas*, 294–95
and Hindu nationalism, 153n6
and *kolus*, 265, 267
and praise of Durgā, 153n3
as prince of Ayodhyā, 3, 142
and the *Rām Līlā*, 139, 142, 143, 152
and return to Ayodhyā, 318
rule of, 142, 143, 326
See also *Rāmāyaṇa* (Vālmīki); *Rām Līlā*
Rāmāyaṇa (Tulsīdās), 14, 140, 142
Rāmāyaṇa (Vālmīki), 3, 14, 185, 212n2, 249, 301
Rām Līlā
in the 18th. century, 143
of Assi, 152
of Benares, 139–40, 141, 143–48, 150–51, 153n2
and Brahmanical hierarchy, 142–43
in Chaitganj neighborhood, 150–51
decline of, 145
and defeat of Rāvaṇa, 139
government control of, 151
and Hindi vernacular *Rāmāyaṇa*, 140
and Hindu society, 143, 152
and Hindu symbolism, 149
and identity, 140, 151
and Mahārāja's power, 139
and military campaigning, 144
and performance of *Rāmcaritmānas* (Tulsīdās), 139, 143
popularity of, 14, 140, 145
in public places, 140, 141, 147, 150–51
and Rāma, 139, 142, 143, 144
Rāmnagar *Rām Līlā*, 144, 145, 152
royal patronage of, 14, 143–44
spectacle of, 150–51
and tradition, 140, 144, 151–52
and Tulsīdās, 4, 14, 140, 144
and *Vijayadaśamī*, 139
Raṅgamahal (Hall of Color)
Dasara mural of, 77–79, 80
and "Everlasting Lotus" painting, 73–74, 75, 77, 79
and "Family Tree" painting, 74–75, 77, 81n6
in Jaganmōhan Palace, 65, 68, 71, 73, 76, 78
mural paintings of, 65, 68, 71, 73–80, 81n6

Raṅgamahal (Hall of Color) *(continued)*
and *Rās Līlā* mural, 75–77, 80
and royal lineage, 73–75, 77, 79, 80
and virility of Kṛṣṇarāja III, 75–76, 79, 80
religion
and ancestors, 158, 173, 292–95
ancient religion, 9, 318, 319
and astrological mythology, 30–35
and atonement, 167–69
and belief, 127
and Bengal Institute of Art & Culture, 128
and Bonaigarh, 86, 96
and Buddhism, 57n2, 96, 292
Buddhism, 328n2
caste dynamics in, 47
and Christianity, 66, 118n3, 272n1, 322–23
and Christmas season, 40, 105, 109, 246
and community's identity, 135, 149
and cultural heritage, 127
and the *Devī Māhātmya*, 24–25, 47
and *dharma*, 105
and diaspora traditions, 9, 10, 132
and diversity of belief, 16, 16n1, 109
and divinity of goddesses, 169, 170
and dolls *(kolus)*, 159
and domestic religion, 9–11
and Durgā Pūjā, 130, 132, 207, 211
and faith, 228
family (including ancestors) in, 9
and feminist movements, 328n9
and festivals, 10, 105–7, 116, 122–25, 127, 128, 130, 133, 135, 139–50, 152, 153n2, 157–59, 168, 176n11, 179–80, 182–85, 186, 188, 189–90, 191–192n16, 191n7, 191n14, 228, 230–31, 238, 252, 284–85, 317–19, 327
and former princely Indian states, 14, 84, 92, 99n1
and gift giving, 248
and heterogeneity of practices, 16n1
and Hindu-Muslim riots, 149
and Hindu-Muslim tensions, 152
and Hindu society, 146, 152
and Holi festival, 1, 317, 318
and ideas of the sacred, 17n6
and ideological concerns, 12
and Indian religious thought, 35
and individual actors' media use, 127
and Jains, 328n2
and *kolus*, 246–47, 266–67
and Mahendra Sanskrit University, 46
and Mamata Banerjee as artist, 110–13
and manus, 35
and marriage festival, 191n14
materiality of, 157
mediatized religion, 122, 125, 127–128
and minority religious groups, 7
and modernity, 249–50
and monastic establishments, 171
and Muslims, 17n5, 118n2, 118n3, 123, 144, 149, 152
and Mylapore, Chennai, 272n1
and mythology, 142–143, 168
and nature, 9
and neo-Vedantin Hinduism, 146
and Nepal's royal rituals, 13, 39, 40–50, 55–57
and notions of divinity, 207–8
and piercing ceremony, 166–67
and political capital, 115
and political deification, 108–9
and power of king, 10, 39, 56, 106
as promoted by state, 39, 40–41, 50, 56, 115
and public or civic religion, 9, 122–23, 124, 125, 141
and *pūjās*, 106, 107, 115, 116, 122–23, 124, 125, 128, 130, 133–36, 140–41, 149, 152, 162, 189–90, 197–98, 199, 206–8, 251, 262, 283, 299–313, 323, 325
and Purāṇic texts, 69
and *Rām Līlā*, 144
and religious authority, 136
and religious doctrine, 127
and ritual practice, 9–13, 39–50, 55–57, 87–92, 97–98, 144, 147, 157, 173, 175n8

and rituals and social power, 140, 142
and role of priests, 9, 10, 43, 45, 48–49, 88, 89, 91–92, 94, 97, 183–84, 185, 189, 190n2, 192n22, 198, 202–3, 204, 205 fig. 10.2, 206, 207–8, 212n4, 302, 319, 323
and royal courts, 9, 10, 11, 13–14, 16, 39–50
saints in, 181, 216
and secularism, 14, 118n3
and Sikhs, 118n3
and social status, 238
and solar mythologies, 36n3
in South Asia, 9–13, 106
and status negotiation, 123
and symbols, 199–200, 208–11, 211n1, 294, 327
and temple images, 167–71
and temples, 9, 10, 11, 12, 48–49, 58n7, 64, 72, 90, 93, 96, 97, 98, 106, 109, 121, 124, 141, 147, 157, 158, 159, 163–71, 172, 173, 179, 180, 186, 188, 189–90, 191n5, 192n19, 197, 210, 216, 228, 241, 303–6, 317–18, 323–24
and theologies of transformation, 319, 325–26
and "tribal deities," 84, 97–98
and urbanization, 238
See also Buddhism; Durgā Pūjā; goddesses; gods; Hinduism; kings; *King's Two Bodies, The* (Kantorowicz); media; Muslims; Navarātri; Sūrya (Sun)
ritual timing
and Dasara, 80
and the *Devī Māh2ātmya*, 33, 35
and Mahānavamī, 5
in Malla period diaries, 56
and *Mārkaṇḍeya Purāṇa*, 30, 35
and Navarātras, 310–11
in Nepal, 49–50, 55, 56
and performance of *Rām Līlā*, 144
and Shah period, 56
and worship of Ugracaṇḍā, 55
Rodrigues, Hillary, 15, 16, 34, 57, 154n13, 189, 291
Roy, B. C., 112

śakti
as divine female energy, 108, 114
and Durgā, 109, 117, 146, 153n3, 204
and *mantras*, 226
and Navaratri, 161, 167, 231
and Patavēttammaṉ, 170
and power, 224–25, 248
and royal tutelary goddesses, 141
and *śakti pīṭhas* (seats of the goddess), 147
and Śāktism, 179
triadic nature of, 209
San Francisco Bay, CA, 258, 259, 272n2
Sanskrit
and the *Amarakośa*, 209
and auspicious moments, 44
and Brahminical culture, 240–41
and classical sources, 1, 3
and Dasara terms, 64
and the *Devī Māhātmya*, 158
and early textual history of Navarātri, 3–7
and goddess' name, 53
and gods, 186
and instructions for *kolus*, 245
literary tradition of, 2, 34, 36n3, 52, 65
at Mahendra Sanskrit University, 46
and Mahiṣāsura, 241
mantras in, 244, 251
and Navarātri, 277
and Pāncarātra *saṃhitās*, 15
prayers in, 200
and *Rāmāyaṇa* (Vālmīki), 3
and ritual practice, 166
and *śakti*, 141
and Sanskrit *daśāhan*, 57n1
and Sanskritic deities, 168
and Sanskritization, 240
and *ślokas*, 3
and texts on royal Navarātra, 43–44
and treatises on Jyotiṣa, 31–33
See also *Devī Māhātmya* (*Glorification of the Goddess*)
Sen, Moumita, 14, 57, 96, 147, 148, 190

Shah dynasty
adoption of religious elements by, 13, 49, 322
at Hanuman Dhoka palace, 48
of Kathmandu, Nepal, 13, 41, 42, 46, 48, 49–50
and Kathmandu Valley, 55
and libraries, 58n10
and main goddess Kālikā, 42, 47, 54, 322
and palace of Gorkha, 54
and Parbatiya priests, 48–49
ritual procedures of, 13, 42–48, 49, 50, 54, 55, 322
and seat of power, 55, 56
and worship of Brahmin girls, 48
Shankar, Jishnu, 15, 325
Simmons, Caleb, 13, 57, 190, 295, 321, 322
Sivakumar, Deeksha, 16, 324
Skoda, Uwe, 13–14, 321
Smith, Jonathan Z., 9, 10, 11, 12
South Asia
and astrological mythology, 31
devotional practices in, 106, 299
Hindu/Buddhist calendars of, 292
and Indian caste identities, 239–40
middle class of, 238
and Navarātri celebrations, 1, 299
and social status, 252
and theories of the gift, 311, 312
Śrīman Mahārājavara Vaṃśāvaḷi (The Annals of the Royal Family of Mysore), 65, 68, 69–72, 74, 77, 79, 80
Sultān, Ṭippu, 64, 65, 287, 288
Sūrya (Sun)
and Āśvin twins, 26, 31, 32, 33
children of, 26, 27, 30, 31, 32, 33, 35
and color red, 253n4
cosmic role of, 141
and court astrologers, 30
and equine myth, 26, 27, 30, 31, 32, 33
and equinoxes, 33, 37n8
and "Everlasting Lotus" painting, 74
and family with Chaya, 26
and manus, 35
narratives of, 13, 24, 25–30, 31, 32–33, 34, 35, 36n3, 37n9
power of, 27, 32, 33, 34–35
and relationship with Goddess, 25, 26, 27, 35
and ritual practice, 33–34, 35
role in creation of, 28 table 1.1, 32
royal caste of, 35, 37n11
and son Sāvarṇi (a manu), 24, 25, 26
as soul, 31, 32, 36n5
and *Sūrya (Sun) Māhātmya*, 27–29
and *Sūrya Gītā*, 36n3
and wife Saṃjñā, 26–27, 30, 31, 32–33
worship of, 3, 24, 27, 32, 36n3
and zodiac, 31–33, 37n9

Tagore, Rabindranath, 105, 118n1
Trinamool Congress (TMC), 14, 107–8, 110, 112, 115–17, 118n3
Tulsīdās
and biography *Gautamacandrikā* (Miśra), 4
and *līlā* tradition, 144
and *Rāmāyaṇa* in Hindi, 14
Rāmcaritmānas of, 4, 139, 153n6
and *Rām Līlā* in Benares, 140

Vajpayee, Atal Behari, 17n4
Vijayadaśamī
and atonement, 167–69
Bhārat Mīlāp scene after, 145
and birth *nakṣatra* of Vedānta Deśika, 191n9
and fight with demon Makiṣāsuraṉ, 165, 169, 171
as final day of Durgā Pūjā, 149
and forms of the goddess, 170, 174
honoring of teachers during, 288
and *kolus*, 161
and Pommai Kolu, 267
and Rāma's defeat of Rāvaṇa, 3, 4, 139, 318
rites of, 206
royal celebration of, 4, 77, 78 fig. 3.4, 91, 144, 287
and royal power, 144
in Sanskrit and Kannada, 81n1
and state of Karnataka, 278

as tenth day of victory, 1, 79, 89, 139, 159, 176n11, 241, 288, 318
and victory of good over evil, 139, 259
and worship of the *vaṉṉi* tree, 164–65
See also Dasara
Vijayanagara Empire
and the *Ānanda Rāmāyaṇa*, 294–95
court of, 284–87
and Dasara, 282, 286
demise of, 65
and Hampi, 187–88, 285
kings of, 80, 141, 187, 285
and Navarātri, 277, 287–88, 291
and royal *darbār*, 285, 287–88
state deity of, 188
and viceroy of Śrīraṅgapaṭṭaṇa, 70
Viśvakarman, 26, 28
vrata, 6, 147, 218, 301

Weber, Max, 136, 328n6
Wilson, Nicole A., 15, 162, 324
Woḍeyar dynasty
Ādi Yadurāya Woḍeyar of, 74
during British period of Kṛṣṇarāja III's reign, 80
Cāmarāja Woḍeyar X of, 77, 81n6
Cikkadēvarāya Woḍeyar of, 65
and continuity of lineage, 64–65, 68–69, 70, 72, 73–75, 77, 78–79, 80
and "Curse of Taḷakāḍu," 70, 75, 77, 80, 81n5
and *darbār*, 72
and Dasara, 65, 68–69, 70–71, 72, 77–79, 80
devotional deities of, 74
and divine kingship, 64, 65, 67–69, 70, 72, 77, 79, 80
and genealogical accounts or pictures, 13, 65, 68–80
and goddess Cāmuṇḍēśvari, 63, 74
history of, 65, 69–72
hunting of, 79
insignia of, 78
and *kolus*, 284
Kṛṣṇarāja Woḍeyar III of, 13, 64, 65–68, 69, 70, 72, 73, 74–77, 79, 80, 81n6, 287
literature of, 64, 65, 67–72, 77, 79, 80, 82n6
paintings of, 64, 65, 67, 68, 73–80, 81n6
palace of, 81n2
Rāja Woḍeyar of, 65, 69–72, 81–82n6, 81n5
reinstallation of, 64, 65, 68
and royal adoptions, 66, 68, 70, 81n6
and rulers in Mysore, 321
and the *Śrīman Mahārājavara Vaṃśāvaḷi*, 82n6
and Yadu Vaṃśa (lineage of Yadu), 68, 69, 73, 74, 79, 80
See also Raṅgamahal (Hall of Color); *Śrīman Mahārājavara Vaṃśāvaḷi*; Yadu Vaṃśa (lineage of Yadu/Lunar lineage)

Yadu Vaṃśa (lineage of Yadu/Lunar lineage), 68, 69, 73, 74, 79, 80

Zeiler, Xenia, 14, 96
Zotter, Astrid, 13, 50, 322, 323

Printed in Great Britain
by Amazon

33517495R00222